# Microfoundations of Financial Economics

*Microfoundations of Financial Economics:*
*An Introduction to General Equilibrium Asset Pricing*
IS A PART OF THE
PRINCETON SERIES IN FINANCE

---

SERIES EDITORS



Finance as a discipline has been growing rapidly. The number of researchers in academy and industry, of students, of methods and models have all proliferated in the past decade or so. This growth and diversity manifests itself in the emerging cross-disciplinary as well as cross-national mix of scholarship now driving the field of finance forward. The intellectual roots of modern finance, as well as the branches, will be represented in the Princeton Series in Finance.

Titles in the series will be scholarly and professional books, intended to be read by a mixed audience of economists, mathematicians, operations research scientists, financial engineers, and other investment professionals. The goal is to provide the finest cross-disciplinary work, in all areas of finance, by widely recognized researchers in the prime of their creative careers.

OTHER BOOKS IN THIS SERIES

*Financial Econometrics: Problems, Models, and Methods* by Christian Gourieroux and Joann Jasiak
*Credit Risk: Pricing, Measurement, and Management* by Darrell Duffie and Kenneth J. Singleton
*Credit Risk Modeling: Theory and Applications*, by David Lando
*Quantitative Risk Management: Concepts, Techniques, and Tools* by Alexander J. McNeil, Rudiger Frey, and Paul Embrechts

# Microfoundations of Financial Economics

## An Introduction to General Equilibrium Asset Pricing

Yvan Lengwiler

Princeton University Press
Princeton and Oxford

Published by Princeton University Press,
41 William Street, Princeton, New Jersey 08540

In the United Kingdom: Princeton University Press,
3 Market Place, Woodstock, Oxfordshire OX20 1SY



Second printing, and first paperback printing, 2006
Paperback ISBN-13: 978-0-691-12631-9
Paperback ISBN-10: 0-691-12631-3

The Library of Congress has cataloged the cloth edition of this book as follows
Lengwiler, Yvan.
Microfoundations of financial economics : an introduction to general equilibrium asset pricing / Yvan Lengwiler.
p. cm. — (Princeton series in finance)
Includes bibliographical references and index.
ISBN 0-691-11315-7 (cloth : alk. paper)
1. Finance. 2. Economics. 3. Capital assets pricing model. I. Title. II. Series.
HG173.L46 2004
332'.01'5195—dc22 2003066415



British Library Cataloging-in-Publication Data is available

This book has been composed in New Baskerville by
Deerpark Publishing Services, Republic of Ireland

Printed on acid-free paper. ∞

pup.princeton.edu

Printed in the United States of America

10 9 8 7 6 5 4 3

*To Brigitte,*

*with love*

# Contents

# List of boxes

# Preface

## Dear reader

This book takes you from the level of microeconomics principles through a sequence of carefully elaborated and detailed steps to modern topics in finance. The book is for you if you have been exposed to indifference curves, budget constraints, and maximization but would like to know about the consumption capital asset pricing model, the theory of the term structure of interest rates, the equity premium puzzle, and the social cost of the business cycle. Even if you have not taken a course in basic microeconomics, you can still read this book, because it reviews the part of microeconomics and general equilibrium theory that is relevant for the topics covered in this book.

The book was written with three groups of readers in mind:

- graduate students with a focus on macroeconomics, financial economics, or monetary economics;
- MBA students specializing in finance;
- professionals of the financial community with a sufficient prior knowledge of mathematics and economics.

Essentially, it is suitable for everyone who is seriously interested in financial economics and its relation to the macroeconomy, and has an appetite for the formal analysis of these issues.

## Dear instructor

The book is geared to the needs of MA/MSc or PhD students specializing in financial economics. It can also be used for undergraduate students with a sufficient appetite for formal analysis as an introduction to general equilibrium theory, macroeconomics, or finance—three terms that have begun to overlap increasingly over the last two decades.

The material covered fits comfortably into a two semester course. For students with sufficient prior exposure to economics (knowledge of general equilibrium theory and expected utility theory), chapters 2–4 can be reviewed quickly and the remainder of the book should then fit into one semester.

Some knowledge of mathematics is required. This becomes quickly obvious simply by looking at the density of the equations in the book: there are fewer than a typical mathematics textbook would have, but considerably more than what someone who is not used to mathematics will feel comfortable with. We use Euclidean spaces (finite-dimensional real vector spaces), basic statistics (mean, variance, covariance), maximization subject to constraints, and calculus. More precisely, knowledge of mathematics at the level of Bartle (1976), Simon & Blume (1994), Sundaram (1996), Weintraub (1982), or any other slightly advanced "Mathematics for Economists" text is more than enough.

## Use in combination with other books

Depending on the class level you may wish to emphasize or de-emphasize different aspects or topics, and it may make sense to combine this text with another one.

For a more applied audience and for practitioners, I recommend Cornell (1999) or Siegel (1998) as a starting point. Both books contain detailed discussions of the equity premium puzzle, yet both manage to do away almost completely with mathematics and econometrics. Another good place to start is AIMR's (2002) published forum on the topic. In this forum, several prominent researchers in the field present their ideas in not too technical a fashion. These ideas are then discussed by a panel.

LeRoy & Werner (2001) and Danthine & Donaldson (2002) are comparable in style and difficulty to the present book, should you wish to offer an alternative presentation of the material. The main differences are that these two books put less emphasis on aggregation conditions and cover empirical issues to a lesser extent (Danthine & Donaldson) or not at all (LeRoy & Werner).

If you want to focus somewhat more on empirical work and your students are technically well-trained, the textbooks by Cochrane (2001) and Campbell, Lo & MacKinlay (1997) should provide nice complements, containing much more information on econometric issues related to financial market data.

The present book can also be used as a supplement to modern macroeconomics courses. For instance, Ljungqvist & Sargent (2000) contains two chapters on equilibrium asset pricing; if you want to focus more on this topic that would be a valuable addition, especially since, unlike Ljungqvist & Sargent, we develop the topic at sub-sonic speed.

For the more theory-minded reader, Gollier (2001*a*) has created an outstanding research book on the theory of decisions under risk and relations to general equilibrium and asset pricing. An older classic in this domain is Duffie (1988). These titles are clearly more advanced than the present.

Finally, Brunnermeier (2001) presents a book that would be very appropriate as a basis for a follow-on course from this one. He explores the consequences of asymmetric information in general equilibrium asset pricing theory, a topic we touch upon here only marginally.

## Website and supporting material

The book's website[1] offers supporting material for instructors. First of all, there is a list of all the references made in the book, with links to online sources where available. This should help instructors collect material for a reader accompanying their course, and should help students collect the relevant literature on their own. The same website offers some Excel files in connection with the problem sets. Finally, there is a collection of PowerPoint files that should help instructors prepare their lectures. These files can easily be amended using PowerPoint.

I also maintain a list of errors. If you find any errors or omissions, please let me know (see the email address on the book's website).

## Acknowledgements

The editor of Princeton University Press, Richard Baggaley, who guided this project, did a great job—never late, always precise and supportive. Among other services, he selected the anonymous referees, who deserve a big thank you. Their comments and suggestions have made this a far better book. I am also grateful to my colleagues Simon Benninga, Christian Ghiglino, Michael Gratwohl, Matthias Hagmann, Carlos Lenz, Elmar Mertens, Fabienne Peter, Richard Porter, Paul Söderlind, Rob Sproule, and Andy Sturm for many sug-

[1]pup.princeton.edu/titles/7724.html

gestions, and for the encouragement they gave me. Sue Hughes enhanced my mediocre English. I am sure her effort will make your life easier.

## (S)he

Throughout I use the male pronoun. This is not intended as a sexist statement. I find it clumsy to keep using "she or he." Alternating between the sexes—"She chooses a portfolio that maximizes expected utility . . . Higher interest rates therefore incite him to save more"—is confusing and keeps reminding readers of important issues of gender inequality, when they should be focusing their minds on asset pricing.

# 1 Introduction

## 1.1 What finance theory is about

*How much should you save?* and *How much risk should you bear?* When we think about these questions, it becomes clear pretty quickly that they are of great importance to our overall material well-being. Saving is essential because most of us will retire at some point. From that point onwards, although we will still be consuming, we will receive no more labor income. Moreover, we will all face significant economic risks during our lives—the risk of losing our job, for instance, or—much worse—of becoming unable to work because of illness or other misfortunes. Clearly, the risks we are exposed to can have a huge effect on our future life, and it is therefore essential to make rational decisions about how much risk to bear.

Important as these questions are for each one of us, individuals' decisions about saving and risk-taking also matter for society as a whole. Total saving determines the amount of investment that the economy as a whole can realize and thus affects future production possibilities. The amount of risk that people are willing to bear determines whether risky projects will be undertaken. Individual decisions in the face of future retirement and risk and the capital requirements of more or less risky investment projects are coordinated through financial markets. If markets work well, risk is allocated to those people who are least hurt by it, impatient people get to consume before they earn (by taking out a loan), and capital is allocated to those projects that generate the most attractive risk-return profile. Finance is concerned with the determination of those prices that equalize demand and supply on these markets and with their effect on the allocation of capital and risk across agents in the economy.

Finance theory is also useful in interpreting financial market prices in ways that are of interest for public policy and social welfare issues. Robert Lucas

(1987), for instance, has examined the social costs of business cycles. This is obviously important for economic policy making, but it is also important for macroeconomic theory. To learn the answer to this question, we need to know how much people dislike risk, that is, variations in income. More specifically, in order to judge how expensive business cycles are, we need to determine a price that people would be prepared to pay to avoid the income variations caused by business cycles. Modern asset pricing theory allows us—at least in principle—to do just that.

## 1.2 Some history of thought

General equilibrium theory, macroeconomics, and asset pricing theory are three fields in economics that have converged more and more over the last thirty years or so. In this section we consider how this convergence came about.

### *1.2.1 General equilibrium theory*

General equilibrium theory is an approach to describing the behavior of an economy as a whole by working out the optimal behavior of each member of the set of *agents* that make up the economy, and looking for a point of mutual compatibility or consistency. The theory assumes that individuals do not interact with each other directly. Interaction occurs only indirectly, through *anonymous markets* on which prices (exchange rates for different commodities) are posted. A second assumption that goes hand in hand with anonymity is that each individual is small in relation to the market, so that everyone neglects his own influence on market prices. This assumption is called *perfect competition*. Models that make these two assumptions are called *Walrasian*, in honor of Léon Walras (1874) who was the first to formulate such a model. We say that the economy is in *equilibrium* if, at a certain price, each individual buys or sells the optimal quantities (given his tastes and possibilities) of all commodities and the total supply of each commodity equals the total demand for it.[1]

Modern general equilibrium theory in the tradition of Arrow & Debreu (1954) accommodates a large number of different goods and very diverse preferences of individuals. This research has established conditions that guarantee the existence of an equilibrium. It has also developed properties of equilibrium allocations, such as the welfare theorems. The two welfare

[1]Note that it is left unspecified in this model who posts the prices, since everyone takes them as given.

theorems demonstrate that market equilibrium allocations and socially efficient allocations are equivalent, under some conditions. This equivalence will be extremely useful for our purposes.

This theory was significantly advanced by Hirshleifer (1965, 1966) and Radner (1972). These authors built financial markets into the model and thus provided the first crucial ingredient for making general equilibrium theory applicable to finance. Moreover, their work opened up the possibility of analyzing financial markets that are incomplete in the sense that the available financial instruments may not be sufficient to trade all individual risks efficiently. This incompleteness opens the door to various sorts of coordination failures in a market economy.

By the late 1950s, general equilibrium theory had become the cornerstone of microeconomics, and remained so until it was slowly pushed aside by advances in game theory and information economics in the 1970s. General equilibrium theory has, however, received a new lease of life through its applications to the theory of macroeconomic fluctuations and the theory of asset pricing.

### *1.2.2 Macroeconomics*

When John Maynard Keynes (1936) developed his *General Theory*, the world was in disarray. Mass unemployment and mass bankruptcy had erupted—first in the U.S.A. but then quickly spreading throughout the capitalist world. Possibly because of these events, Keynes chose a style of model that broke with the tradition of classical economics. His model did not feature individual agents explicitly, nor did it feature dynamics of any sort. Instead, he focused on the interdependence between different aggregate variables. In that sense, Keynes's model is a general equilibrium model, yet one in which the aggregate demand and supply functions are not developed from an individual optimization perspective. This became most clear in Hicks's (1937) version of Keynes's model, which came to dominate macroeconomic thinking.

This lack of microfoundation led to problems associated with the endogenous determination of expectations. Clearly, expectations should affect an individual's decisions. We would expect that rational decision makers will try to collect information if faulty decisions are costly. Hicks's version of Keynes's model really lacked a convincing theory of expectations. This omission led to increasing dissatisfaction with the model on purely theoretical grounds and ultimately to a dramatic empirical failure with the stagflation of the 1970s, which was an impossible event in the Keynes–Hicks orthodoxy.

These developments gave impetus to a new, or rather renewed old, approach,[2] namely to construct dynamic models of aggregate economic fluctuations based on individual decisions together with shocks of some sort (most prominently to technology). The *rational expectations revolution* in macroeconomics is nothing but a simplified version of Radner's (1972) idea of an "equilibrium of plans, prices, and price expectations." The early macro versions of this idea were simplified, in the sense that agents were assumed to have an unbiased expectation of the mean of stochastic variables only, whereas in Radner's model agents have correct state-contingent expectations.

In essence, this is what the *New Classical* and later *Real Business Cycle* theory consist of: computable dynamic stochastic general equilibrium models. Compared with traditional general equilibrium theory, the macroeconomic variants are typically simpler because they feature only one good and one agent, and give scant attention to the conditions for aggregation. They also make much stronger assumptions concerning preferences and technology in order to get easily computable equilibria. Modern *New Keynesian* theory and the *New Neoclassical Synthesis* models deviate from the Walrasian orthodoxy by introducing various frictions into the model. But they, too, work within the general equilibrium framework and assume representative goods and agents.[3,4]

### *1.2.3 Finance*

Finance theory started out as a field of business administration. Sensible decision making about how to finance operations is obviously vital for any firm, and the placement of free reserves into financial assets can have a substantial impact on the profitability of the enterprise. Markowitz's (1952) *mean–variance mechanics* was a breakthrough, offering a much more sophisticated decision rule than was common at the time, but one that was still simple to apply.

Markowitz's contribution serves as a tool for decision making; accordingly, his research is silent about the determination of asset prices. Their stochastic properties are taken as given. Subsequently, emphasis shifted away from

[2]Ramsey (1928) is a precursor to real business cycle theory and therefore an early contributor to a theory that only much later became part of "modern macroeconomics."

[3]Despite the fact that frictions render the first welfare theorem inoperative and thus remove the basis for aggregation!

[4]See Woodford (forthcoming) for an excellent survey of the development of macroeconomics.

using properties of asset prices to guide decisions, towards *explaining* asset prices. The *capital asset pricing model* (CAPM) of Sharpe (1964) and others assumes that the economy is populated by Markowitzian mean–variance decision makers. With the help of some additional assumptions, Sharpe concludes that the market portfolio must be mean–variance efficient, and that every agent must hold a mixture of the risk-free asset and the market portfolio (*two-fund separation theorem*). Most significantly, this theory implies that only that part of the risk of an asset that is correlated with the whole market carries a premium in equilibrium.

Today finance is largely concerned with the implications of *no arbitrage conditions* for asset prices. Absence of arbitrage opportunities is a weak form of rationality or equilibrium requirement.[5] An arbitrage portfolio is a portfolio that guarantees positive payoffs but whose price is zero or negative. If such a portfolio exists, it is possible to generate infinite payoffs without taking any risk. An absence of arbitrage opportunities means that asset prices must be such that no arbitrage portfolio exists. This is certainly reasonable, but the no arbitrage assumption alone does not allow one to incorporate all the economic fundamentals of preferences and endowments which arguably drive the decisions about intertemporal allocation and risk exposure; nor does it fully exploit the implications of market equilibrium. Equilibrium requires more: namely that the total supply of each asset equates the total demand for it. Relating asset prices to the extensive data of the economy in this way not only makes for a more complete (and hopefully more precise) theory, but also allows for interpretations of these prices that are beyond the range of possibilities when using just the assumption of arbitrage conditions alone.

### *1.2.4 Macrofinance: a unified general–equilibrium–asset–pricing–business–cycle–theory*

Traditional general equilibrium theory as well as macroeconomics focuses on the description of properties of equilibrium allocations. The scope is different, with macroeconomics concentrating on the time series (dynamical) aspects of aggregate measures of economic activity and traditional general equilibrium theory targeting questions of existence and efficiency of equilibria. But general equilibrium theory is also able to make statements about equilibrium prices. General equilibrium theory that focuses on the explanation of prices of financial assets may be called *equilibrium asset pricing theory*.

[5] Bachelier (1900), Fisher (1907), and Bronzin (1908) were very early contributors to this theory. I thank Heinz Zimmermann for pointing out Bronzin's book to me.

Equilibrium asset pricing theory in this generality (heterogeneous goods and agents and general preferences) has not enough structure to yield interesting results, though, and it has proved very fruitful to impose more structure on preferences.

It was (one of) Stiglitz's (1970) contribution(s) to connect finance more closely with economic theory. By explaining the demand for financial assets with a utility maximization problem whose ultimate goal is the optimal choice of consumption, he paved the way to Lucas's (1978) *tree model* and Breeden's (1979) *consumption capital asset pricing model* (CCAPM). Here we will call this model the *finance economy*, because it is a general equilibrium model that is simplified and specialized in exactly the way that financial economists have found useful. This model is the result of the combination of Arrow–Debreu–Radner general equilibrium theory and von Neumann–Morgenstern expected utility theory. The first welfare theorem of general equilibrium theory allows us to transform the general version of the model into a much simpler one-good, one-agent economy. We will discuss in detail how this aggregation can be performed. Expected utility theory gives much more structure to the behavior of people with respect to risk taking, and thus allows for a theory with more concrete predictions about equilibrium asset prices.

What exactly does the finance economy look like? First of all, there is only one agent, hence the equilibrium allocation is trivial: the single agent eats the output. Moreover, we are dealing with an exchange economy; that is to say, there is no production,[6] so the endowment is exogenous (but still stochastic). Thus, the equilibrium allocation is also exogenous: the single agent eats his own endowment.

What's the point of this? Why should a model like this be of interest? Since quantities are not the focus of the analysis, it is natural to choose a model in which the equilibrium allocation is given beforehand. Thus, moving from the traditional general equilibrium model to the finance economy simplifies the model in exactly the way we want: we lose information on items that we do not aim to explain, such as equilibrium trades, distribution, and allocations, but we keep all the information on equilibrium prices. Such a model is perfectly geared for investigating how changes of stochastic properties of endowments affect equilibrium prices of different kinds of securities.

The field that studies these relationships could be called *macrofinance*, because the objective is to explain financial market data with aggregate or macroeconomic shocks. By building on a complete (if simplified) general

[6] In fact, this is an exchange economy in which there is not even any exchange going on, because there is only one agent and the poor chap has no one to trade with.

equilibrium model, macrofinance provides microeconomic foundations for more conventional theories of finance. This microeconomic foundation helps us to gain deeper insights, because it relates asset price data to individual preferences over risk and time and aggregate consumption fluctuations, and thus allows us to interpret asset prices in terms of structural data of the economy.

## 1.3 The importance of the puzzles

This general model can be applied to a quite diverse set of objects. For instance, we can make predictions about the return rates of bonds of different maturities, thereby generating an equilibrium model of the term structure of interest rates. The model also makes predictions about the equilibrium return rate of risk-free bonds and of risky shares. The difference between the two is called the equity premium. Unfortunately, this application of the model fails miserably: it predicts a much higher risk-free return rate than what we observe in the data, and it predicts a very low (almost zero) equity premium, which is not at all what we typically observe in the data.

It is puzzling why anyone would invest in bonds rather than shares, given the large premium that equities offer. Standard theory could justify this if agents were subject to very large risks, or were very averse to being exposed to risk. National income accounting data tell us, however, that aggregate risk is small, and the assumption of very strong risk aversion contradicts experimental evidence. This empirical failure is called the *equity premium puzzle*. Similarly, consider that an impatient person's optimal consumption path is decreasing through time: he would rather consume early than late. The optimal consumption path of an infinitely patient person (having a discount factor of one) would be flat, because he would prefer to consume the same amount every year. But it is a fact that on average income grows every year. Thus, there is a tendency for people to dissave in order to transfer consumption from the future to the present. Of course, not everyone can dissave at the same time, and in equilibrium a high enough interest rate must provide an incentive for agents to postpone consumption. The trouble is that standard assumptions (a discount factor not exceeding one, moderate risk aversion) imply that the equilibrium interest rate should be much larger than the current market rate. This empirical failure has been named the *risk-free rate puzzle*.

The puzzles have initiated an extraordinary research effort. We will review some of this large literature dedicated to resolving the empirical failure of the model. Correcting this failure, as well as the question *how* we correct it, is important in three dimensions. First, since modern macroeconomic

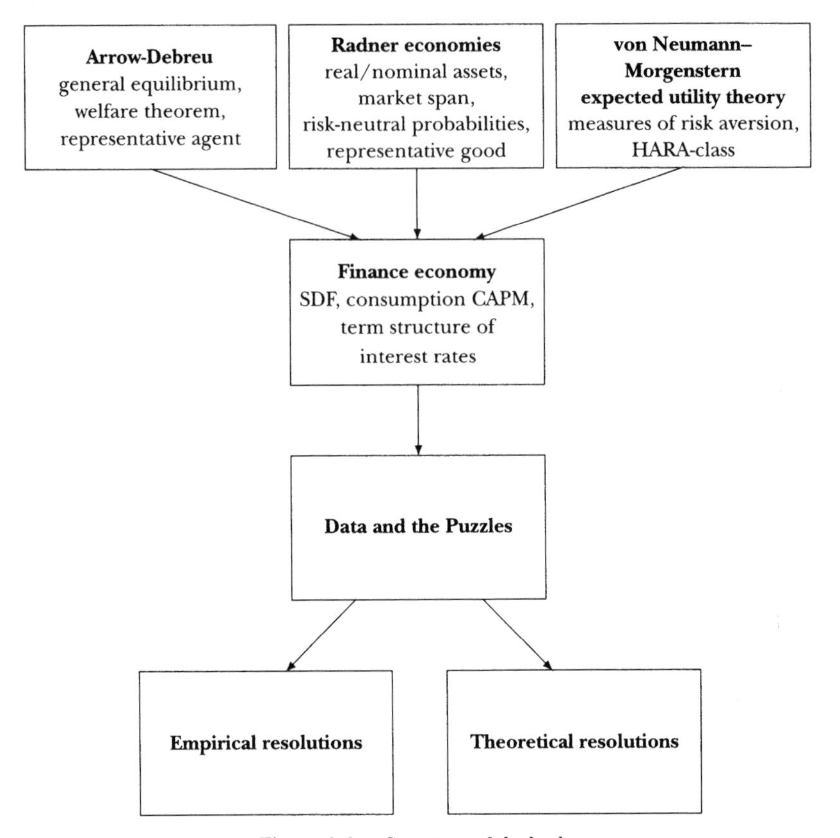


***Figure 1.1.*** *Structure of the book.*

theory is an application of the same model as the one underlying asset pricing theory, the way we resolve the puzzles will ultimately also influence our thinking about the mechanics of growth and business cycles. Second, different approaches taken to resolving the puzzles will result in different predictions about the future return to capital we can expect. Whether this will be 10% or only 3% per year has an enormous effect on pension systems and, more generally, on the appropriate amount of saving that each of us should undertake. And third, the fashion in which the model has to be changed to match the empirical data will also affect our view about the average attitude toward risk and, accordingly, the social cost we attribute to aggregate risk.

## 1.4 Outline of the book

The book develops general equilibrium asset pricing theory from the bottom up. We start with Arrow–Debreu (chapter 2) and Radner general equilibrium theory (chapter 3). Combining this with von Neumann–Morgenstern utility theory (chapter 4), we derive a model that we call finance economy (chapter 5). This model is the workhorse of macrofinance. We consider several special cases, and also extend the model to cover many periods (chapter 6). Only at this point do we confront the model with the data and identify the asset pricing puzzles (chapter 7). We then explore some of the avenues researchers have taken to bring the theoretical predictions closer to empirical evidence (chapter 8). The last chapter concludes by offering three directions in which the asset pricing puzzles can be interpreted, and speculating on what these interpretations imply for the future development of the theory, and the likely future performance of financial assets. Figure 1.1 shows the structure of the book and relates the different parts to each other.

# 2
# Contingent claim economy

Economists use the word *commodity* in a very precise way. Their definition of a commodity may seem peculiar to the non-initiated, but it is a powerful notion that is very helpful for thinking about economic problems. So we will begin this introductory chapter with a discussion of this important concept. After that we move on to the notion of a *general equilibrium of a contingent claim economy*. This, too, is a fundamental notion. At the same time, it is, in a way, the most simple and the most abstract representation of a complex economy. It is essential to have a solid understanding of these concepts. All that follows is built on top of them.

## 2.1 The commodity space

We call anything that people want to have but that costs something a *commodity* or a *good*. There are three rather obvious categories of properties that define a commodity. First is its *physical characteristics*. An apple is not the same commodity as a haircut or a car. A red pickup truck is not the same as a blue compact car.

Second is the *geographical place of availability*. An umbrella that is available in London is hardly the same commodity as one available in Togo, so the definition of a commodity needs also to include the geographical location of its availability. For some non-tangible goods (such as payment services or asset management services) this may not make much sense, but for many the distinction is relevant. The theory that concentrates on exchanges of commodities having different geographical specifications is called international trade if there is a national border between the geographical specifications.

The third property is the *time of availability*. Anyone who is at all impatient knows that income tomorrow is not the same as income today. Trading today's wealth for tomorrow's is called saving. Thus, by a broad enough definition of what a commodity is, we can view an inherently dynamic decision (such as saving) as a simple trade, much like an exchange of apples for bananas.

Besides physical properties, location, and time of availability, there is a fourth, and maybe less obvious, class of properties that define a commodity. This is the *conditionality* of commodities. Conditionality means that a good may or may not be useful or available, conditional on a specific event. To understand why it is useful to define a commodity by its conditionality, consider the following example. In many big cities, as soon as it starts to rain you can see people selling umbrellas at street corners or at the exits of metro stations. You do not see those traders on a nice sunny day—or if you do they may be selling flowers or ice cream rather than umbrellas. Why is this? Well, obviously, an umbrella is much more useful when it rains than when the sun is shining. For this very same reason, the price of an umbrella could be expected to change with the weather: on a sunny day the price may drop to near zero, but on rainy days it should be sufficiently high to enable the umbrella sellers to make a profit—which is why they appear on street corners. So it seems that the same commodity, an umbrella, can have two different prices, depending on meteorological conditions. But in standard microeconomics a commodity is supposed to have just one price, not many. How do we get rid of this predicament? We say that "an umbrella" is not a well defined commodity. Rather, we have to distinguish two commodities, "umbrella when it rains" and "umbrella when it is not raining." The first commodity is much more useful than the second, and thus carries a significantly higher price.

More generally, there is no harm in defining a commodity as a physically differentiated good or service, *conditional on random events.* By "random events" we mean things that we consider to be exogenous to our decision making, like the weather, the outbreak of war,[1] or the last winner of the national lottery.[2]

Formally, let $\mathcal{S}$ denote the set of possible states of the world. We assume that $\mathcal{S}$ is a finite set with $S$ elements.[3] For each period $t$ there is a partition

[1]Which is not truly exogenous (someone does start the war), but is often treated as being exogenous.

[2]Which also is not really exogenous. At least the set of players and, therefore, the set of potential winners, is endogenous.

[3]Conceptually, we could assume an infinite number of states, but the mathematics would be more difficult, so we avoid this.

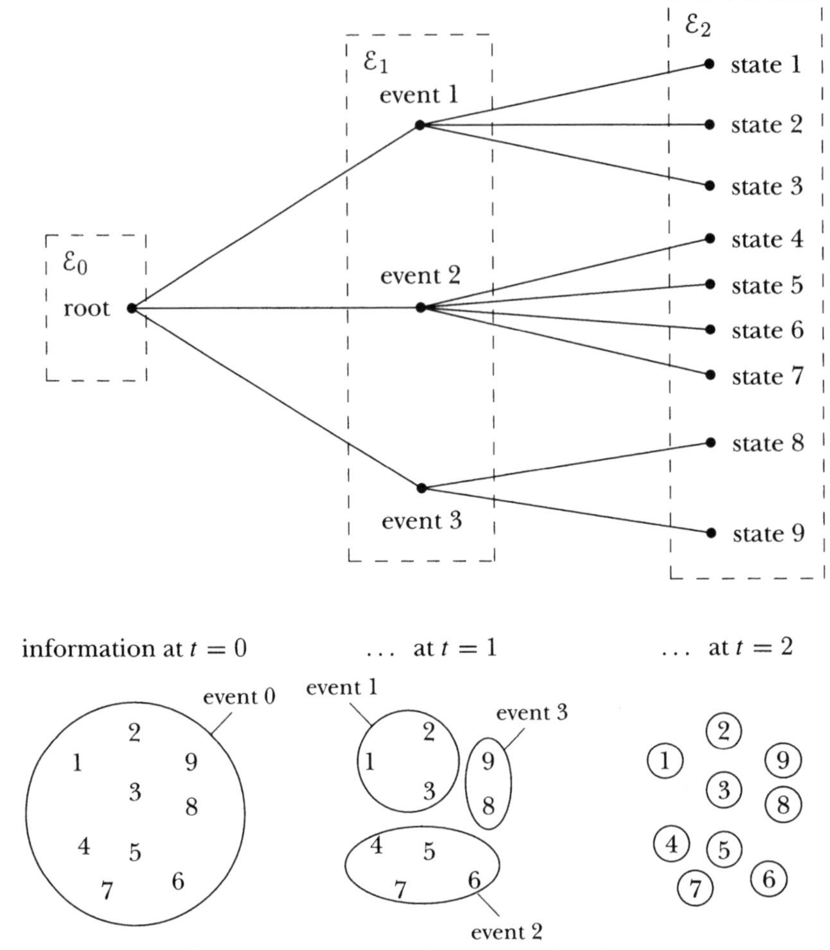


***Figure 2.1.*** *Resolution of uncertainty through time.*

$\mathcal{E}_t$ of $\mathcal{S}$.[4] The elements of $\mathcal{E}_t$ are the events that can happen at time $t$. At each point in time all agents know the event that has taken place, i.e., they know which event, $e \in \mathcal{E}_t$, is realized; but the agents do not know which state within this event, $s \in e$, is realized. $\mathcal{E}_0$ is the root, meaning that at this time no information about the state of the world is known. Thus, $\mathcal{E}_0$ has just one

[4]A partition is a collection of non-empty and pairwise disjoint subsets whose union makes up the whole set (like the pieces of a cake). Formally, to say that $\mathcal{E}_t$ is a partition of $\mathcal{S}$ means that $\mathcal{E}_t := \{e_1, e_2, \ldots, e_m\}$ such that $\forall j \; e_j \subset \mathcal{S}$, $e_j \neq \emptyset$, $\forall (j, i) \; e_j \cap e_i = \emptyset$ if $i \neq j$, and $\cup_{j=1}^{m} e_j = \mathcal{S}$.

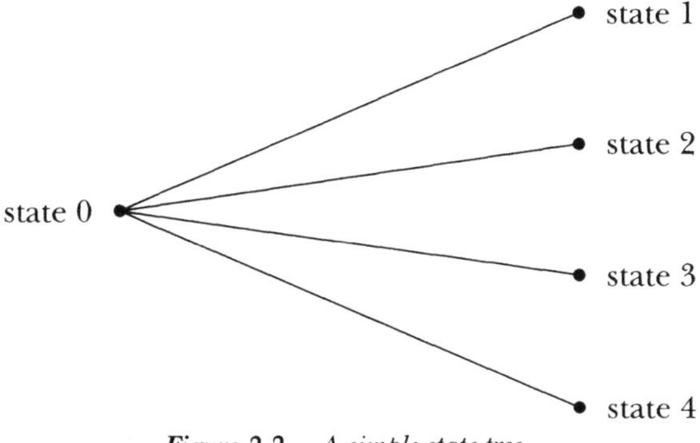


***Figure 2.2.*** *A simple state tree.*

element, namely $\mathcal{E}_0 = \{\mathcal{S}\}$. Let time proceed sequentially from $0, 1, 2, \ldots, T$. As time progresses, the partition of events becomes ever finer,[5] indicating that the initial uncertainty resolves slowly through time. If we consider a model with finite time, there is a final period $T$ in which all uncertainty is resolved, $\mathcal{E}_T = \{\{1\}, \{2\}, \ldots, \{S\}\}$. The upper half of Figure 2.1 depicts such an event tree. The lower half shows the same thing in an alternative way: at each point in time people know in which component of the information partition they are, but they do not know the true state of the world until the end of time.

When we say that commodities are event contingent, we mean that for each point in time there is an umbrella, but it is available if and only if a specific event of this period of time is realized.

The event tree simplifies considerably in a two-period model. In the first period there is complete uncertainty about the state of the world. In the second period all the uncertainty is resolved and the state of the world is known.[6] Thus, uncertainty is resolved in one step in a two-period model. Figure 2.2 depicts a two-period event tree. In this case we can talk about state contingency instead of event contingency. Until chapter 6 we will use two-period models only, so for the time being it is sufficient for us just to consider this simpler situation.

[5]Formally, this means that, for all $e \in \mathcal{E}_t$ and $t \geqslant 1$, there exists $e' \in \mathcal{E}_{t-1}$ such that $e' \supset e$. So $\mathcal{E}_0, \mathcal{E}_1, \ldots$ is a nested sequence of partitions. Such a structure is called a *filtration*.

[6]We often refer to the root of the event tree in a two-period model as state 0, meaning that this is the event in which nothing is known about the true state.

**Box 2.1** *Definition of a commodity*

A complete description of a commodity requires a specification of the following components;

- physical specification,
- place of availability,
- event contingency (or state contingency in a two-period model).

Where is the time contingency we mentioned in the beginning of this section? Well, since events belong to a specific time period, event contingency already embodies time contingency, so there is no need to specify the time of availability separately if the event the commodity is contingent on has been specified.

## 2.2 Preferences and ordinal utility

With such an extensive definition of a commodity, it is pretty clear that there ought to be a huge number of commodities. In fact, a particular combination of commodities comes close to defining the biography of a person: 1971–1973: lots of milk, pacifiers, a room in a four-bedroom flat in the city, clothing, many diapers, various toys; 1974–1975: electric toy train, new bed, a bicycle; 1976–1979: "cool" clothing, a bigger bike, skateboard, various books, stereo; 1980–1982: a room in a semi-detached house in the suburbs, 550 train rides, 400 visits to McDonald's, a pair of skis and five trips to ski resorts; 1983–1985: a motorbike, a helmet, lots of gas, 250 visits to various cinemas and clubs, more books; and so on.

Notice that this bundle of commodities does not specify any events. By making these commodities event-contingent, we could also cover different biographies depending on random events, such as, "If I have an accident with the motorbike, I will receive $X$ type of medical treatment," or "If there is a major earthquake in my neighborhood and I survive, I will stay on there or I will move away".

The economic person we are studying is supposed to be able to rank these different "lives" (or, more precisely, consumption bundles) in the sense that, when he faces a choice between two of them, he is able to express which one he prefers.

Let $\ell$ be the number of different commodities. Then a *consumption bundle* is a list of $\ell$ numbers, indicating the quantities of each commodity. Thus, a consumption bundle is a point in $\mathbb{R}^\ell$. If an agent prefers bundle 1 over bundle 2 we write

$$\text{bundle 1} \succ \text{bundle 2},$$

where the symbol $\succ$ expresses preference. Under some axioms, which will not be of interest here,[7] one can show that this implies that the preferences of the agent can be represented by a utility function, $u\colon \mathbb{R}^\ell \to \mathbb{R}$, such that

$$\text{bundle 1} \succ \text{bundle 2} \iff u(\text{bundle 1}) > u(\text{bundle 2}).$$

We assume that the utility function is continuous (it has no jumps.), it is increasing (more of any commodity is better than less), strictly quasi-concave (some of everything is better than lots of something and nothing of other things), and smooth differentiable arbitrarily many times).

The utility function serves to order the points in $\mathbb{R}^\ell$ (the set of commodity bundles) in the right way. For every preference relation $\succ$ there are many utility functions that achieve that. Suppose $u$ represents $\succ$. Then $v\colon x \mapsto 2u(x)$ also represents $\succ$ because $v$ orders the points in $\mathbb{R}^\ell$ in the same way as $u$ does. In fact, any positive transformation of $u$ will have this same property and thus will represent $\succ$ equally well.

**Box 2.2** ***Equivalent utility functions***

The representation of a preference ordering by a utility function is determined only up to a positive transformation. In other words, two utility functions are equivalent if one can be obtained from the other by a positive transformation.

Technically speaking, $v$ is a positive transformation of $u$ if there exists a strictly increasing function $f\colon \mathbb{R} \to \mathbb{R}$ such that for all $x$ it is true that $v(x) = f(u(x))$. If this is the case, $v$ and $u$ induce *the same indifference curves.* Here is an example: the utility functions $\sqrt{x_1 x_2}$ and $\ln x_1 + \ln x_2$ are equivalent.

A utility function that represents a preference ordering is sometimes said to be *ordinal.* That means that the utility function can be used only to "order" or "rank" different commodity bundles with respect to the satisfaction they provide; the level of the utility itself does not provide any information, nor

[7]These axioms say that the preference relation is asymmetric ($a \succ b \Rightarrow b \not\succ a$), that the preference relation and its negation are transitive ($a \succ b$ and $b \succ c$ implies $a \succ c$; $a \not\succ b$ and $b \not\succ c$ implies $a \not\succ c$), and that, for every consumption bundle $x$, the set of strictly better and the set of strictly worse consumption bundles are open sets; see Kreps (1988, chapters 2 and 3) or Kreps (1990, chapter 2) for a detailed presentation.

does the difference of the utilities associated with different bundles carry any information. For instance, it does not mean anything to say that bundle $x$ provides "twice as much satisfaction" than bundle $x'$ because $u(x) = 2u(x')$. Likewise, it does not make any sense to say that $x$ is better than $x'$ "by the same amount" that $y$ is better than $y'$, because $u(x) - u(x') = u(y) - u(y')$. Why does this not make sense? A simple monotonic transformation of $u$ would not change the preferences that are being characterized by the utility function, but it would mess up those equalities. Hence, these equalities have no meaning in terms of the underlying preferences. In chapter 4 we will encounter a stronger form of utility function which is more than just ordinal: it is *cardinal*.

## 2.3 Maximization

The most basic notion of rationality is that of choosing the option you like the best from all available alternatives. Economics is built on this assumption. In the context of markets and perfect competition, rationality simply means that everyone chooses the consumption bundle he deems the best among the set of consumption bundles he can afford. We know what "deems best" means: it is an expression of taste or preferences, and is mathematically modelled as a preference relation or utility function. It remains for us to define what "affords" means.

### *2.3.1 Endowment, trade, and rate of exchange*

We have learned about the economists' notion of commodities, and we know how economists model tastes. The third fundamental notion is *endowment*. An agent's endowment is simply a list of the quantities of all the commodities he owns, before any trade has taken place. For most of us, the biggest item in this list is the labor service we are able to provide over our lifetime.

Consider a situation with $\ell$ commodities. You are endowed with some amount of each of the commodities, $\omega_1, \omega_2, \ldots, \omega_\ell$. Suppose that you consider your initial endowment as not a very satisfactory combination of goods. For instance, it might contain a large capacity to work and the car you received from your parents for your eighteenth birthday, but no housing, food, or gas. It would make sense to trade some of your labor power for those missing commodities. But how much do you have to work, and how much housing, food, and gas will you get in exchange?

In a perfectly competitive economy, this is determined by market prices. Suppose that for each commodity there is a market and hence a price,

$p_1, p_2, \ldots, p_\ell$. The monetary value of your endowment, your *wealth*, equals the monetary value of each thing you own, so your wealth is $\sum_{c=1}^{\ell} p_c \omega_c$. As a shortcut for that term, we may simply write $p \cdot \omega$ (the inner product). The *budget constraint* says that you can consume any combination of goods, $x_1, x_2, \ldots, x_\ell$, whose monetary value does not exceed your wealth. So, you will be able to buy food, housing, and gas that is worth (at most) as much as the value of labor you sell in exchange for it. Formally, the budget constraint requires

$$p \cdot x \leqslant p \cdot \omega, \quad \text{or more compactly,} \quad p \cdot (x - \omega) \leqslant 0.$$

$x - \omega$ is your *excess demand*. It is the amount you consume in excess of your endowment. The budget constraint requires that the value of your excess demand must be non-positive. Note that if all prices are positive then, if some component of your excess demand is positive, $x_i - \omega_i > 0$ (you buy food), some other component must be negative, $x_j - \omega_j < 0$ (you sell labor) in order for the budget constraint to be satisfied.

Depending on how the commodities we are looking at are defined (in terms of physical specification, time of availability, and state of availability), we may give prices different names. We may talk about interest rates, exchange rates, or insurance premia instead of prices, but these terms are really equivalent. Most generally, we call the rate of exchange between two commodities (how much food for one unit of labor) the *relative price*, $p_i/p_j$.

### 2.3.2 Maximizing preference subject to a budget

The fundamental assumption of economics, what we call *rationality*, is that everyone ought to choose the bundle he likes best given the constraints that are imposed on him. Your endowment and the market prices together define the set of commodity bundles (or *lives*, given the broad definition of commodities) that you can afford. Within a market the only constraint individuals are subject to is their budget, so in a market setting rationality just means that you should choose what you like most among the things you can afford; or in techno-speak, we assume that agents maximize preference subject to a budget constraint. Formally, the problem is

$$\max \{u(x) \mid p \cdot (x - \omega) \leqslant 0\}. \tag{2.1}$$

To make this problem easy to deal with, we impose two additional assumptions on top of those needed to represent preferences with an ordinal utility function: we assume that preferences are strictly *convex*, and that the indifference curves have no kinks. Strict convexity means that, if a person is indifferent between two rides on the roller coaster and two bungee jumps, then he strictly prefers one of each of these thrills. This assumption will make sure that the best consumption bundle is a continuous function of prices. (Strict) convexity of preferences is equivalent to (strict) quasi-concavity of the utility function. The no-kinks-in-the-indifference-curves assumption is equivalent to the possibility of representing these preferences with a *differentiable* utility function. This allows us to use calculus. The assumptions of *strict* convexity and differentiability are made just for convenience.

Maximization of a monotonic, strictly quasi-concave, differentiable utility function, $u$, subject to a budget constraint, $p \cdot (x - \omega) \leqslant 0$, implies (assuming an interior solution) that there exists a positive number $\lambda$ such that[8]

$$\partial_c u(x) = \lambda p_c, \qquad \text{for } c = 1, \ldots, \ell,$$

or, in vector notation,

$$\nabla u(x) = \lambda p. \tag{2.2}$$

This is the Kuhn–Tucker theorem; see e.g. Sundaram (1996, Theorem 6.1). $\lambda$ is some scalar (the Lagrangian multiplier) that measures the marginal utility of wealth, and $\nabla u(x) := (\partial_1 u(x), \ldots, \partial_\ell u(x))$ is the vector of partial derivatives of $u$ at the point $x$, and is called the *gradient* of $u$ at $x$.[9] This equation simply says that the gradient of the utility function at the optimal consumption bundle $x$ points in the same direction as the price vector; in math-speak, the gradient and the price vector must be collinear (i.e. they point into the same direction).[10] Figure 2.3 shows why this must be so: if it were not, then there would be another consumption bundle that was affordable (i.e. in the budget set), yielding a higher satisfaction.

From (2.2) it follows that for any pair of commodities $(i, j)$ we have

$$\frac{\partial_i u(x)}{\partial_j u(x)} = \frac{p_i}{p_j}. \tag{2.3}$$

This says that the marginal rate of substitution (the left-hand side of the equation) equals the relative price (the right-hand side). This is an important relationship which we will use repeatedly.

[8] $\partial_i f$ denotes the partial derivative of function $f$ with respect to its $i$th argument (see Appendix A for a list of symbols and their meaning).

[9] Geometrically, the gradient is an arrow that points into the direction of the steepest climb up the utility hill.

[10] Eq. (2.2) is the first-order condition of the maximization of the Lagrangian, $\max_{x,\lambda} L(x, \lambda)$ with $L(x, \lambda) := u(x) - \lambda(p \cdot (x - \omega))$. The gradient at $x$ is a vector that is orthogonal to the hyperplane, which is tangent to the indifference curve through $x$.

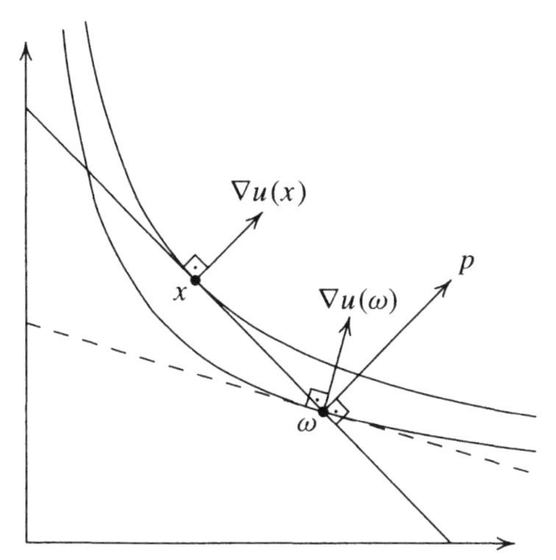


***Figure 2.3.*** *Maximization of a standard preference subject to a budget requires that the gradient of the utility at the maximum be collinear to the price vector, i.e.* $\nabla u(x) = \lambda p$ *for some* $\lambda > 0$.

**Box 2.3** ***Maximality condition***

In the utility maximum, the decision maker's marginal rate of substitution between two commodities equals the relative price of these two goods. Equivalently, the price vector is collinear to the gradient of the utility function at the consumption point.

Note that the maximization problem (2.1) can have a solution only if all prices are strictly positive, because we assume that preferences are monotonic. Thus, $\nabla u(x) \gg 0$ for any $x$, and since the gradient must be collinear to the price it must be that $p \gg 0$.[11] Less technically, suppose there is a commodity with a zero or even negative price, $p_c \leqslant 0$. If $p_c = 0$ the agent can increase utility by demanding ever more of this commodity (by the monotonicity assumption). So his objective function is monotonically increasing in one of its arguments and, since the price is zero demand, is not constrained by the budget. But that means that there is no choice that maximizes utility subject to the budget. The situation is even more extreme if a price is negative, $p_c < 0$. The agent could then increase his purchasing power by "buying" more of this commodity $c$, and spending the amount of money he gets from this purchase (the price is negative) on other goods

[11]We use $\leqslant$ and $<$ to denote inequalities of numbers. For vectors $x, y \in \mathbb{R}^n$, we say $x \leqq y \iff \forall i (x_i \leqslant y_i)$, we say $x \ll y \iff \forall i (x_i < y_i)$, and we say $x \leq y \iff \forall i (x_i \leqslant y_i)$ and $\exists i (x_i < y_i)$. See Appendix A for a list of symbols.

with positive prices. But there is no limit to this scheme. Thus, the individual could increase his purchase of all commodities indefinitely. This again means that there is no maximum.

### 2.3.3 Dichotomy

Notice also that the budget constraint (that is, the set of affordable consumption bundles) does not change if we re-scale the price vector by multiplying each price $p_c$ with some positive constant $\mu$. This will simply make the price vector longer or shorter, but it will not affect the hyperplane that is orthogonal to it. You can see this graphically: making the arrow labelled $p$ in Figure 2.3 longer or shorter, without changing its direction, leaves the budget set, and hence the maximum, unaffected. In fact, changing $\mu$ is like a currency reform in which you add or remove a zero from all prices. Such a change has no economic meaning (in this model). This is why the standard competitive equilibrium theory is unable to analyze the general price level. We can only say something about relative prices and real allocations. This fact has been coined the *classical dichotomy* in the literature (Patinkin, 1965).

> **Box 2.4** *Classical dichotomy*
>
> Only the relative prices affect behavior. The price level is irrelevant.

Because of classical dichotomy, we can normalize prices without affecting any economically relevant data. For instance, often we consider price vectors with components that sum to unity, $\sum_{c=1}^{\ell} p_c = 1$. We say that such price vectors are in the *unit simplex*.

### 2.3.4 Interpretations of relative prices

In our everyday lives we come across many prices, for instance as tags on a loaf of bread or a car, but not all of them are as straightforward as those. Some of the most important prices for our purpose are interest rates and insurance premiums. We discuss how these prices relate to the prices of state-contingent commodities discussed above.

**Interest rates as relative prices**

Consider a decision problem that looks more "dynamic." To make the problem simple, suppose there are just two periods, today and tomorrow. Suppose also that you have some wealth $w$ today, and you want to decide how much to save in order to consume today and tomorrow. If you save the amount $s$, you will be able to consume the remaining part of your endowment, $w - s$, today. You can invest your savings either in a savings account or in a bond or similar asset, which pays a (non-random) gross interest rate of $\rho$,[12] so you will be able to consume $\rho s$ tomorrow. Your decision problem can thus be written as

$$\max_{s} u(w - s, \rho s). \tag{2.4}$$

The first-order condition of this problem is

$$-\partial_1 u + \rho \partial_2 u = 0.$$

Thus the marginal rate of substitution equals

$$\frac{\partial_1 u}{\partial_2 u} = \rho, \tag{2.5}$$

but by (2.3) this must equal the relative price. Therefore, the gross interest rate $\rho$ can be expressed with period prices $p_1$ and $p_2$ as,

$$\rho = \frac{p_1}{p_2}. \tag{2.6}$$

$p_1$ is the price of an asset that delivers \$1 today. Such an asset obviously costs \$1. $p_2$ is the price of an asset that pays \$1 tomorrow. It is a *bond.* If the interest rate is, say, 4%, then a bond that matures in the next period costs $p_2 \approx 0.9615 (\text{because} p = 1.04 = p_1/p_2 = 1/p_2)$.[13]

Note that $\rho - 1$ is the gross *real* interest rate, that is, the gross interest rate in terms of commodities, or the terms of trade of tomorrow's versus today's real purchasing power. In principle, the (net) real interest rate can be negative ($\rho - 1 < 0$), but it cannot fall below minus one[14] in equilibrium because then no one would save (if utility is increasing). If the interest rate is negative it means that $p_1 < p_2$; that is, tomorrow's consumption is more valuable than today's consumption. Typically, we would expect a positive interest rate ($\rho - 1 > 0$) because people tend to be impatient. A positive interest rate implies $p_1 > p_2$, which means that today's consumption is more valuable than tomorrow's, in accordance with the assumed impatience of the people.

[12]If the interest rate is 4%, then $\rho = 1.04$.

[13]To be a little bit more precise, the period–2 asset we are considering here does not simply pay \$1 tomorrow, but it delivers tomorrow the purchasing power that \$1 has today. In other words, we consider an *inflation indexed bond.* It may not be perfectly clear what this means, but we will discuss this later in section 3.1.

[14]To accept an interest rate $\rho - 1$ of minus one (or equivalently a gross interest rate $\rho = 0$) is like burning money. Such an "investment" is never reasonable.

**Box 2.5** ***Interest rate as relative price***

The gross real interest rate is the relative price of consumption today versus that of consumption tomorrow. Conversely, the price of an inflation-indexed bond is the relative price of tomorrow's consumption versus that of today's.

### Insurance premia as relative prices

Consider now a situation with no time dimension, but with two states of the world. Suppose you have wealth $w$. If you are lucky (if state 1 occurs) you will keep that wealth. If you are unlucky (if state 2 occurs) you will suffer a damage $d$. So your endowment is $w$ in state 1 and $w - d$ in state 2, or more compactly $(w, w - d)$. There is an insurance company that offers to cover the loss, if it materializes, in exchange for a premium which you will have to pay to the insurer independent of the state of the world. If you choose full coverage you will receive the amount $d$ in state 2 and zero in state 1. This insurance costs a premium $\mu$. Let us assume, however, that you can choose any coverage rate $c$ (also less than zero or greater than one). If you choose a coverage $c$ (say 60%), you will receive $cd$ in state 2 from the insurance company, and you will receive zero in state 1. The premium for this partial coverage is $c\mu$. Your decision problem is this:

$$\max_c u(w - c\mu, w - c\mu - d + cd). \tag{2.7}$$

The first-order condition yields

$$\frac{\partial_1 u}{\partial_2 u} = \frac{d - \mu}{\mu}. \tag{2.8}$$

But by (2.3) we know that this must equal $p_1/p_2$. We can rearrange this to get

$$\frac{\mu}{d} = \frac{p_2}{p_1 + p_2}. \tag{2.9}$$

This means that the *premium per damage*, $\mu/d$ (this is the premium expressed in percentage of the damage), can be expressed in terms of the state prices $p_1$ and $p_2$.

**Box 2.6** ***Insurance premium as relative price***

The insurance premium, expressed as a percentage of the damage, is the relative price between consumption that is contingent on the bad state and state-independent (or certain, or safe) consumption.

What is a safe asset? It is an asset that pays one unit of income no matter what state occurs. It is, in fact, a bundle of state-contingent commodities, one for each possible state, so that the delivery of the commodity is not contingent on the state anymore. With only two states, such a bundle costs $p_1 + p_2$, which is the denominator of the right-hand side of (2.9).

## 2.4 General equilibrium

We have learned what an economic commodity is, and we have learned the classical economic model of individual choice between commodity bundles. These individual choices need to be compatible with each other. For instance, if everyone preferred to consume more leisure and work less at the going wage, a serious deficiency in production would emerge.

General equilibrium theory studies the interaction of optimizing agents through markets. Classical questions posed by general equilibrium theory all concern specific properties of the set of equilibria. For instance, does an equilibrium exist? (Yes.) Is the equilibrium unique? (Usually not.) If it is not unique, are there at least only a small number of equilibria? (Typically, yes.) Are the equilibrium allocations efficient? (Yes.)

In macrofinance we are not really concerned with existence. Nor are we much interested in equilibrium allocations. Our focus is equilibrium prices, and how they relate to utilities and endowments of the agents. More specifically, we would like to know how equilibrium prices relate to aggregate data, such as "average tastes" and "average endowments." It is sufficiently clear what an average endowment could be. It is far less clear what average tastes should be. This is the aggregation problem: to find a single artificial agent—the representative agent—that behaves in the same way as the diverse agents behave on average when faced with the same prices.

It is worth noticing that microeconomists and macroeconomists tend to use the term "representative agent" somewhat differently. For a microeconomic general equilibrium theorist, the representative agent is supposed to behave the same as the aggregate not only in equilibrium, but everywhere (Mas-Colell et al., 1995, chapter 4.D) also at off-equilibrium prices. Such a *global representative* is required when we want to do comparative statics. In contrast, financial economists and macroeconomists are usually happy with a *local representative*, i.e. an artificial agent that behaves the same as the aggregate only at equilibrium prices. The reason for this less demanding definition is that it is used only to relate aggregate data, such as average endowment, to asset prices in equilibrium. In this chapter we will learn how to construct a local representative.

In chapter 3 we will learn also how to simplify a model of an economy with many commodities into a model featuring only one *aggregate commodity*, namely wealth. Combining this with a representative agent, we wil end up with a one-good, one-agent economy. This will be very helpful for studying the macroeconomic determinants of asset prices.

### 2.4.1 Abstract exchange economy

Generally—and certainly empirically—an economy provides a home for many agents, each having different tastes and endowments, and trading many commodities. Formally, we define a *contingent claim economy* (Debreu, 1959) by making a list of all its relevant elements. In addition to what we have discussed so far, an economy also contains different production technologies which transform one set of commodities (land and labor) into other commodities (bananas). Yet, for the most part, we abstract from production.

For simplicity we stick to a two-period model—today and tomorrow—with $S$ states tomorrow and $M$ commodities in each state, so that together there are $(S+1)M$ contingent commodities ($M$ spot commodities today and $M$ spot commodities in each of the $S$ states tomorrow). To ease manipulation of the elements of the theory, let us reorder endowments, consumption bundles, and prices so that they are matrices and not vectors, as they were before. We write

$$\omega(i) := \begin{bmatrix} \omega_1^0(i) & \cdots & \omega_1^S(i) \\ \vdots & \ddots & \vdots \\ \omega_M^0(i) & \cdots & \omega_M^S(i) \end{bmatrix}, \qquad x(i) := \begin{bmatrix} x_1^0(i) & \cdots & x_1^S(i) \\ \vdots & \ddots & \vdots \\ x_M^0(i) & \cdots & x_M^S(i) \end{bmatrix},$$

$$p := \begin{bmatrix} p_0^1 & \cdots & p_0^M \\ \vdots & \ddots & \vdots \\ p_S^1 & \cdots & p_S^M \end{bmatrix}.$$

**Box 2.7** ***Contingent claim economy***

An agent is defined by his utility function, $u_i : \mathbb{R}^{(S+1)M} \to \mathbb{R}$, and his endowment, $\omega(i) \in \mathbb{R}^{(S+1)M}$. Thus, the pair $(u_i, \omega(i))$ characterizes an agent. A *contingent claim economy* is simply a collection of all agents, $\{(u_i, \omega(i)) : i = 1, \ldots, I\}$. For short, we may simply write $(u, \omega)$.

As discussed in section 2.3, the decision problem of an agent in a contingent claim economy is to choose a consumption bundle today ($x^0(i)$) and a state-contingent consumption bundle tomorrow ($x^1(i), \ldots, x^S(i)$) such as to maximize utility subject to the budget constraint. Formally,

$$\max \left\{ u_i(x(i)) \;\middle|\; \sum_{s=0}^{S} p_s \cdot (x^s(i) - \omega^s(i)) \leqslant 0 \right\}. \tag{2.10}$$

This is the same as (2.1), only the constraint is formulated a little bit less compactly.

The problem is that the decisions of Mr. X and Mr. Y might not be compatible with each other. If a good is too cheap, most people will want to buy it since it is so cheap, but only few people will be willing to sell it. Demand will exceed supply. For another good, which is too expensive, the situation will be opposite: most people will want to sell it, but only few desperate people will be able and willing to purchase it at such inflated prices. An *equilibrium price* is a price vector at which aggregate demand equals aggregate supply for each commodity simultaneously.

**Box 2.8** ***Competitive equilibrium***

An *equilibrium* is a pair $(p, x)$, consisting of a matrix of prices, $p \in \mathbb{R}^{(S+1)M}$, and a collection of consumption bundles, $x(i)$, one for each agent, such that, for each $i$, $x(i)$ maximizes $i$'s utility subject to the budget constraint, given $p$ (i.e. it is a solution to (2.10)), and all markets clear:

$$\sum_{i=1}^{I} x^s_m(i) = \sum_{i=1}^{I} \omega^s_m(i), \qquad s = 0, 1, \ldots, S;\; m = 1, \ldots, M.$$

### 2.4.2 Excursion: Existence of an equilibrium

The question of existence of an equilibrium is important for any model because it answers the question about the possibility of internal consistency of a model. A model that cannot even guarantee that an equilibrium exists is a model that is inconsistent or at least incomplete in some sense, because it does not specify what happens outside of equilibrium.

We need a few additional definitions in order to consider why the existence of equilibrium may be a problem in our model or, more precisely, what assumptions are sufficient to ensure existence. Let us define $i$'s *demand function*, $d^i$, as the function that maps the prices $p$ to the consumption bundle $x(i)$ that solves $i$'s problem given $p$, so $d^i(p)$ maximizes utility subject to the budget. Because preferences are assumed to be continuous and strictly convex, they can be represented by a continuous and strictly quasi-concave utility function. Thus, by the Maximum Theorem (Bartle, 1976, page 153ff.), the demand functions that result from (2.1) are continuous. Let the aggregate demand function be the sum of all individual demand functions, $D(p) := \sum_{i=1}^{I} d^i(p)$. Aggregate endowment is denoted with $\Omega := \sum_{i=1}^{I} \omega(i)$. $p$ is an equilibrium price if and only if $D(p) = \Omega$.

The literature on existence is extensive. Why is that so? After all, suppose there are $\ell$ commodities ($\ell$ equals $(S+1)M$ in a two-period model with uncertainty); then $D(p) = \Omega$ is a system of $\ell$ equations ($D_c(p) = \Omega_c$ for $c = 1, \ldots, \ell$) in $\ell$ unknowns $(p_1, \ldots, p_\ell)$. Is that not sufficient to make sure that there is precisely one solution? Well, no. To see why, it suffices to consider "systems" of one equation in one unknown. In the following we will always try to

$$\text{find an } x \text{ such that } f(x) = 0.$$

Consider the following examples of $f$ (make a graph for each of these examples):

1. $f(x) := 3 - x$,
2. $f(x) := x^2 - 1$,
3. $f(x) := 0$,
4. $f(x) := 1$,
5. $f(x) := \begin{cases} x - 1 & \text{if } x < 0, \\ x + 1 & \text{if } x \geqslant 0. \end{cases}$

There is a simple solution in case 1 ($x = 3$). There are two solutions in case 2 ($x = -1$ and $x = +1$). Case 3 is a little pathological because every $x$ is a solution. There are no solutions in cases 4 and 5. The same cases can occur in a multi-dimensional setting when there is more than just one commodity. To prove existence, we need to make sure that the excess demand function $D(p) - \Omega$ does not belong to case 4 or 5. This is the topic of the literature on existence of a general equilibrium.

What do we know about $D$? We have already argued that the individual demand functions $d^i$ are continuous functions, hence the aggregate demand function $D$ is also continuous, ruling out situations like case 5 above. Further, if preferences are monotonic and the endowments are strictly positive (everyone owns something of everything), then excess demand explodes near the boundary, that is to say, if $p_s^m$ converges to zero, then excess demand for state-$s$ contingent commodity $m$ diverges to infinity, ruling out situations like case 4.

We conclude that existence is now guaranteed because all remaining cases 1–3 do have a root. To make this argument rigorous and prove that there are no other cases that we might have forgotten, we need to invoke a fixed point theorem. The simplest such theorem is the *intermediate value theorem* (IVT) (Bartle, 1976, page 153). It states that a continuous function from the real line into itself, and which has a positive value at some point and a negative value at another, also has a point in between at which it is zero. Figuratively, this theorem says that the chicken has to cross the road somewhere. We can use this theorem to prove existence of a general equilibrium if we restrict ourselves to economies with only two commodities. We know from classical dichotomy (Box 2.4) that we can normalize prices as we like so long as we do not distort relative prices, so let us normalize a price vector $(p_1, p_2)$ by setting $p_2 = 1$. $p_1$ is then just the relative price of good 1 vis-à-vis good 2. Suppose that everyone believes that having more of a good is always better than having less (technically, preferences are monotonic), and consider a sequence of relative prices $p_1$ that converge to zero. This means that good 1 becomes increasingly cheaper than good 2. Buying more of good 1 will thus imply giving up less and less of good 2, and because preferences are monotonic demand for good one will diverge to infinity. Likewise, if we consider a sequence of relative prices $p_1$ that become increasingly greater, demand for good one will eventually converge to zero. This convergence will hold for each individual as well as for the aggregate demand. If we also assume that aggregate endowment is positive, this means that, for a sufficiently small relative price $p_1$, excess demand $[D_1(p_1, 1) - \Omega_1]$ for good 1 will be positive, and for a sufficiently large relative price excess demand will be negative. Therefore, by the IVT, there must be at least one (maybe many) relative price $p_1$ at which excess demand vanishes. This point is an equilibrium.

With more dimensions (more than two commodities), the IVT must be replaced with a more advanced argument. The boundary behavior allows us to restrict attention to a compact set of prices, bounded away from zero, because we know that there cannot exist a root on the boundary (when some relative price is zero). Brouwer's Theorem (Bartle, 1976, page 161ff.) establishes that a continuous map from a compact set into itself has a fixed point, i.e. a price $p$ at which $D(p) - \Omega + p = p$; hence $D(p) = \Omega$, an equilibrium. Notice, however, that we cannot rule out multiple equilibria (situations similar to cases 2 and 3 above).[15]

Existence of an equilibrium of a contingent claim economy is not our main concern here, though. We use general equilibrium theory only because we want to aggregate individuals' decisions so as to relate asset prices to the aggregate data that are available to us. If you want to get the whole detailed picture of existence proofs, there are many good sources you can consult. The classic reference is Debreu (1959). A very clean step-by-step development can be found in Hildenbrand & Kirman (1988). A quick but thorough treatment is provided by Mas-Colell et al. (1995, chapter 17).

### 2.4.3 *Pareto efficiency and the welfare theorem*

Suppose you live in an economy with $I$ agents. There is some aggregate endowment $\Omega$, not associated with any particular agent. Suppose there are no markets, prices, or budgets. Instead, people gather at some central place to vote about the best way to distribute the endowments of the economy. The people start by randomly assigning an endowment to each agent, $(\omega(1), \ldots, \omega(I))$, such that $\sum_{i=1}^{I} \omega(i) = \Omega$. Then voting begins. Every allocation $x := (x(1), \ldots, x(I))$ that is feasible, $\sum_{i=1}^{I} x(i) \leqq \Omega$, can be proposed. The voting rules require unanimity; that is, as long as one agent disagrees with the proposed reallocation, it will not be implemented. We call an allocation $x$ *Pareto efficient* if there is no alternative allocation $y$ that could be unanimously accepted given any initial distribution $\omega$. This is the weakest sense in which we may define efficiency. It requires only that it is not possible to redistribute consumption among agents so that no one is worse off and at least someone is made better off by the redistribution.

From its very beginning, general equilibrium theory has been concerned not only with existence of an equilibrium, but also with properties of equilibrium allocations. The most important result in this domain is that equilibrium allocations are Pareto efficient. Why? We know that everyone's maximum indifference curve is tangent to the budget hyperplane in equilibrium (Box 2.3).[16] This implies that there are no unexploited gains from

[15] A continuum of solutions (as in case 3) can be shown to be very exceptional, though. Also, a situation like case 2 is impossible, because excess demand $\to +\infty$ as price $\to 0$, but excess demand $< 0$ as price $\to \infty$. Therefore, typically, there is an odd number of roots (Mas-Colell et al., 1995, chapter 17).

[16] If utility is differentiable, this means that everyone's utility gradient points in the same direction, or in other words, everyone has the same marginal rates of substitution; but differentiability is not essential for the argument.

trade. By this simple geometric argument we see that the equilibrium allocation must be Pareto efficient.

**Box 2.9** ***First welfare theorem***

Everyone is marginally identical in equilibrium. For that reason there are no further gains from trade and the equilibrium allocation is Pareto efficient.

This is equivalent to saying that, given a competitive equilibrium allocation, there is no redistribution that would be accepted unanimously.

Given the utility functions of the agents and an aggregate endowment, we can generate all Pareto-efficient allocations with the help of a *social welfare function* (SWF). An SWF is a weighted sum of individual utilities which is maximized subject to the feasibility constraint. Formally,[17]

$$U(z) := \max \left\{ \frac{1}{I} \sum_{i=1}^{I} \sigma_i u_i(y(i)) \;\middle|\; \sum_{i=1}^{I} (y(i) - z) \leqq 0 \right\}. \tag{2.11}$$

The numbers $\sigma_1, \ldots, \sigma_I > 0$ are the weights we assign to the respective individual's utility. Notice that (2.11) features a vector of feasibility constraints, one for each commodity. Accordingly, there will also be a vector of Lagrange multipliers. $z$ is the average endowment that each individual has. Setting $z$ equal to the mean endowment of the original economy, $z := \Omega/I$, we can generate every Pareto-efficient allocation $(y(1), \ldots, y(I))$ by an appropriate choice of weights, $\sigma_1, \ldots, \sigma_I$.[18]

If the equilibrium allocation is Pareto efficient there must be a social welfare function $U$ that is maximized in equilibrium. How do we choose the weights $\sigma_1, \ldots, \sigma_I$ to construct the social welfare function that is maximized in the competitive equilibrium? These weights can be inferred from the first-order conditions of the individuals' maximization problems (2.2). In equilibrium there exist Lagrange multipliers, $\lambda_1, \ldots, \lambda_I > 0$, one for each agent, so that

$$p = \lambda_1^{-1} \nabla u_1(x(1)) = \cdots = \lambda_I^{-1} \nabla u_I(x(I)). \tag{2.12}$$

Those $\lambda_i$ measure agent $i$'s marginal utility of wealth.

[17]The $1/I$ term at the front of the objective function does not make a difference in terms of economics but will provide us with a nice normalization.

[18]This technique goes back to Negishi (1960); see also e.g. Mas-Colell et al. (1995, chapter 16).

Now consider the first-order conditions of problem (2.11). They are

$$\frac{1}{I}\sigma_i \nabla u_i(y(i)) = \mu, \qquad i = 1, \ldots, I, \tag{2.13}$$

$$\mu_c \sum_{i=1}^{I} (y_c(i) - z_c) = 0, \qquad c = 1, \ldots, (S+1)M, \tag{2.14}$$

where $\mu$ is the vector of Lagrange multipliers of the constraints in (2.11). We search for weights $\sigma_1, \ldots, \sigma_I$ such that $y = x$ is a solution if $z = \Omega/I$.

Consider the candidate $\sigma_i := \lambda_i^{-1}$. Substitute $x$ for $y$ and $\Omega/I$ for $z$ in (2.13) and (2.14). Because preferences are assumed to be monotonic, the Lagrange multipliers of the material constraints are strictly positive, $\mu \gg 0$. Then, (2.13) and (2.14) become

$$\frac{1}{I}\lambda_i^{-1} \nabla u_i(x(i)) = \mu, \qquad i = 1, \ldots, I, \tag{2.15}$$

$$\sum_{i=1}^{I} (x(i) - \Omega/I) = 0. \tag{2.16}$$

First, (2.16) is simply the market clearing condition and therefore satisfied in equilibrium. Second, there is a strictly positive vector $\mu$ such that (2.15) is also satisfied. Just consider the Pareto criterion given by (2.12). We know that the equilibrium allocation $x$ satisfies this condition because it is an efficient allocation (by the welfare theorem). Thus, $\mu = p/I$ is a solution.

We conclude that the equilibrium allocation maximizes a social welfare function that weights agents according to the reciprocal of their marginal utility of wealth,

$$U(z) := \max \left\{ \frac{1}{I} \sum_{i=1}^{I} \lambda_i^{-1} u_i(y(i)) \;\middle|\; \sum_{i=1}^{I} (y(i) - z) \leqq 0 \right\}. \tag{2.17}$$

We call this the *competitive SWF.*

The marginal increase of the objective function that can be achieved if the constraint is marginally eased is called the *shadow price.* It is a fact of calculus that the Lagrange multiplier is equal to the shadow price. But the constraint is $\sum_{i=1}^{I} y(i) \leqq Iz$, so enlarging $z$ by $dz$ actually eases the constraint by $I$ times $dz$. As a result, $\nabla U(z) = I\mu = p$. This equality provides an important interpretation: equilibrium prices ($p$) measure the marginal social value ($\nabla U$) of the goods. If loaves of bread were falling from heaven, one for every person living on earth, social welfare would increase by the price of a loaf of bread.

Moreover, the competitive weighting function, $\sigma_i = \lambda_i^{-1}$, has a desirable property. Since utilities are only ordinal, any monotonic transformation of $u_i$ represents the same preferences, and is therefore equivalent. Such a monotonic transformation should not change social preferences, since it is merely a change of how we as theorists represent an agent in the language of our model. Luckily, the competitive SWF is independent of monotonic transformations. Suppose we multiply person $i$'s utility by 2, so that $\tilde{u}_i(x(i)) := 2u_i(x(i))$. This is equivalent in (2.17) to keeping the original utility function $u_i$ but weighing person $i$ twice as much (using $2\sigma_i$ instead of $\sigma_i$ as $i$'s weight). But since $i$'s utility is multiplied by 2, so will be the Lagrange multiplier of his budget constraint, $\tilde{\lambda}_i := 2\lambda_i$, and accordingly, the competitive SWF will weight $i$'s inflated utility $\tilde{u}_i$ by only half as much as before. The inflation of $i$'s utility is just cancelled by the deflation of the weight he gets according to (2.17). Formally, $\lambda_i^{-1}u_i(x(i)) = \tilde{\lambda}_i^{-1}\tilde{u}_i(x(i))$.

The weighting in (2.17) also demonstrates that the competitive equilibrium has nothing to do with an equitable distribution. Suppose that all agents have identical preferences, so that we can represent each agent's tastes with the same utility function $u$. Assume, however, that not all people are equally wealthy, $w(i) := p \cdot \omega(i)$. Let $v$ be the *indirect utility function*, mapping $w(i)$ to the maximum utility that agent $i$ can achieve. The marginal indirect utility is the shadow price of wealth, hence $v'(w(i)) = \lambda_i$. If the utility function $u$ is concave,[19] then, by the Maximum Theorem (Sundaram, 1996, theorem 9.17), $v$ is a (weakly) concave function, so $v'$ is (weakly) decreasing. In other words, wealth has a (weakly) decreasing marginal utility. As a consequence, the competitive SWF (weakly) assigns greater weight to rich agents than to poor ones. But we need to be aware that the interpretation of these weights is a tricky matter. Suppose all agents have the same Cobb–Douglas utility function, $u(x) := x_1^{\gamma_1} x_2^{\gamma_2} \cdots x_\ell^{\gamma_\ell}$ with $\gamma_1 + \cdots + \gamma_\ell = 1$. Then the shadow price of wealth is independent of wealth, and therefore all agents, rich and poor, receive the same weight in the competitive SWF. Consider now rescaling the utilities by applying the logarithm, $u(x) := \gamma_1 \ln x_1 + \cdots + \gamma_\ell \ln x_\ell$. No economic change is involved here; only the preferences of the agents are simply represented by another, equivalent, ordinal utility function (Box 2.2). Now, however, the shadow price of wealth is decreasing in wealth, and rich agents get a larger weight than poor agents in the competitive SWF.

[19]There is in general no reason to believe that it is. The usual convexity assumption on preferences is equivalent to quasi-concavity of $u$, but does not imply concavity.

### *2.4.4 Summing up*

In this section we have studied abstract contingent claim economies. We have discussed a Pareto-efficient allocation, and a competitive equilibrium of a contingent claim economy. A social welfare function, or SWF, is the value of a problem that maximizes a weighted sum of individual utilities subject to the material limitations of the economy. An allocation is Pareto efficient if and only if it is the solution to some SWF. A competitive equilibrium is a price–allocation pair in which all markets clear and every agent maximizes utility subject to a budget constraint. The key result of general equilibrium theory, which will be useful for the further development of asset pricing theory, is the first welfare theorem. This theorem establishes that a competitive equilibrium allocation is Pareto efficient. It implies that an equilibrium allocation is the solution to an SWF. In fact, the equilibrium allocation solves a specific SWF, where the weights given to the individual agents are determined by their shadow prices on wealth. We call this specific SWF the competitive SWF. We will see that the competitive SWF is key in simplifying the model, but retains all the information we need to determine equilibrium asset prices.

## 2.5 The representative agent

### *2.5.1 What representative agents are good for*

If we could observe an individual's endowment and his decisions, we might be able to deduce some facts about his preferences. But usually we do not have access to such micro data. In fact, as economists, we are not particularly interested in a single person's preferences. Instead, we are interested in the relation between the aggregate data that we can observe and equilibrium prices, in particular asset prices. We know what aggregate saving, aggregate consumption, and aggregate (i.e. market) portfolios are, and we are interested in "society's utility function", in the sense of characterizing how the market equilibrium is affected by, say, business cycles, and the uncertainty it causes.

Consider an economy $(u, \omega)$ with $I$ agents. In order to calculate a competitive equilibrium $(p, x)$ of this economy, we would normally have to solve the maximization problem of each agent as a function of prices, and search for a fixed point. This is very cumbersome.

If, instead, there were only one agent in the economy, we would know at the outset what the equilibrium allocation was, namely, the endowment of this lonely chap, because there is no one he could trade with. The equilibrium prices are then just given by the gradient of this single agent's utility at his endowment point.

Given a multi-agent economy $(u, \omega)$ and a competitive equilibrium $(p, x)$, we define a *(locally) representative agent* as an artificial agent $(u^\circ, \omega^\circ)$ such that $(p, \omega^\circ)$ is a competitive equilibrium of the one-agent economy $(u^\circ, \omega^\circ)$. Notice that the equilibrium allocation in this economy is $\omega^\circ$, which implies no trade, as must be the case in a one-agent economy.

**Box 2.10** ***Loss of distributional information***

If we work with a representative agent, we lose all information on the interpersonal equilibrium distribution; that is, we can no longer determine who consumes what. But in fact, in macrofinance we are not interested in this micro information.[20] All we want is to characterize equilibrium prices, and using a representative agent allows us to do precisely that with a simpler model.

### 2.5.2 *An arbitrary representative agent*

Such a representative agent is clearly useful for determining equilibrium prices, but how can we construct such a representative? If there are no further requirements, this is simple. Take an arbitrary (monotonic, quasi-concave, differentiable) utility function $v$ and a point $x$ such that $\nabla v(x) = \lambda p$ for some $\lambda > 0$. For convenience we could scale $v$ so that $\lambda = 1$. Then $(v, x)$ is a representative agent, because if he is faced with prices $p$ he will not want to trade, thus forming a one-person general equilibrium.

### 2.5.3 *Everyone is a representative*

The mere existence of a local representative agent is no problem, since an arbitrary representative can always be constructed. Yet, this arbitrary guy, $(v, x)$, is not very useful, because he has no relation to the data of the original multi-person economy. How can we construct a representative from the data of the original economy? This, too, is fairly straightforward. Observe that

[20] To be more precise, in macrofinance we are not interested in the allocation of consumption among agents *per se*. But it is possible that the inter-personal distribution of endowments has an influence on equilibrium prices. In that case, distribution becomes important as an explanatory variable; see chapter 8.

*everyone is marginally identical in equilibrium.* This is a consequence of the Pareto efficiency of equilibrium (Box 2.9). Each agent's utility gradient is collinear to the price in equilibrium (Box 2.3). That is to say, for all $i$, $\nabla u_i(x(i)) = \lambda_i p$; thus, $(u_i, x(i))$ is a representative agent. In other words, *everyone is a representative agent in equilibrium.* Intuitively, the reasoning is straightforward: if you face prices $p$, and your endowment is the bundle that maximizes your utility subject to the original budget constraint (i.e. $p \cdot x(i) \leqslant p \cdot \omega(i)$), then there is no reason for you to trade further. So, even though each of us is different, in an efficient allocation we are all marginally identical.

Although this is interesting philosophically (I think), for empirical analyses it is usually not very helpful because we often do not have micro data on individual endowments, preferences, and consumption bundles. And even if we had, an individual person can make mistakes. Most economists (today) would agree that rationality (i.e. maximization of preferences subject to contraints) is a good description of average human behavior, but not necessarily of an individual instance of a decision of a single agent.

### 2.5.4 The competitive SWF as a representative

So what the macroeconomist really wants is to construct a representative agent using *only aggregate data* of the original economy. How can we do that? The answer is, with the help of the competitive social welfare function. Remember that, by construction, the gradient of the competitive SWF (2.17) at the point $z = \Omega/I$ just equals the equilibrium prices, $\nabla U(\Omega/I) = p$; thus, $(U, \Omega/I)$ is a representative agent. This is quite good, because the endowment of this representative is just the average per capita endowment of the original economy, and these are data that are usually available to us. The construction of $U$, however, still requires micro data, because it depends on the inter-personal joint distribution of preferences and endowments. There are two possible ways out of this: (1) we might be able to estimate $U$, or (2) we could assume that everyone has the same utility function $u$, but different endowments $\omega(i)$, and then use data on endowment distributions (which may be available) to compute $U$. In chapter 5, after integrating the von Neumann–Morgenstern utility theory into the model, we will acquaint ourselves with a class of utility functions that can be aggregated without knowledge of the distribution of endowments (Rubinstein, 1974).

## Notes on the literature

Much of section 2.1 is taken from chapters 2 and 7 of Debreu (1959). Discussions of the rest of the material presented in this chapter can be found in any good microeconomics text; Kreps (1990, chapter 2 and 6) and Mas-Colell et al. (1995, chapters 2 to 4 and 10) are especially instructive.

## Problems

**Problem 2.1** Let $p \in \mathbb{R}^\ell$ be a price vector, let $\omega \in \mathbb{R}^\ell$ be an agent's endowment, and let $x$ and $x'$ be two distinct consumption bundles. Prove the following.

($a$) If both $x$ and $x'$ satisfy the budget constraint with equality, then any linear combination $z := \lambda x + (1 - \lambda)x'$, with $\lambda \in \mathbb{R}$, also satisfies the budget constraint with equality.

($b$) If both $x$ and $x'$ satisfy the weak budget constraint, then any convex combination $z := \lambda x + (1 - \lambda)x'$, with $\lambda \in [0, 1]$, also satisfies the weak budget constraint.

**Problem 2.2** Consider a situation with just two commodities. Let the endowment of some agent be $\omega := (3, 2)$, and let the price vector be $p := (1, 2)$.

($a$) Draw a two-dimensional coordinate system. Make a dot at $\omega$, and draw the price vector as an arrow, starting at the point $\omega$. Now compute different combinations of quantities of commodities 1 and 2 that the agent can just afford. The resulting set is called the budget line. Judging by visual inspection, is the budget line you have drawn a straight line? Is the price vector orthogonal to the budget line?

($b$) Consider now a utility function $u(x_1, x_2) := x_1 x_2$. Compute the utility of the initial endowment. Try to find some other combinations $(x_1, x_2)$ that give the same utility level.[21] Connect these utility-equivalent points you have found with a smooth line. Then use a ruler to draw a straight line that is tangent to this indifference curve and that goes through $\omega$.

($c$) The gradient of the utility at endowment is $\nabla u(\omega) = (2, 3)$. Draw an arrow into your graph starting from $\omega = (3, 2)$ and ending at $\omega + \nabla u(\omega) = (6, 6)$. Is this arrow (the gradient) orthogonal to the line that is tangent to the indifference curve?

[21] Fix $x_1 = 1.0, 1.5, 2.0, 2.5, 3.0, 3.5, 4.0, 4.5, 5.0$. For each of these values, compute how large $x_2$ must be for the agent to reach the same utility as derived from consuming his endowment.

**Problem 2.3** Consider an agent who lives for two periods and who faces the decision problem of how much to consume now and how much to save, just as in (2.4). $w$ is his first period income, his second period income is zero (he's retired then), and there is a guaranteed gross real interest rate $\rho$ on any savings.

($a$) Suppose the agent has an additively separable utility function of the following form:

$$u(x_1, x_2) = \ln x_1 + \delta \ln x_2.$$

We use the logarithm as the period utility function, indicating the amount of utils you get from consuming some quantity in one period. $\delta$ is a weight which measures your relative valuation of consuming now versus consuming later. It measures therefore your *time preference* and is usually called the *discount factor.* We typically assume that $0 < \delta < 1$, meaning that people are not patient and would rather enjoy consumption now than later. With these preferences, compute his optimal saving, as a function of $\rho$ and $\delta$?

($b$) Now consider the preferences represented by this utility function,

$$\tilde{u}(x_1, x_2) = x_1^{\gamma} x_2^{\varepsilon}.$$

Do you have any prior about the solution? If yes, write it down. If no, or if you are unsure, compute the optimal saving, as a function of $\rho$, $\gamma$, and $\varepsilon$. Compare your result with your answer to the previous problem and comment.

# 3
# Asset economy

The trading arrangements we have studied so far bear little resemblance to our practical everyday experience. Many contingent claims markets do not exist. For instance, there is no market for bananas next Christmas provided it rains. What we see, roughly, is a set of *spot markets* combined with a set of *financial markets.* This chapter is about how to solve our individuals' decision problems facing these more involved markets, and how to reformulate our notion of a general equilibrium. We will also learn how the notion of a complete financial market allows us to work with a *representative commodity.*

## 3.1 Financial assets

### *3.1.1 A more realistic trading arrangement*

Spot markets are markets for physically specified commodities that are available today. They are not contingent on any event other than the one we are experiencing at present. Suppose the world evolves according to an event tree such as the one represented in Figure 2.1, and suppose today is $t = 0$. A spot market is a market for a commodity that is contingent on the root of the event tree (or on state 0 in Figure 2.2). This means that we can buy bananas, tomatoes, suits, and cars now, but usually we cannot buy tomorrow's bananas today.

The spot markets are complemented by a set of financial markets. Financial assets are contracts that deliver some state-contingent amount of money in the future. For instance, a bond delivers a positive cash flow every time a coupon is due, and it delivers the principal when it matures. Of course, the issuer could go bankrupt—a bad event—in which case the bond will not deliver any further cash flow, so the cash flow is contingent on the event.

More generally, a financial asset is defined by the event-contingent cash flow it delivers.

For simplicity, consider a two-period model with $S$ states, as shown in Figure 2.2. A financial asset, call it $j$, is a vector,

$$r^j = \begin{bmatrix} r_1^j \\ r_2^j \\ \vdots \\ r_S^j \end{bmatrix},$$

where the components are the state-contingent cash flows which the asset delivers.

Suppose there are $J$ different assets. We can collect the cash flows of all financial assets and thus represent the whole financial market as a return matrix,

$$\begin{array}{c} \\ \textit{states} \end{array} \begin{array}{c} \\ 1 \\ \vdots \\ S \end{array} \overset{\begin{array}{c}\textit{securities}\\ 1 \quad \cdots \quad J\end{array}}{\begin{bmatrix} r_1^1 & \cdots & r_1^J \\ \vdots & \ddots & \vdots \\ r_S^1 & \cdots & r_S^J \end{bmatrix}} =: r.$$

### 3.1.2 Real and nominal assets

The cash flows of some financial assets are defined as functions of the spot prices of real commodities. For instance, a wheat forward contract as traded on the Chicago Board of Trade specifies the payment of an amount of money that is equal to the price of wheat at some future point in time. Formally, $r_s^j := p_s^m$, if $m$ is the index for wheat. More generally, let $x$ be some bundle of spot commodities. An asset whose cash flow is a linear function of spot prices, $r_s^j := p_s \cdot x$, is called a *real asset* because it delivers the purchasing power necessary to buy some specific commodity bundle $x$ on tomorrow's spot markets (Magill & Quinzii, 1996*b*, definition 33.1). A bundle with returns given by $p_s \cdot x$ is a *forward* for the commodity bundle $x$.

The cash flows of some assets, however, are independent of spot prices. A nominal bond is an example. A bond typically just delivers some specified (state-contingent) amount of money. Such securities are called *nominal assets* because they deliver not wheat[1] which you can consume, but money, which you cannot consume but can only spend, and whose purchasing power is uncertain (Magill & Quinzii, 1996*b*, definition 33.2).

Real and nominal assets are polar cases. Some assets belong to neither of these categories. Consider a share. Typically, a share is modelled as a claim on the firm's profits. Let $y^s$ denote the firm's input–output vector in state $s$. That means that inputs constitute negative components of $y^s$ and outputs constitute positive components of $y^s$. The market value of this input–output vector, $p_s \cdot y^s$, is the profit that the firm generates in state $s$. Thus, if a share is a claim on the firm's profit, then $r_s^j := p_s \cdot y^s$. If this is an accurate description of the dividends a share pays, then it is a real asset; but there are two problems with this description. First, shareholders have only limited liability. They are not required to make up for losses of the firm. If $p_s \cdot y^s < 0$ in some state $s$, then $r_s^j = 0 \neq p_s \cdot y^s$. This property makes a share look like a call option on corporate profit (Merton, 1974). It means that the linear relationship between corporate profit and dividends is lost. Second, in practice, dividend policy is subject to discretionary decisions by the managers, the board, or the shareholder assembly, so that in general we should not expect a linear relationship between profits (or spot prices) and dividends. For these two reasons, a share is not a real asset in the sense defined above.

As another example, consider a corporate bond. This is a bond that pays, say, one unit in all states in which the firm survives, and zero otherwise. We may consider this to be a nominal asset. However, the firm survives if and only if its profits are greater than minus its equity. The profit is a linear function of state prices. Consequently, the payoff of a corporate bond is some function of spot prices. It is not a linear function, so a corporate bond is not a real asset; but neither is it a nominal asset, because the payoff of the bond depends in some fashion on the spot prices.[2]

It should be mentioned that there is a well developed theory of economies with real assets. There is an equally well developed theory of economies with nominal assets.[3] But there are very few contributions that examine the properties of equilibria of economies with assets that are not of these polar

[1] Or the purchasing power necessary to buy wheat.

[2] The nomenclature is not uniform in the literature. Some researchers prefer to define real assets as assets that pay goods instead of money. An option on wheat would be a real, but non-linear asset. In this sense, a share is also a non-linear real asset. In this book, however, we follow Magill & Quinzii (1996*b*), so in our terminology an option on wheat and a share are neither purely real nor purely nominal assets.

[3] See Magill & Shafer (1991) or Magill & Quinzii (1996*b*) for comprehensive treatments of this field.

types (the case of options, for instance, is studied by Polemarchakis & Ku (1990) and Krasa & Werner (1991)), or of economies that contain real and nominal assets at the same time (see e.g., Neumeyer, 1999).

### 3.1.3 *What is a risk-free asset?*

A naive way of defining a risk-free asset is to associate it with an asset that delivers a fixed amount of money in all states. When talking about a bond, we fix this constant amount of money to be unity,[4]

$$r^{\text{risk-free bond}} := \begin{bmatrix} 1 & 1 & \cdots & 1 \end{bmatrix}'.$$

But this asset just delivers money, and money is not something that enters the preferences of people directly. It only allows agents to buy things that give them "utils," and how much of these utility-providing goods can be bought with the proceeds of a risk-free nominal bond depends on tomorrow's spot prices of the real goods.

Suppose a person is interested only in eating broccoli. "Risk-free broccoli" is a contract that delivers the purchasing power to buy one unit of broccoli in all states (a broccoli forward), so that

$$r^{\text{risk-free broccoli}} := \begin{bmatrix} p_1^{\text{broccoli}} & \cdots & p_S^{\text{broccoli}} \end{bmatrix}'.$$

Now consider another person who is interested only in eating carrots. Risk-free carrots are defined analogously. But note that, in general, there is no $\lambda$ such that

$$r^{\text{risk-free broccoli}} = \lambda r^{\text{risk-free carrots}}.$$

The two definitions of a risk-free asset are not collinear. Risk-freeness means different things to a broccoli-lover and to a carrot-enthusiast. The concept of a risk-free asset depends on the consumption habits or preferences of the individual, and accordingly there is no universal definition.

So what is a risk-free bond? Well, to put it bluntly, this concept is not well-defined in a model featuring more than one commodity! Economists follow a very pragmatic approach to deal with this problem. Some *normalizing consumption bundle* is defined, for instance the average consumption bundle of some population in some base period. The *price level* is then defined as the value of this normalizing consumption bundle in each of the states. Nominal cash flows of assets are then divided by this (state-contingent) price

[4]Ordinarily a bond periodically delivers a coupon to its owner, and when it matures it pays the principal as well. We assume here that the coupon is zero; that is, we consider zero-coupon bonds, so-called discount bonds, and we assume that the principal is one.

level. The resulting cash flows are called *deflated.* Deflated money is sometimes also called *purchasing power.* A bond that delivers constant deflated cash flows (constant purchasing power) through all states is considered to be risk-free. Effectively, a risk-free asset is a forward on the normalizing consumption bundle. This example shows most clearly that the concept of risk-freeness is not independent of the bundle used to normalize the purchasing power of money. If you change the normalizing bundle, you also change the definition of risk-freeness.

This is, of course, not completely satisfactory. Individuals will be subject to idiosyncratic inflation risk (or, you might say, relative price risk). People really do bear this risk, but it will not show up in any aggregate measure of risk, and so will lead to an underestimation of the risk that people are exposed to. To my knowledge, no attempt has been made yet to address this problem and to tackle its consequences for equilibrium asset pricing, and so we swim with the crowd here and follow the usual deflation mechanics. In the back of our heads there will always be the normalizing consumption bundle that is used for computing the price level. All asset returns are to be understood as deflated according to the value of this normalizing bundle.

## 3.2 Pricing by redundancy

### *3.2.1 Arrow securities*

An especially simple—one could say elementary—financial asset is an *Arrow security* (Arrow, 1953). It delivers one unit of purchasing power conditional on a specific event $s$, and zero otherwise. We denote the vector of state-contingent cash flows of a state-$s$ Arrow security by $\mathbf{e}^s$:

$$\mathbf{e}^s = \begin{bmatrix} 0 \\ \vdots \\ 0 \\ 1 \\ 0 \\ \vdots \\ 0 \end{bmatrix}.$$

Thus, the payoff matrix of the collection of all $S$ Arrow securities is the $S$ times $S$ identity matrix:

$$\mathbf{e} := \begin{bmatrix} 1 & 0 & \cdots & 0 \\ 0 & 1 & \cdots & 0 \\ \vdots & \vdots & \ddots & \vdots \\ 0 & 0 & \cdots & 1 \end{bmatrix}.$$

These securities are hardly ever traded, but some (maybe all) of them can be generated by combining other assets.[5] Because of their simplicity, Arrow securities come in very handy when pricing more general assets. This is because a general financial asset can be represented by a portfolio of Arrow securities. For instance, a financial asset that pays one in state 1, three in state 2, and zero in state 3 has the same state-contingent payoff as a portfolio consisting of one state-1, three state-2, and zero state-3 Arrow securities.

### 3.2.2 *The law of one price*

On the financial markets there is usually a spread between the highest bid price and the lowest ask price for a specific security. This spread is due to temporary mismatches and the profit motive of the market maker. Also, people who are not members of the exchange have to use a broker, and the broker takes some fees for trading. The effect of this is that an ordinary agent cannot sell a security for the same price as he can buy it.

Very often, it is also the case that the same asset, which may be traded at different places, commands slightly different prices at each place. This allows arbitrageurs to make an extra profit by buying at the low-price place and simultaneously selling at the high-price place. It is the activity of these arbitrageurs that keeps this mispricing within narrow bands.

In all that follows we will ignore these imperfections. Instead, we will assume that the markets work perfectly well.

[5]So-called "delta securities" (Breeden & Litzenberger, 1978) or "butterfly spreads" (Luenberger, 1998, section 12.3) or "digital contracts" (Ingersoll, 2000) are the same as Arrow securities (as long as we work with a finite set of states).

**Box 3.1** *Law of one price*

We assume that there are no transaction costs and no bid–ask spreads. Thus, an asset can be bought and sold at the same price. We denote the period 0 price of asset $j$ with $q_j$. We also assume that the *law of one price* holds. This assumption says that two assets with the same payoff vector have the same price. More generally, if a combination of assets (a portfolio) produces the same payoff vector as another combination of assets (another portfolio), then the two portfolios cost the same. Formally, if two portfolios, $z$ and $z'$, produce the same cash flow, $r \cdot z = r \cdot z'$, they must also cost the same, $q \cdot z = q \cdot z'$.

Remember that we can artificially reproduce the cash flow of an arbitrary asset $r^j$ with a portfolio of Arrow securities, consisting of $r_s^j$ state $s$ Arrow securities, for each $s$. We denote the prices of the Arrow securities with a row vector,

$$\alpha = \begin{bmatrix} \alpha_1 & \cdots & \alpha_S \end{bmatrix}.$$

Arrow securities need not exist as traded assets, though, so we may not be able to observe these prices directly. But if they do exist, or if we are able to compute the Arrow prices in other ways (more on that later), then we can use them to compute the prices of arbitrary assets using the law of one price.

**Box 3.2** *Decomposition*

A security with payoff $r^j$ can be decomposed into a portfolio, containing $r_s^j$ state $s$ Arrow securities, for each $s$. By the law of one price, the original security $j$ costs the same amount as this portfolio of Arrow securities. Formally, $q_j = \alpha \cdot r^j$, or, collecting this for all assets,

$$q = \alpha \cdot r.$$

As an important application of this principle, consider the price of a risk-free asset. A risk-free asset is a security or a portfolio of securities that guarantees one unit of purchasing power no matter what event (or, in a two-period model, what state) is realized. Formally, the cash flow of a safe asset is given by

$$\begin{bmatrix} 1 \\ \vdots \\ 1 \end{bmatrix}.$$

This asset corresponds to the definition of a bond that never defaults (see page 21). Because the price of such a risk-free bond is so important for the development of the theory, we denote it with a new symbol, $\beta$. From the considerations of Box 2.5, there is a simple relationship between $\beta$ and the gross risk-free interest rate: one is just the reciprocal of the other, $\beta = \rho^{-1}$. Considering the cash flow vector, a risk-free bond can be created by holding a portfolio of one unit of each Arrow security (assuming that these securities are traded). Thus, the price of this bond must be the same as the sum of the prices of all Arrow securities:

$$\beta = \rho^{-1} = \sum_{s=1}^{S} \alpha_s, \tag{3.1}$$

### *3.2.3 Risk-neutral probabilities*

It leads to an interesting concept if we multiply the Arrow security prices by $\rho$.

> **Box 3.3** ***Risk-neutral probabilities***
>
> Let $\rho$ be the risk-free interest rate and let $\alpha$ be the vector of Arrow security prices. The numbers
>
> $$\tilde{\alpha}_s := \rho \alpha_s$$
>
> are called the *risk-neutral probabilities*, even though these are not really probabilities in the sense of assigning likelihoods to the states.

Note that the components of $\tilde{\alpha}$ sum to unity by (3.1). Furthermore, they are all positive. We will see this a little later when we encounter the idea of arbitrage freeness in Box 3.7. Thus, the $\tilde{\alpha}_s$ have the structure of probabilities over the set of states (hence their name). Let $\tilde{E}$ be the expectation operator using the risk-neutral probabilities. Then the pricing formula of Box 3.2 can be written compactly.

**Box 3.4** ***Risk-neutral pricing***

The price of a security with cash flow $r^j$ equals the expected cash flow of the security, using the risk-neutral probabilities, discounted with the risk-free interest rate. Formally,

$$q_j = \beta \tilde{E}\{r^j\}.$$

Often we are interested not in prices, but in rates of return on assets. The rate of return is the gain in percentage of the investment. Let $R_s^j$ denote the gross rate of return of asset $j$ if state $s$ occurs. There is a simple defining relationship between price and rate of return:

$$R_s^j := \frac{r_s^j}{q_j}.$$

Dividing both sides of the equation in Box 3.4 by $q_j$, remembering that $\beta = \rho^{-1}$, and rearranging leads to an interesting formula for the rates of return of arbitrary assets.

**Box 3.5** ***Risk-neutral returns***

The expected rate of return of any asset, evaluated with the risk-neutral probabilities, equals the risk-free rate of return. Formally,

$$\tilde{E}\{R^j\} = \rho.$$

Boxes 3.4 and 3.5 give the key pricing equations. The reason why the $\tilde{\alpha}$ are called risk-neutral probabilities will become clear later when we discuss asset pricing using von Neumann–Morgenstern utility theory (in chapter 5). Without that theory we cannot go much further in asset pricing theory than the risk-neutral pricing formulae. Von Neumann–Morgenstern utility theory will allow us to use information about the true probability distribution over the states. Combining this with the risk-neutral pricing formula will lead to a pricing equation involving so-called *stochastic discount factors* (section 5.5) or the *martingale measure* (chapter 6). Doing the same with the formula of the risk-neutral returns will lead to the consumption based capital asset pricing model, or CCAPM. All three elements—stochastic discount factors, martingale measure, and CCAPM—are central to asset pricing theory and are special cases of the two risk-neutral valuation equations we have developed here.

## 3.3 Radner economies

### 3.3.1 Definition

An economy is described by the properties of the people that live in it, i.e. by the endowments $\omega$ and the preferences of all agents $u$, just as in a contingent-claim economy, plus a description of the financial assets that are available for trading, $r$.

**Box 3.6** *Asset economy*

An *asset economy* consists of a contingent claim economy and a cash flow matrix, $(u, \omega, r)$. The matrix $r$ has $S$ rows and $J$ columns, with $J$ denoting the number of financial assets.

Even though it is not made explicit in the above definition, there is in addition some fixed normalizing bundle whose value defines the state-contingent price level. The cash flows as defined in $r$ are deflated; i.e., they are the money cash flows of the assets divided by the price level.

### 3.3.2 The market span

The law of one price assumption, Box 3.1, is responsible for making the choice sets of the agents' linear spaces. With this assumption, therefore, some basic knowledge of real vector spaces takes us a long way into finance.

Consider a return matrix $r$ and a vector of financial asset prices $q$. A portfolio (collection of assets) $z$ costs $q \cdot z$ today (produces a cash flow of $-q \cdot z$ today), and yields a cash flow of $r_s \cdot z$ in state $s$ tomorrow. Collecting all today's and tomorrow's cash flows that can be achieved in this way by an appropriate choice of portfolio produces the *market span* $\mathcal{M}(q)$, which is defined as

$$\begin{aligned} \mathcal{M}(q) &:= \operatorname{span}\begin{bmatrix} -q \\ r \end{bmatrix} \\ &:= \left\{ \begin{bmatrix} -q \\ r \end{bmatrix} \cdot z \;\middle|\; z \in \mathbb{R}^J \right\}. \end{aligned} \tag{3.2}$$

$\mathcal{M}(q)$ is a linear space with at most $J$ dimensions. It captures the choice set of the agents, i.e. the set of allocations of purchasing power through time and the states that can be achieved by some portfolio, and among which the agents choose the best one. If two different return matrices and security price vectors give rise to the same market span, they are equivalent. All that happens when we switch from one to the other is a change of basis.

Define $\alpha_+ := \begin{bmatrix} 1 & \alpha_1 & \dots & \alpha_S \end{bmatrix}$; this is the same as the $\alpha$, but with a leading 1. It will be useful to note that $\alpha_+$ is orthogonal to $\mathcal{M}(q)$, for the following reason. Consider some $x \in \mathcal{M}(q)$, that is to say,

$$x = \begin{bmatrix} -q \\ r \end{bmatrix} \cdot z$$

for some $z$. Then

$$\begin{aligned}\begin{bmatrix} 1 & \alpha_1 & \dots & \alpha_S \end{bmatrix} \cdot x &= \begin{bmatrix} 1 & \alpha_1 & \dots & \alpha_S \end{bmatrix} \cdot \begin{bmatrix} -q \\ r \end{bmatrix} \cdot z \\ &= \underbrace{(-q + \alpha \cdot r)}_{=0} \cdot z = 0\end{aligned}$$

by the decomposition formula (Box 3.2). Therefore, $\alpha_+$ is orthogonal to $x$, for arbitrary $x \in \mathcal{M}(q)$.

### *3.3.3 Decision problem and beliefs*

An agent in an asset economy maximizes utility by choosing a consumption bundle today ($x^0$) and the planned consumption bundles in all the states that will possibly materialize tomorrow ($x^1, \dots, x^S$), as well as an appropriate portfolio of securities ($z$) to fulfill the budget constraint at every time and in every state. We could say that an agent in such an economy faces an *integrated consumption-portfolio problem.* Of course, the future spot prices, $p_1, \dots, p_S$, are not observable at the point in time when decisions must be made because those future spot markets do not operate at time 0. Thus, we assume that the decision-maker has a *belief* about the spot prices for each of the possible states. We denote these beliefs by $B(p_1), \dots, B(p_S)$. Note that these beliefs are *conditional on the state* and are therefore not subject to uncertainty. If an agent figures that different spot price vectors are conceivable for a given state, then we treat these two cases as two different states of the world! Formally, the integrated consumption-portfolio problem is now given by

$$\max \left\{ u(x) \;\middle|\; \begin{array}{ll} \overbrace{p_0 \cdot (x^0 - \omega^0)}^{-\text{saving}} + \overbrace{q \cdot z}^{\text{investment}} \leqslant 0 & \\ \underbrace{B(p_s) \cdot (x^s - \omega^s)}_{\substack{\text{value of excess}\\ \text{consumption}}} - \underbrace{r_s \cdot z}_{\text{return}} \leqslant 0 & \text{for } s = 1, \dots, S \end{array} \right\}. \tag{3.3}$$

Since the constraints will hold with equality because of the monotonicity of the utility function, we can write this somewhat more compactly as

$$\max\{u(x) \mid B(p) \cdot (x - \omega) \in \mathcal{M}(q)\}, \tag{3.4}$$

setting $B(p_0) := p_0$. This is the maximization problem of an agent as of time 0, i.e. before uncertainty is resolved.

Now note that the beliefs will also affect the implied expected price level (the value of the normalizing bundle), and thus the return matrix $r$, since the cash flows of the financial assets are deflated with the price level. If different people have different price-level expectations, they will also use different return matrices! We disregard this problem here completely. In fact, we do not hypothesize at all about how people form their beliefs: all we do is to formulate the decision problem of an agent, *given* some contingent spot price beliefs $B(p_1), \ldots, B(p_S)$. Later, in the definition of a Radner equilibrium, we will make an assumption about the mutual consistency of beliefs.

### 3.3.4 Arbitrage (and positivity of Arrow prices)

From Weierstrass's Maximum Theorem (Bartle, 1976, page 154 f.), we know that a maximization problem has a solution if the objective function is continuous and the constraint gives rise to a compact (closed and bounded) set on which we maximize. In (3.3), utility is continuous by assumption, and the budget set is closed. There is, however, nothing here that guarantees that the budget set is bounded.

**Example.** Suppose there are two states, $S = 2$, and two assets, $J = 2$. One is a bond paying 1 unit in each state, the other is a share paying 1.5 units in state 1 and 0.5 unit in state 2. Assume further that the bond costs 1 unit of account today, and the share costs 2, $q = (1, 2)$. Consider then the payoff of an investor who buys two bonds and sells one share short:

| **asset** | | **cash flow** | |
|---|---|---|---|
| | **now** | **in state 1** | **in state 2** |
| +2 bonds | −2 | +2 | +2 |
| −1 share | +2 | −1.5 | −0.5 |
| portfolio | 0 | +0.5 | +1.5 |

The investor gets a positive payoff in the future and pays nothing today. This is obviously a good deal. We call it *arbitrage*. An even better deal would be to buy 20 bonds and sell 10 shares short, or to buy 200 bonds and sell 100 shares short, or—well, there are no limits. If arbitrage is possible, the investor can achieve unlimited consumption, implying that the budget set is unbounded and, owing to monotonicity of utility, the maximization problem (3.3) has no solution.

More generally, we say that $(q, r)$ contains *arbitrage opportunities* if there exists a portfolio $z$ such that

$$\begin{bmatrix} -q \\ r \end{bmatrix} \cdot z \geq 0.$$

This means that the payoff today or in any future state is not negative, and that it is strictly positive either today or in at least one future state. Formally, absence of arbitrage opportunities is equivalent to the statement that the market span must not intersect the positive orthant except at the origin:

$$\mathcal{M}(q) \cap \mathbb{R}_+^{S+1} = \{0\}.$$

As we demonstrated before, $\begin{bmatrix} 1 & \alpha \end{bmatrix}$ is orthogonal to $\mathcal{M}(q)$. Thus, arbitrage opportunities are absent if and only if there are strictly positive Arrow prices, $\alpha \gg 0$, that are compatible with $(q, r)$.[6]

**Box 3.7** ***Absence of arbitrage opportunities***

$(q, r)$ is arbitrage-free if and only if there exists an $\alpha \gg 0$ such that $\alpha \cdot r = q$.

To see why, note two things. First, an arbitrage portfolio $z$ yields a cash flow $y := \begin{bmatrix} -q & r \end{bmatrix}' \cdot z$ that points into the positive orthant. Second, any two vectors in the positive orthant form an acute angle. It follows from this that any strictly positive Arrow price vector, $\alpha_+ \gg 0$, forms an acute angle with any arbitrage cash flow ($\alpha_+ \cdot y > 0$ if $y \geq 0$), thus violating decomposition. Conversely, if the market allows for arbitrage, then this arbitrage cash flow (and thus the market span as a whole) cannot be orthogonal to any strictly positive $\alpha_+$. We conclude that the existence of strictly positive Arrow prices rules out arbitrage, and the possibility of arbitrage rules out strictly positive Arrow prices.

The absence of arbitrage opportunities is a minimum requirement for consistency. If there are arbitrage opportunities, the consumption-portfolio problem (3.3) does not even have a solution. There can be prices, however,

[6] Note that we move onto shaky grounds if we allow for heterogeneous conditional spot price beliefs (or for idiosyncratic price level definitions), because then some portfolio might offer an arbitrage for one agent, given his beliefs (his definition of price level), but not to another agent, given his different beliefs (his different price level definition).

that do not allow arbitrage, but still do not generate individual decisions that are compatible with each other. Put differently, arbitrage-free prices need not clear markets. The opposite, however, is always true: equilibrium prices never allow arbitrage. Equilibrium is therefore a stronger requirement than just the absence of arbitrage opportunities.

### 3.3.5 Radner equilibrium

As in the contingent claim economy, we will require that demand equals supply for each commodity in each state in equilibrium. But there are also financial assets. What does market clearing mean for financial assets? Well, every security that is bought by an investor must first be issued. Usually it is firms or government agencies that issue shares or bonds, banks that issue options, and insurance companies that issue insurance contracts. If someone issues such an asset, he is "short" in this asset. For instance, if I hold a bond I will receive, say, \$100 tomorrow. But the person that issued the bond will have to pay out \$100. So we could say that the portfolio of the issuer contains $-1$ bond. Aggregating over all individuals, the portfolios must sum to zero: every financial asset that is bought by an investor has to be issued by someone else. In tech-speak, we say that assets are "in zero net supply." This is the market clearing condition for financial assets.[7]

Box 3.8 summarizes what Radner (1972) calls an "equilibrium of plans, prices, and price expectations." By "plans" he means the consumption bundle today ($x^0$) and the planned consumption bundles in all the states that will possibly materialize tomorrow ($x^1, \ldots, x^S$). "Prices" are the spot prices that can be observed today ($p_0$) and the prices of the financial assets ($q$). "Price expectations" concern tomorrow's spot prices ($p^1, \ldots, p^S$), which depend on the state and are not observable today, because tomorrow's spot markets do not operate today. Each agent $i$ forms beliefs about these prices, $B^i(p_s)$ for $s = 1, \ldots, S$. In addition to market clearing, an equilibrium requires that everyone has the same beliefs and that these beliefs are correct, i.e. $p_s = B^i(p_s)$ for each $i = 1, \ldots, I$; $s = 1, \ldots, S$.

This assumption may look extreme, since it seems to imply perfect foresight. However, it implies perfect foresight only *conditional on the state.* Since

[7] Assets are often assumed to be in "positive net supply." This is appropriate for partial equilibrium models. For instance, if we take the outstanding shares of a firm as given, and the firm is not an active player of the model, then the short position of the firm in its own shares does not enter our accounting and the shares are in positive net supply for the rest of the economy. Likewise, the monetary base is often modelled as being in positive net supply, because the central bank may not be part of the model. Equilibrium then requires that the aggregate money holdings equals the amount of base money that has been issued (which is a short position of the central bank).

there is still uncertainty about the state, we do *not* assume *unconditional perfect foresight.*

**Box 3.8** ***Radner equilibrium***

Let $B^i(p_s)$ denote agent $i$'s state-$s$ conditional belief about spot prices. A *Radner equilibrium* is a four-tuple $(p, q, x, z)$, consisting of a matrix of spot prices $p$, a vector of security prices $q$, a collection of consumption matrices $x(i)$, one for each agent, and a collection of portfolios of securities $z(i)$, one for each agent, such that $(x(i), z(i))$ solves $i$'s optimization problem (3.3),

$$x(i) \in \arg\max\{u(y) \mid B^i(p) \cdot (y - \omega) \in \mathcal{M}(q)\}, \quad i = 1, \ldots, I;$$

aggregate consumption equates aggregate endowment today and in each state tomorrow,

$$\sum_{i=1}^{I} x_m^s(i) = \sum_{i=1}^{I} \omega_m^s(i), \quad s = 0, 1, \ldots, S; \; m = 1, \ldots, M;$$

each security is in zero net supply,

$$\sum_{i=1}^{I} z_j(i) = 0, \qquad j = 1, \ldots, J;$$

and everyone has perfect conditional foresight,

$$B^i(p_s^m) = p_s^m, \qquad i = 1, \ldots, I; \; s = 1, \ldots, S; \; m = 1, \ldots, M.$$



### 3.3.6 *The representative commodity*

In this section, we will show that we can divide the decision problem of the agent in a Radner economy into two parts, one that could be called the *consumption-composition problem,* and the other the *financial problem.* The decision problem (3.4), replacing $B^i\{p_s\}$ with $p_s$, is

$$\max\{u(x) \mid p \cdot (x - \omega) \in \mathcal{M}(q)\}. \tag{3.5}$$

Denote with $w$ the state-contingent value of the agent's endowment, evaluated at the spot market prices,

$$w^s := p_s \cdot \omega^s \qquad \text{for } s = 0, \ldots, S. \tag{3.6}$$

$w^0$ is the income of the agent today and $w^1, \ldots, w^S$ is his state-contingent future income. Define the indirect utility function $v$ as follows:

$$v(y) := \max\left\{u(x) \;\middle|\; p_s \cdot x^s \leqslant y^s \quad \text{for } s = 0, \ldots, S\right\}. \tag{3.7}$$

$v(y)$ is the maximized utility if at most $y^s$ can be spent in state $s$. The choice of $x$ is the choice about the composition of consumption, that is to say the kinds of commodities that should be bought in each state. $y := (y^0, y^1, \ldots, y^S)$ is a distribution of incomes spent today and tomorrow in each of the states; it summarizes the allocation of the financial means of the agent over time and across states. The choice of $y$ characterizes the decisions of the agent about saving and risk exposure, i.e. his financial decisions. Consider then only the financial decision problem,

$$\max\left\{v(y) \;\middle|\; y - w \in \mathcal{M}(q)\right\}. \tag{3.8}$$

This requires the agent to maximize his indirect utility function $v$ over $y$, subject to staying within the transfers that the market span allows. This problem is equivalent to the original decision problem (3.5). To see this, notice that the state-contingent budget constraints $p_s \cdot x^s \leqslant y^s$ must be binding by monotonicity of $u$, and thus are satisfied with equality. Substituting (3.7) into (3.8) (with the inequality constraints replaced by equality constraints) transforms the problem into the problem we started with,

$$\begin{aligned}
&\max\left\{v(y) \;\middle|\; y - w \in \mathcal{M}(q)\right\} \\
&\quad = \max\left\{\max\left\{u(x) \;\middle|\; p \cdot x = y\right\} \;\middle|\; y - w \in \mathcal{M}(q)\right\} \\
&\quad = \max\left\{u(x) \;\middle|\; p \cdot (x - \omega) \in \mathcal{M}(q)\right\}.
\end{aligned} \tag{3.9}$$

This is the same as (3.5).

Magill & Quinzii (1996*b*, chapter 1, section 5) have noticed that this separation of the integrated consumption-portfolio problem into a financial part and a consumption-composition part can be used to drastically simplify the original economy, $(u, \omega, r)$. Let $(p, q, x, z)$ be an equilibrium of this economy. Consider the new economy $(v, w)$, where $w^s(i)$ and $v_i$ are defined as in (3.6) and (3.7), respectively. This is a contingent claim economy with $I$ agents but featuring only one commodity—namely *income* or *consumption*—today and in each of the future states. Let $\alpha$ be any Arrow price vector that is compatible with $q$, i.e. $q = \alpha \cdot r$, and let $\alpha_+ := \begin{bmatrix} 1 & \alpha \end{bmatrix}$. By construction, $(\alpha_+, y)$, with $y^s(i) := p_s \cdot x^s(i)$, is a competitive equilibrium of this one-good economy. To see why, consider the definition in Box 2.8 of a competitive equilibrium. We need to show that the market clears (this is trivially true by the market clearance assumption in the definition of the Radner equilibrium) and that, for all $i$,

$$y(i) \in \arg\max \left\{ v_i(\tilde{y}) \;\middle|\; (\tilde{y}^0 - w^0(i)) + \sum_{s=1}^{S} \alpha_s(\tilde{y}^s - w^s(i)) \leqslant 0 \right\}.$$

In the maximum, the constraint is satisfied with equality due to monotonicity. Note further that $(\tilde{y}^0 - w^0(i)) + \sum_{s=1}^{S} \alpha_s(\tilde{y}^s - w^s(i)) = \alpha_+ \cdot (\tilde{y} - w(i))$, so the constraint is equivalent to the statement that $\alpha_+$ be orthogonal to $\tilde{y} - w(i)$. But this again is equivalent to saying that $\tilde{y} - w(i) \in \mathcal{M}(q)$ (see page 47). Hence,

$$y(i) \in \arg\max \left\{ v_i(\tilde{y}) \;\middle|\; \tilde{y} - w(i) \in \mathcal{M}(q) \right\}.$$

By (3.9), this is satisfied in the Radner equilibrium $(p, q, x, z)$.

As with the introduction of the representative agent (Box 2.10), by using income as a representative good, we lose some information about the equilibrium.

**Box 3.9** ***Loss of information on composition***

By using a representative commodity, we lose all the information on the composition of consumption; i.e., we can no longer tell if people are consuming pizzas or movies. But again, we are not interested in this type of information in macrofinance. Thus, using a representative commodity makes our model simpler, but still allows us to characterize equilibrium asset prices.

## 3.4 Complete markets (and uniqueness of Arrow prices)

### *3.4.1 Definition, reverse decomposition, and canonical basis*

We have seen in section 3.2 that a general financial asset can be represented by a portfolio of Arrow securities. Is the converse also true? Can we construct an artificial Arrow security with a combination of general financial assets? And is it true that the price of an Arrow security can be computed from the prices of general financial securities? In other words, is *reverse decomposition* possible?

In general we cannot answer this question in the affirmative. The answer depends on the size and structure of the return matrix $r$. As a straightforward example, suppose there are five states, but only one financial asset.

Clearly, we cannot generate five Arrow security prices $\alpha_1, \ldots, \alpha_5$ from just one observed price $q_1$.

More generally, reverse decomposition is possible if and only if the financial assets provide diverse enough state-contingent cash flows. What we need is that the financial assets allow us to insure each state separately.

**Box 3.10** *Complete markets*

We say that *markets are complete* if agents can insure each state separately, that is if they can trade assets in such a way as to affect the payoff in one specific state without affecting the payoffs in the other states.

If markets are complete, there is a portfolio—for each state $s$ a different one—that generates the state-contingent cash flows of the state-$s$ Arrow security. Formally, for each $s$ there exists a portfolio $z^s$ such that $r \cdot z^s = \mathbf{e}^s$. Collecting these portfolios for each state, we can write

$$r \cdot \begin{bmatrix} z^1 & \cdots & z^S \end{bmatrix} = \mathbf{e}.$$

If $r$ is invertible, we can compute the $z^s$ portfolios,

$$\begin{bmatrix} z^1 & \cdots & z^S \end{bmatrix} = r^{-1}.$$

Thus, reverse decomposition works if and only if $r$ is invertible.

**Box 3.11** ***Reverse decomposition and uniqueness of Arrow prices***

Markets are complete if and only if $r$ is invertible. In this case, the Arrow prices can be computed from the financial market prices as $\alpha = q \cdot r^{-1}$. If markets are not complete, then there are many possible Arrow prices that are compatible with a return matrix $r$ and financial market prices $q$.

The proof of this claim is a simple fact of linear algebra.[8] The economic significance of this result is that all complete asset markets are equivalent,

[8]We have seen that $\alpha_+$ is orthogonal to $\mathcal{M}(q)$. In fact, $\alpha$ satisfies decomposition if and only if $\alpha_+$ is orthogonal to $\mathcal{M}(q)$. Let $\mathcal{M}(q)^\perp$ be the collection of all such vectors $\alpha_+$. $\mathcal{M}(q)^\perp$ is itself a linear space, and it is a fact of linear algebra that $\mathcal{M}(q)$ and $\mathcal{M}(q)^\perp$ together span the whole space $\mathbb{R}^{S+1}$, and that the sum of their dimensions is $S+1$. We say that $\mathcal{M}(q)$ and $\mathcal{M}(q)^\perp$ are a *direct sum.* Now, all vectors $\alpha_+$ for $\alpha$ that satisfy decomposition are collinear if and only if $\mathcal{M}(q)^\perp$ is one-dimensional. Moreover, the length of $\alpha$ is determined by the price of a risk-free bond. As a consequence, given the price of a risk-free bond, $\alpha$ is unique if and only if the dimension of $\mathcal{M}(q)$ equals $S$, i.e. the market is complete. For proofs, see e.g. Halmos (1993).

because they are all equivalent to an economy containing every Arrow security. As long as the financial assets span $S$ dimensions, full insurability can be achieved by an appropriate choice of portfolio. Exchanging one complete asset market with another amounts only to a change of basis with no change of effective constraints.

**Example.** Suppose there are two states. State 1 is a boom, state 2 is a recession. There are also two assets, both risky. Asset 1 is a share of a risky start-up firm. Asset 2 is a share of an established firm. Both firms pay a dividend of 1 in the boom. In the recession the dividend is reduced, but the start-up firm's dividend is affected much more than the established firm's dividend. The return matrix is

$$r := \begin{bmatrix} 1 & 1 \\ 0.2 & 0.8 \end{bmatrix}.$$

A person would like to save without being exposed to any risk, so he would like to buy a risk-free bond, but such an asset is not traded. However, a portfolio with a risk-free payoff can easily be constructed with the existing assets. The payoff of a portfolio $z$ is given by $r \cdot z$. We want the payoff to equal 1 in both states, i.e.

$$\begin{bmatrix} 1 \\ 1 \end{bmatrix} = r \cdot z \Rightarrow r^{-1} \cdot \begin{bmatrix} 1 \\ 1 \end{bmatrix} = z.$$

The inverse of the return matrix is

$$r^{-1} := \begin{bmatrix} 4/3 & -5/3 \\ -1/3 & 5/3 \end{bmatrix},$$

thus, the portfolio that yields the required risk-free payoff is

$$z = r^{-1} \cdot \begin{bmatrix} 1 \\ 1 \end{bmatrix} = \begin{bmatrix} -1/3 \\ 4/3 \end{bmatrix}.$$

To save without being exposed to risk, you must buy (a multiple of) $4/3$ shares of the established firm and sell short (a multiple of) $1/3$ shares of the startup firm. Mathematically, what is happening here is a change of basis, from the canonical basis given by the elementary Arrow securities to the twisted basis provided by the two different shares. Figure 3.1 illustrates this.

The canonical basis formed by the Arrow securities, $r = \mathbf{e}$, is an especially simple basis. Thus, as long as we work with complete markets, we can just as well make life a little easier and work with this particularly nice asset structure.

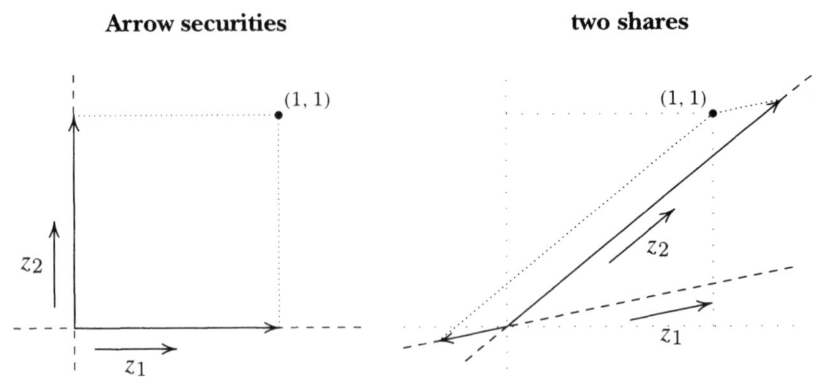


*Figure 3.1.* *Change of basis.*

For most of this text we will assume that markets are complete, even though this is counterfactual (Shiller, 1993). Note that incompleteness does not invalidate our pricing relationships (Boxes 3.4 and 3.5). It only invalidates their uniqueness. More specifically, suppose you know the payoffs $r$ and the prices $q$ of all existing financial assets. Now you would like to price a new asset, call it $J+1$, which is defined by its state-contingent cash flow, $r^{J+1}$. If markets are incomplete, the Arrow prices that are compatible with our data, $r$ and $q$, are not unique. Yet we can still use our pricing equations. Decomposition still holds, so the price of the new asset is $p_{J+1} = \alpha \cdot r^{J+1}$ for *some* Arrow prices $\alpha$ that are compatible with $r$ and $q$. If the new asset is *redundant* in the sense that it could be artificially reproduced by a portfolio of the existing $J$ assets (formally, $r^{J+1} \in \mathcal{M}(q)$), then this pricing equation will yield the same result for all Arrow prices that are compatible with $r$ and $q$. In other words, the pricing equations we have developed are well defined only for securities that do not change the market span (and thus are redundant). If the market is complete to begin with, then all new securities are redundant, and the pricing equations always yield a definite answer.

A new security that does expand the market span (and thus makes the market more complete) cannot, however, be priced with these pricing equations for two reasons. First, the price $p_{J+1} = \alpha \cdot r^{J+1}$ depends on which Arrow prices we choose. Second, by introducing a new security that enlarges the market span, the equilibrium allocation will most likely change, and with it the prices of all assets $q$.

### 3.4.2 Equivalence to contingent claim economy

The decision problem with markets for contingent claims is

$$\max\left\{u(x)\ \middle|\ \sum_{s=0}^{S}\tilde{p}_s\cdot(x^s-\omega^s)\leqslant 0\right\}. \tag{2.1}$$

Now consider the agent's decision problem if the contingent claims markets are not available. Rather, we assume that there are spot markets, one for today and one for each of tomorrow's states, and there are markets for each of the $s$ Arrow securities. $z$ denotes the *portfolio* of Arrow securities that the agent chooses to hold.[9] We assume that the assets are perfectly divisible and that there are no short sale constraints. Thus, the components of $z$ can be any positive or negative real number, depending on whether the agent is long or short in the respective securities. We can now formalize the decision problem of the agent,

$$\max\left\{u(x)\ \middle|\ \begin{array}{ll} p_0\cdot(x^0-\omega^0)+\alpha\cdot z\leqslant 0 & \\ p_s\cdot(x^s-\omega^s)\leqslant z^s & \text{for } s=1,\ldots,S \end{array}\right\}. \tag{3.10}$$

$\alpha\cdot z$ is the value of the portfolio. It equals the amount that the agent saves between today and tomorrow (the amount of wealth he transfers from today to tomorrow). This amount can be negative, indicating that the agent takes a loan. $z^s$ is the payoff of his saving in state $s$. We do not assume that the spot prices $p_0$, $p_1$, etc. are the same in this problem as in the contingent claims problem, $\tilde{p}_0$, $\tilde{p}_1$, etc., hence the different notation.

Now notice that the second-period budget constraints, $p_s\cdot(x^s-\omega^s)\leqslant z^s$, must be binding by the monotonicity assumption. Hence, at the maximum, they must hold with equality. Substituting this into the period zero constraint yields

$$\max\left\{u(x)\ \middle|\ p_0\cdot(x^0-\omega^0)+\sum_{s=1}^{S}(\alpha_s p_s)\cdot(x^s-\omega^s)\leqslant 0\right\}. \tag{3.11}$$

Notice that there is now a classical dichotomy principle in each state separately, meaning that we can normalize spot prices state-wise and use the Arrow prices for controlling the intertemporal marginal rates of substitution. All that matters is the combination of the two, $\alpha_s p_s$. If this equals $\tilde{p}_s$ for each $s=1,\ldots,S$, the two decision problems we have considered in this section, i.e. (2.1) and (3.11), are the same.

[9]A portfolio is the equivalent of a consumption bundle, but containing financial assets instead of commodities.

**Box 3.12** ***State-wise dichotomy***

In an asset economy with a complete set of Arrow securities, the spot prices can be normalized for each state separately. That is, we can choose arbitrary positive numbers $\mu_1, \ldots, \mu_S$, rescale spot prices, $p_s \mapsto \mu_s p_s$, and adjust the Arrow prices accordingly, $\alpha_s \mapsto \alpha_s/\mu_s$, without changing anything of economic substance. If there exist multipliers $\lambda, \mu_1, \ldots, \mu_S$ such that $p_0 = \lambda \tilde{p}_0$ and $\alpha_s p_s = \lambda \tilde{p}_s$, then the decision problem in the complete market asset economy, (3.11), and the decision problem of an agent who faces contingent claims markets, (2.1), are the same.[10]

The state-wise multipliers $\mu$ are fixed by the way we normalize prices (section 3.1). A state-$s$ Arrow security is supposed to deliver an amount of money that is sufficient to buy one unit of the normalizing bundle in state $s$. This normalization fixes a specific $\mu$, $p$, and $\alpha$.

Arrow (1953) was the first to notice the simplification that financial markets provide for the infrastructure of the market system. Suppose there are $S$ states in the future, and in each state there are $M$ spot commodities. Then a contingent claim economy needs $(S+1)M$ markets for state-contingent commodities. An asset economy with complete markets, in contrast, requires only $M$ spot markets today and $S$ financial markets, plus $M$ spot markets tomorrow, when the true state $s$ has been revealed. These are $2M + S$ markets together, even though the two systems are equivalent. This is a little bit of a cheat, though, because in the asset economy we require much more computational abilities of the agents, since they are required to make correct conditional forecasts of tomorrow's spot prices. In period 0 they have to compute the period 1 spot prices conditional on each of the future states. Of course, only one of these states will actually materialize, and therefore only one price vector will become reality tomorrow. Thus, physically, there is a smaller number of markets open, but in the minds of the people all state-contingent markets are present and they optimize using as many prices as people living in an ordinary state-contingent economy.

### *3.4.3 The one-good one-agent economy*

We have seen how we can simplify an economy with many state-contingent commodities into a simpler economy in which state-contingent income is a representative commodity. We have also seen earlier (section 2.5) that we can make use of a local representative agent if the equilibrium allocation

[10] $\lambda$ is an overall normalization which is possible by the classical dichotomy (Box 2.4).

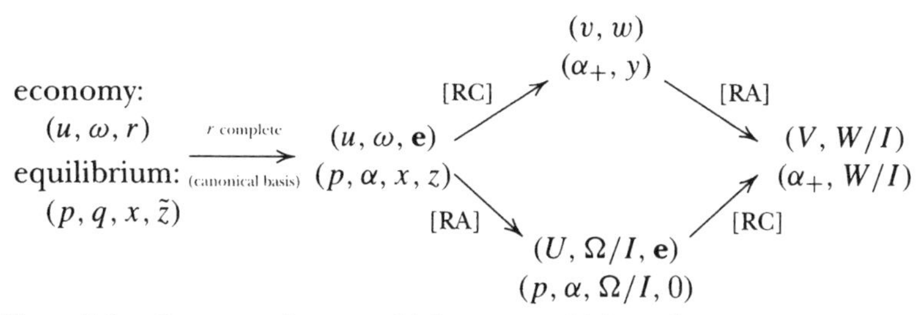


*Figure 3.2.* *Two routes from a multiple-agents multiple-goods asset economy to a one-agent one-good economy ([RC] means "make a representative commodity"; [RA] means "make a representative agent").*

is Pareto efficient.[11] We can actually do both, i.e. use a representative commodity and a representative agent. From the one-good economy $(v, w)$ we can compute a representative agent $(V, W/I)$. By definition, $(\alpha_+, W/I)$ is a competitive equilibrium of the one-good one-agent economy $(V, W/I)$.

Notice how far we have gotten. We have through several steps transformed an asset economy with general financial assets and complete markets, featuring many agents and many commodities, into a contingent claim economy with just one agent and one state-contingent commodity, and we have done it in such a way that the equilibrium prices of the financial assets are not changed.

**Box 3.13** ***The one-good one-agent economy***

Consider an asset economy $(u, \omega, r)$ with many commodities, many agents, and complete markets. Let $(p, q, x, z)$ be a Radner equilibrium of this economy. We can generate a one-good one-agent economy $(V, W/I)$ with equilibrium $(\alpha_+, W/I)$. The equilibrium prices of this simpler economy are the Arrow prices of the Radner equilibrium of the more complex asset economy $(\alpha = q \cdot r^{-1})$. This allows us to study the relationships between mean state-contingent income $W/I$, representative utility of income $V$, and asset prices $q = \alpha \cdot r$ within a much simpler model.

We could also first generate a multiple commodity representative agent economy, and then in the second step generate the representative commodity. The diagram in Figure 3.2 depicts this.

[11] If markets are complete, the Radner equilibrium allocation is necessarily efficient, because such an economy is equivalent to a contingent claim economy, as argued in the previous section, and therefore the first welfare theorem applies.

## 3.5 Complications arising from market incompleteness

### *3.5.1 What typically does not work with incompleteness . . .*

*Complete markets* means that the financial markets are such that individual states can be insured (Box 3.10). If this is the case, the individuals' decision problem in an asset economy, (3.3), is the same as in a contingent claim economy, (2.1). As a result, for every competitive equilibrium of an abstract exchange economy there is a corresponding asset economy with a Radner equilibrium. Formally, let $(\tilde{p}, x)$ be a competitive equilibrium of the contingent claim economy $(u, \omega)$, and let $r$ be a regular payoff matrix (markets are complete); then the asset economy $(u, \omega, r)$ has a Radner equilibrium $(p, q, x, z)$. What is important here is that $x$, the equilibrium allocation, is the same in the competitive contingent claim equilibrium and the Radner equilibrium. As a consequence, the welfare theorem (Box 2.9) holds also in an asset economy, provided markets are complete. For the same reason, we can construct the competitive SWF and the representative agent in the same way.

Can we construct such a representative also if markets are incomplete? We can if the equilibrium allocation is Pareto efficient, because then we could again use the competitive SWF. So the question is really this: is the Radner equilibrium allocation of an asset economy with incomplete markets necessarily efficient?

The answer is "generally no," for the following reason. If the return matrix of the assets is singular, the market space as defined in (3.2) has less than $S$ dimensions. This singularity means that some income transfers, from one state to another or from one time period to another, are not possible, or cannot be accomplished independently from one another. This problem has profound effects on the properties of equilibrium. The first-order conditions of (3.3) still imply that everyone's marginal rates of state-contingent intertemporal substitution of wealth are given by the Arrow prices. The problem is that the Arrow prices are not uniquely defined in a Radner equilibrium if the market is incomplete because there is an infinite combination of Arrow prices that are orthogonal to $\mathcal{M}(q)$. As a consequence, different agents can have different marginal rates of substitution. If two agents have different marginal rates of substitution, they would like to trade with each other because there is unexploited room for mutually beneficial trade between them; but they cannot perform this trade because the financial markets do not provide the infrastructure that is necessary for this trade to work. As a consequence, the equilibrium allocation is not Pareto efficient.

Such an example is depicted in Figure 3.3. We consider a one-commodity, two-period, two-person economy with two future states. The endowment of agent 1 is $\omega(1) := (2, 1, 0)$ and the endowment of agent 2 is $\omega(2) := (0, 1, 2)$, so aggregate endowment is $(2, 2, 2)$. This situation can be represented with a three-dimensional Edgeworth box (see left half of Figure 3.3). We use Basu's (1992) method for reducing the relevant space to two dimensions so that we can easily depict the situation on a two-dimensional paper surface. We assume that both agents have identical preferences. The preferences we use may seem somewhat unusual at first, but they will simplify the graphical representation and will not violate any of the usual assumptions. Let $x(i) := (x_0(i), x_1(i), x_2(i))$ denote agent $i$'s consumption. We assume that the preferred distribution is to have equal consumption today and in both future states. Such preferences can be represented with the following utility function;

$$u(x(i)) := \sigma(i) - \sqrt{\sum_{s=0}^{2}\left(x_s(i) - \frac{\sigma(i)}{3}\right)^2},$$

with

$$\sigma(i) := x_0(i) + x_1(i) + x_2(i).$$

Utility is the sum of consumption in the three states, minus the Euclidean distance from the point with the same total consumption but no cross-state variability. With a complete market,[12] the unique (and efficient) equilibrium allocation is $(1, 1, 1)$ for each agent; the equilibrium prices of the contingent claims 1 and 2 are $(1, 1)$. Thus, the equilibrium budget surface of each agent is an equilateral triangle. Because agent 2's coordinate system points in the opposite direction to agent 1's system, 2's budget surface is upside down compared with the budget surface of agent 1.

The circles in the picture on the right-hand side of Figure 3.3 represent the intersections of indifference surfaces with the budget plane. The closer to the center a consumption bundle is, the better it is. Usually we would have separate systems of indifference curves for each agent, but since in our example both agents have the same preferences, and since these indifference curves are unaffected by rotations (owing to the fact that cross-state variation of consumption is penalized with the Euclidean metric, and that the budget planes are parallel to the unit simplex), these circles represent the preferences of both agents.

Suppose now that there is only one asset, a risk-free bond which pays one unit in each of the two future states. Suppose the price of this bond is $q := 2$.

[12] In fact, in this case a single Arrow security for state 2 is sufficient for achieving efficiency. It is an example of a quasi-complete market (see Box 3.15).

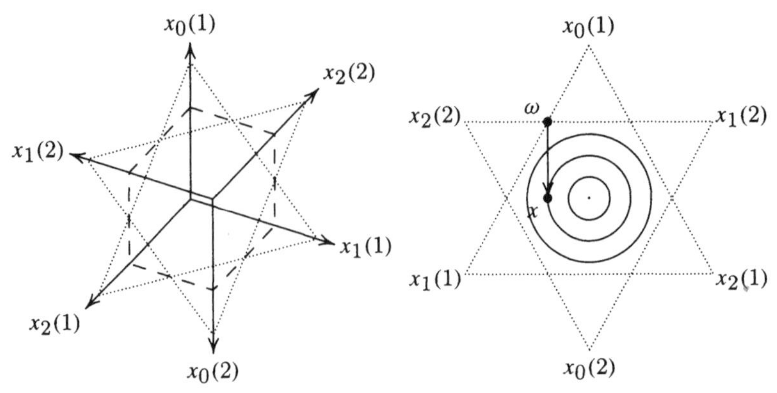


***Figure 3.3.*** *Pareto-inefficient equilibrium in an Edgeworth box with two agents, $I = 2$, two future states, $S = 2$, but only one asset.*

Then the portfolios $z(1) := 1/2$ and $z(2) := -1/2$, giving rise to the Pareto-inefficient allocation, $x(1) = (1, 3/2, 1/2)$, $x(2) = (1, 1/2, 3/2)$, constitute an equilibrium. The arrow on the right-hand side of Figure 3.3 depicts the net trade. This is an equilibrium because the net trade is tangent to the indifference surfaces of both agents (i.e., the utility gradients of both agents are orthogonal to the market space), which makes it an equilibrium; but the gradients are not identical, making the equilibrium allocation inefficient.[13]

The lack of efficiency of the equilibrium allocation has a grave impact on the representative agent. If the equilibrium allocation is not efficient, there is no SWF that is maximized in equilibrium. Hence, no representative agent can be computed on the basis of an SWF. This result does not render obsolete the pricing principles that we have seen in section 3.2, such as decomposition (Box 3.2) and risk-neutral pricing (Boxes 3.4 and 3.5), but it does invalidate the aggregate asset pricing formulae that we will develop in chapter 5 (such as SDF and CCAPM).

Incompleteness has an additional important effect which we have not touched upon. We have not considered productive economies (i.e. economies in which there are firms that transform one vector of commodities (input) into another one (output)). If markets are complete, there is unanimity among everyone that the firm should maximize profit (the difference between the value of output and the value of input). In that case, the management of the firm can easily be transferred to some specialist, implying that ownership and control of the firm can be separated. Unanimity fails if markets are incomplete. Agents differ in the production plans they pre-

[13] $\nabla u(x(1)) = \begin{bmatrix}1 & 0.293 & 1.707\end{bmatrix}$, $\nabla u(x(2)) = \begin{bmatrix}1 & 1.707 & 0.293\end{bmatrix}$. You can check that these two gradients are both orthogonal to the market space spanned by $\begin{bmatrix}-2 & 1 & 1\end{bmatrix}$.

fer for the firms, depending on their endowments and preferences because they are subject to non-diversifiable idiosyncratic risks, and this affects their preferred production plan. As a result, people will not agree on a production plan, so shareholders will not agree in general about the best course of action, let alone whom to delegate the management of the firm to (Ekern & Wilson, 1974; Radner, 1974).

**Box 3.14** ***Effects of incomplete markets***

If markets are incomplete, then

- Arrow prices associated to an equilibrium are not unique,
- typically, the equilibrium allocation is not Pareto efficient,
- typically, there is no locally representative agent based on an SWF,
- typically, there is no unanimous production plan for firms.

The consequences of this are, first, that the pricing of arbitrary new assets (that are not in the span of the existing return matrix) is not well defined; second, that aggregate models do not exist; and third, that multilateral ownership of a firm leads to conflict.

Note, however, that using purchasing power as a representative good does not depend on the efficiency of the equilibrium allocation. The transformations we did in (3.9) do not require full spanning.

Incompleteness can also jeopardize the very existence of an equilibrium that has only real assets (Hart, 1975), but this result was later shown to be non-generic (Duffie & Shafer, 1985, 1986). Also, existence is not in jeopardy in economies that feature only nominal assets (Werner, 1985). The same cannot be said about economies with options where non-existence may be robust (Polemarchakis & Ku, 1990).

### *3.5.2 ... and the exceptional cases in which it works nevertheless*

The equilibrium allocations of incomplete market economies are typically not efficient, and so we cannot aggregate the economy into a representative agent. But this is a statement that is only generically true. An incomplete market economy could be *accidentally* efficient. If the span of the incomplete market structure contains a Pareto-efficient point, then this allocation is an equilibrium of this economy, which also happens to be efficient. In this case, all the aggregations can be performed despite the incompleteness of the market. Such a market structure is called *quasi-complete.* Unlike a complete market, a quasi-complete market does not permit the independent insurance of each state, but the structure is rich enough for a Pareto-efficient allocation to be achieved and nothing more is required for aggregation.

**Box 3.15** ***Equilibrium in a quasi-complete market***

Suppose $x$ is a Pareto-efficient allocation and suppose $\exists q$ such that for each agent $i$, $p \cdot (x(i) - \omega(i)) \in \mathcal{M}(q)$. If this is the case we say that the asset market $r$ is *quasi-complete.* Then $\exists z$ such that $(p, q, x, z)$ is a Radner equilibrium.

We have to show that

($i$) goods markets clear, $\sum_{i=1}^{I} x(i) - \omega(i) = 0$,

($ii$) asset markets clear, $\sum_{i=1}^{I} z(i) = 0$,

($iii$) everyone behaves optimally, i.e.

$$x(i) \in \arg\max\{u_i(y) \mid p \cdot (y - \omega(i)) \in \mathcal{M}(q)\}.$$

Condition ($i$) follows directly from the fact that $x$ is an allocation (since it is Pareto efficient). For ($ii$), observe that $p \cdot (x(i) - \omega(i)) \in \mathcal{M}(q)$, which simply means that, for each $i$,

$$p \cdot (x(i) - \omega(i)) = \begin{bmatrix} -q \\ r \end{bmatrix} \cdot z(i) \tag{3.12}$$

for some $z(i)$; that is, the net trade that allows agent $i$ to exchange his endowment $\omega(i)$ for the bundle $x(i)$ can be performed with the available assets and asset prices. We need to show that there exists such a $(z(1), \ldots, z(I))$ that clears the financial markets. For each agent $i \in \{1, \ldots, I-1\}$, pick a $z(i)$ satisfying (3.12) and let $z(I) := -\sum_{i=1}^{I-1} z(i)$. We need to show that $z(I)$ satisfies (3.12) as well. Summing (3.12) over the first $I-1$ agents and using goods market clearing, we obtain

$$\begin{aligned} -p \cdot (x(I) - \omega(I)) &= p \cdot \sum_{i=1}^{I-1} (x(i) - \omega(i)) \\ &= \begin{bmatrix} -q \\ r \end{bmatrix} \cdot \sum_{i=1}^{I-1} z(i) \\ &= -\begin{bmatrix} -q \\ r \end{bmatrix} \cdot z(I); \end{aligned}$$

hence $z(I)$ satisfies (3.12) as well. Finally, (*iii*) follows from the assumed Pareto efficiency of $x$. Pareto efficiency means that the utility gradients of all agents are collinear at $x$. Thus, for each $i$, $x(i)$ maximizes $i$'s utility in a larger space, $\tilde{\mathcal{M}} \supset \mathcal{M}(q)$, where $\tilde{\mathcal{M}}$ is a complete market space which is orthogonal to the common utility gradient of all agents. Since $x \in \mathcal{M}(q) \subset \tilde{\mathcal{M}}$ and $x(i)$ solves $i$'s problem in the larger space $\tilde{\mathcal{M}}$, it also solves the problem in the restricted space $\mathcal{M}(q)$, establishing (*iii*).

The span of a quasi-complete set of assets can have far fewer dimensions than a complete market, but it is sufficient to allow the agents to reach a Pareto-efficient allocation. Spanning more dimensions would not permit any further gains from trade. For that reason, quasi-completeness is an important property, and Box 5 . 4 will set out a sufficient condition for quasi-completeness.

## Notes on the literature

The material of sections 3.1, 3.2, and 3.4 can be found in financial economics textbooks, such as Eichberger & Harper (1997, chapter 3), Danthine & Donaldson (2002, chapter 7), and LeRoy & Werner (2001, chapters 2, 3, 5, 6). Thorough but mathematically more demanding treatments are provided by Magill & Quinzii (1996*b*) (see sections 5–11, 18, and 33 in various chapters) and Mas-Colell et al. (1995, chapter 19).

## Problems

**Problem 3.1** (*a*) Consider a risk-free bond paying today's purchasing power of \$100 a year from now. This means that the bond will pay tomorrow an amount of money that suffices to buy a bundle of commodities that cost \$100 today, so this is a real or inflation indexed bond. Suppose this bond costs \$97.73. What is the real interest rate?

(*b*) Suppose there is a second bond, paying two years from now the purchasing power that \$100 has today. Suppose this bond costs \$95.02 today. On the basis of these figures, is the real interest rate next year lower or higher than this year?

**Problem 3.2** Suppose there are two states and three financial assets, a risk-free bond with state-contingent cash flows (100, 100), a risky bond that pays only in state 2, with cash flow (0, 100), and a share with cash flow (20, 35). Can you find a portfolio containing only shares and risky bonds that reproduces 40 risk-free bonds?

**Problem 3.3** Consider a situation in which there are five states, and suppose you can observe the prices of the Arrow securities. They are (0.1225, 0.2451, 0.3676, 0.0613, 0.1838).

(*a*) Compute the price of a risk-free bond and the risk-free rate of return.

(*b*) What are the risk-neutral probabilities of the five states?

(*c*) How much does a hypothetical asset cost with cash flow (5, 5, 2, 7, 4)?

**Problem 3.4** Consider a two-period economy with five possible states in the future. There are no markets for Arrow securities, so you cannot observe the Arrow security prices. Yet, you can observe the prices of the following financial assets:

| **asset** | **price** | **cash flow in state...** | | | | |
|---|---|---|---|---|---|---|
| | | **1** | **2** | **3** | **4** | **5** |
| share of company X | 2.857 | 8 | 5 | 2 | 0 | 0 |
| share of company Y | 4.048 | 12 | 8 | 0 | 0 | 4 |
| bond of company X | 0.774 | 1 | 1 | 1 | 1 | 0 |
| bond of company Y | 0.893 | 1 | 1 | 1 | 0 | 1 |
| option on share X | 1.429 | 6 | 3 | 0 | 0 | 0 |

The option on the share of company X is a call option with exercise price 2.

(*a*) Is the market complete? (Probably you need to use a computer to answer this and the following questions.)

(*b*) Compute the prices that Arrow securities would have if they were traded.

(*c*) Are there arbitrage opportunities in this market? Prove your claim.

(*d*) Compute the risk-free rate of return.

(*e*) Compute the risk-neutral probabilities.

(*f*) Consider a call option on a share of company Y with exercise price 5. What state-dependent cash flow does this option have? How much does it cost?

(*g*) Using a spreadsheet program, compute a graph of the price of a call option on shares of companies X and Y as a function of the exercise price.

**Problem 3.5** (*a*) Suppose now that we had a continuum of states—say, the state could be any positive number. Consider some arbitrary asset with price $q(s)$. Assume that $q$ is strictly increasing and differentiable. In fact, to simplify matters, assume that $q(s) = s$; that is, we name the state $s$ after the price of our asset in this state, $q(s)$.[14] Let $c(x)$ be the price of a call option on this asset with strike price $x$. Using the decomposition principle (or continuous analogue of it), write down an explicit formula for $c(x)$.

(*b*) What can you say about the second derivative of this price, $c''(x)$?

(*c*) Suppose you observe the following prices of call options on some stock:

| **strike** | 1 | 2 | 3 | 4 | 5 | 6 | 7 |
|---|---|---|---|---|---|---|---|
| **price of call** | 7.01 | 5.46 | 4.88 | 4.46 | 3.30 | 1.55 | 1.02 |

Can you do arbitrage? How?

[14] In general there can be many states of the world in which a specific asset has some price $q$; for instance, a Microsoft share costs $43 and it rains in New York, and a Microsoft share costs $43 and New York enjoys sunny weather, or, Microsoft $43 and Nestlé $205, and Microsoft $43 and Nestlé $210. Thus, when we assume that the price is strictly increasing in the state, we do not really consider the complete collection of all the states of the world, but rather a partition of this set in which each component of the partition is the collection of all states in which a given asset has a specific price.

# 4
# Risky decisions

In chapter 2 we defined commodities to be contingent upon events or states. This framework provides us with a powerful tool for thinking and theorizing about decisions under risk. In fact, within the theory we have been using so far, decisions that concern risky outcomes are formally identical to decisions concerning the time or the place that some commodity will be available, or its physical characteristics. In other words, choosing whether to buy health insurance is formally the same as the decision to buy a vacation in Hawaii or a new car.

Yet, decisions about risk exposure have a special property which we have not exploited until now, namely probabilities.[1] When talking about something like insurance the concept of probabilities makes sense, but it is not sensible for decisions involving cars or vacation. Probabilities are only a part of those decisions that involve uncertainty. This additional structure can help us develop sharper statements about the behavior of people in the face of risk.

We have seen in the previous chapter how to reduce a multi-good economy into a one-good economy. Because finance is primarily about money, rather than, say, apples and bananas, we are ultimately interested in these kinds of simplified problems where income is the only good. So we will consider risky decisions about wealth only, not about bundles of real goods.[2]

[1]We have used the word *probability* in the last section when discussing *risk-neutral probabilities* (Box 3.3), but this is something quite different from the objective odds of a state occurring. Risk-neutral probabilities are in fact transformed equilibrium prices, and we call these things "probabilities" only because they have the mathematical structure of probabilities.

[2]A few contributions generalize this to situations involving risky commodity bundles, but we will not use this here (Stiglitz, 1969; Kihlstrom & Mirman, 1974; Karni, 1979).

## 4.1 Bernoulli's St. Petersburg paradox

The modern theory of risk preferences starts with the great Swiss mathematician Daniel Bernoulli, when he discussed a puzzle that was suggested by his cousin Nicolas.[3] Suppose someone proposes the following:

> "I have a fair coin here. I'll flip it, and if it's tails I pay you $1 and the gamble is over. If it's heads, I'll flip again; if it's tails then I pay you $2, if not I'll flip again. With every round, I double the amount I will pay to you if it's tails."

Obviously, this gamble sounds like a good deal. After all, you cannot lose. So, how much are you willing to pay to take this gamble?

The gamble is risky because the payoff is random. So, intuitively, this risk should be taken into account. If the expected payoff is $X$, you will most likely want to pay at most $X$ minus some risk premium. But notice that the expected payoff of this gamble is *infinite*!

$$E\{\text{payoff}\} = \sum_{t=1}^{\infty} \underbrace{\left(\frac{1}{2}\right)^t}_{\text{probability}} \cdot \underbrace{2^{t-1}}_{\text{payoff}} = \frac{1}{2}\sum_{t=1}^{\infty} 1^t = \infty.$$

So it seems that you should be willing to pay everything you own *and more* to purchase the right to take this gamble. Yet, in practice, no one is prepared to pay such a high price. Why? Well, even though the expected payoff is infinite, the distribution of the payoff is not particularly attractive (Figure 4.1). There is a more than 99% probability that we will end up with $64 or less. How can we decide in a rational fashion about such gambles?

Bernoulli's idea was that utility increments of large payoffs are smaller then utility increments of small payoffs, and that these utilities should then be weighted with their probabilities.[4] He favored a weighting function that

[3]Nicolas Bernoulli suggested this problem, known as St. Petersburg paradox, between 1708 and 1713 in a letter to Pierre Rémond de Montmort; see Daniel Bernoulli (1954, page 31).

[4]It is fascinating to read how Bernoulli states the principles of decreasing marginal utility and of expected utility. He writes: "the determination of the *value* of an item must not be based on its *price*, but rather on the *utility* it yields. The price of the item is dependent only on the thing itself and is equal for everyone; the utility, however, is dependent on the particular circumstances of the person making the estimate. Thus, there is no doubt that a gain of one thousand ducats is more significant to the pauper than to a rich man though both gain the same amount." Only a few lines later he writes: "If the utility of each possible profit expectation is multiplied by the number of ways in which it can occur, and we then divide the sum of these products by the total number of possible cases, a mean utility [moral expectation] will be obtained, and the profit which corresponds to this utility will be equal to the risk in question," (Bernoulli, 1954, both quotations from page 24).

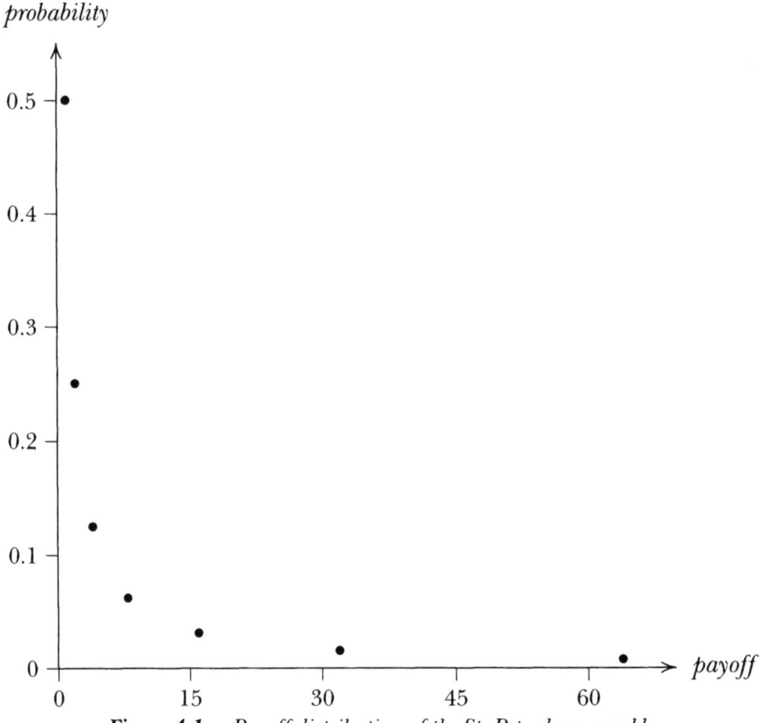


***Figure 4.1.*** *Payoff distribution of the St. Petersburg gamble.*

would value a payoff of $x$ dollars as $\ln x$. The natural logarithm, he argued, would provide a natural measure of the utility that any given payoff provides to the receiver.[5] The true value of the gamble, according to this idea, is then

$$E\{\text{utility}\} = \sum_{t=1}^{\infty} \underbrace{\left(\frac{1}{2}\right)^t}_{\text{probability}} \cdot \underbrace{\ln(2^{t-1})}_{\text{utility}} = \ln 2 < \infty.$$

Bernoulli would have paid at most $e^{\ln 2} = \$2$ for the right to participate in this gamble.[6] This idea was much later given an axiomatic basis by John von

[5]"Now it is highly probable that any increase in wealth, no matter how insignificant, will always result in an increase in utility which is inversely proportionate to the quantity of goods already possessed," (Bernoulli, 1954, page 25). In other words, $v'(x) = x^{-1}$.

[6]Earlier, Gabriel Cramer, another famous Swiss mathematician, had suggested using the expected square root of the payoff. With this utility function he would have paid at most \$2.90. At the end of this chapter, we will see that both Bernoulli's $\ln(x)$ and Cramer's $\sqrt{x}$, belong to the class of constant relative risk aversion utility functions.

Neumann and Oskar Morgenstern in connection with the development of game theory. Their theory is the topic of the next section.[7]

## 4.2 Using more structure: probabilities and lotteries

Consider a coin flipping gamble. Heads means that you win an amount $x$ of money, tails that you lose $x$. Or consider driving your car from A to B because you have an appointment. If you get there in time with probability, say, 95%, you will get some payoff $x$. If there is a traffic jam (with probability 4.8%) you will be late and your payoff will be zero. If you have an accident (with probability 0.2%) you will not only be late for your appointment but will have to repair your car, so your damage will be $y$. Such gambles or risky situations can be represented by a list of possible outcomes and their respective probabilities. For instance, the coin flipping gamble can be represented as $[+x, 0.5; -x, 0.5]$; the risky travel is described by $[+x, 0.95; 0, 0.048; -y, 0.002]$. More generally, we say that

$$[x_1, \pi_1; \ldots; x_S, \pi_S], \quad \text{with } \pi_s \geqslant 0 \text{ and } \sum_{s=1}^{S} \pi_s = 1,$$

is a *lottery*. The prizes $x_1, \ldots, x_S$ are real numbers (amounts of money). For simplicity we consider situations with a finite set of possible outcomes only ($S$ is some finite number).

Let $\mathcal{L}$ denote the set of all lotteries. We assume that agents have preferences over this set; that is, just as in ordinal utility theory (section 2.2), we assume that an agent has a preference relation $\prec$ on $\mathcal{L}$ that satisfies the usual assumptions of ordinal utility theory (asymmetric, negatively transitive, and continuous).[8] These assumptions imply that we can represent

[7]Using a concave utility function does not suffice in general to shield us from St. Petersburg paradoxes. If the utility function is unbounded, it is always possible to design a gamble with infinite expected utility. With,for instance, the log-utility function, the paradox reappears if we substitute the prize $2^{t-1}$ with $e^{2^{t-1}}$, as first noted by Carl Menger (1967) (see also Weirich, 1984). Yet, we often encounter unbounded utility functions, such as ln, in economics and finance. How can this be? The distribution of prizes used for Menger's example is extremely skewed. If we consider only bounded distributions of prizes, or distributions that are sufficiently well behaved (unlike $e^{2^t}$), then St. Petersburg paradoxes cannot occur. This is the strategy that the literature has followed.

[8]Continuity implies, among other things, the Archimedean axiom (Kreps, 1988, page 44f): let $[x_1, 1] \prec [x_2, 1] \prec [x_3, 1]$; then there exists a $p$ such that $[x_1, 1-p; x_3, p] \sim [x_2, 1]$.

such preferences with a continuous utility function $\mathcal{V}: \mathcal{L} \to \mathbb{R}$ so that $L \prec L' \iff \mathcal{V}(L) < \mathcal{V}(L')$.[9]

As in ordinary utility theory, we assume that people prefer more to less. Since the prizes are just money, this simply means that people prefer to have more money rather then less—an assumption that should not be too controversial. Therefore we assume that preferences are monotonic in the prizes that have positive probability; i.e., [10]

$$\pi_1 > 0,\ a > 0 \Rightarrow \mathcal{V}([x_1, \pi_1; x_2, \pi_2]) < \mathcal{V}([x_1 + a, \pi_1; x_2, \pi_2]).$$

We also assume that people dislike risk. This assumption should only be slightly more controversial than monotonicity. Let $E\{L\}$ denote the expected value of the prize of lottery $L$,

$$E\{L\} := \sum_{s=1}^{S} \pi_s x_s.$$

In the following, we assume that $L$ is not degenerate in the sense that it does contain some variation.[11] Now consider the degenerate lottery $[E\{L\}, 1]$. This lottery pays $E\{L\}$ with certainty. We say that an agent is *risk neutral* if $\mathcal{V}(L) = \mathcal{V}([E\{L\}, 1])$; that is, the risk in $L$ (the variation of payoffs between states) is irrelevant to the agent—he cares only about the expectation of the prize. We say that the agent is *risk averse* if $\mathcal{V}(L) < \mathcal{V}([E\{L\}, 1])$. Such an agent would rather have the average prize $E\{L\}$ for sure than to bear the risk embodied in the lottery $L$. Put another way, the agent is willing to give up some wealth on average in order to avoid the randomness of the prize of $L$.

[9]There is a mnemotechnical reason for this strange choice of symbols. In accordance with previous chapters, I use a "V" instead of a "U" to represent utility because the prizes are money, not real commodities. I use a script symbol because this utility function is defined over the set of lotteries, which is denoted with a script letter.

[10]Note that this assumption rules out an extreme, but conceivable, form of risk aversion. A person might dislike uncertainty to such an extent that he will forgo an opportunity of gaining something, just because the gain is uncertain. One can imagine that the disappointment if the gain did not occur would be so great as to more than offset the increase in happiness if the gain did materialize. This person would not pick up a $100 bill from the street because it might be counterfeit. We do not cover such preferences.

[11]Formally, we assume that there are $s, s'$ with $\pi_s, \pi_{s'} > 0$ and $x_s \neq x_{s'}$.

**Box 4.1** ***Certainty equivalent and risk premium***

Let $\mathcal{V}$ be some utility function on $\mathcal{L}$, and let $L$ be some lottery with expected prize $E\{L\}$. The *certainty equivalent* of $L$ under $\mathcal{V}$ is defined as

$$\mathcal{V}([\mathrm{CE}(L), 1]) := \mathcal{V}(L).$$

In words, $\mathrm{CE}(L)$ is the level of (non-random) wealth that yields the same utility as the lottery $L$. The *risk premium* is the difference between the expected prize of the lottery, and its certainty equivalent,

$$\mathrm{RP}(L) := E\{L\} - \mathrm{CE}(L).$$

If preferences are increasing and risk averse, each lottery has precisely one certainty equivalent.[12] Risk aversion is equivalent to the assumption that the risk premium is positive, $\mathrm{CE}(L) < E\{L\}$.

This situation can be visualized by considering the set of lotteries with just two possible outcomes ($s = 2$), and holding the probabilities fixed ($\pi_1, \pi_2$ given). A lottery $[x_1, \pi_1; x_2, \pi_2]$ is then just a point in the two-dimensional space of outcomes $(x_1, x_2)$, and as such is amenable to graphical representation in two dimensions. In the following we fix $\pi := (0.4, 0.6)$, and we write $\overline{\mathcal{V}}(x_1, x_2) := \mathcal{V}([x_1, 0.4; x_2, 0.6])$.

In the $(x_1, x_2)$-space, the lotteries on the 45°-line are risk-free because they pay some non-random prize. The lotteries with expected prize $z$ are located on a straight line that is orthogonal to the vector of probabilities; see Figure 4.2. Why? By definition of orthogonality, a point $z$ is in the affine space which is orthogonal to $\pi$ and goes through $x$ if $\pi \cdot z = \pi \cdot x$, but $\pi \cdot x = \sum_{s=1}^{S} \pi_s x_s = E\{L\}$.

We can also draw indifference curves in this space. What would they look like? By monotonicity, they must be strictly decreasing from left to right. Moreover, risk aversion implies that the expected prize of any lottery $L$ that has the same utility level as some degenerate risk-free lottery $[z, 1]$ must be greater than $z$. This implies that the indifference curve that goes through the point $(z, z)$ must lie to the right and above the line connecting all lotteries with expectation $z$. Thus, the indifference curve is tangent to the constant-expected-prize line at the point $(z, z)$. Formally, $\nabla\overline{\mathcal{V}}(z, z) = \lambda\pi$

[12]In order to avoid confusion, note that macroeconomists sometimes use a mathematical result known as "certainty equivalence," which deals with the simplifications that are possible when maximizing the expected value of a quadratic objective function subject to linear constraints (Malinvaud, 1969). This has nothing to do with the certainty equivalent we study here.

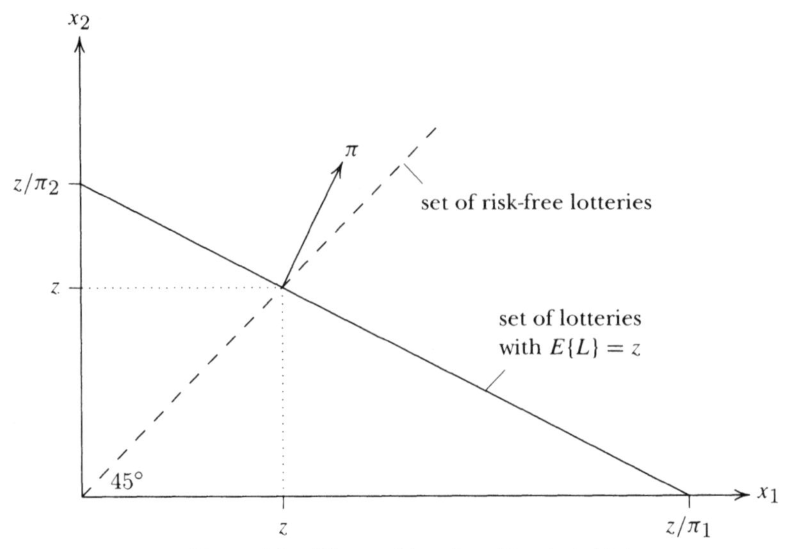


***Figure 4.2.*** *The set of lotteries with expected prize z.*

for some $\lambda > 0$. Likewise, consider some non-degenerate lottery $L$ (one not on the 45°-line) and consider the indifference curve to which it belongs. Given monotonicity and continuity, this indifference curve cuts through the 45° line at exactly one point. This point is the certainty equivalent of the lottery $L$ (Figure 4.3).

Notice that the preferences that give rise to the indifference curve in this figure are not convex. Risk aversion *per se* does not imply convexity of $\prec$. It implies only that the indifference curve is above the constant-expected-prize line, as in Figure 4.3, so that the risk premium is positive, as depicted in Figure 4.4. Likewise, convexity of $\prec$ does not imply risk aversion. Of course, in order to prove the existence of a general equilibrium, we have to make sure that the aggregate demand function is continuous, which we would usually ensure by assuming that $\prec$ is convex. Note, however, that this is an additional assumption, which does not imply nor is implied by risk aversion. Convexity is not necessary to define the certainty equivalent, which is the aim of this section, so we do not make this assumption now. On the other hand, convexity is not sufficient for the von Neumann–Morgenstern expected utility representation, which we develop in the next section. When we do this, we will impose stronger assumptions which imply convexity of $\prec$ (see footnote 13 on page 77).

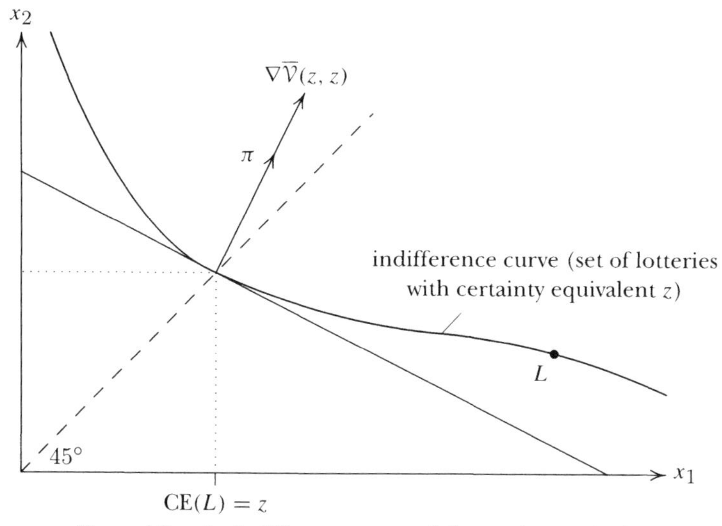


*Figure 4.3.* *An indifference curve and the certainty equivalent.*

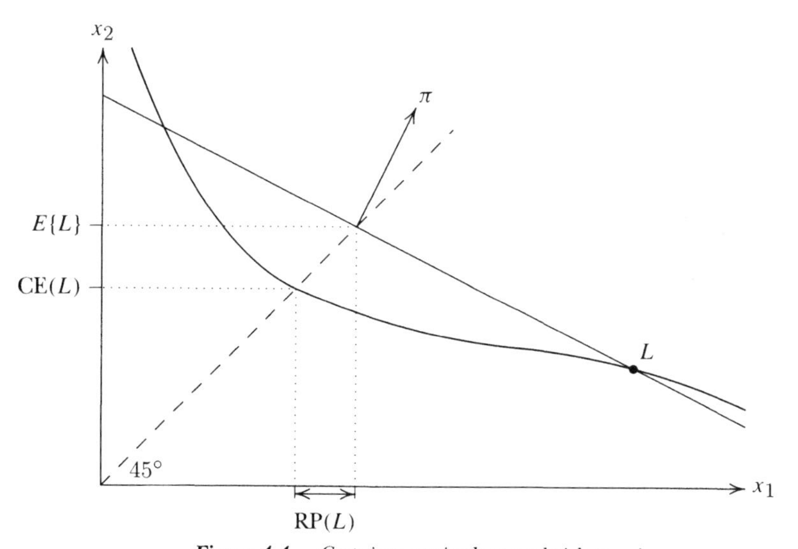


*Figure 4.4.* *Certainty equivalent and risk premium.*

## 4.3 The von Neumann–Morgenstern representation

So far we have not done anything different from the ordinary ordinal utility theory. We will now begin to exploit the additional structure given by the probabilities. The aim is to represent the preferences of the agent by eval-

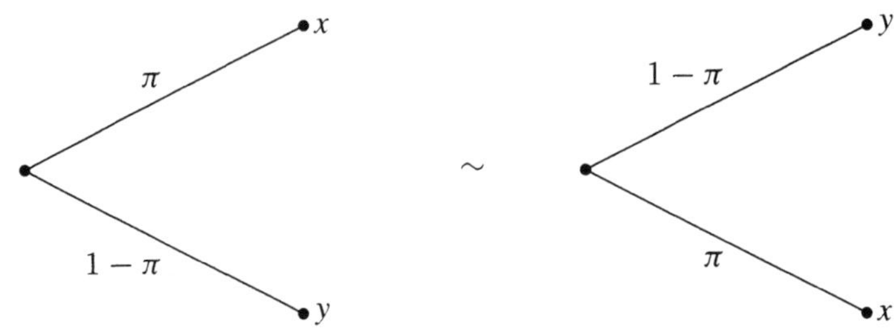


*Figure 4.5.* State-independence.

uating the expected utility of a lottery. More precisely, we seek a function $v$ that maps a single outcome $x_s$ to some real number $v(x_s)$, and will then compute the expected value of $v$. Formally, the function $v$ is the *expected utility representation* of $\mathcal{V}$ if $\mathcal{V}([x_1, \pi_1; \ldots; x_S, \pi_S]) = \sum_{s=1}^{S} \pi_s v(x_s)$.

The great advantage of using $v$ instead of $\mathcal{V}$ is that it is a much simpler object. $\mathcal{V}$ maps $\mathcal{L}$ into $\mathbb{R}$, but $\mathcal{L}$ is a large set; $v$, in contrast, maps $\mathbb{R}$ into $\mathbb{R}$. It is therefore a lot easier to work with $v$ instead of $\mathcal{V}$. Von Neumann & Morgenstern (1944) were the first to develop this idea formally.

### 4.3.1 State independence

A basic assumption that is clearly needed for an expected utility representation of preferences is that all that matters to an agent is the statistical distribution of outcomes. The state itself is just a label with no significance *per se.* So what we assume is that $[x, \pi; y, 1-\pi] \sim [y, 1-\pi; x, \pi]$. Figure 4.5 shows this axiom graphically.

### 4.3.2 Consequentialism

Probabilities allow us to mix lotteries in a way that is not sensible for ordinary commodity bundles. Consider a lottery whose prizes are themselves lotteries,

$$L := [L_1, \pi_1; L_2, \pi_2],$$

with

$$L_1 := [x_{11}, \pi_{11}; x_{12}, \pi_{12}],$$
$$L_2 := [x_{21}, \pi_{21}; x_{22}, \pi_{22}].$$

$L$ is a *compound lottery,* i.e. a lottery whose outcomes are lotteries. We assume that the agent is indifferent between $L$ and a "one-shot lottery" with the four

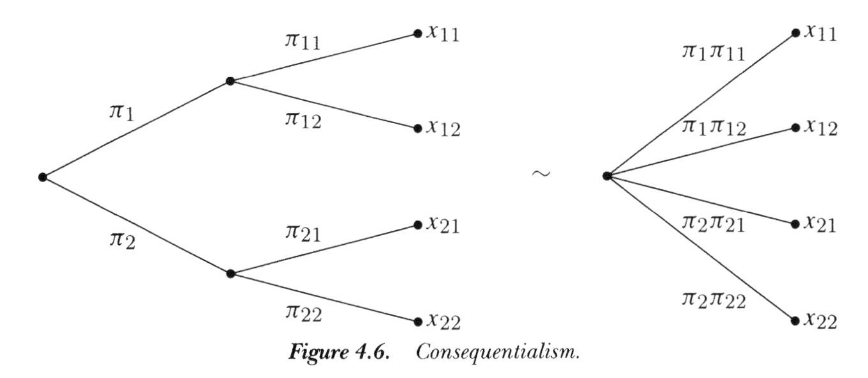


**Figure 4.6.** *Consequentialism.*

possible prizes and compounded probabilities. More precisely, we assume that the agent is indifferent between the compound lottery $L$ and the simple lottery

$$[x_{11}, \pi_1\pi_{11}; x_{12}, \pi_1\pi_{12}; x_{21}, \pi_2\pi_{21}; x_{22}, \pi_2\pi_{22}].$$

This assumption is called *consequentialism* (Figure 4.6) because only the consequences (distribution over prizes) are supposed to matter, and not the way we get there (through a one-shot lottery or a sequence of lotteries). Consequentialism says, basically, that the act of gambling is irrelevant. Only the probability distribution of the prizes matters for the agent.

### 4.3.3 Irrelevance of common alternatives

The *axiom of the irrelevance of common alternatives* (Figure 4.7) is another assumption about the preferences of agents over $\mathcal{L}$ which has no counterpart in ordinal utility theory.[13] This axiom says that compounding two arbitrary lotteries with a third one does not change their relative preference order. More formally, consider three arbitrary lotteries and a probability $\pi_3 < 1$. Irrelevance of common alternatives means that

$$L_1 \precsim L_2 \iff [L_1, 1-\pi_3; L_3, \pi_3] \precsim [L_2, 1-\pi_3; L_3, \pi_3].$$

Intuitively, this axiom says that there are two worlds: in one world, which has probability $\pi_3$, $L_3$ will be played. In the other world, which has probability $1-\pi_3$, $L_3$ will not be played. Either $L_1$ or $L_2$ will be played, depending on whether I choose the lottery $[L_1, 1-\pi_3; L_3, \pi_3]$ or $[L_2, 1-\pi_3; L_3, \pi_3]$. The

[13]We did not assume that the preference relation over lotteries is convex in section 4.2; see page 74. The irrelevance axiom, however, guarantees convexity [cf. page 80 and the digression on page 181 of Mas-Colell et al. (1995)].

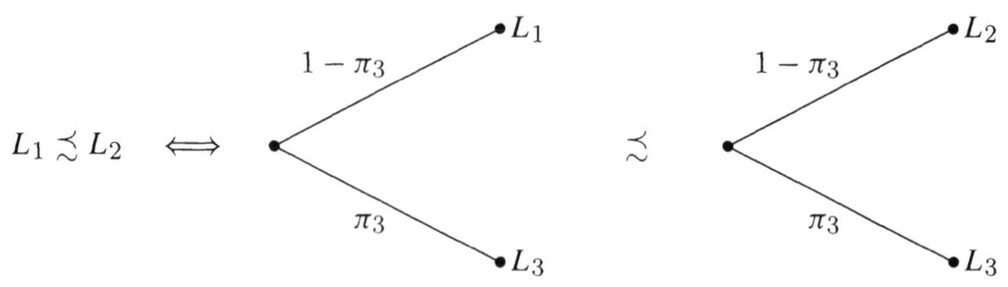


***Figure 4.7.*** *Irrelevance of common alternatives.*

irrelevance axiom says that the choice between these two lotteries should be independent of this alternative world in which $L_3$ is played. Rather, the compound lotteries should be evaluated by considering only those cases in which they differ, that is to say, when $L_3$ is not played.

For example, suppose you have to travel tomorrow. You can go by either bus or train, but you have to choose now because you need to buy the ticket one day in advance. The irrelevance axiom says that your choice of train or bus should not be affected by some independent outside possibility, like becoming ill tonight or the occurrence of an earthquake between now and tomorrow morning, in which case you will not travel at all.

### *4.3.4 The von Neumann–Morgenstern (NM) utility*

State-independence, consequentialism, and irrelevance of common alternatives, together with the usual assumptions on the preference $\prec$ (asymmetry, negative transitivity, continuity[14]), give rise to von Neumann and Morgenstern's famous result.

**Box 4.2** ***Expected utility representation***

The utility function $\mathcal{V}$ has an expected utility representation $v$ such that

$$\mathcal{V}([x_1, \pi_1; \ldots; x_S, \pi_S]) = \sum_{s=1}^{S} \pi_s v(x_s).$$

[14]In ordinal utility theory, continuity is meant with respect to consumption bundles. Here we need continuity in the space of lotteries. Formally, this is the same: if $L_1 \prec L_2 \prec L_3$, then $\exists \lambda \in (0, 1)$ such that $L_2 \sim \lambda L_1 + (1-\lambda)L_3$. But in terms of economics, something more is involved. We assume here that there is always a probability that makes one outcome equivalent to a mixture of other outcomes. For instance, consider three degenerate lotteries, $L_1 := [x_1, 1]$, $L_2 := [x_2, 1]$, $L_3 := [x_3, 1]$, such that $L_1 \prec L_2 \prec L_3$. The continuity assumption implies that there is a certain mixture between $L_1$ and $L_3$, a non-degenerate lottery $[x_1, \lambda; x_3, 1-\lambda]$, which is equivalent to the risk-free outcome $x_2$ (= the degenerate lottery $L_2$).

The proof is omitted here. Kreps (1988, chapter 5) provides an extensive proof. A shorter proof can be found in Gollier (2001*a*, chapter 1, theorem 1).

The utility function on the space of lotteries, $\mathcal{V}$, which represents the preference relation between lotteries, $\prec$, is an ordinal utility function in precisely the same sense as discussed in section 2.2. This means that $\mathcal{V}(L)$ is an ordinal measurement of satisfaction, and the utility levels of two lotteries can be compared only in the sense of ranking the lotteries, e.g. with $\mathcal{V}(L_1) < \mathcal{V}(L_2)$ meaning $L_2$ is better than $L_1$. As a consequence, any monotonic transformation of $\mathcal{V}$ is equivalent because it does not change the ranking and thus represents the same preferences (Box 2.2).

The von Neumann–Morgenstern utility function $v$ has more structure than that. It is such that it represents $\mathcal{V}$ as a linear function of probabilities. This structure would be lost by applying an arbitrary monotonic transformation on $v$. Hence, $v$ is not invariant under arbitrary monotonic transformations. It is invariant only under positive affine transformations, meaning that $\tilde{v}$ is equivalent to $v$ if and only if $\exists a \ \exists b > 0 \ \forall x \ \tilde{v}(x) = a + bv(x)$. For this reason, we say that the von Neumann–Morgenstern utility is *cardinal*. Cardinal numbers are measurements that are ordinal, but whose difference can also be ordered. Suppose we have $v(x_1) > v(x_2)$, $v(x_3) > v(x_4)$, and $v(x_1) - v(x_2) > v(x_3) - v(x_4)$. If $v$ were an ordinal utility, this last inequality would be meaningless. Not so with cardinal utility. With NM utility it does make sense to say that $x_1$ is better than $x_2$ "by a larger amount" than $x_3$ is better than $x_4$. As an example, consider the utility functions $v(w) := \sqrt{w}$ and $\tilde{v}(w) := \ln w$. $v$ and $\tilde{v}$ are equivalent if they are ordinal utility functions, but not if they are cardinal.

### 4.3.5 Risk aversion and concavity

Consider a binary lottery $[x_{low}, \pi; x_{high}, 1 - \pi]$. Let us evaluate $v$ at the two prizes, $v(x_{low})$ and $v(x_{high})$. Expected utility is

$$E\{v(x)\} = \pi v(x_{low}) + (1 - \pi)v(x_{high}).$$

The points $(x_{low}, v(x_{low}))$, $(E\{x\}, E\{v(x)\})$, and $(x_{high}, v(x_{high}))$ lie on one straight line, by definition (see Figure 4.8).

Now, the certainty equivalent is the level of wealth that gives the same utility as the lottery gives on average. Formally,

$$v(\mathrm{CE}(x)) = E\{v(x)\}.$$

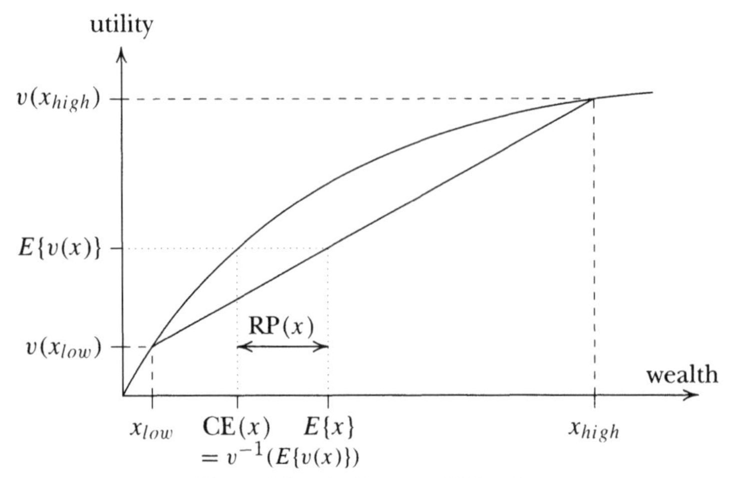


***Figure 4.8.*** *A risk-averse NM utility is concave.*

By inverting $v$, we can solve explicitly for the certainty equivalent,

$$\mathrm{CE}(x) = v^{-1}(E\{v(x)\}).$$

It becomes clear from Figure 4.8 that the agent is risk averse if and only if $v$ is a concave function. In fact, this follows formally from *Jensen's inequality*, which states that the strict convex combination of two values of a function is strictly below the graph of the function if the function is concave. For this reason, the risk premium is positive (and thus the agent is risk averse) if $v$ is strictly concave. The curvature of $v$ is therefore a measure of risk aversion.

As a borderline case, suppose that $v$ has no curvature ($v'' = 0$, i.e. $v$ is an affine function). Then $\mathrm{CE}(x) = E\{x\}$ and the risk premium is zero. This is the utility function of a risk-neutral agent.

### 4.3.6 Risk aversion and convexity

We have seen that risk aversion imposes only a very weak restriction on the ordinal utility function $\mathcal{V}$. In fact, all that it implies is that the gradient of $\mathcal{V}$ in the outcome space at a point without uncertainty be collinear to the probabilities of the outcomes ($\nabla\overline{\mathcal{V}}(z, z) = \lambda\pi$; see page 74). A risk-averse ordinal utility that is representable as a NM expected utility, however, has more structure. In fact, the NM axioms together with risk aversion imply that the ordinal utility is convex in the outcome space; i.e., the upper contour sets (the sets above the indifference curves of Figures 4.3 and 4.4) are convex sets.

Consider two lotteries, each with $S$ possible outcomes and with the same probability distribution $\pi := (\pi_1, \ldots, \pi_S)$. The two lotteries differ only in the possible outcomes, $x := (x_1, \ldots, x_S)$ and $y := (y_1, \ldots, y_S)$. Assume that lottery $[y, \pi]$ is weakly better than lottery $[x, \pi]$, i.e. $\mathcal{V}([x, \pi]) \leqslant \mathcal{V}([y, \pi])$, or, using the same notation as in section 4.2, $\overline{\mathcal{V}}(x) \leqslant \overline{\mathcal{V}}(y)$. Convexity means that $\overline{\mathcal{V}}(x) \leqslant \overline{\mathcal{V}}(\lambda x + (1-\lambda)y)$ for all $0 \leqslant \lambda \leqslant 1$. Let $v$ be the NM representation of $\mathcal{V}$. By risk aversion (the concavity of the NM utility representation), we know that $v(\lambda x_s + (1-\lambda)y_s) \geqslant \lambda v(x_s) + (1-\lambda)v(y_s)$ for all $s$. Thus, taking expectations, we also have $\overline{\mathcal{V}}(\lambda x + (1-\lambda)y) = E\{v(\lambda x + (1-\lambda)y)\} \geqslant \lambda E\{v(x)\} + (1-\lambda)E\{v(y)\} \geqslant E\{v(x)\} = \overline{\mathcal{V}}(x)$, proving convexity of $\overline{\mathcal{V}}$.

## 4.4 Measures of risk preference

### *4.4.1 Absolute risk aversion*

Consider again the problem an agent faces when deciding how much coverage of a risk to buy from an insurance company. We saw this problem in section 2.3 (on page 22);

$$\max_c u(w - c\mu, w - c\mu - (1-c)d), \tag{2.7}$$

where $v$ was some ordinal utility function. But now suppose that the agent has a von Neumann–Morgenstern utility $v$, and let $\pi$ denote the probability that the damage occurs. Then the problem becomes

$$\max_c (1-\pi)v(w - c\mu) + \pi v(w - c\mu - (1-c)d). \tag{4.1}$$

The first-order condition of this problem yields

$$\frac{1-\pi}{\pi} \cdot \frac{v'(w - c\mu)}{v'(w - c\mu - (1-c)d)} = \frac{d-\mu}{\mu}. \tag{4.2}$$

If the agent buys full coverage, $c = 1$, this collapses to

$$\frac{1-\pi}{\pi} = \frac{d-\mu}{\mu}. \tag{4.3}$$

Solving for $\mu$ yields

$$\mu = \pi d. \tag{4.4}$$

The right-hand side is the damage, $d$, times the probability that the damage occurs, $\pi$, so $\mu$ just equals the expected value of the loss. We say that an insurance premium that is equal to the expected loss is *statistically* or *actuarially fair.*

**Box 4.3** ***Demand for full coverage***

A risk-averse agent demands full coverage if and only if the premium is statistically fair. For any premium greater than that, the agent will demand less than full coverage.

Next time your insurance agent recommends that you buy full coverage auto insurance, ask him if his company has a gross markup on this insurance (for paying its employees, for instance). If it does, you should not buy full insurance.[15]

We have already proved the first half of the statement in the box above. What about the second half? Suppose

$$\mu := (1+m)\pi d, \quad \text{with} \quad m > 0; \tag{4.5}$$

that is to say, suppose the insurance costs more than the expected loss. $m$ is similar to a gross *markup* of the insurer. A positive markup implies that the right-hand side of (4.3), which is $(d-\mu)/\mu$, is smaller than $(1-\pi)/\pi$ because

$$\frac{d-\mu}{\mu} = \frac{1-(1+m)\pi}{(1+m)\pi} < \frac{1-\pi}{\pi} \quad \text{if} \quad m > 0.$$

Thus, to restore equality, the second part of the left-hand side of (4.2) must be smaller than 1,

$$v'(w - c\mu) < v'(w - c\mu - (1-c)d).$$

If the agent is risk averse, then $v'$ is a decreasing function of its argument (i.e. $v'' < 0$), so the condition can be rewritten as

$$w - c\mu > w - c\mu - (1-c)d,$$

which is true if and only if $c < 1$. This proves the second half of the statement in Box 4.3.

If the insurance premium is high enough, the agent will forego insuring himself altogether. Denote the markup at which demand for the insurance vanishes with $m_0$. Combining the first-order condition (4.2) with the definition of the markup (4.5) yields

$$\frac{1-\pi}{\pi} \cdot \frac{v'(w - c\mu)}{v'(w - c\mu - (1-c)d)} = \frac{1-(1+m)\pi}{(1+m)\pi}.$$

[15]If it does not, this insurance company will soon go out of business and you should not buy any coverage from it.

We look for the level of $m$ that makes $c = 0$ the solution to this equation. Substituting $c = 0$ and solving for $m$ yields

$$m_0 := \frac{(1-\pi)(v'(w-d) - v'(w))}{\pi v'(w-d) + (1-\pi)v'(w)} > 0. \tag{4.6}$$

If the premium $\mu$ equals $(1 + m_0)\pi d$, the agent is just indifferent between bearing the whole risk ($c = 0$) and consuming the certain (non-random) income $w - (1 + m_0)\pi d$. Thus, this last amount is the *certainty equivalent* of the lottery, $(1-\pi)v(w) + \pi v(w-d) = v(w - (1+m_0)\pi d)$. For a very risk-averse agent, the certainty equivalent is very small (meaning that the agent will still buy some coverage even if the markup is rather large). For this reason we can view $m_0$ as a measure of risk aversion: $m_0 = 0$ means that the agent is risk neutral because he values the risky income as high as the expected income $w - \pi d$; i.e., his satisfaction is not affected by the risk. If $m_0 > 0$, the agent is willing to pay a premium for avoiding some of the risk.

It is clear that $m_0$ converges to zero when the expected damage $\pi d$ diminishes, but it is less clear whether $m_0$ or $\pi d$ diminish more rapidly as we let $d$ converge to zero. As a local measure of risk aversion, let us consider

$$\lim_{d \to 0} \frac{m_0}{\pi d} = \lim_{d \to 0} \frac{1-\pi}{\pi} \cdot \frac{(v'(w-d) - v'(w))/d}{\pi v'(w-d) + (1-\pi)v'(w)}.$$

For symmetric risks ($\pi = 0.5$), this becomes

$$\lim_{d \to 0} \frac{m_0}{0.5d} = \lim_{d \to 0} \frac{(v'(w-d) - v'(w))/d}{0.5(v'(w-d) + v'(w))}.$$

The denominator converges to $v'(w)$. The numerator is a quotient whose numerator and denominator both converge to zero,

$$\lim_{d \to 0} \frac{v'(w-d) - v'(w)}{d}.$$

Note that this is the definition of (minus) the second derivative of $v$ at the point $w$. Thus we have

$$\lim_{d \to 0} \frac{m_0}{0.5d} = -\frac{v''(w)}{v'(w)} =: A(w). \tag{4.7}$$

This fraction was independently discovered by Pratt (1964) and Arrow (1965), and is known as the *Arrow-Pratt coefficient of absolute risk aversion.*[16]

[16]Note that for *asymmetric* risk ($\pi \neq 0.5$) the expression converges to $\frac{(1-\pi)}{\pi} A(w)$. This is an appropriate local measure of aversion against asymmetric risk.

**Box 4.4** *ARA*

The coefficient of *absolute risk aversion* ARA is a local measure of the degree that an agent dislikes risk. It is defined as

$$A(w) := -\frac{v''(w)}{v'(w)}.$$

$A$ has several desirable properties. First, it is invariant under affine transformations of the utility function, meaning that, if $v$ and $\tilde{v}$ are equivalent von Neumann–Morgenstern utility functions (in the sense that $v$ is an affine transformation of $\tilde{v}$), then $A_v(w) = A_{\tilde{v}}(w)$ for all $w$. This means that the coefficient of absolute risk aversion can be used for interpersonal comparisons.

Second, suppose two persons have the same endowment but different preferences. Mister X's utility function $v$ is more concave than Mister Y's utility function $\tilde{v}$, in the sense that there exists a concave function $g$ such that $v(w) = g(\tilde{v}(w)))$, so Mister X will always demand a larger risk premium than Mister Y for exposing himself to some given risk. In other words, X is globally more risk averse than Y. But it is also true that $A_v(w) > A_{\tilde{v}}(w)$ for all $w$. Thus, $A$ does indeed measure the degree of risk aversion.

**Box 4.5** *CARA—DARA—IARA*

We say that the utility function $v$ exhibits *constant absolute risk aversion*, or CARA, if $A$ does not depend on wealth, $A'(w) = 0$. $v$ exhibits *decreasing absolute risk aversion*, or DARA, if richer people are less absolutely risk averse than poorer ones, $A'(w) < 0$. Likewise, $v$ exhibits *increasing absolute risk aversion*, IARA, if $A'(w) > 0$.

What does CARA or DARA or IARA mean economically? Consider a simple binary lottery in which you cannot win anything, but you may lose \$10 with, say, 50% probability. CARA means that a millionaire requires the same payment to enter this lottery as a beggar would. IARA means that the millionaire requires a larger payment than the beggar. For most people this seems not very probable. Most people would expect the millionaire to enter this lottery in exchange for a significantly smaller payment than the beggar, which is DARA.

### 4.4.2 Relative risk aversion

Now consider a variation of the binary lottery we saw before. Instead of losing $10 with some probability, the game is now that you have a 50% probability of losing 10% of your wealth. For the beggar this amounts to something like 50 cents; for the millionaire it would be $100,000. Who requires a larger payment up front, in percentage of his wealth, to enter this gamble? This is not an easy question. Suppose the millionaire requires $70,000, which is not totally absurd, and the beggar requires 30 cents, which again may make sense. Then the millionaire requires a larger payment in percentage of his wealth than the beggar. In that case, we say that the millionaire is more relatively risk averse than the beggar. The coefficient that measures this is the *coefficient of relative risk aversion*, defined as

$$R(w) := wA(w).$$

If $R$ is independent of wealth, we say that the utility function is in the *constant relative risk aversion*, or CRRA, class. Similarly, some utilities exhibit increasing (IRRA) or decreasing (DRRA) relative risk aversion.

### 4.4.3 Precautionary saving and prudence

The coefficients of risk aversion measure the disutility that small amounts of risk impose on the agent, so these are measures of how much an agent dislikes risk. But such measures do not tell us how the behavior of the agent changes when we vary the amount of risk the agent is forced to bear. For instance, it may seem reasonable to assume that an agent accumulates some precautionary savings when facing more uncertainty. Risk aversion *per se*, however, does not imply such comparative statics. An agent is said to be *prudent* if his optimal saving increases with the amount of uncertainty of his future wealth. In other words, more risk induces a prudent agent to accumulate precautionary savings. Kimball (1990) defines the *coefficient of absolute prudence* as $P(w) := -v'''(w)/v''(w)$ and establishes that an agent is prudent in the above sense if and only if this coefficient is positive. To see why, consider a simplified saving problem. Suppose there is only a risk-free bond with price $\beta$, but there are two states of the world, each equally likely. The state-contingent endowment of the agent is $w^0$ today and $(w^1 - x, w^1 + x)$ tomorrow. $x$ is endowment risk, and because there is only a risk-free bond, this risk cannot be hedged; the agent must bear the risk. He maximizes intertemporal utility by choosing an optimal amount of bonds $z$,

$$\max\{v(w^0 - \beta z) + \delta(0.5v(w^1 - x + z) + 0.5v(w^1 + x + z))\},$$

where $\delta$ is the agent's discount factor. The first-order condition of this problem is

$$\beta v'(w^0 - \beta z) = \delta(0.5v'(w^1 - x + z) + 0.5v'(w^1 + x + z)).$$

The left-hand side is the marginal utility today of reducing bond holdings, and the right-hand side is the discounted expected marginal utility tomorrow of increasing bond holdings. $x$ is only part of the right-hand side. If an increase of $x$ increases tomorrow's expected marginal utility (the right-hand side), then the optimal bond holdings should increase in order to shift consumption away from today's relatively low marginal utility into tomorrow's higher expected marginal utility. Starting from $x = 0$, a marginal increase of $x$ has this effect on the right-hand side of the first-order condition if and only if $v'$ is convex (by Jensen's inequality). More formally, totally differentiating the first-order condition yields

$$\frac{dz}{dx} = (-v''(w^1 - x + z) + v''(w^1 + x + z)) \cdot \phi,$$

where

$$\phi := \frac{-0.5\delta}{\beta^2 v''(w^0 - \beta z) + 0.5\delta v''(w^1 - x + z) + 0.5\delta v''(w^1 + x + z)} > 0.$$

Thus, $dz/dx > 0$ if and only if $v''(w^1 + x + z) > v''(w^1 - x + z)$, that is to say, $v''' > 0$ (for small $x$).

The precautionary saving motive is important because it implies that uncertainty induces agents to save more. If agents are prudent, then the aggregate supply of saving increases (and thus the equilibrium risk-free interest rate decreases) with aggregate uncertainty, as we will see later (Box 5.10).

## 4.5 Assumptions and evidence

### 4.5.1 A priori *assumptions*

We certainly assume that people do not like to be constrained in their choices by scarcity of any kind. When you are faced with a choice between a bottle of very good wine and an exquisite meal, you would certainly prefer to have both.[17] So we will assume that the utility function is strictly increasing in wealth.

We also assume that people dislike risk. This may not be true for everyone—there may be risk addicts—but it is probably true for most of us. So we assume that utility is a strictly concave function of wealth.

[17] At least, I would.

Having dealt with the meaning of ARA, it seems quite clear that ARA should be decreasing in wealth: rich people find it easier to be exposed to a $1000 risk than poor people. Note also that risk aversion plus DARA or CARA implies prudence, but not vice versa.[18] Thus, for risk-averse utility, prudence is a strictly weaker assumption than DARA, so we definitely want reasonable utility functions to exhibit prudence.

There is, however, much less consensus or clear evidence about the behavior of RRA, so we may not have a clear prior in favor of DRRA, CRRA, or IRRA.

### 4.5.2 *Experimental and survey evidence*

There is a large body of evidence regarding the typical shape of the utility function stemming from experimental research. The usual result is that most people are indeed risk averse. There is also some evidence supporting DARA. Also, CRRA can usually not be rejected, but the evidence concerning relative risk aversion is often less conclusive.

An especially interesting series of experiments has been performed by biologists using animals![19] The advantage of using animals instead of humans is that one can control the environment very well and easily make a great number of experiments, because animal subjects are cheaper to work with than humans. Payoff is—of course—not money, but food. Kagel et al. (1995) report on this research. They find overwhelming evidence for risk aversion (see especially their chapter 6). There is also some evidence for DARA. Unfortunately, the authors do not deal with relative risk aversion.

Friend & Blume (1975) study revealed risk preferences of US households by analyzing survey data collected by the Federal Reserve Board. The data contain information on the values of assets and liabilities and on the sources of income of 2100 households for the years 1962 and 1963. They report that a utility function that is DARA and approximately CRRA, with a coefficient of relative risk aversion in the neighborhood of 2, is compatible with these data. Another, more recent field experiment with high stakes involving humans is Fullenkamp, Tenorio & Battalio (2003). They use data from a televised game show in which very large amounts of money are at stake. They find evidence for a small degree of risk aversion and estimate the

[18]More precisely, it is not difficult to check that DARA implies $P(w) > A(w)$, and since the right-hand side is positive by risk aversion, the left-hand side must also be positive.

[19]In the light of these experiments, it seems that entities that, we might think, do not have *ratio* still optimize and behave economically. Economic behavior does not seem to hinge upon reason or reflection, so *rationality* is a misnomer for this behavior. Alternatively, we may conclude that animals do have reason.

coefficient of relative risk aversion to be between 0.6 and 1.5. Abdulkadri & Langemeier (2000) find significantly larger values. Using data on farm household consumption, they locate relative risk aversion in the range 2.8–6.3. Van Praag & Booji (2003) use results from a large survey conducted by Dutch newspapers which contained questions about hypothetical behavior in the face of risk, and have more than 9000 respondents. They find that the coefficient of relative risk aversion seems to be more or less log-normally distributed, with a mean of 1.54 and a standard deviation of 3.78.

### 4.5.3 *Introspection*

To understand the equity premium puzzle, it is necessary to have an idea about reasonable assumptions concerning the degree of risk aversion. An easy way to achieve this is to determine your own degree of risk aversion. Box 4.6 is designed to help you do that (assuming a CRRA utility function).

Now you have an estimate of your own personal degree of relative risk aversion. Mathematically, you are asked in Box 4.6 to find the $s$ that satisfies

$$0.5 \cdot v(w(1-r)) + 0.5 \cdot v(w(1+r)) = v(w(1-s)).$$

Assuming a CRRA utility function (with $\gamma \neq 1$) this becomes

$$0.5\frac{(w(1-r))^{1-\gamma}}{1-\gamma} + 0.5\frac{(w(1+r))^{1-\gamma}}{1-\gamma} = \frac{(w(1-s))^{1-\gamma}}{1-\gamma},$$

which simplifies to

$$0.5(1-r)^{1-\gamma} + 0.5(1+r)^{1-\gamma} = (1-s)^{1-\gamma}.$$

Table 4.1 on page 90 was computed with this equation.

### 4.5.4 *Evolutionary stability*

Introspection (Box 4.6), experiments (Kagel et al., 1995), and revealed preferences (Friend & Blume, 1975) all reach a similar conclusion; namely, that a reasonable average utility function exhibits some moderate amount of risk aversion. A new field of research, called *evolutionary finance*, reaches the same conclusion, but with a very different reasoning. Moreover, the conclusion that follows from this literature is much sharper. Evolutionary finance views the utility functions that investors maximize as the result of natural selection: unsuccessful investment strategies eventually die out (become poor) and only the successful strategies survive (become rich). For this reason, we do not have to research or introspect plausible utility functions.

**Box 4.6** ***Determine your preferences***

1. How much do you consume every year on average (in money units)? $y =$ __________
2. Compute 10%, 20%, 30% of your yearly consumption. For enhanced concreteness, think of an item that is worth that much.
   $r_1 := y \cdot 10\% =$ ______ item ______________
   $r_2 := y \cdot 20\% =$ ______ item ______________
   $r_3 := y \cdot 30\% =$ ______ item ______________
3. Suppose you are subject to a lottery. This lottery takes place only once and the odds are 50–50. If you win the lottery, you will receive a tax rebate of $r$ every year from now on. If you lose the lottery you will be subject to an additional tax every year. This gives rise to three lotteries, every year from now on, depending on $r$:
   $L_1$ : 50–50 chance of consuming _____ $(y - r_1)$ or _____ $(y + r_1)$
   $L_2$ : 50–50 chance of consuming _____ $(y - r_2)$ or _____ $(y + r_2)$
   $L_3$ : 50–50 chance of consuming _____ $(y - r_3)$ or _____ $(y + r_3)$
4. Suppose you can avoid this risk and exchange it for some safe amount of consumption. What safe level of yearly consumption feels equivalent to the risky situation shown above? Try to make this feel as real as possible. Think of a risk-free consumption level that you would clearly prefer relative to the risky lottery. Then think of a consumption level that would clearly make you feel worse, so that you would rather be subject to the uncertainty of the lottery. Then narrow the boundaries. Try to determine the consumption level at which your decision switches.
   The safe consumption level of _____ $(=: c_1)$ feels equivalent to $L_1$.
   The safe consumption level of _____ $(=: c_2)$ feels equivalent to $L_2$.
   The safe consumption level of _____ $(=: c_3)$ feels equivalent to $L_3$.
5. Compute the implicit risk premia by subtracting $c_1$, $c_2$, $c_3$ from your initial consumption $y$, then dividing these by $y$. Express the results in percentage points:
   $s_1 := (y - c_1)/y =$ _____ %
   $s_2 := (y - c_2)/y =$ _____ %
   $s_3 := (y - c_3)/y =$ _____ %
6. Look up the corresponding $\gamma$s from Table 4.1,
   $\gamma(s_1) =$ _______, $\gamma(s_2) =$ _______, $\gamma(s_3) =$ _______.

*Note*: An electronic version of this experiment may be downloaded from the book's website.

*Table 4.1. Determining γ.*

| $\gamma$ | $s_1$ | $s_2$ | $s_3$ | $\gamma$ | $s_1$ | $s_2$ | $s_3$ |
|---|---|---|---|---|---|---|---|
| 0 | 0.0% | 0.0% | 0.0% | 3 | 1.5% | 5.9% | 12.8% |
| 0.25 | 0.1% | 0.5% | 1.1% | 3.5 | 1.7% | 6.7% | 14.5% |
| 0.5 | 0.3% | 1.0% | 2.3% | 4 | 2.0% | 7.6% | 16.0% |
| 0.75 | 0.4% | 1.5% | 3.5% | 5 | 2.4% | 9.1% | 18.4% |
| 1 | 0.5% | 2.0% | 4.6% | 6 | 2.9% | 10.4% | 20.3% |
| 1.25 | 0.6% | 2.5% | 5.7% | 7 | 3.3% | 11.5% | 21.7% |
| 1.5 | 0.8% | 3.0% | 6.9% | 10 | 4.4% | 13.8% | 24.4% |
| 1.75 | 0.9% | 3.5% | 7.9% | 15 | 5.8% | 16.0% | 26.4% |
| 2 | 1.0% | 4.0% | 9.0% | 20 | 6.8% | 17.0% | 27.4% |
| 2.5 | 1.2% | 5.0% | 11.0% | 30 | 7.8% | 18.1% | 28.2% |

Instead, we have to determine which investment strategies are evolutionary stable, in the sense of not disappearing in the evolutionary selection process.

In a path-breaking contribution, Blume & Easley (1992) have shown that the only evolutionary stable strategy is to maximize the expected logarithm of wealth.[20] In other words, the single strategy that asymptotically attracts all the wealth of the economy is a von Neumann–Morgenstern utility maximizer with a log utility function.[21] All other strategies are eventually extinct. The reason for this result is that maximizing the expected value of the logarithm of wealth is the same as maximizing the expected growth rate of wealth.[22]

Evolutionary decision theory thus gives a very clear-cut answer to the question what utility functions we should work with: either you are a log-person, or you eventually become marginalized. This is a very strong argument in favor of the assumption that almost all the wealth is controlled by people with utility functions that are close to the log-function. Researching the utility of random people (with questionnaires or using revealed preferences) is irrelevant for explaining market prices because asymptotically only the log-persons make the music.

[20]Sinn & Weichenrieder (1993) find the same result, but their presentation is much easier to follow; see also Sinn (2002).

[21]Recall that Bernoulli (1954) suggested this particular utility function by introspection. Arrow (1971) advocates the same utility function on purely formal grounds. Another supporter of the (generalized) log utility is Rubinstein (1976); he advocates this choice essentially on the basis of convenience.

[22]This was actually known for a long time, see e.g., Hakansson (1971).

## 4.6 Often used specifications

### 4.6.1 The HARA class

Summing up these different sources of evidence, we have a rather detailed view of the properties of a plausible utility function.

> **Box 4.7** ***Likely utilities***
>
> We believe that the utility function of most agents is (1) strictly increasing; (2) strictly concave; (3) DARA [$A'(w) < 0$]; (4) with not too large relative risk aversion ($0 < R(w) < 4$ for all $w$, or $R(w) \approx 1$ if following the evolutionary finance approach).

In the literature one finds only a handful of specifications. The most common are linear (or affine), quadratic, power, log, and exponential. How do these specifications fare with respect to our idea of what a utility should look like? Table 4.2 gives an overview of the properties of these functions. Note that the quadratic utility implies zero prudence, so a quadratic expected utility maximizer has no precautionary saving motive. The power utility function with not too large $\gamma$ seems to satisfy the requirements of Box 4.7 best.[23] All these standard specifications of Table 4.2 share an interesting property. They all belong to the so-called HARA class, which stands for *hyperbolic absolute risk aversion.* (Absolute) *risk tolerance* is defined as the reciprocal of absolute risk aversion,

$$T(w) := 1/A(w).$$

A utility is HARA if and only if absolute risk tolerance is an affine function of wealth.[24] The derivative of absolute risk tolerance, $T'(w)$, is sometimes called *cautiousness.* HARA utility functions are therefore sometimes also called constant cautiousness utility functions, because $T'(w) = b =$ constant. Still another name is *linear risk tolerance* (or LRT) utility functions.

[23]The power utility function is not defined for $\gamma = 1$, but the log function is the limit of the power function as $\gamma$ converges to one. To see this, first note that $v(y) := (y^{1-\gamma} - 1)/(1-\gamma)$ is an affine transformation of the power utility function defined in Table 4.2 and therefore represents the same preferences. We consider the limit of this function as $\gamma \to 1$. The numerator and the denominator converge to zero; thus, de l'Hôpital's rule applies:

$$\lim_{\gamma\to 1} \frac{y^{1-\gamma}-1}{1-\gamma} = \lim_{\gamma\to 1} \frac{\partial(y^{1-\gamma}-1)/\partial\gamma}{\partial(1-\gamma)/\partial\gamma} = \lim_{\gamma\to 1} \frac{y^{1-\gamma}}{-1}\frac{\partial \ln(y^{1-\gamma})}{\partial\gamma} = \ln y,$$

where we have used the fact that $[\ln(f(\gamma)+1)]' = f'(\gamma)/(f(\gamma)+1)$.

[24]Strictly speaking, the affine utility function does not satisfy this definition, but it is the limiting case as $a \to \infty$ and $b$ arbitrary but bounded.

*Table 4.2. Often used utility functions.*

| Name | Formula | $A(y)$ | $R(y)$ | $P(y)$ | $a$ | $b$ |
|---|---|---|---|---|---|---|
| affine | $\gamma_0 + \gamma_1 y$ | 0 | 0 | undefined | undefined | undefined |
| quadratic | $\gamma_0 y - \gamma_1 y^2$ | increasing | increasing | 0 | $\gamma_0/(2\gamma_1)$ | $-1$ |
| exponential | $-\frac{1}{\gamma} e^{-\gamma y}$ | $\gamma$ | increasing | $\gamma$ | $1/\gamma$ | 0 |
| power | $\frac{1}{1-\gamma} y^{1-\gamma}$ | decreasing | $\gamma$ | decreasing | 0 | $1/\gamma$ |
| Bernoulli | $\ln y$ | decreasing | 1 | decreasing | 0 | 1 |

$a = 0$ is the power (CRRA) specification, $b = 0$ is the exponential (CARA) specification. $a > 0$ and $b = -1$ is the quadratic utility. This negative $b$ indicates that the quadratic utility features increasing absolute risk aversion (IARA). The HARA class also contains not-so-standard specifications, for instance with $a \neq 0$ and $b > 0$. An example of this is the power specification with a subsistence level, $v(x) := (x - \underline{x})^{1-\gamma}/(1-\gamma)$, with $a = -\underline{x}\gamma^{-1}$ and $b = \gamma^{-1}$. $a$ is negative if the subsistence level $\underline{x}$ is positive. This indicates that this utility function exhibits decreasing relative risk aversion (DRRA).[25]

**Box 4.8** *HARA (Merton, 1971)*

A utility function $v$ belongs to the *hyperbolic absolute risk aversion*, or HARA, class if $T$ is an affine function of wealth; formally,

$$T(w) = a + bw,$$

for some $a$ and $b$. $v$ features DARA if and only if $b > 0$. It is CARA if $b = 0$, with a coefficient of absolute risk aversion equal to $a^{-1}$. $v$ features DRRA if and only if $a < 0$; it is CRRA if $a = 0$, with a coefficient of relative risk aversion equal to $b^{-1}$. As a special case, $a = 0$ and $b = 1$ is the log-utility. A HARA utility function that is in accordance with Box 4.7 should exhibit $b > 1/4$.

[25]Kagel et al. (1995, page 150f) find some weak evidence for this specification in their animal experiments. Ogaki & Zhang (2001) find evidence for the same specification in a study about risk sharing in India and Pakistan. Much earlier, Cohn et al. (1975) have reported evidence for DRRA based on data collected with a questionnaire from customers of a brokerage firm. However, the study of Fullenkamp et al. (2003) mentioned before, which exploits data from a high-stakes televised game show, reports some evidence for IRRA. In their data, higher initial wealth agents tend to have a larger coefficient of relative risk aversion.

A general HARA utility function takes the form

$$v(y) := \begin{cases} \ln(y + a), & \text{if } b = 1, \\ -ae^{-y/a}, & \text{if } b = 0, \\ (b - 1)^{-1}(a + by)^{(b-1)/b}, & \text{otherwise.} \end{cases} \tag{4.8}$$

The first line ($b = 1$) requires $y > -a$. The second line ($b = 0$) is well defined for all $y$. The domain using the third line depends on the sign of $b$. If $b > 0$ (DARA), $y$ must be sufficiently large for the function to be defined, $y > -a/b$. If $b < 0$ (IARA), then $y$ may not exceed a certain threshold to avoid entering negative absolute risk aversion, $y < -a/b$.

The HARA class is of great importance in finance and macroeconomics. It is a convenient class of utility functions because it is simple enough and gives sufficient structure to ease theoretical and empirical work, but at the same time it encompasses all major specifications found in the literature. Log, power, exponential, and quadratic all belong to it. Many results of finance and macroeconomics are valid only under the assumption of HARA utility. Whether this is a good assumption empirically remains debatable.

### 4.6.2 CRRA and homotheticity

Of all these specifications, the CRRA assumption is particularly popular with financial economists and macroeconomists, for both theoretical and empirical studies (see for instance Mehra & Prescott (1985) and the large body of literature that followed them). One reason may be the partially favorable empirical evidence for this assumption (e.g. Friend & Blume, 1975). The other reason is certainly the technical simplifications that CRRA buys.

Homothetic (ordinal) utility functions have the convenient property that the marginal rates of substitution do not change along a ray originating in the origin. As a consequence, the composition of the optimal consumption bundle of an agent is not affected by the agent's wealth, but depends only on the relative prices. A homothetic agent simply consumes twice as much of everything if his wealth doubles. The same is true if we work with state-contingent consumption of an aggregate good. If an agent's lifetime income doubles, then his optimal consumption doubles in each state, and the share of his wealth that he allocates to the different states is independent of his wealth. One important reason why CRRA is so popular may be that $\overline{V}$ (as defined on page 73) is a homothetic ordinal utility function if and only if $v$ is CRRA. We establish this fact in the remainder of this section.[26]

[26]Precisely the same statement was proven by Brennan & Kraus (1976, corollary on p. 179). An early precursor which seems to reach the same conclusion is Burk (1936).

Consider a lottery $[x, \pi]$. Fix the probabilities $\pi$ with $\pi \gg 0$, and let $\overline{V}(x) := \sum_{s=1}^{S} \pi_s v(x_s)$ be the expected utility given these probabilities. $\overline{V}$ is homothetic if and only if

$$\forall x \;\; \forall \lambda > 0 \;\; \exists \mu > 0 \quad \nabla \overline{V}(\lambda x) = \mu \nabla \overline{V}(x). \tag{4.9}$$

We show that $\overline{V}$ is homothetic if and only if $v$ is CRRA. This can be proven in three steps.

1. "Homotheticity $\iff$ $v'(\lambda y)/v'(y)$ is independent of $y$." The definition of homotheticity, together with the expected utility representation, $\overline{V}(x) := \sum_{s=1}^{S} \pi_s v(x_s)$, allows us to restate what homotheticity means. Consider the gradient,

$$\nabla \overline{V}(\lambda x) = \begin{bmatrix} \pi_1 v'(\lambda x_1) & \cdots & \pi_S v'(\lambda x_S) \end{bmatrix}. \tag{4.10}$$

(4.9) says that $\overline{V}$ is homothetic if and only if there exists a scalar $\mu$ such that $\nabla \overline{V}(\lambda x) = \mu \nabla \overline{V}(x)$; thus, according to (4.10), $\pi_s v'(\lambda x_s) = \mu \pi_s v'(x_s)$ for all $s$. This is equivalent to requiring that $v'(\lambda x_s)/v'(x_s)$ is independent of $s$. This must be true for a general outcome vector $x$; hence $\overline{V}$ is homothetic if and only if $v'(\lambda y)/v'(y)$ is independent of $y$.

2. "CRRA $\Rightarrow$ Homotheticity." If $v$ is the power utility function, then

$$\frac{v'(\lambda y)}{v'(y)} = \frac{(\lambda y)^{-\gamma}}{y^{-\gamma}} = \lambda^{-\gamma}. \tag{4.11}$$

This is independent of $y$; thus, $\overline{V}$ is homothetic.

3. "Homotheticity $\Rightarrow$ CRRA." Fix $\lambda$ and suppose $\exists \mu > 0$ such that $\forall y$,

$$v'(\lambda y) = \mu v'(y); \tag{4.12}$$

i.e. $\overline{V}$ is homothetic. Totally differentiating yields

$$\lambda v''(\lambda y) dy = \mu v''(y) dy. \tag{4.13}$$

Dividing (4.13) by (4.12), we have

$$\begin{aligned} \lambda \frac{v''(\lambda y)}{v'(\lambda y)} dy &= \frac{v''(y)}{v'(y)} dy \\ \iff -\lambda A(\lambda y) dy &= -A(y) dy \\ \iff -\lambda \frac{R(\lambda y)}{\lambda y} dy &= -\frac{R(y)}{y} dy, \end{aligned}$$

which is equivalent to

$$R(\lambda y) = R(y).$$

Relative risk aversion is independent of wealth; thus, $v$ is CRRA.

### *4.6.3 Mean–variance analysis*

Much of the theory of finance describes investors' risk preferences in terms of mean and variance. Higher mean return increases utility; higher variance of return decreases utility. How does this relate to the von Neumann–Morgenstern utility theory?

Clearly, mean–variance analysis is not always a sensible or useful description of behavior in the face of risk. For instance, for the St. Petersburg gamble it cannot even be applied, because neither the mean nor the variance of the payoff is defined in that case. But mean–variance can be used in some cases. In this section we demonstrate that mean–variance analysis is a special case of the von Neumann–Morgenstern utility theory, which applies only if we make some additional assumptions. In these cases, mean–variance analysis is appropriate.

**Case 1: *v* is quadratic.** There is one straightforward, but irrelevant, case in which mean–variance analysis works. Suppose the von Neumann–Morgenstern utility is quadratic, $v(w) := aw - bw^2$. This function increases monotonically in wealth as long as $w < a/2b$. Let $x$ be some random variable (i.e., $x$ is a function of the state, $x_1, \ldots, x_S$, with associated probabilities $\pi_1, \ldots, \pi_S$); then expected utility is[27]

$$\begin{aligned} E\{v(x)\} &= \sum_{s=1}^{S} \pi_s v(x_s) \\ &= aE\{x\} - bE\{x^2\} \\ &= aE\{x\} - b(E\{x\}^2 + \mathrm{var}(x)) \\ &= aE\{x\} - bE\{x\}^2 - b\mathrm{var}(x). \end{aligned}$$

[27]The third line follows from $\mathrm{var}(x) = E\{(x - E\{x\})^2\} = E\{x^2 - 2xE\{x\} + E\{x\}^2\} = E\{x^2\} - E\{x\}^2$.

This function increases monotonically in the mean as long as $E\{x\} < a/2b$ (i.e. as long as the mean is in the region where utility increases in wealth), and it decreases monotonically in the variance.

This justification for mean–variance analysis is not a good one, though, because quadratic utility implies IARA (see Table 4.2), which is highly implausible.[28]

**Case 2: *r* is jointly normal.** This second case is potentially more relevant than the unappealing quadratic utility. Suppose the returns of all assets are jointly normal.[29] Then, any portfolio of those assets will have returns that are also normally distributed. The normal distribution, however, is fully described by its first two moments, the mean and the variance. Thus, in this case we can find an equivalent representation of the von Neumann–Morgenstern utility function $v$, taking only the mean and the variance of the returns as arguments, $f(\mu_x, \sigma_x) = E\{v(x)\}$, where $\mu$ and $\sigma$ denote the mean and the standard deviation.

Suppose there are no other financial assets than stocks, and their returns are jointly normal.[30] Then mean–variance analysis can be used. But now suppose someone issues an option on a stock. The return of the option is not normal, but truncated normal, so mean–variance analysis cannot be used anymore.

**Case 3: Linear distribution classes.** Meyer (1987) points out that the case of jointly normal distributions is just a special case of a more general one.[31] Two distribution functions $F_1$ and $F_2$ belong to the same *linear distribution class* if there exist parameters $a$ and $b > 0$ such that $F_1(x) = F_2(a + bx)$ for all $x$. $F_1$ is just a stretched and dislocated version of $F_2$. Several families of distribution functions have this property, for instance the uniform and the normal. Others do not; most notably, if $F_1$ and $F_2$ are log-normal with different mean or variance, they do not belong to the same linear distribution class.

[28]Notice that this justification for mean–variance analysis implies that the mean enters quadratically, contrary to the linear-in-mean linear-in-variance specification ordinarily used. This is not so in case 4 below.

[29]But note that the normal distribution implies that the support of the asset returns is not bounded above or below. Thus, assets with limited liability (such as almost all financial assets we know) are excluded.

[30]Or rather, approximately normal, assuming that the probability that a stock price falls to zero is very small, so that the truncated normal is almost normal.

[31]Meyer (1987, page 422) does not claim that the idea is new: "Surprisingly, the condition presented here has been stated before, and yet seems to have been misunderstood or ignored." Sinn (1989) is more specific in pointing out who reported this insight earlier; see also Meyer's (1989) reply.

Let $y_1, y_2, \ldots$ be random variables drawn from $F_1, F_2, \ldots$, respectively, and assume that all $F_i$ belong to the same linear distribution class. Furthermore, let $\mu_i := E\{y_i\}$ and $\sigma_i^2 := E\{(y_i - \mu_i)^2\}$ be the mean and the variance of $y_i$.[32] Define then the new random variable $x := (y_i - \mu_i)/\sigma_i$. $x$ is distributed according to the same distribution $F$, no matter what $y_i$ is used to generate it, and $F$ is in the same linear distribution class as $F_1, F_2, \ldots$ and has zero mean and unit variance.

Suppose now that an agent faces a decision problem in which his payoff is some random variable, and he gets to choose the distribution of this payoff out of a choice set. Suppose further that all the distribution functions he can choose from belong to the same linear distribution class. Then, clearly, each possible choice is completely characterized by its mean and variance, since they are all transformations of the normalized distribution of this linear distribution class. Because of this, the normalized distribution can be used to evaluate the expected utility of some choice $y_i$,

$$E\{v(y_i)\} = \int_a^b v(\mu_i + \sigma_i x) dF(x) =: u(\mu_i, \sigma_i),$$

where $F$ is the normalized distribution, and $a$ and $b$ are the boundaries of the support of $F$. The expected NM utility $E\{v(\cdot)\}$ can be computed via the mean–standard deviation utility function $u(\cdot)$.

From this equation, Meyer (1987) deduces several interesting connections between the properties of $v$ and of $u$. For instance, if $v$ is monotonic and risk averse, then $u$ is increasing in $\mu$ and decreasing in $\sigma$. If $v$ is CARA, then the indifference curves in $(\sigma, \mu)$-space are vertically parallel copies of each other. If $v$ is CRRA, then the slopes of the indifference curves in $(\sigma, \mu)$-space do not change as we travel along a ray from the origin. Note that these properties are independent of which linear distribution class we work with. As long as we work with some linear distribution class, these qualitative properties of the $u$ function are determined only by the properties of the NM utility function $v$.

**Case 4: Small risks.** Any smooth function $f : \mathbb{R} \to \mathbb{R}$ can be locally decomposed into an infinite polynomial. The formula that does this is the *Taylor expansion*:

$$\begin{aligned} f(x) &= f(x_0) + \sum_{i=1}^{\infty} \frac{\partial^i f(x_0)}{\partial x_0{}^i} \frac{(x - x_0)^i}{i!} \\ &= f(x_0) + f'(x_0)(x - x_0) + f''(x_0)\frac{(x - x_0)^2}{2} + \cdots, \end{aligned}$$

[32] We assume that all $\mu_i$ and $\sigma_i$ are finite.

where $x_0$ is a point close to $x$. By evaluating only the first $n$ terms of the sum, this decomposition becomes the *$n$th-order Taylor approximation.*

Now consider a utility $v$, initial wealth $w$, and a zero mean risk (i.e. some $x$ with $E\{x\} = 0$). For small risks, expected utility is close to $v(w)$. Consider the second-order Taylor approximation of expected utility around $w$,

$$\begin{aligned} E\{v(w+x)\} &\approx v(w) + v'(w)E\{x\} + v''(w)\frac{E\{x^2\}}{2} \\ &= v(w) + v''(w)\frac{\text{var}(x)}{2}. \end{aligned}$$

Let $c := \text{CE}(w+x)$ be the certainty equivalent. For small risks, $c$ is close to $w$. Consider the first-order Taylor approximation of $c$ around $w$,

$$v(c) \approx v(w) + v'(w)(c-w).$$

Since by definition $v(c) = E\{v(w+x)\}$ we have, for small risks,

$$v(w) + v''(w)\frac{\text{var}(x)}{2} \approx v(w) + v'(w)(c-w),$$

which simplifies to

$$w - c \approx A(w)\frac{\text{var}(x)}{2}. \tag{4.14}$$

$w - c$ is the risk premium and therefore a measure of the utility cost of the small risk. This means that small risks can be evaluated approximately just by their variance.

In these calculations the risk $x$ is additive; it is simply added to the initial wealth, $w+x$. Now consider a multiplicative risk. Let $g$ be a positive random variable with unit mean, $E\{g\} = 1$. The prize of the lottery is $gw$. You can view $g$ as a random gross rate of return or growth factor (one plus the growth rate). Repeat the same steps as before, i.e.

$$\begin{aligned} E\{v(gw)\} &\approx v(w) + v'(w)wE\{g-1\} + v''(w)w^2\frac{E\{(g-1)^2\}}{2} \\ &= v(w) + v''(w)w^2\frac{\text{var}(g)}{2}. \end{aligned}$$

Let $\kappa$ be the certainty equivalent growth factor, $v(\kappa w) = E\{v(gw)\}$, and consider the first-order Taylor approximation of $v(\kappa w)$ around $w$,

$$v(\kappa w) \approx v(w) + v'(w)w(\kappa - 1).$$

Then

$$v(w) + v''(w)w^2\frac{\text{var}(g)}{2} \approx v(w) + v'(w)w(\kappa - 1),$$

which simplifies to

$$1 - \kappa \approx R(w)\frac{\text{var}(g)}{2}. \tag{4.15}$$

**Box 4.9** ***Approximate mean–variance analysis***

The risk premium associated to a small additive risk is approximately equal to half the variance multiplied by the coefficient of absolute risk aversion (4.14). The risk premium (in terms of a reduced growth rate) of a small multiplicative risk is approximately equal to half the variance times the coefficient of relative risk aversion (4.15).

Equations (4.14) and (4.15) are called *Arrow–Pratt approximations.* They are very handy because they allow us to evaluate the cost of small risks at very little computational expense. An important application of this idea, due to Lucas (1987), is the evaluation of the social welfare cost of the aggregate risk imposed upon society by the existence of business cycles. Problem 4.4 asks you to do just this.

For large curvatures of the utility function, or for somewhat bigger risks, the second-order approximation may not be satisfactory. But that does not imply that in these cases we must necessarily recur to full-fledged expected utility maximization. Instead, the quality of the approximation can be improved by taking more than just the first two terms of the Taylor series, thereby generating an approximate utility function in terms of an arbitrary number of moments. For instance, we could work with mean-variance-*skewness* utility, or with mean-variance-skewness-*kurtosis* utility (Samuelson, 1970).

## Notes on the literature

Excellent presentations of this material are provided by Gollier (2001*a*, chapters 1–4), Chambers & Quiggin (2000, chapter 3), Kreps (1990, chapter 3), and Mas-Colell et al. (1995, chapter 6). Kreps and Mas-Colell et al. also cover state-dependent utility functions, which we have not considered here. A comprehensive source for the whole field is Kreps (1988).

## Problems

**Problem 4.1** Suppose you face some uncertainty against which you can buy insurance. The premium of the insurance is just the expected value of the loss.

($a$) Suppose your utility function is $\frac{1}{1-\gamma}x^{1-\gamma}$. Will you buy no insurance, positive but incomplete insurance, or full coverage?

($b$) How does your answer depend on $\gamma$, or on the general form of your utility function?

($c$) How does your answer depend on your initial wealth?

($d$) Consider questions ($a$) to ($c$), but this time assume that the premium is 10% higher than the expected value of the loss. (Note: Only a qualitative answer is asked for. You do not have to compute anything for this. Think about the logic of the coefficients of risk aversion, and, for problem ($c$), distinguish between additive and multiplicative risk.)

**Problem 4.2** Consider a binary risk: you will either win $H$ with probability $\pi$ (e.g., the jackpot of the national lottery), or lose $L$ (the price of participating in the lottery) with probability $1-\pi$. You can expose yourself in a continuous manner to this risk, meaning that you can buy $x$ tickets, where $x$ is any real number. Assume that you have preferences that can be represented with a risk-averse von Neumann–Morgenstern utility function.

($a$) **Prove** that you will take some of this risk ($x > 0$) if the expected payoff, $\pi H - (1 - \pi)L$, is positive.

($b$) The expected payoff of the national lottery is negative. Why do some people participate? Have you personally participated in the past?

**Problem 4.3** Consider the insurance problem (4.1) and let the premium $m$ be defined as in (4.5). For each of the following cases, compute the demand for insurance (i.e. the optimal coverage $c$) as a function of the markup $m$.

1. $v$ is Bernoulli,
2. $v$ is CRRA,
3. $v$ is CARA,
4. $v$ is quadratic,
5. $v$ is affine.

[Hint: In cases 1 and 2, express the damage $d$ as portion of initial wealth, $d := rw$.]

**Problem 4.4** Between 1930 and 1999, real GDP per capita in the USA grew 2.24% per year on average, with a standard deviation of 5.21%.[33] Suppose

[33] These statistics are computed from data collected by the US Department of Commerce and the US Census Bureau. A spreadsheet containing the data is available from the book's website.

the coefficient of relative risk aversion of the representative agent (the one constructed with the competitive SWF) is 2.

(*a*) What is the certainty equivalent growth rate?

(*b*) How do you think the result would change qualitatively if we considered real consumption instead of real GDP?

(*c*) Given this, do you think that business cycles are a major economic problem for society?

(*d*) Try to think of arguments why something might be wrong with this analysis.

**Problem 4.5** Provide a functional form for a strictly increasing and risk-averse NM utility function that is *not* in the HARA class, and prove that it is not HARA.

# 5
# Static finance economy

This is the key theory chapter of this book. We now combine the Arrow–Debreu–Radner economy of chapters 2 and 3 with the von Neumann–Morgenstern utility of chapter 4. The payoff of this combination is considerable. We will be able to obtain much more concrete asset pricing formulas with more interpretations and content, and more empirically testable relationships. This marriage of general equilibrium theory and NM utility theory is a cornerstone of modern asset pricing theory. This is why we call the structure a *finance economy*.

But the finance economy is not only the playground of modern asset pricing theory. It also allows us to measure the social disutility of risk, that is to say, how much society as a whole is willing to pay for a marginal reduction of risk. Such a measure is of utmost interest for evaluating economic policy in general. What is the social cost of specific risks, such as unemployment risk, diseases, or natural disasters? What is the social value of stabilization policies, such as countercyclical monetary or fiscal policy?

## 5.1 An economy with von Neumann–Morgenstern agents

### *5.1.1 Intertemporal NM utility*

In the previous chapter, a risky decision was characterized by the agent's NM utility function $v$, his initial wealth $w$, and the properties of the lottery under review, $[x_1, \pi_1; \ldots; x_S, \pi_S]$. The objective function of the agent is the expected utility of this situation, $\sum_{s=1}^{S} \pi_s v(w + x_s)$. Alternatively, we could view wealth as state contingent, i.e. $(w + x_1, w + x_2, \ldots, w + x_S)$. The objective is then the expected utility of state-contingent wealth.

In order to apply this machinery to a general equilibrium model, we need to make two adaptations. First, uncertainty in an economy is not well captured by an arbitrary set of lotteries. Instead, we have modelled uncertainty as states of the world (or, with more than two periods, as an event-tree, or filtration—see Figure 2.1). It seems therefore natural to restrict the set of lotteries to contain only lotteries with $S$ possible outcomes and a fixed probability distribution over these outcomes, corresponding to the probability distribution of the states of the world. An asset is then a lottery in the sense that it assigns different payoffs—$r_s^j$ in the notation of chapter 3, $x_s$ in the notation of chapter 4—to different states of the world. A portfolio of securities is then in fact the same as a mixture of lotteries.

Second, in our general equilibrium model we have considered two periods, today and tomorrow, so the agent can choose not only how much purchasing power to allocate to the different states tomorrow, but also how much to consume now and how much to save for consumption tomorrow. Combining the two-period general equilibrium model with NM utility therefore requires the specification of a utility over consumption today and state-contingent consumption tomorrow. The simplest, and for this reason most usual, way to do this is to postulate a NM utility function that is additively separable through time. In other words, there is a NM utility function $v$, mapping today's consumption to today's utility, and a NM utility function $u$, mapping tomorrow's consumption to tomorrow's utility. The total expected utility is then just the sum of both expected utilities,[1]

$$v(y^0) + E\{u(y)\}.$$

$v(y^0)$ is not in the expectations operator because today's consumption is not subject to uncertainty. This formulation allows us in principle to model changing aversion to risk (choosing different curvatures for $v$ and $u$), but we have no theories about the evolution of utility functions through time. It seems natural therefore to assume that $v$ and $u$ are equal in terms of risk aversion, i.e. to choose $u$ to be a linear transformation of $v$, $u(y) := \delta v(y)$.[2]

$\delta$ is a *time preference* parameter, indicating a preference for the intertemporal allocation of consumption. The agent maximizes

$$v(y^0) + \delta E\{v(y)\}.$$

Typically, we assume that $\delta \leqslant 1$, implying *impatience* in the sense that consumption tomorrow produces less utility than consumption now.

[1]In this chapter, expectations are always taken over the future states $s = 1, \ldots, S$, so $E\{u(y)\} = \sum_{s=1}^{S} \pi_s u(y^s)$.

[2]We could also allow $u$ to be an *affine* (not necessarily *linear*) transformation of $v$. The agent would then maximize $v + \alpha + \delta E\{v\}$, but this is equivalent to assuming $\alpha = 0$.

### 5.1.2 Asset economy with NM agents

If we take the time-separable NM utility for granted, an agent $i$ is described by his period NM utility $v_i$, by his rate of impatience $\delta_i$ and by his income today and his state-contingent income tomorrow, $w(i) := (w^0(i), \ldots, w^S(i))$. Moreover, we can (for a moment) also allow different agents to have different beliefs about the likelihoods of different states of the world, so everyone will have a different $\pi(i) := (\pi_1(i), \ldots, \pi_S(i))$. An economic agent is then a four-tuple, collecting all of his properties, $(v_i, \delta_i, \pi(i), w(i))$.

An asset economy is just the collection of all agents, plus the return matrix of the financial assets,

$$(\{(v_i, \delta_i, \pi(i), w(i)) : i \in \{1, \ldots, I\}\}, r).$$

We will usually assume that asset markets are complete ($r$ is regular), in which case we can replace $r$ by the identity matrix, indicating that there is a market for each Arrow security,

$$(\{(v_i, \delta_i, \pi(i), w(i)) : i \in \{1, \ldots, I\}\}, \mathbf{e}).$$

### 5.1.3 The portfolio problem

Take a situation in which you know your income today, and you know you will have income tomorrow, but you don't know how much income you will have. In terms of our model, income tomorrow is state-contingent, and tomorrow's state is unknown as of today. In other words, you are subject to a lottery. You can undo this lottery by buying lottery tickets (financial assets) whose payoff is high in states where your income is low, and vice versa. Such an operation is called *hedging*, and is in effect nothing more than purchasing insurance. But you have two problems to solve here: how much you should save, and how far you should go in insuring your income tomorrow. In other words, you may want to move wealth through time (to save or borrow) and between states (to insure or take bets). These are precisely the problems we set out to explain, and both can be understood by studying the trading of financial assets.

Formally, the decision problem of a NM agent operating in a finance economy is to maximize total intertemporal expected utility,[3]

$$\max \left\{ v_i(y^0) + \delta_i E^i\{v_i(y)\} \;\middle|\; \begin{array}{ll} y^0 - w^0 \leqslant -q \cdot \tilde{z} & \\ y^s - w^s \leqslant r_s \cdot \tilde{z}^s & \text{for } s = 1, \ldots, S \end{array} \right\}, \tag{5.1}$$

[3] $E^i$ is the expectation over the states $s = 1, \ldots, S$, using $i$'s beliefs.

Because the budget constraints are all binding in the maximum, we can write this more succinctly as $\max\left\{v_i(y^0) + \delta_i E^i\{v_i(y)\} \mid y - w \in \mathcal{M}(q)\right\}$. In (5.1), $y$ is the consumption (in terms of the aggregate commodity) and $z$ is the portfolio of the agent. If the market is complete, or, equivalently, if all Arrow securities are traded, we can collapse the $S+1$ constraints into a single one,

$$\max\left\{v_i(y^0) + \delta_i E^i\{v_i(y)\} \;\middle|\; (y^0 - w^0) + \sum_{s=1}^{S} \alpha_s(y^s - w^s) \leqslant 0\right\}. \tag{5.2}$$

### 5.1.4 Equilibrium

Let $W$ and $Y$ be aggregate endowment and aggregate consumption, respectively,

$$W^s := \sum_{i=1}^{I} w^s(i), \quad Y^s := \sum_{i=1}^{I} y^s(i), \quad \text{for } s = 0, \ldots, S.$$

As before, a Radner equilibrium of this asset economy is a pair consisting of a price for each asset $\alpha$, and an allocation $(y(1), \ldots, y(I))$, such that $y(i)$ solves (5.2) for each $i$, and all markets clear: $Y - W = 0$.

### 5.1.5 Common beliefs

We have until now allowed for the possibility that agents may differ in their beliefs about the likelihood of tomorrow's state of the world. The story behind such a possibility is as follows. Suppose there is a true, objective probability distribution over the set of states, but this true distribution is not known. Each agent receives an imperfect signal about the true distribution. This signal is correlated with the true distribution, but it also contains some noise, indicating that an agent may get the true distribution somewhat wrong. Of course, in such a situation it would be valuable to know not only your own signal, but also the signal of other people, because that would enhance your ability to estimate the true probability distribution. In other words, it is valuable not only to have an opinion, but also to know other people's opinions. For simplicity, we assume that signals are private information. There could be markets for opinions (and in fact we see such markets in reality), but there are tricky moral hazard problems here: a famous stock-picker guru might have an incentive to recommend stocks he owns himself.

Now suppose that everyone uses his own assessment of the probabilities when maximizing his expected utility, as stated in (5.2). The problem is that the resulting equilibrium prices will contain information about the average opinion of the other agents. But that means that everyone will want to revise their probability assessments. In fact, we see this happening: a common activity of finance 'Quants' is to extract risk-neutral or objective probabilities from financial market data. These estimates are then fed into investment decisions, which affect prices, and so on. Central banks often do the same, interpreting interest rate and exchange rate movements to assess the degree of monetary policy tightness. These findings are then fed back into a monetary policy decision.

The problem is that our definition of equilibrium is not complete. What would be required is a combination of allocation, prices, and beliefs, so that all markets clear and no one has an incentive to revise beliefs. In this book we will follow the simplest way out and ignore this problem, simply by assuming that everyone has the same beliefs. In that case, equilibrium prices will be compatible with these common beliefs, and no one will have a reason to revise them. This is not completely satisfactory, but at least it is consistent. Models that do not make this assumption are much more difficult and lead to some paradoxes. The problem is that prices have two roles: to measure the scarcity of goods and allocate them, and to convey private information to the public. A *fully revealing rational expectations equilibrium* is a Radner equilibrium of an economy with heterogeneous beliefs, which is such that market prices are a sufficient statistic for all information of all agents. In such an equilibrium it seems rational for an agent simply to use this commonly available information in making his decisions, and to ignore his private information altogether. But if all agents ignored their private information, how could such information be channelled into market prices? This is the *Grossman paradox* (Grossman, 1976). Brunnermeier's (2001) survey may be a good place to enter this more advanced field.

Since we will usually assume common beliefs, we define the beliefs $\pi$ as part of the economy, not as a property of an agent. So from now on an agent with intertemporal NM utility is a triple $(v_i, \delta_i, w(i))$, and an economy is the collection of all agents, plus beliefs and an asset matrix,

$$(\{(v_i, \delta_i, w(i)) : i \in \{1, \dots, I\}\}, \pi, r).$$

## 5.2 Efficient risk-sharing

### 5.2.1 *Mutuality principle*

Consider two states that have the same aggregate endowment, though they may differ with respect to the state-contingent distribution of income among agents. Such states, we say, differ only with respect to *idiosyncratic risk.* There is no aggregate risk between them. A fundamental principle of any efficient allocation in such a situation is that everyone should consume the same in both states.

**Box 5.1** *Mutuality principle*

An efficient allocation of risk requires that only aggregate risk be borne by the agents. All idiosyncratic risk is diversified away by mutual insurance among the agents.

In other words, this principle says that agents should not bet on anything but aggregate risk. An individual's consumption is a function of aggregate endowment only. This principle is due to Wilson (1968).

A consequence of the mutuality principle is that no one bears any risk whatsoever if there is no aggregate risk (i.e., if aggregate endowment is the same in all states), because then all the risk there is in the economy is idiosyncratic and is therefore diversified away; there is complete mutual insurance.

The mutuality principle is most easily understood by considering an economy with just two agents and two states—an Edgeworth box—without any aggregate risk (Figure 5.1). From Figure 4.3 we know that the marginal rates of substitution along the certainty line are given by the relative probabilities of the states. As a consequence, indifference curves are tangent to each other along the certainty line. Thus, the contract curve (the set of Pareto-efficient allocations) is equal to the certainty line. The two agents mutually insure each other's idiosyncratic risk and neither one bears any risk in an efficient allocation.

From the second welfare theorem, we know that every efficient allocation can be supported by a competitive equilibrium. Depending on the distribution of initial incomes, we will end up at different points on the contract curve, but the equilibrium allocation is always such that no one bears any risk. The equilibrium prices are just collinear to the probabilities, $\alpha_s = \lambda\pi_s$. Normalizing prices so that they sum to one gives us the risk-neutral probabilities $\tilde{\alpha}$. Thus, in equilibrium, if there is no aggregate risk, then $\tilde{\alpha} = \pi$. The risk-neutral probabilities are just the common beliefs.

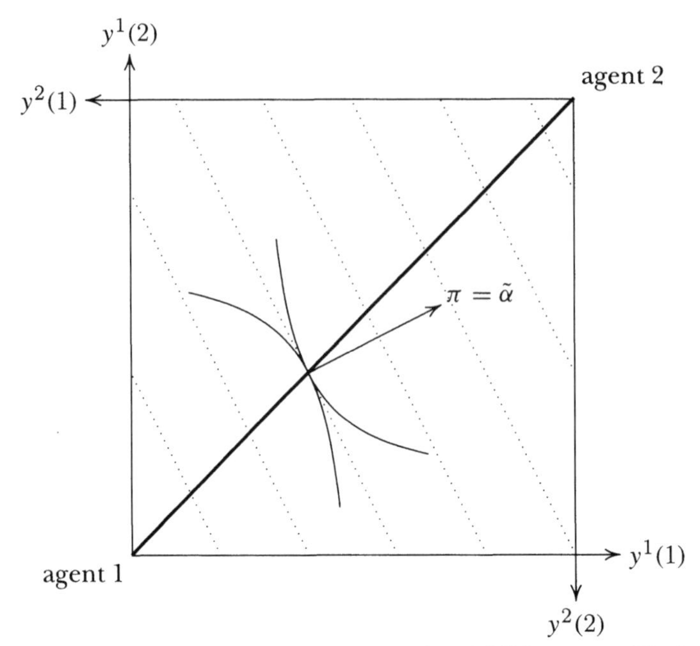


*Figure 5.1. An Edgeworth box with no aggregate risk and full insurance. The dotted lines are iso-expected wealth lines, the fat line is the contract curve.*

### 5.2.2 Failure of the mutuality principle

The mutuality principle fails if beliefs are heterogeneous.[4] This is the principle underlying racetrack betting. Mr. X believes that 'Pegasus' is in exceptionally good shape and therefore has a good chance of winning. But Mrs. Y thinks that 'In the Wings' is better prepared for this kind of terrain. Thus, they will bet against each other. Such betting is usually done through a bookmaker. Mr. X buys the 'Pegasus' Arrow security, Mrs. Y buys the 'In the Wings' Arrow security, and the bookmaker sells both securities. Mr. X and Mrs. Y do that not in order to hedge some idiosyncratic risk—their income (outside of the race court) is not correlated with the outcome of the race (unless they are the owners of the horses).[5] Rather, they do that

[4]We take beliefs as exogenous and disregard the problem of equilibrium belief formation.

[5]Suppose the market value of a horse increases with every win, and falls with every defeat. The owner of a race horse then bears some idiosyncratic risk. To hedge this risk, the owner should bet *against* his own horse.

because they have different probability assessments of the odds of winning.[6] For this reason they bet on non-aggregate risk, thus violating the mutuality principle.

The mutuality principle is a normative statement because it is a property that every efficient allocation must necessarily possess. As a positive description of the data, the mutuality principle can be used only if we can make sure that the equilibrium allocation is Pareto efficient. For this reason, we should expect the mutuality principle to fail empirically if some sort of frictions impede Pareto efficiency or if markets are incomplete. For instance, incomplete information typically destroys first-best efficiency because there is a tension between the allocation of risk and incentives. As an example, executives are often payed to a significant extent with non-tradable options on their firm's stock, to give them financial incentives to create shareholder value. Yet, such contracts force the manager to bear a large amount of risk because the value of his employee options and the probability of his keeping his job both depend on the fate of his company (which he can influence, but not completely control), and he cannot hedge this risk. It is just as if the aforementioned horse owner was forced to bet a large share of his fortune on the event that his horse wins. This fact makes (non-tradable) stock options particulary unattractive to executives, who are willing to take them only for a large premium. Thus, the use of such instruments for executive pay significantly increases the cost for the company (Hall & Murphy, 2002). Effectively, this is just one aspect of how incomplete information decreases the payoff of the principal (the firm), but it is important for our topic because it also destroys efficiency, and along with it invalidates the mutuality principle.

Townsend (1994; 1995) provides an empirical test of the mutuality principle using micro data from India, Thailand, and the Ivory Coast. He finds that much of the individual income fluctuation is indeed idiosyncratic. Only a small part of the income variation is aggregate risk. Thus, there is considerable scope for diversification. But despite the lack of well functioning financial markets, he finds a surprisingly large (but less than perfect) amount of mutual insurance. Clearly, there are other ways to insure than through organized financial exchanges.

### 5.2.3 *The SWF*

By the mutuality principle, we know that in an efficient allocation people bear only aggregate risk. But who bears how much of it? How should the

[6] Or simply because they like the thrill of betting, thus violating the consequentialism axiom.

burden of aggregate risk be allocated in order to be efficient? We can get insight into this problem by considering a social welfare function (equation (2.11)). For every Pareto-efficient allocation, there is a vector of weights, one for each agent, such that the SWF constructed with these weights is maximized by the allocation.

With NM agents and common beliefs, the SWF takes this form:

$$V(z) := \max \left\{ \frac{1}{I} \sum_i \sigma_i \left[ v_i(y^0(i)) + \delta_i E\{v_i(y(i))\} \right] \,\middle|\, \sum_i (y(i) - z) \leqq 0 \right\}.$$

$\sigma_i$ is $i$'s weight. The objective function is additively separable between states, and there is one constraint for every state, without any interaction. This allows us to write this problem as a sum of simple one-dimensional maximization problems,

$$\begin{aligned} V(z) := & \underbrace{\max \left\{ \frac{1}{I} \sum_i \sigma_i v_i(y^0(i)) \,\middle|\, \sum_i (y^0(i) - z^0) \leqslant 0 \right\}}_{=:v(z^0)} \\ & + \sum_{s=1}^{S} \pi_s \underbrace{\max \left\{ \frac{1}{I} \sum_i \sigma_i \delta_i v_i(y^s(i)) \,\middle|\, \sum_i (y^s(i) - z^s) \leqslant 0 \right\}}_{=:u(z^s)} \\ = & \; v(z^0) + E\{u(z)\}. \end{aligned} \tag{5.3}$$

Thus, the SWF takes the form of an additively separable NM utility.

Note in the definition of $u$ how patient people (large $\delta_i$) get a relatively larger weight ($\sigma_i \delta_i$) in tomorrow's consumption than impatient ones (small $\delta_i$).

### 5.2.4 *Efficient allocation of aggregate risk: Wilson's theorem*

The mutuality principle tells us that only aggregate risk matters, but it does not tell us how aggregate risk is allocated among the agents. Some qualitative insights are possible from the Edgeworth box: suppose there is aggregate risk as in Figure 5.2. Someone has to bear some risk, because by definition aggregate risk can not be diversified away. The convex shape of the indifference curves implies that if they are tangent somewhere it will be in the shaded area. In other words, the contract curve "lives" inside the shaded area.[7] This means that both agents bear some of the aggregate risk—or,

[7]This is true if at least one agent is strictly risk averse. If both agents are risk-neutral, every allocation is efficient, and thus the contract "curve" is the whole Edgeworth box.

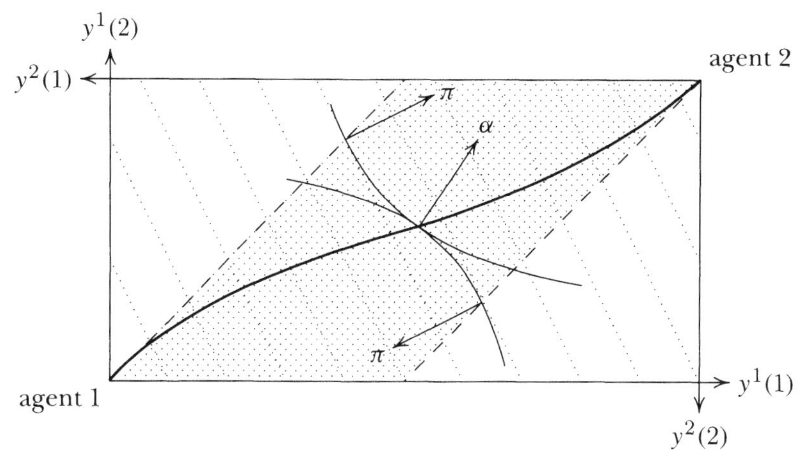


**Figure 5.2.** *The biotope of the contract curve.*

if we end up on the edge of the shaded area, that all the aggregate risk is borne by one agent and the other bears no risk. But it is never the case that some agent is overinsured in the sense of enjoying higher consumption in the poor state than in the rich state. In other words, the state-contingent consumption of all agents are positively correlated with each other: every agent consumes more in the boom than in the recession.

The second result of Wilson's (1968) paper (the first result is the mutuality principle) provides a much more precise answer to the question how aggregate risk is efficiently shared among the members of society. Consider the definition of $u$ in (5.3) (to ease notation we drop the superscipt $s$):

$$u(z) := \max_{y(1),\dots,y(I)} \left\{ \frac{1}{I} \sum_i \sigma_i \delta_i v_i(y(i)) \;\middle|\; \sum_i (y(i) - z) \leqslant 0 \right\}.$$

The first-order condition of this problem is

$$\frac{1}{I} \sigma_i \delta_i v_i'(y(i)) = \mu,$$

where $\mu$ is the Lagrange multiplier of the feasibility constraint, so $\mu$ measures the marginal increase of $u$ when the constraint is marginally eased. Expanding $z$ by $dz$ eases the constraint $I$ times $dz$; thus $u'(z) = I\mu$ and therefore

$$\sigma_i \delta_i v_i'(y(i)) = u'(z). \tag{5.4}$$

Totally differentiating yields

$$\sigma_i \delta_i v_i''(y(i)) dy(i) = u''(z) dz. \tag{5.5}$$

Solving for $i$'s marginal share of aggregate risk, $dy(i)/dz$, yields

$$\frac{dy(i)}{dz} = \frac{u''(z)}{\sigma_i \delta_i v_i''(y(i))}. \tag{5.6}$$

But by (5.4), $\sigma_i \delta_i = u'(z)/v_i'(y(i))$; thus,

$$\begin{aligned}\frac{dy(i)}{dz} &= \frac{u''(z)}{u'(z)} \cdot \frac{v_i'(y(i))}{v_i''(y(i))} \\ &= \frac{T_i(y(i))}{T(z)},\end{aligned} \tag{5.7}$$

where $T_i$ is $i$'s absolute risk tolerance and $T$ is the risk tolerance associated with the utility function $u$. Equation (5.7) says that the marginal share of aggregate risk borne by agent $i$ is proportional to the agent's absolute risk tolerance.

Feasibility requires that the average change of consumption $dy(i)$ equals the change of per capita endowment $dz$. Taking averages of (5.7) (i.e. summing over all $i$ and dividing by $I$) thus yields

$$T(z) = \frac{1}{I} \sum_{i=1}^{I} T_i(y(i)). \tag{5.8}$$

The risk tolerance of $u$ is the average risk tolerance of the population.

**Box 5.2** ***Efficient allocation of aggregate risk (Wilson, 1968)***

The marginal aggregate risk borne by an agent equals the ratio of his absolute risk tolerance to the average risk tolerance of the population.

In an efficient allocation, aggregate risk is allocated to people that are less hurt by it. The more risk averse someone is, the less risk he bears at the margin.

## 5.3 A representative NM agent

An economy with NM agents is just a special case of an economy of agents with ordinal utility functions, and we know that this more general economy admits a local representative if markets are complete. So we could use the same procedure to generate a local representative for the NM economy (section 2.5). The result would be unsatisfactory, though, because the representative thus obtained would have an *ordinal* utility function, which means that we could not use the NM machinery with him.

Instead, what we are looking for is a representative whose preferences adopt the expected utility representation. Consider an economy $(\{(v_i, \delta_i, w(i)) : i \in \{1, \ldots, I\}\}, \pi, r)$, and an equilibrium $(\alpha, y)$. We say that $(v, \delta, w)$ is a *NM representative* if $(\alpha, w)$ is an equilibrium of the one-agent economy $((v, \delta, w), \pi, r)$. Does such a representative $(v, \delta, w)$ exist, and if so how does he relate to the individuals' characteristics $(v_i, \delta_i, w(i))$?

### 5.3.1 Everyone is a representative

As in section 2.5, everyone is a representative. If we assign to an agent his optimal choice (given some prices) as endowment, clearly he will not want to make further trades at these same prices. Thus, $(\alpha, y(i))$ is an equilibrium of the one-agent economy $((v_i, \delta_i, y(i)), \pi, r)$. But, as before, this is not too useful if we have no microdata.

### 5.3.2 A risk-neutral representative

We know from section 3.2 that asset prices are described by risk-neutral probabilities even in the absence of NM agents. We can generate a risk-neutral NM representative by twisting the common beliefs $\pi$.

Consider a risk-neutral NM utility function. To make it as simple as possible, let $v(y) := y$. Let the time-preference be given by the price of a risk-free bond $\beta := \sum_{s=1}^{S} \alpha_s$. Let the beliefs be the risk-neutral probabilities $\tilde{\alpha}_s := \alpha_s / \beta$. Let $W$ denote aggregate state-contingent income. Consider this one-person economy, $((v, \beta, W/I), \tilde{\alpha}, r)$. The claim is that $(\alpha, W/I)$ is an equilibrium of this economy, for the following reason. The maximization problem of this single agent is

$$\max \left\{ y^0 + \beta \sum_{s=1}^{S} \tilde{\alpha}_s y^s \;\middle|\; (y^0 - W^0/I) + \sum_{s=1}^{S} \alpha_s (y^s - W^S/I) \leqslant 0 \right\}.$$

Note that $\beta \tilde{\alpha}_s = \alpha_s$, so the objective function can be simplified somewhat. The first-order conditions of this problem are

$$\begin{aligned} 1 &= \lambda, \\ \alpha_1 &= \lambda \alpha_1, \\ &\vdots \\ \alpha_S &= \lambda \alpha_S, \end{aligned}$$

so anything that fulfills the budget constraint with equality is a maximum. Clearly, $y = W/I$ is such a point. Thus, $(\alpha, W/I)$ is an equilibrium of the one-agent economy, and the agent $(v, \beta, W/I)$ is indeed a *risk-neutral NM representative.*

It now becomes clear why $\tilde{\alpha}$ are called risk-neutral probabilities: they are the beliefs of the risk-neutral representative.

### 5.3.3 Social risk preference

If we assume that the equilibrium allocation is efficient (that is, that the market is complete, or is quasi-complete and we consider the efficient equilibrium), then we can also generate a local representative via the intertemporal NM social welfare function (5.3). Assign weights $\sigma_i := \lambda_i^{-1}$, where $\lambda_i$ is $i$'s Lagrange multiplier of his budget constraint in his portfolio problem (5.2). By construction, the resulting functions

$$\begin{aligned} v(z) &:= \max\left\{\frac{1}{I}\sum_i \lambda_i^{-1} v_i(y(i)) \,\middle|\, \sum_i (y(i) - z) \leqslant 0\right\}, \\ u(z) &:= \max\left\{\frac{1}{I}\sum_i \lambda_i^{-1} \delta_i v_i(y(i)) \,\middle|\, \sum_i (y(i) - z) \leqslant 0\right\}, \end{aligned} \tag{5.9}$$

are such that the marginal utility of expected utility $v(z^0) + E\{u(z)\}$, evaluated at per capita income $z := W/I$, is collinear to equilibrium prices. Thus, a NM agent with utility $v$ today and utility $u$ tomorrow and mean per capita endowment is a NM representative. Moreover, this representative has the same beliefs as the common beliefs of all agents.

By Wilson's Theorem, we know that the absolute risk tolerance of this representative, for risk borne tomorrow (i.e. the risk tolerance of utility $u$), is equal to the mean absolute risk tolerance of the population as a whole; see (5.8). This is important because it tells us something about society's risk preference: the absolute risk tolerance associated to $u$ is society's absolute risk tolerance.[8]

[8]To be sure, the fact that society's absolute risk tolerance is equal to the arithmetic mean of the absolute risk tolerance of the population does not imply that the same is true for absolute risk aversion. For instance, if all agents have utilities that are HARA and DARA, then the representative's coefficient of absolute risk aversion is smaller than the average coefficient of absolute risk aversion of the population. To understand why, just note that in this case the coefficient of absolute risk aversion is a convex function of consumption (make a graph to see this more clearly), thus, if there is income heterogeneity, mean absolute risk aversion will exceed absolute risk aversion of the mean by Jensen's inequality. (To be precise, the representative's absolute risk aversion equals the *harmonic* mean of the individuals' coefficients of absolute risk aversion.)

### 5.3.4 Social time preference

Can we say something similar about society's time preference? Can we compute a $\delta$ such that $u(z) = \delta v(z)$? Such a $\delta$ would have to satisfy

$$\delta = \frac{u(z)}{v(z)} = \frac{\max\left\{\frac{1}{I}\sum_i \lambda_i^{-1}\delta_i v_i(y(i)) \,\middle|\, \sum_i (y(i) - z) \leqslant 0\right\}}{\max\left\{\frac{1}{I}\sum_i \lambda_i^{-1} v_i(y(i)) \,\middle|\, \sum_i (y(i) - z) \leqslant 0\right\}}. \tag{5.10}$$

Clearly, in general, there is no $\delta$ satisfying this for all $z$. Thus, in general social time preference is not well defined.

In the special case where everyone in the population has the same time preference, $\delta_1 = \cdots = \delta_I$, the representative has this same common time preference $\delta$. In that case we may say that $(v, \delta, W/I)$ is a NM representative of the economy who preserves the common beliefs.

### 5.3.5 Distribution independent aggregation I: No aggregate risk

In general, the representative's tastes depend on all aspects of the economy, including the inter-personal income distribution. This is a problem for macrofinance because it implies that asset prices will in general depend not only on aggregate endowment, but on the distribution as well. What assumptions suffice to make the representative's utility independent of the distribution?

One case in which this is possible is if there is no aggregate risk. By the mutuality principle, in a Pareto-efficient allocation no-one bears any risk in that case. Thus, if the equilibrium allocation is efficient, then, independently of the income distribution, there is a risk-neutral representative agent whose beliefs are equal to the objective probabilities, because in that case $\tilde{\alpha} = \pi$.

Likewise, suppose there is some aggregate risk, but there is also a group of risk-neutral agents who are jointly rich enough to be able to absorb the whole aggregate risk without hitting a corner (i.e., the non-negativity constraint is not binding); and suppose that the financial market is able to assume a Pareto-efficient equilibrium. In this case all the aggregate risk is assigned to these "natural insurers" in any efficient equilibrium, and there is no risk left to bear for the risk averse agents, making their risk-aversion irrelevant. This follows from Wilson's Theorem as well: the risk-neutral agents are infinitely risk tolerant, $T_i(y(i)) = +\infty$; thus, average (= representative) risk tolerance is also infinite, and the representative is risk-neutral, no matter what the income distribution is.

### 5.3.6 Distribution independent aggregation II: Rubinstein

Under some conditions, aggregation can be achieved independently of the income distribution even if there is aggregate risk, as was shown by Rubinstein (1974). This is most easily understood as an application of Wilson's theorem. Suppose that everyone has HARA utility, possibly with different constants $a_i$ and cautiousness parameters $b_i$. Then, by Wilson's theorem, (5.7), and (5.8), risk tolerance of the representative is given by

$$T(W^s/I) = \frac{1}{I}\left[\sum_i a_i + \sum_i b_i y^s(i)\right].$$

Risk tolerance depends on the distribution $(y^s(1), \ldots, y^s(I))$.

Define social cautiousness $b$ to satisfy

$$\begin{aligned} T(W^s/I) &= \frac{1}{I}\left[\sum_i a_i + b\sum_i y^s(i)\right] \\ &= \frac{1}{I}\left[\sum_i a_i + bW^s\right]. \end{aligned}$$

The constant $a$ of the representative is simply the mean of the population, but cautiousness $b$ depends on the state-specific interpersonal income distribution, and therefore on the state. As a consequence, the representative is not HARA in general.

If all agents have the same cautiousness $b_1 = \cdots = b_I$, however, then the representative's cautiousness will equal this common individual cautiousness. In that case, the representative's utility no longer depends on the distribution and his cautiousness is independent of the state; i.e., the representative is HARA.

**Box 5.3** *A distribution-independent representative (Rubinstein, 1974)*

If all agents have utilities in the HARA class with a common cautiousness $b$, then the representative's utility does not depend on the distribution of income. In fact, the representative's utility is $v(W^0/I) + E\{u(W/I)\}$, where $u$ is HARA with the common cautiousness $b$ and the absolute equal to the population average, $a = \sum_i a_i/I$.

If, moreover, all agents share a common time preference $\delta$, then the representative shares this common time preference and his utility can be written as $v(W^0/I) + \delta E\{v(W/I)\}$.[9]

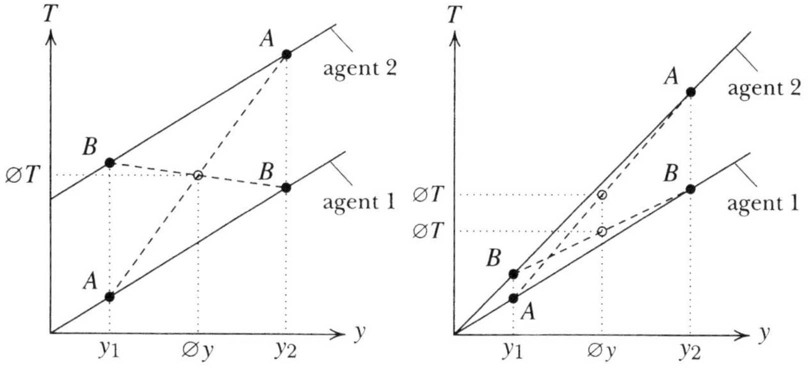


***Figure 5.3.*** *Why the common cautiousness assumption is needed.*

Why is common cautiousness required? Consider an economy with two agents, both CRRA, but with different degrees of relative risk aversion. Thus, agent $i$'s absolute risk tolerance is $T_i(y_i) = b_i y_i$, where $b_i$ is the reciprocal of $i$'s coefficient of relative risk aversion. According to Wilson's theorem, the absolute risk tolerance of the representative equals $(b_1 y_1 + b_2 y_2)/2$. It is quite clear that this risk tolerance depends on the interpersonal distribution of income $(y_1, y_2)$ if the cautiousness parameters are not the same.

Figure 5.3 illustrates this fact. The two figures depict situations with two agents and two alternative distributions. Agent 1 is less risk tolerant than agent 2. In one distribution ($A$–$A$) agent 2 is richer than agent 1; in the other distribution ($B$–$B$) this is reversed. Aggregate income ($\varnothing y$) is the same in both distributions. In the left picture, it does not matter how we distribute income among the two agents. The mean absolute risk aversion is a function only of mean income, not of the distribution. In the right picture, on the contrary, the slopes of the $T_i$-functions are different, and average absolute risk aversion depends not only on average income, but also on the distribution of income among the agents.

Note that, if the representative is independent of the interpersonal distribution, then equilibrium prices are also independent of the interpersonal distribution. This means that the price vectors that support a Pareto-efficient allocation are all collinear to each other. Consider two arbitrary Pareto-efficient allocations, and consider the hyperplanes generated by the equilibrium prices that support these two allocations. Since the equilibrium prices at the two efficient allocations are collinear, the supporting hyperplanes are parallel to each other, so they do not intersect. This is true for arbitrary pairs of efficient allocations. As a consequence, if Rubinstein's aggregation works, equilibrium is unique for all initial distributions. This

[9] Rubinstein's result is somewhat more general than this.

shows most clearly that Rubinstein aggregation is very convenient, but at the same time is a very special case.

### 5.3.7 *Quasi-complete markets*

We have discussed in section 3.5 the effects of market incompleteness, and the exceptional cases in which incomplete markets effectively work just as well as complete markets do. Such quasi-complete markets are exceptional in the sense that the equilibrium allocation is Pareto efficient, despite the incompleteness of the market, and accordingly all the aggregations can be performed. In this section we discuss a sufficient condition for quasi-completeness, and we also discuss how quasi-completeness makes distribution-independent aggregation possible.

Quasi-completeness is just as good as completeness for all our purposes, but it may be less demanding. By the mutuality principle, we know that in an efficient allocation everyone bears only aggregate risk. Thus, if the financial market allows each agent to hedge his idiosyncratic risk by buying some aggregate endowment in each state, and also allows agents to allocate their consumption through time according to their time preferences, then the market is quasi-complete. Formally, let $\hat{w}(i) := (w^1(i), \ldots, w^S(i))$, so this is $i$'s contingent *future* income. (It is the same as $w(i)$ but without the first component $w^0(i)$.)

> **Box 5.4** *Sufficient condition for quasi-completeness (Ross, 1976)*
>
> Suppose that $\hat{w}(i)$ is in the asset span, for each $i$, so that each agent can sell (a fraction of) his idiosyncratic risk, or buy a fraction of someone else's. Suppose further that there is a complete set of call options on the aggregate endowment.[10] Then the market is quasi-complete.

To see why these assets are sufficient, note that, by selling asset $i$ short, agent $i$ can hedge his idiosyncratic risk. The options on aggregate endowment allow the agents to buy a share of aggregate endowment, conditional on how much aggregate endowment there is. One might think that the agents would also need a risk-free asset to get the intertemporal allocation right, but this is not necessary, because the risk-free cash flow is contained in the span of options on aggregate endowment.

[10] A call option on aggregate endowment $\hat{W}$ with strike price $x$ is an asset with cash flow $r_s := \max\{0, \hat{W}^s - x\}$. If such call options are traded with strike prices equal to each possible value of future aggregate endowment, $x_1 = \hat{W}^1, \ldots, x_S = \hat{W}^S$, then we say that the set of call options is complete.

Note that this market structure is actually complete if aggregate endowment is different in each state.[11] As a result, options will most likely not allow us to economize much in terms of the number of assets needed for a (quasi- ) complete market. Only if there are at least two states in which aggregate endowment is the same can we reduce the number of assets, because, by the mutuality principle, the consumption of each agent in the two states with equal aggregate endowment will also be the same.

A complementary result was recently given by Aliprantis & Tourky (2002). These authors turn the question that Ross was interested in upside down. They ask instead under what conditions an incomplete market can be used to replicate an option. Of course, the incomplete market structure could contain options as assets, but this is not a generic situation because it requires a very specific (piecewise-linear) cash flow of the asset as a function of the underlying asset's cash flow. Aliprantis & Tourky find that, if there are less than half as many independent assets as there are states and the risk-free asset is marketed, then, generically, *no* option can be replicated.[12]

In practice, we do not normally observe options on aggregate endowment. Essentially, these would be options on business cycle data of different regions or of the world at large. Shiller (1993) discusses how this type of assets could and should be designed. Individual endowment processes also are hardly ever traded, although some hedging of idiosyncratic risk can be achieved with existing assets.[13] A person working for an auto maker, a bank, an airline, or any other type of business could sell shares of his employer short to hedge his unemployment risk. Similarly, firms operating in markets that are affected by weather conditions (such as agriculture, tourism, clothing, movies) can hedge this risk with weather contracts. These are assets whose payoff depends on specific weather data (temperature, precipitation, wind speed, etc.). Standard weather assets are currently traded on LIFFE (www.liffe.com) and on the Chicago Merchantile Exchange (www.cme.com). Custom-made weather related assets are traded over the counter. Other useful assets with payoffs conditioned on some non-financial data are conceivable. Life insurance companies, for instance, face a significant increase in their expenses if the death ratios of their clients decline and life expectancy increases accordingly. They may be able to hedge some

[11]Because in that case *all* Arrow securities can be generated with "butterfly spreads." This is a portfolio consisting of 1 call option with strike price $x - 1$, 1 call option with strike price $x + 1$, and $-2$ call options with strike price $x$. It has the same payoff as a security that has a cash flow of 1 if and only if aggregate endowment is equal to $x$.

[12]More precisely, no non-trivial option can be replicated, meaning an option that is neither always out-of-the-money nor always in-the-money.

[13]Shiller (2003) has recently proposed the construction of financial assets that are designed to enhance the ability of individuals to hedge idiosyncratic risk.

of this risk (in a very imperfect manner) by holding shares of major drug companies. A more useful asset for them, however, would be options whose underlying are demographic statistics. But such options do not currently exist.

Box 5.4 says that options can be used to make any market quasi-complete, independently of the microeconomic data (preferences and endowments) of the economy. It is interesting that these conditions can be weakened in cases assuming a distribution-independent representative, i.e. in the absence of aggregate risk, or if the Rubinstein conditions are satisfied.

Before we discuss the result, note that in case $(i)$ of Box 5.4 a risk-free asset would be redundant: a portfolio consisting of equally many units of each of the assets $r^1$ through $r^I$ is in fact risk-free. By holding a constant share of each agent's endowment, one holds a share of aggregate endowment, which by assumption does not contain any risk in case $(i)$. Therefore, we can assume that for all three cases the asset structure is $r := \begin{bmatrix} \hat{w} & 1 \end{bmatrix}$.

Box 5.5 says that the options that we used in Box 5.4 are not used in these particular cases. This is most easily understood for the cases $(i)$ and $(ii)$. By the mutuality principle, any efficient allocation simply assigns to each agent a certain share of aggregate endowment in these cases. For quasi-completeness, the financial market must allow each agent only to hedge his idiosyncratic risk, to purchase a share of aggregate endowment, and to allocate his consumption through time according to his time preferences. This can clearly be achieved by the proposed assets. More directly, the absence of aggregate risk (or the complete absorption of aggregate risk by the risk-neutral agents) implies that a risk-free bond *is* "a complete set of call options on aggregate endowment" in the sense of Box 5.4.

**Box 5.5** ***Quasi-completeness without options***

As before, assume that $\hat{w}(i)$ is in the asset span, for each $i$. If in addition

$(i)$ there is no aggregate risk, or

$(ii)$ there is also a risk-free asset and there is a group of agents that are jointly rich enough to absorb all the aggregate risk without running into a non-negativity constraint, or

$(iii)$ there is also a risk-free asset and all agents have HARA utility with the same cautiousness,

then $r$ is quasi-complete.

For case (*iii*), we need to establish that the Rubinstein conditions imply that each agent's future state-contingent consumption lies in the span of the risk-free asset and the aggregate endowment; that is to say, an agent's future consumption contingent on a certain state is an affine function of aggregate income in that state. This result goes back to Pye (1967) (see also Cass & Stiglitz (1972) and Rubinstein (1974), section 2), and will be proved in the next section. But before we do that we should bring to mind that, if the simple asset structure of Box 5.5 is quasi-complete, then no options on aggregate endowment will be traded in any efficient equilibrium, even if they are available. They are simply useless in that case, and therefore no-one holds them long or short in equilibrium.

## 5.4 Who holds what kind of portfolio?

### 5.4.1 *Portfolio selection of a HARA person*

An agent's optimal portfolio is a solution to his maximization problem (5.2), but not much can be said without imposing more structure. Some insights can be gained by considering the problem of a HARA utility maximizer, because this class of utility functions simplifies the solution considerably, but is still rich enough to accommodate many different cases. Consider first an agent with non-zero cautiousness ($b \neq 0$), and recall that in this case $v'(z) = (a + bz)^{-1/b}$. Define the present value of his endowment as $\bar{w} := w^0 + \sum_{s=1}^{S} \alpha_s w^s$. Using this, the portfolio problem (5.2) can be written as

$$\max \left\{ v(y^0) + \delta E\{v(y)\} \;\middle|\; y^0 + \sum_{s=1}^{S} \alpha_s y^s - \bar{w} \leqslant 0 \right\}.$$

The first-order conditions are

$$(a + by^0)^{-1/b} = \lambda, \quad \delta\pi_s (a + by^s)^{-1/b} = \lambda\alpha_s.$$

Dividing the second by the first yields

$$\delta\pi_s \left( \frac{a + by^s}{a + by^0} \right)^{-1/b} = \alpha_s.$$

Because the budget constraint binds, we have $y^0 = \bar{w} - \sum_{s=1}^{S} \alpha_s y^s$. Thus, after a few transformations,

$$y^s = \alpha_s^{-b} \pi_s^b \delta^b \left( \frac{a}{b} + \bar{w} - \sum_{\bar{s}=1}^{S} \alpha_{\bar{s}} y^{\bar{s}} \right) - \frac{a}{b}. \tag{5.11}$$

We multiply by $\alpha_s$ and sum over all $s$ to arrive at

$$\sum_{s=1}^{S} \alpha_s y^s = \delta^b \sum_{s=1}^{S} (\alpha_s^{1-b} \pi_s^b) \left( \frac{a}{b} + \bar{w} - \sum_{s=1}^{S} \alpha_s y^s \right) - \frac{a}{b} \sum_{s=1}^{S} \alpha_s.$$

We can solve for saving,[14] $\sum_{s=1}^{S} \alpha_s y^s$,

$$\sum_{s=1}^{S} \alpha_s y^s = \phi_0 + \phi_1 \bar{w}, \tag{5.12}$$

where

$$\phi_0 := \frac{a}{b} \left( \frac{\delta^b \sum_{s=1}^{S} \alpha_s^{1-b} \pi_s^b - \sum_{s=1}^{S} \alpha_s}{1 + \delta^b \sum_{s=1}^{S} \alpha_s^{1-b} \pi_s^b} \right), \tag{5.13}$$

$$\phi_1 := \frac{\delta^b \sum_{s=1}^{S} \alpha_s^{1-b} \pi_s^b}{1 + \delta^b \sum_{s=1}^{S} \alpha_s^{1-b} \pi_s^b}. \tag{5.14}$$

Saving for a HARA agent is an affine function of his wealth, with slope $0 \leqslant \phi_1 < 1$. For CRRA ($a = 0$), saving is proportional to wealth ($\phi_0 = 0$). We also see a special property of Bernoulli's utility function ($a = 0$ and $b = 1$). This implies that $\phi_0 = 0$ and $\phi_1 = \delta/(1+\delta)$ is independent of asset prices $\alpha$. Thus, the log person's saving does not depend on asset prices.

Note further that saving is monotonically increasing in patience. We find

$$\frac{d}{d\delta} \sum_{s=1}^{S} \alpha_s y^s = \frac{\phi_1}{\delta} \left( \frac{a \left(1 + \sum_{s=1}^{S} \alpha_s\right) + b\bar{w}}{1 + \delta^b \sum_{s=1}^{S} \alpha_s^{1-b} \pi_s^b} \right). \tag{5.15}$$

If $b > 0$ (DARA), wealth must be at least sufficient to allow the agent to reach his subsistence level in both periods for his utility to be well defined. This means that $\bar{w}$ must be sufficient to consume $-a/b$ in the first and second periods with certainty. This consumption stream costs $-(a/b)(1+\sum_{s=1}^{S} \alpha_s) =: \underline{w}$. To ensure that the agent's maximization problem has a solution, we need to assume $\bar{w} > \underline{w}$. As a consequence, (5.15) is unambiguously positive. If $b < 0$ (IARA), then $\bar{w} < \underline{w}$, for otherwise we enter a region where risk aversion is negative; cf. the explanation following (4.8). But this again implies that (5.15) is positive.

[14]This is not saving in the sense of today's endowment minus today's consumption, $w^0 - y^0$, but rather present value of endowment minus today's consumption, $\bar{w} - y^0$.

Using (5.11) and (5.12), we can compute the demand of this agent for Arrow security $s$,

$$y^s = \bar{\varepsilon}_s + \varepsilon_s \bar{w} \tag{5.16}$$

where

$$\bar{\varepsilon}_s := (a/b)(\delta^b \alpha_s^{-b} \pi_s^b - 1) - \phi_0 \delta^b \alpha_s^{-b} \pi_s^b, \tag{5.17}$$

$$\varepsilon_s := (1 - \phi_1)\delta^b \alpha_s^{-b} \pi_s^b. \tag{5.18}$$

HARA utility gives rise to demand functions that are affine in wealth (Brennan & Kraus, 1976, theorem 1).

The solutions for CARA utility ($b = 0$) have the same qualitative features but have to be derived separately:

$$\phi_0 := \frac{a\left[(\ln \delta)\sum_{s=1}^{S} \alpha_s + \sum_{s=1}^{S} (\alpha_s \ln(\alpha_s/\pi_s))\right]}{1 + \sum_{s=1}^{S} \alpha_s}, \tag{5.19}$$

$$\phi_1 := \frac{\sum_{s=1}^{S} \alpha_s}{1 + \sum_{s=1}^{S} \alpha_s}, \tag{5.20}$$

$$\bar{\varepsilon}_s := -\phi_0 + a \ln(\delta \pi_s/\alpha_s), \tag{5.21}$$

$$\varepsilon_s := 1 - \phi_1. \tag{5.22}$$

### 5.4.2 Two fund separation

The fact that the demand functions for assets are affine implies that each agent holds a mixture of two portfolios, which we call $A$ and $B$. Portfolio $A$ consists of $\bar{\varepsilon}_1$ units of state 1 Arrow security, $\bar{\varepsilon}_2$ units of state 2 Arrow security, etc. Portfolio $B$ consists of $\varepsilon_1$ units of state 1 Arrow security, $\varepsilon_2$ units of state 2 Arrow security, etc. Both portfolios are affected by the security prices and by the preferences of the agent, but not by his wealth. His wealth only influences how much of portfolio $B$ he buys.

Add a risk-free bond to the Arrow securities. The bond is of course redundant, but it will nevertheless be useful to have a risk-free asset, because the optimal portfolio can be split into a share invested in the risk-free bond and a share invested in a risky portfolio whose composition is independent of wealth. The choice of a HARA agent can therefore be dichotomized into a selection of the composition of the risky portfolio, and a decision on how much to invest in it (Pye, 1967).

We know that the HARA agent's optimal portfolio satisfies (5.16). Let $z_0$ be the number of bonds the agent holds, and define $z_s := y^s - z_0$, so that

$$z_s = \bar{\varepsilon}_s + \varepsilon_s \bar{w} - z_0. \tag{5.23}$$

The portfolio consisting of $z_0$ risk-free bonds and, for all $s$, $z_s$ state $s$ Arrow securities produces the same, optimal, cash flow $y$. By an appropriate choice of $z_0$ we can make the composition of the risky part of the optimal portfolio independent of wealth $\bar{w}$; that is to say, we can choose $z_0$ in such a way that $\alpha_s z_s / \sum_{\tilde{s}=1}^{S} \alpha_{\tilde{s}} z_{\tilde{s}}$ is independent of $\bar{w}$. We will verify that

$$z_0 := -\frac{a}{b} \tag{5.24}$$

satisfies this requirement. From (5.17), (5.18), (5.23), (5.24), we compute the risky portfolio,

$$z_s = \delta^b \alpha_s^{-b} \pi_s^b (1 - \phi_1) \left[ \bar{w} + \frac{a}{b} \left( 1 + \sum_{\tilde{s}=1}^{S} \alpha_{\tilde{s}} \right) \right]. \tag{5.25}$$

The shares of the risky portfolio are

$$\frac{\alpha_s z_s}{\sum_{\tilde{s}=1}^{S} \alpha_{\tilde{s}} z_{\tilde{s}}} = \frac{\alpha_s^{1-b} \pi_s^b}{\sum_{\tilde{s}=1}^{S} \alpha_{\tilde{s}}^{1-b} \pi_{\tilde{s}}^b}, \tag{5.26}$$

and thus are only a function of asset prices $\alpha$, probabilities $\pi$, and cautiousness $b$, but are independent of wealth $\bar{w}$, of $a$, and of patience $\delta$. In particular, with unit cautiousness (log utility is a special case of this), the share of the state $s$ Arrow security in the risky portfolio simply equals the probability of this state. Furthermore, we conclude from (5.24) that CRRA agents ($a = 0$) hold no risk-free assets ($z_0 = 0$), and by (5.25) their holding of the risky Arrow securities are proportional to their wealth. This is an implication of the fact that CRRA preferences are homothetic; thus, optimality implies that the state-contingent consumption $(y^1, \dots, y^S)$ is proportional to wealth. Therefore, the optimal portfolio consists only of the risky components, $z_1, \dots, z_S$.

For CARA agents ($b = 0$), the solution is

$$z_0 := (1 - \phi_1)\bar{w}, \tag{5.27}$$

$$z_s := -\phi_0 + a \ln(\delta \pi_s / \alpha_s). \tag{5.28}$$

Thus, the CARA person's holding of the risk-free bond is proportional to his wealth, but the amount of risky assets he holds is independent of his wealth.

### 5.4.3 *Who holds options?*

We have seen that a HARA agent holds a mixture of the risk-free asset and some portfolio of risky assets. The composition of this risky part of the optimal portfolio depends only on the agent's cautiousness (and on asset prices and probabilities). Therefore, if everyone is equally cautious, everyone will choose a mixture of the risk-free bond ($z_0$) and the *same* risky portfolio ($z_1, \dots, z_S$), although the weight given to these two may be individually different. In equilibrium, the aggregate portfolio of all agents must yield the state-contingent period 2 endowment as cash flows. Therefore, the common risky portfolio with the shares given by (5.26) is a linear combination of the aggregate endowment and the risk-free bond.

This is the reason why economies with HARA agents who share the same cautiousness do not need any options on aggregate endowment for implementing a quasi-complete market, as claimed in Box 5.5. Once the asset markets allow trading of idiosyncratic risk (i.e. once $\hat{w}(i)$ is in the market space for each $i$), the aggregate endowment is also marketed, since it consists simply of one unit of each of the endowment assets, $\sum_i \hat{w}(i)$. In addition, only a risk-free asset is required to allow all agents to implement their optimal payoff vector, thus making the market quasi-complete.

We conclude from this that Rubinstein's common cautiousness assumption implies that no options are traded in equilibrium, as claimed in Box 5.5.[15] The consumption of all agents is perfectly correlated among them because they are mixtures of the same two portfolios. Options on aggregate endowment can be used to implement any consumption pattern as a function of aggregate endowment, but if Rubinstein's conditions are satisfied there is no need for that.

Options are useful for implementing an efficient allocation only if agents have different degrees of cautiousness. The question of which agents hold options in equilibrium was investigated by several authors (see Leland, 1980; Brennan & Solanki, 1981; Dumas, 1989; Huang, 2002). This literature concludes that the agent with the highest cautiousness has a globally convex sharing rule; that is to say, his state-contingent consumption $y^s$ is a convex function of aggregate wealth.[16] The person with the lowest cautiousness has a globally concave sharing function. All agents in between have sharing functions that are convex for low-income states and concave for high-income states. In equilibrium, the least cautious person sells all options on aggregate endowment short, the most cautious person holds all options long. All other agents buy options with low strike prices, but sell options with high strike prices short (see e.g. Dumas (1989), Propositions 9 and 12; or Huang (2002), Propositions 1 and 2). Benninga & Mayshar (2000) establish that the representative agent of a population with heterogeneous cautiousness

[15]More precisely, no options on aggregate endowment are traded. It is still possible that, in an economy that satisfies Rubinstein's condition, some options (not on the aggregate endowment) are traded for hedging idiosyncratic risk.

[16]Recall that, assuming CRRA, high cautiousness is equivalent to low relative risk aversion.

necessarily exhibits DRRA. Representative relative risk aversion equals the highest relative risk aversion in the population at low income levels, and decreases to the lowest relative risk aversion in the population for high income levels. Hara & Kuzmics (2002) extend the analysis to heterogeneous preferences outside of the HARA class. They show that the same conclusions apply also in this more general case.

## 5.5 The stochastic discount factor

### 5.5.1 *Definition*

We can derive all the pricing relationships we will receive from the marriage of the asset economy and NM utility theory simply by assuming that we know the objective probabilities of the states, $\pi$, and combining this knowledge with the risk-free pricing relationships (Box 3.4, Box 3.5).

**Box 5.6** *SDF*

The *stochastic discount factor*, or SDF, is defined as

$$M_s := \frac{\alpha_s}{\pi_s}.$$

"Stochastic discount factor" is a strange name for this. The above definition rather suggests a name like "state price per probability." It will become clear later why SDF is an appropriate name.

Note that the SDF is positive if and only if there are no arbitrage opportunities (Box 3.7). The SDF associated with an equilibrium is unique if and only if markets are complete (Box 3.11).

The SDF is to a NM agent similar to what Arrow prices are to an ordinal utility maximizer. Instead of summing Arrow prices, the NM agent computes expected stochastic discount factors. For instance, the price of a risk-free bond is the sum of the Arrow prices (see equation (3.1)). But this just equals the expected value of the SDF, i.e.

$$\beta = \sum_{s=1}^{S} \alpha_s = \sum_{s=1}^{S} \pi_s M_s = E\{M\}. \tag{5.29}$$

Risky assets can also be priced with the SDF. Remember that $q_j = \alpha \cdot r^j$ (Box 3.2) or, equivalently, $q_j = \beta \tilde{E}\{r^j\}$ (Box 3.4), where we use the risk-neutral probabilities to evaluate the expectation. With the SDF we can transform this into an expectation using the objective probabilities $\pi$,

$$q_j = E\{Mr^j\}. \tag{5.30}$$

Dividing both sides by $q_j$ and substituting $r^j/q_j$ with $R^j$, this becomes

$$E\{MR^j\} = 1. \tag{5.31}$$

These pricing formulae may look just like mindless transformations of the risk-neutral pricing relationships we have developed much earlier, but we will be able to fill these equations with much content by relating the SDF to aggregate data, such as utility functions, state-contingent aggregate income, and objective probabilities.

### 5.5.2 *The representative's first-order conditions*

The representative's portfolio problem is

$$\max \left\{ v(y^0) + \delta E\{v(y)\} \;\middle|\; (y^0 - w^0) + \sum_{s=1}^{S} \alpha_s (y^s - w^s) \leqslant 0 \right\}. \tag{5.32}$$

By market clearing, we know that the equilibrium net trade of the representative is zero. Thus, the first-order conditions must be satisfied at the endowment point,

$$\delta \pi_s \frac{v'(w^s)}{v'(w^0)} = \alpha_s.$$

Alternatively, the SDF can be used to express this.

> **Box 5.7** ***Equilibrium SDF as function of aggregate data***
>
> Let $(v, \delta, w)$ be a NM representative. Then, in equilibrium,
>
> $$M_s = \delta \frac{v'(w^s)}{v'(w^0)}.$$

This is significant. It means that the SDF can be expressed in terms of aggregate data only. But the SDF holds all the information that is contained in asset prices. Thus, asset prices can be computed from macro data alone. The entire asset pricing theory of modern finance is contained within these first-order conditions and this interpretation of the SDF.

Conversely, the SDF is a transformation of aggregate consumption data. How this transformation is achieved depends on the representative utility function. Thus, from aggregate consumption data and information about the state contingent payoff and the prices of assets, we can in principle estimate the representative's utility function. More generally, there are six items involved here:

- today's endowment per capita ($w^0$),
- tomorrow's contingent endowment per capita ($w^1, \ldots, w^S$),
- asset prices ($q$ or $\alpha$),
- common beliefs (objective probabilities $\pi$),
- the representative's time preference ($\delta$),
- the representative's utility function ($v$).

Equations (5.30) and (5.31) and Box 5.7 relate these six items to each other. If we know five of the items, we can compute the sixth.

Box 5.7 also gives a meaning to the name we have given $M_s$. In fact, an accurate term would be "discounted state-contingent intertemporal marginal rate of substitution," but this is far too long to be useful. The much shorter term "stochastic discount factor" is equally accurate: *M* is stochastic because it is state contingent. *M* is also a discount factor, because it relates future purchasing power to present purchasing power.

### 5.5.3 Relationship between risk-neutral and objective probabilities

Our interpretation of the SDF, which is based on a representative agent with NM utility, helps us to generate an interpretation of risk-neutral probabilities which would not be possible using ordinal utility functions alone. Remember the risk-neutral pricing formula given in Box 3.4. According to this formula, which follows simply from the first-order conditions of the integrated consumption-portfolio optimization problem, the price of a security is the discounted expected return of the security, using not the objective probabilities $\pi$, but the risk-neutral probabilities $\tilde{\alpha}$, to evaluate the expected payoff of an asset. Someone who maximizes expected return does not care about risk—he is risk neutral. This is the reason why this method of pricing securities is called risk-neutral pricing.

It is important to understand, however, that we do not need to assume risk neutrality when using the risk-neutral pricing formula. In fact, this formula can be used for any kind of agent, whether risk averse, neutral, or risk loving. How does this work? In effect, risk aversion of the representative agent enters the Arrow security prices $\alpha$ and thus also the risk-neutral probabilities $\tilde{\alpha}$. Consider a situation with random endowment (endowment is a function of the unknown state). The more risk averse an agent is, the more he will value additional income in low-income states. This is because his marginal utility is larger at low income levels than at high income levels (owing to the concavity of his von Neumann–Morgenstern utility function). Thus, the more risk averse the representative agent is, the greater will be the Arrow security prices of the low endowment states; conversely, the smaller will be the Arrow security prices of the high-endowment states. Thus, with increasing risk aversion, low-endowment states receive an increasing weight when computing the expected return of a security with the risk-neutral pricing formula, because income is especially valuable in those states.

Formally, we have $\alpha_s = \pi_s M_s$ and $\tilde{\alpha}_s = \rho \alpha_s$, thus

$$\frac{\tilde{\alpha}_s}{\pi_s} = pM_s = \frac{\delta}{\beta} \cdot \frac{v'(w^s)}{v'(w^0)}.$$

But

$$\beta = E\{M\} = \delta \frac{E\{v'(w)\}}{v'(w^0)}, \tag{5.33}$$

hence

$$\frac{\tilde{\alpha}_s}{\pi_s} = \frac{v'(w^s)}{E\{v'(w)\}}. \tag{5.34}$$

These equations contain interesting information. First, (5.33) shows that the equilibrium price of time, $\beta$, can deviate from the time preference parameter $\delta$. Second, (5.34) captures how risk aversion transforms objective into risk-neutral probabilities.

**Box 5.8** ***Risk-neutral probabilities are pessimistic***

Suppose the representative agent is risk averse. Then the risk-neutral probability distribution is *pessimistic* in the sense that it puts excessive weight on low-income states ($\tilde{\alpha}_s > \pi_s$ if $w^s$ is small), and little weight on high-income states ($\tilde{\alpha}_s < \pi_s$ if $w^s$ is large).

We have seen this qualitative relationship in Figure 5.2. As a special case, if the representative agent is risk neutral ($v'$ is constant), the risk-neutral probabilities are the same as the objective probabilities, $\tilde{\alpha} = \pi$ (Figure 5.1).

The intuitive reason why the risk-neutral probability must be pessimistic is as follows. One can evaluate a risky situation either by computing the expected return, using the best guess one has about the probabilities of the different states of the world, and then subtracting a premium for bearing the risk; or simply by considering its expected payoffs, just as a risk-neutral agent would do, but using distorted probabilities that exaggerate the probability of bad outcomes. Equation (5.34) tells us exactly how much pessimism makes these two evaluation methods equivalent.

## 5.6 The equilibrium price of time

Equation (5.33) tells us all about the determination of the equilibrium risk-free interest rate,

$$\beta = \delta \frac{E\{v'(w)\}}{v'(w^0)}. \tag{5.33}$$

We now investigate some comparative statics of this price.

### *5.6.1 The effect of growth*

Consider first an economy with no uncertainty and no growth, so that income tomorrow is the same as income today and is independent of the state of the world: $w^0 = w^1 = \cdots = w^S$. Then

$$\beta = \delta \frac{v'(w^0)}{v'(w^0)} = \delta.$$

Suppose now there is growth, but still no uncertainty, so $w^s := (1+g)w^0$ for $s = 1, \ldots, S$. $g > 0$ is the growth rate of income. Then

$$\beta = \delta \frac{v'((1+g)w^0)}{v'(w^0)} < \delta.$$

The last inequality is due to risk aversion (the concavity of $v$). Hence, with growth, the price of a risk-free bond is smaller than without growth, or, equivalently, the risk-free interest rate is greater with growth.

This finding remains qualitatively valid if we reintroduce uncertainty: a right shift of tomorrow's income also increases the risk-free rate of return if there is uncertainty.

**Box 5.9** *Growth and the risk-free rate*

Suppose the representative agent is risk averse ($v'' < 0$). Consider an alternative state-contingent income, $\bar{w}$, that stochastically dominates $w$ in the first degree (more growth);[17] then the corresponding price of a risk-free bond decreases, $\bar{\beta} < \beta$, or, equivalently, the risk-free interest rate increases, $\bar{\rho} > \rho$.

The intuition is as follows. The faster the economy grows (per capita), the more people would like to transfer wealth from the future to today, in order to smooth consumption intertemporally. In the aggregate, wealth cannot be moved through time, so the faster the economy grows per capita, the higher the interest rate must be in order to prevent the people from trying to move wealth through time in the aggregate.

An example of the effect of growth on the real risk-free interest rate is provided by the fall of the Berlin wall 1989. The collapse of the Soviet system led to much increased growth expectations because it opened up the prospect of utilizing previously ill used resources in the former communist countries in a much more efficient way. Consequently, real interest rates rose.

### 5.6.2 *The effect of aggregate risk*

Suppose now that again there is no growth, and add uncertainty in the form of a mean-preserving spread, i.e. $\exists(s, s')\ w^s \neq w^{s'}$, but $E\{w\} = w^0$. Consider (5.33), and suppose that $v'$ is a linear function (which is equivalent to $v''' = 0$). In that case, the mean-preserving spread of income has no effect on $\beta$. If, however, $v'$ is an convex function (so that, accordingly, the representative agent is prudent, $v''' > 0$), then the mean-preserving spread increases $E\{v'(w^s)\}$ and therefore also $\beta$. This finding, too, is more generally true.

[17]The distribution function of $w$ is defined as $F(z) := \text{prob}\{w \leqslant z\}$; in words, $F(z)$ is the probability that tomorrow's income does not exceed $z$. Let $\bar{F}(z) := \text{prob}\{\bar{w} \leqslant z\}$, so this is the distribution function of the alternative state-contingent income $\bar{w}$. We say that $\bar{w}$ first-order stochastically dominates $w$ if $F(z) \geqslant \bar{F}(z)$ for all $z$. In words, for any number $z$, tomorrow's income is more likely to be smaller than $z$ under $w$ than under $\bar{w}$.

**Box 5.10** ***Aggregate risk and the risk-free rate***

Suppose the representative agent is prudent ($v''' > 0$), and consider a mean preserving spread added to $w$, generating a new state-contingent income distribution $\bar{w}$ with the same mean but more risk. Then the corresponding price of a risk-free bond increases, $\bar{\beta} > \beta$, or, equivalently, the risk-free interest rate decreases, $\bar{\rho} < \rho$.

More aggregate risk increases the supply of savings if the representative agent is prudent. In equilibrium, aggregate saving cannot increase, but future consumption becomes relatively more valuable than present consumption. In other words, the more aggregate risk there is, the more valuable is a risk-free bond, and the lower the risk-free interest rate.

The terrorist attacks on the Twin Towers and the Pentagon of September 11, 2001 is an example of this effect. In the aftermath of this event, real interest rates decreased considerably. These attacks certainly led to more pessimistic growth expectations, which by themselves should reduce real interest rates, according to Box 5.9. But it also increased the general uncertainty, which further contributed to a reduction in the real interest rates.

## 5.7 The equilibrium price of risk

Consider (5.31) (which we repeat here for completeness), which was generated by combining the idea of risk-neutral returns from chapter 3 (Box 3.5) with the definition of the SDF (Box 5.6):

$$E\{MR^j\} = 1. \tag{5.31}$$

Before doing anything with this, remember how the covariance of two random variables is defined:

$$\begin{aligned} \operatorname{cov}(x, y) &:= E\{(x - E\{x\})(y - E\{y\})\} \\ &= E\{xy\} - E\{x\}E\{y\}. \end{aligned} \tag{5.35}$$

Applied to our equation, this means that we can split $E\{MR^j\}$ into two terms:

$$\begin{aligned} 1 &= E\{M\}E\{R^j\} + \operatorname{cov}(M, R^j) \\ &= \beta E\{R^j\} + \operatorname{cov}(M, R^j). \end{aligned}$$

Multiplying by $\rho$ and rearranging, we can express the expected rate of return of asset $j$ in excess of the risk-free interest rate—$j$'s *risk premium*—as

$$E\{R^j\} - \rho = \rho \operatorname{cov}(-M, R^j). \tag{5.36}$$

In equilibrium, the SDF is given by the first-order condition of the portfolio-problem of the representative (Box 5.7). Substituting this gives rise to the *consumption-based capital asset pricing model,* (CCAPM).

**Box 5.11** *CCAPM*

The risk premium of any asset is proportional to minus the covariance of its state-contingent rate of return with the SDF,

$$\begin{aligned} E\{R^j\} - \rho &= \rho \operatorname{cov}\left(-M, R^j\right) \\ &= \rho\delta \operatorname{cov}\left(-\frac{v'(w)}{v'(w^0)}, R^j\right) \\ &= \frac{\operatorname{cov}(-v'(w), R^j)}{E\{v'(w)\}}, \end{aligned}$$

where the last line follows from (5.33).

Notice what this says: if the rate of return of an asset is not correlated with aggregate risk, then the risk premium is zero and the expected return rate of this asset equals the risk-free rate. This is true even though the asset's return may be stochastic. Yet no premium is paid for this risk. Why is this so? It is because the risk inherent in such an asset can be diversified away, since it is unrelated to aggregate risk. Hence the risk of this asset will not be borne by anyone in an efficient allocation (by the mutuality principle), and therefore has no effect on the price of the asset.

An asset whose return rate co-varies positively with aggregate endowment will carry a positive risk premium. This is because the return structure of such an asset is unfavorable: it pays out in good times (when $w^s$ is large), but it fails in bad times (when $w^s$ is small). To compensate for this disadvantageous return pattern, the expected return rate must exceed the risk-free interest rate; i.e., such an asset carries a risk premium.

Finally, an asset whose return rate co-varies negatively with aggregate endowment is a *hedge* against aggregate risk. It can be used to insure against aggregate risk. Of course, such insurance is not possible for the aggregate, but an asset of this kind allows its owner to pass the aggregate risk on to his fellow citizens. This makes it especially valuable. Hence such assets are expensive, which means that their expected return rate falls short of the risk-free rate. They carry a negative risk premium.

## 5.8 Some important special cases

In the preceding section(s) we have seen that NM utility theory buys us a lot in terms of interpretation and concreteness of the asset pricing relationships. This is true not only for the risk-free interest rate, but for arbitrary assets as well. Combining the theory developed thus far with a few additional assumptions provides much insight, as well as specific, empirically testable hypotheses.

### *5.8.1 No aggregate risk or risk-neutral representative agent*

The pricing equations become especially simple if there is no aggregate risk. If the representative agent's income is constant in all states, $w^1 = \cdots = w^S$, the stochastic discount factor is a constant and equals $M_s = \delta v'(w^1)/v'(w^0) = \beta$, where $w^1$ is the future (state-independent) income. The price of an asset with returns $r^j$ is therefore simply

$$q_j = \beta E\{r^j\}.$$

This formula says that the price of an asset just equals the *expected present discounted value* (PV) of the cash flow it generates, using the risk-free interest rate for discounting.

Similarly, using the CCAPM, all assets have the same expected return rate in that case:

$$E\{R^j\} = \rho.$$

This shows that only aggregate risk affects asset prices and returns. Idiosyncratic risk is diversifiable if markets are complete, and therefore has no influence on asset prices.

PV is not an appropriate pricing method in general. Yet, if the representative agent is risk neutral, PV is appropriate even in the presence of aggregate risk, because in that case $v'$ is a constant, and therefore the stochastic discount factor is degenerate and equals the plain discount factor $\delta$ in all states,

$$q_j = \delta E\{r^j\}.$$

### 5.8.2 Quadratic utility representative agent and the CAPM

Suppose there is a special asset, call it $m$, whose return rate is perfectly negatively correlated with the state-contingent marginal utility of the representative agent, $R_s^m = -av'(w^s) + b$, with $a > 0$ and $b$ some arbitrary number. Then, $-v'(w^s) = (R_s^m - b)/a$. Using this, the CCAPM formula can be written as

$$E\{R^j\} - \rho = \frac{\text{cov}(R^m, R^j)/a}{E\{v'(w)\}}.$$

Evaluated for $j = m$, this becomes

$$E\{R^m\} - \rho = \frac{\text{var}(R^m)/a}{E\{v'(w)\}}.$$

To get rid of the $v'$, we divide the first equation by the second:

$$\frac{E\{R^j\} - \rho}{E\{R^m\} - \rho} = \frac{\text{cov}(R^m, R^j)}{\text{var}(R^m)}.$$

Defining $\beta_j := \text{cov}(R^m, R^j)/\text{var}(R^m)$ and rearranging yields[18]

$$E\{R^j\} = \rho + \beta_j \left[E\{R^m\} - \rho\right]. \tag{5.37}$$

This equation is known as the *capital asset pricing model*, or CAPM (Sharpe, 1964). To use this formula, we must find an asset whose return is perfectly negatively correlated with marginal utility.

For instance, let $m$ be a claim on aggregate or mean endowment, so that $r_s^m = w^s$. Let $q_m$ be the price of this asset; then $R_s^m = w^s/q_m$. Suppose further that the utility function of the representative agent is quadratic (a heroic assumption), i.e. $v(y) := -cy^2 + dy$. Then $v'(y) = -2cy + d$. In this case $R^m$ is perfectly negatively correlated with marginal utility, $R_s^m = -av'(w^s) + b$, with $a := [2cq_m]^{-1}$ and $b := ad$. Hence, with quadratic utility, the CCAPM collapses to the CAPM.

Typically, however, the special asset $m$ is not defined that broadly. Usually it is taken to be the market portfolio (hence the name $m$), where "market" is narrowly defined as the equity market or some index of the most important equities. With this simplification the CAPM becomes especially amenable to empirical analysis because it contains only observable variables.

Note also that the CAPM is a *special case* of the CCAPM. Therefore it is not sensible to dismiss the CCAPM without at the same time also dismissing the CAPM.

[18] The symbol $\beta$ has been used in this equation because it is traditional. It should not be confused with the price of a bond, to which this symbol refers to in the rest of this book.

### 5.8.3 CARA representative agent

Suppose the representative agent has constant absolute risk aversion, $v(y) = -e^{-\gamma y}/\gamma$. This implies that the SDF obeys $M_s = \delta e^{-\gamma(w^s - w^0)}$, or in logs

$$\ln M_s = \ln \delta - \gamma(w^s - w^0).$$

CARA utility therefore implies that there is an affine relationship between log SDF and the level of consumption. This is an empirically testable hypothesis.

What does this equation imply for the risk-free interest rate? We know that $\beta = \rho^{-1} = E\{M\}$. Taking logs yields

$$\ln \beta = -\ln \rho = \ln E\{M\} \approx E\{\ln M\}.$$

This last transformation is approximately valid only if the variance of $M$ is small, so let us make this assumption. Defining the state-contingent growth rate of per capita income as $1 + g_s := w^s/w^0$, we can reformulate the expression for log SDF as $\ln M_s = \ln \delta - \gamma w^0 g_s$. Substituting this and reordering yields

$$\ln \rho \approx \gamma w^0 E\{g\} - \ln \delta.$$

This equation says that the risk-free interest rate increases with the expected growth rate of endowments, but also with the *level* of endowments. Thus, in a growing economy, the risk-free interest rate should grow indefinitely. This is counter factual, and is therefore evidence against the CARA hypothesis.

### 5.8.4 The benchmark: CRRA representative

Suppose now the representative agent has constant relative risk aversion, $v(y) = y^{1-\gamma}/(1-\gamma)$. This implies that the SDF obeys $M_s = \delta(1 + g_s)^{-\gamma}$, or in logs,

$$\begin{aligned} \ln M_s &= \ln \delta - \gamma \ln(1 + g_s) \\ &\approx \ln \delta - \gamma g_s. \end{aligned}$$

CRRA utility therefore implies that there is an affine relationship between log SDF and log consumption, or, to a first approximation, between log SDF and the rate of aggregate growth. Again, this is an empirically testable hypothesis.

What can we say about the risk-free interest rate? Following the same steps as in the CARA example we get

$$\ln \rho \approx \gamma E\{g\} - \ln \delta. \tag{5.38}$$

This is an attractive relationship: the risk-free interest rate is an affine function of the expected growth rate (in accordance with Box 5.9), but it does not depend on the level of endowments.[19]

Equation (5.38) could in principle be estimated. Regress the real risk-free interest rate on the real growth rate of consumption and on a constant. We expect a positive constant ($\ln \delta$ should be negative if $\delta < 1$) and a positive slope. The slope is the estimate of $\gamma$. We can also use different horizons for estimating (5.38). For instance, we could use the three-month interest rate and the annualized quarterly growth rate of consumption, or we could use the ten-year bond yield (taking care of inflation) and the yearly growth of consumption from decade to decade. Neither the slope nor the constant should change with the horizon. These are testable hypotheses.[20]

Next, consider the equilibrium risk premium. Substituting the CRRA utility into the CCAPM formula yields

$$E\{R^j\} - \rho = \rho\delta \operatorname{cov}(-(1+g)^{-\gamma}, R^j).$$

Unless $g$ is extreme, we can approximate $(1+g)^{-\gamma}$ with $1 - \gamma g$; thus,

$$E\{R^j\} - \rho \approx \rho\delta\gamma \operatorname{cov}(g, R^j).$$

From (5.33), we have

$$[\rho\delta]^{-1} = \frac{E\{v'(w)\}}{v'(w^0)} = E\{(1+g)^{-\gamma}\} \approx 1 - \gamma E\{g\}.$$

Therefore

$$E\{R^j\} - \rho \approx \gamma^* \operatorname{cov}(g, R^j), \qquad (5.39)$$
$$\text{with } \gamma^* := \frac{\gamma}{1 - \gamma E\{g\}}.$$

With moderate growth and not too extreme risk aversion, we have $\gamma^* \approx \gamma$.

We can interpret of (5.39) as follows. The risk premium that an asset carries is approximately equal to its risk, measured as the covariance of its state-contingent return rate with the growth rate of aggregate income, times the price of risk $\gamma^*$, which is almost equal to the coefficient of relative risk aversion of the representative agent.

[19]Note that, according to (5.38), $\rho$ does not depend on the riskiness of the endowment, contrary to Box 5.10. This is due to the first-order approximations we have calculated (switching the log and the expectation operator). If endowment risk is large, this approximation is not valid anymore. A second-order approximation would then be more appropriate and we would also have a term involving the variance of $M$ affecting $\rho$.

[20]Or almost. One difficulty with this estimation is that we should use *expected* real per capita growth, which is not observable. Also, real interest rates are not observable because we can observe only nominal prices or interest rates, but not the expected rate of inflation.

## Notes on the literature

Much of this chapter is reviewed in Campbell (2000). Sargent (1987, chapter 3) and Ljungqvist & Sargent (2000, chapter 10) provide a succinct discussion of the main problems. An excellent discussion for researchers is provided by Gollier (2001*a*, part VII).

## Problems

**Problem 5.1** Consider Figure 5.2. Suppose one agent is risk-neutral and the other is risk averse.

(*a*) Draw the contract curve. Interpret your finding.

(*b*) How risk averse is the representative agent?

(*c*) Now suppose that both agents are risk averse, and each has a CARA utility function, although possibly with different coefficients. Without computing anything explicitly, draw the contract curve simply by using the logic of Wilson's theorem.

**Problem 5.2** Let $\rho$ be the risk-free interest rate and $E\{R\}$ be the expected yield of some (possibly risky) asset. Let the asset we are looking at be an Arrow security that pays out in a state when aggregate endowment is particularly low. This security is clearly risky. Is $E\{R\} > \rho$, $E\{R\} = \rho$, or $E\{R\} < \rho$, and *why*?[21]

**Problem 5.3** Consider a finance economy with two states with probabilities $\pi$ and $1 - \pi$, respectively, and utility function of income $\ln(x)$. Current consumption does not enter agents' utilities; they are interested only in consumption tomorrow.

Compute equilibrium prices, equilibrium allocations, and gains from trade (in terms of ex ante expected utility of the agents), assuming, in turn, that

$$w(1) := \begin{bmatrix} 1 \\ 3 \end{bmatrix}, \quad w(2) := \begin{bmatrix} 3 \\ 1 \end{bmatrix}, \qquad \text{with } \pi = 1/2, \tag{a}$$

$$w(1) := \begin{bmatrix} 1 \\ 3 \end{bmatrix}, \quad w(2) := \begin{bmatrix} 3 \\ 1 \end{bmatrix}, \qquad \text{with } \pi = 2/3, \tag{b}$$

$$w(1) := \begin{bmatrix} 1 \\ 3 \end{bmatrix}, \quad w(2) := \begin{bmatrix} 2 \\ 2 \end{bmatrix}, \qquad \text{with } \pi = 1/2. \tag{c}$$

[21]You do not have to compute anything (you can, of course, if you want to). Only your economic reasoning is of interest in this problem, not your computational skills.

Case $(a)$ is completely symmetric. There is scope for full mutual insurance. Does it happen? Case $(b)$ is similar to case $(a)$ in the sense that there is still no aggregate uncertainty. However, there is an asymmetry between the two agents because agent 2 is richer than agent 1 on average. Will there be full insurance? Case $(c)$ is interesting: now there is aggregate uncertainty, but it is all borne by agent 1. Agent 2 faces no endowment uncertainty. Will he offer (partial) insurance to agent 1?

**Problem 5.4** Consider case $(b)$ of the previous problem, but assume that agent 1's assessment of the probability of state 1 is $\pi(1) := 2/3$, and agent 2's assessment is $\pi(2) := 1/3$.

$(a)$ Compute the equilibrium.

$(b)$ Put yourself into agent 1's shoes. Would you behave as suggested by the equilibrium? What would you think?

**Problem 5.5** Consider again the financial markets of Problem 3.4, but this time we also have information on state-contingent aggregate per capita income and objective probabilities.

| **asset** | **price** | **cash flow in . . .** | | | | |
|---|---|---|---|---|---|---|
| | | **state 1** | **state 2** | **state 3** | **state 4** | **state 5** |
| share of company X | 2.857 | 8 | 5 | 2 | 0 | 0 |
| share of company Y | 4.048 | 12 | 8 | 0 | 0 | 4 |
| bond of company X | 0.774 | 1 | 1 | 1 | 1 | 0 |
| bond of company Y | 0.893 | 1 | 1 | 1 | 0 | 1 |
| option on share X | 1.429 | 6 | 3 | 0 | 0 | 0 |
| income $w$ | | 13 | 11 | 10 | 7 | 8 |
| probability $\pi$ | | 20.42% | 28.96% | 36.08% | 2.97% | 11.57% |

You will need econometrics software or at least a spreadsheet program for questions $(b)$ and $(c)$.

$(a)$ Is the representative agent risk averse?

$(b)$ Can you find a CARA utility that fits these data?

$(c)$ Can you find a CRRA utility that fits these data?

$(d)$ Can you compute the time-preference parameter $\delta$? Would it help if we told you that $w_0 = 10.1$?

**Problem 5.6** Suppose there is a one-year government bond that costs 96.15 today and pays 100 next period. There is also a one-year bond issued by *IT Consulting*, a start-up firm, which costs 76.92. This bond will pay 100 if the firm still exists next period, and will pay zero if it goes bankrupt in the meantime.

(*a*) Suppose IT Consulting's success is independent of the business cycle. What is the probability that the firm will fail between now and one year from now?

(*b*) Suppose that IT Consulting's success is positively correlated with the general economic activity. Would this information change your assessment of the success probability, and if so how?

**Problem 5.7** This is a short excursion into a simple multiple date model. Consider an economy whose representative agent has a power utility function with a subsistence level $v(y) := (y-\underline{w})^{1-\gamma}/(1-\gamma)$, with $\underline{w} > 0$. Suppose there is no aggregate risk and endowment grows at a constant positive rate $g$. Assume also that $w^0 > \underline{w}$. How does the risk-free interest rate evolve over time? *(Hint: Observe that, as the economy grows, consumption y more and more exceeds the subsistence level* $\underline{w}$*.)*

# 6
# Dynamic finance economy

The model of the previous chapter is simplified in that it assumes that there are only two periods. Of course we could interpret these "periods" as present and future, but then the model does not allow us to think about the effects of the gradual resolution of uncertainty. Also, it is not necessarily natural to assume a finite horizon.[1] Luckily, the model generalizes to many periods, thereby increasing the realism and scope considerably. However, moving to an infinite horizon opens up some technical difficulties which require special consideration.

## 6.1 A static dynamic model

### 6.1.1 *Multiple period uncertainty*

The first step in generalizing the model to accommodate many periods is to accommodate our notation. We will interpret an asset as a list of cash flows that are contingent on all *events*, not just on final states. For instance, in the tree of Figure 2.1 (page 12), there are nine final states ($\mathcal{E}_2 = \{\{1\}, \{2\}, \ldots, \{9\}\}$), but there are 12 Arrow securities: the nine that pay out in period 2, conditional on each of the final states, plus the ones that pay out in period 1, conditional on the three events of that period ($\mathcal{E}_1 = \{e_1, e_2, e_3\} = \{\{1, 2, 3\}, \{4, 5, 6, 7\}, \{8, 9\}\}$). Today's event is denoted by $e_0 := \{\mathcal{S}\}$. We use $\mathcal{E} := \bigcup_{t>0} \mathcal{E}_t$ to denote the set of all future events.

[1] A finite horizon requires an agent to be able to name a point in time at which his probability of living for one more period drops to zero. For instance, conditional on reaching the age of 90 years, how would you assess the probability of reaching 91 years? It is clearly strictly positive (unless you have vowed to commit suicide should you reach this age). But by the same argument, the probability of reaching the age of 92 is also strictly positive. The point is that this argument can be applied *ad infinitum*.

Also, we write $\tau(e)$ to denote the time period to which an event $e$ belongs; that is, if $e \in \mathcal{E}_t$ then $\tau(e) := t$. If $\tau(e) < \tau(e')$ and $e \supset e'$, we say that $e$ *precedes* $e'$ and $e'$ *succeeds* $e$.

Next, consider the path in the tree that leads from the root to some event $e \in \mathcal{E}$. Let $\psi_t(e)$ be the event on this path that belongs to period $t$ (with $t \leqslant \tau(e)$). So for instance, the immediate predecessor event of $e$ is denoted with $\psi_{\tau(e)-1}(e)$. Observe also that $\psi_{\tau(e)}(e) = e$. Formally, $\psi$ is defined by the two requirements, first, that it leads to $e$, that is, $\psi_t(e) \supset e$;[2] second, that it belongs to the right period, $\tau(\psi_t(e)) = t$.

If the horizon is finite, $T < \infty$, and each event splits only into a finite number of successor events, then the set of final states $\mathcal{S}$ is also finite. We assume, as in the two-period model, that there is an objective probability distribution over $\mathcal{S}$. From this we can derive probability distributions over the non-terminal events as well, $\pi_e := \sum_{s \in e} \pi_s$. More generally, even if the horizon is infinite, we can still work with probability distributions over all events associated with a certain time period. The distributions are required to be intertemporally consistent only in the sense that the probability of an event, $\pi_e$, must be equal to the sum of the probabilities of all its immediate successor events, $\sum_{\{e' \mid \psi_{\tau(e')-1}(e')=e\}} \pi_{e'}$. If the set of states is uncountable, the same thoughts apply, but we need to work with a more general probability space, introducing technicalities which we wish to avoid here.

If $x$ is some function of events, then $x^{\langle t \rangle}$ is the random variable that consists of the realizations of $x$ in the events that belong to period $t$. For instance, if $w$ is aggregate event-contingent endowment, then $w^{\langle t \rangle}$ is the random aggregate endowment in period $t$. We write $E\{x^{\langle t \rangle}\} := \sum_{e \in \mathcal{E}_t} \pi_e w^e$ for the expected value of the period $t$ component of the random variable $x$. Let $e$ be an event from an earlier period, $\tau(e) < t$. Then $E\{x^{\langle t \rangle} \mid e\}$ is the *expectation conditional on event* $e$. This means that we take expectations only over the part of the event tree following event $e$, or, to put it another way, we consider only paths through the sub-tree that start in node $e$. More formally, $E\{x^{\langle t \rangle} \mid e\}$ weights events $e'$ that succeed $e$ with the probability $\pi_{e'}/\pi_e$, and events that do not succeed $e$ with zero.

### 6.1.2 *Multiple period assets*

With this more general event-tree we can accommodate all real-life financial assets. A risk-free *coupon bond*, for instance, is an asset that pays out the coupon in each event before it matures, and in all the events that belong to the maturity date it pays the coupon and the principal. Formally, consider

[2] Remember the definition of a filtration in footnote 5 on page 13.

a bond with unit face value and let $t^*$ denote the period in which this bond matures. Let $e$ be any future event, $e \in \mathcal{E}$. Then the payoff vector of a risk-free coupon bond is given by

$$r_e := \begin{cases} \text{coupon} & \text{if } 0 < \tau(e) < t^*, \\ 1 + \text{coupon} & \text{if } \tau(e) = t^*, \\ 0 & \text{if } \tau(e) > t^*. \end{cases}$$

A special form of such a coupon bond is a *consol*. This is a coupon bond with infinite time to maturity. Thus, a risk-free consol is an asset that delivers a constant cash flow in each and every future period independently of the event. Formally,

$$r_e := \text{coupon} \quad \text{for all } e \in \mathcal{E}.$$

A *discount bond* (also called *zero-coupon bond*) is the same as a coupon bond except that the coupon is zero. A risk-free discount bond is therefore an asset that delivers a constant cash flow in all events that belong to a certain period (the maturity date), but nothing otherwise,

$$r_e := \begin{cases} 1 & \text{if } \tau(e) = t^*, \\ 0 & \text{otherwise.} \end{cases}$$

From an ordinary coupon bond we can generate STRIPS.[3] These are derivatives of the coupon bond that pay only the coupon at a particular date. They do not pay any earlier or later coupons or the principal. Mathematically, strips and discount bonds are the same, except that the cash flow at maturity is not necessarily unity. More generally, any asset can be stripped: an asset whose event-contingent cash flow is $r^j$ can be decomposed into a portfolio of strips $r^j_{\langle t \rangle}$, for $t \in \{1, \ldots, T\}$, and $r^j_{\langle t \rangle}$ is the part of the cash flows of $r^j$ that are due in period $t$.

The assets we have discussed so far deliver only a small number of different cash flows in all events, such as 0 or 1 or the coupon. This is why these assets are called *fixed income instruments*. A *share*, by contrast, is a claim on the future dividends of the firm, and the cash flows thus depend on ongoing decisions of the management. The number of possible dividends is thus large. Any cash flow vector could describe a share, provided cash flows are non-negative in each event, because shareholders enjoy limited liability.

[3]See http://www.publicdebt.treas.gov/of/ofstrips.htm for a description and for data on the strips market. STRIPS stands for "Separate Trading of Registered Interest and Principal of Securities."

Another example of a non-fixed income security is debt that is issued with a variable interest rate. Variable rate mortgages are an example. These are loans whose interest payment is tied to the yield of some other bonds, such as a Treasury bond or some money market interest rate.

Furthermore, we can define various options on existing assets. For instance, a *European call option* on the underlying asset $r^j$ with strike price $x$ and time to maturity $t$ is an asset that delivers a cash flow of $\max\{0, q_e^j - x\}$ for all $e \in \mathcal{E}_t$, and zero in all other periods. The cash flow of the corresponding *put option* is $\max\{0, x - q_e^j\}$. *Asian options* are the same as European options, except that the payoff is not the difference between the price of the asset at maturity and the strike price, but rather the difference between the average price of the asset during the life span of the option, and the strike price. There are also examples of options whose underlying is an interest rate. *Caps* and *floors*, for instance, are loans that have a variable interest rate, but also a maximum (cap) or a minimum possible (floor) interest rate. More imaginative options (with imaginative names) have also been created, for instance options on the realized volatility of the price of some underlying asset, or options that become effective only if the price crosses some barrier. Yet other options depend on the price or price-paths of more than one underlying asset. A spread option, for instance, is an option on the difference of two asset prices; a rainbow option is on the minimum or maximum of several assets. There are also options whose underlying is itself an option price (so-called compound options).

An analytically more difficult kind of options are *American options*. These are similar to standard European options, but they can be exercised by the agent who holds the option at any point in time at *or before* the expiry date; i.e., the holder of an American call option can exchange the option for $q_e^j - x$ at a time $\tau(e) \leqslant t$ of his choice. This feature makes the cash flow of these options a function of the exercise policy of the holder, so they are no longer simply an exogenous function of the event.[4] Bonds are often bundled with options, in the sense that the issuer of the bond has the right to call the bond before maturity, so the issuer can shorten the time to maturity at will.

### 6.1.3 *Time preference, time consistency, and exponential discounting*

For the two-period model we assumed that an agent's risk aversion would be the same in both periods. Accordingly, we assumed that utility was additively

[4] A more exotic kind of option with an American feature, in the sense that its value depends on the policy of the person who holds it, are "shout options." These are ordinary call or put options but with the added feature that the holder can look in (called "shouting") the minimum payoff of the option at any time during its lifetime (but typically only once).

separable through time, with a weighting factor measuring intertemporal preferences or impatience. A straightforward generalization for multiple periods is

$$v(y^0) + \sum_{t=1}^{T} \delta(t) E\{v(y^{\langle t \rangle})\}. \tag{6.1}$$

If $t$ is calendar time, or, equivalently, the age of the decision maker, then the $\delta$s measure the preferred intertemporal consumption path of the agent. Impatience means that $1 > \delta(1) \geqslant \delta(2) \geqslant \cdots \geqslant \delta(T) \geqslant 0$, i.e. the agent prefers to consume rather early than late.[5]

However, it is often more convenient to work with a model that is formulated in relative time, so that $t = 0$ is always today, $t = 1$ is tomorrow (measured in time units of days, months, years), and so on. But that puts a very strong restriction on the structure of $\delta(\cdot)$.

Suppose you have to make a decision today about your present and future behavior. For instance, when you decide how much to save, you decide how much you are able to consume today and how much tomorrow. We say that such an intertemporal decision is *time consistent* if, when the next period comes along, it will be optimal for you to stick to the same planned path. The decision is *time inconsistent* if a plan that is optimal from the point of view of one period is no longer optimal from the point of view of a later period.

Consider an example. Suppose you have some tedious administrative work to do (filling out an expense claims form, for instance, or filling out IRS forms). The effort required for doing this is large: it costs you 10 "utils." Moreover, each day that you delay the work has a utility cost of 1. (The probability increases that you will not have your expenses reimbursed; it also sends a bad signal about your work ethics.) You know that you will eventually have to do it, but you can still decide whether to do it now or later. Suppose your utility function is additively separable, as in (6.1), with $\delta(t) := \kappa\delta^t$ for some $0 < \delta < 1, 0 < \kappa < 1$. This specification of the discount function is known as *quasi-hyperbolic* (Laibson, 1997). For concreteness, let $\delta = 0.98$ and $\kappa = 0.9$,

$$v(y^0) + 0.9 \sum_{t=1}^{T} 0.98^t v(y^t).$$

[5]Within a model that is formulated in calendar time, this actually means that the agent prefers to consume when young than to consume when old. Personally, I fail to see a clear justification for this assumption.

$v(y^t)$ is zero in all periods not used for the administrative work, and $-(10+t)$ in the period in which you finally do it ($-10$ for the effort and $-t$ for the delay). Doing the work now produces intertemporal utility of $-10$; doing it tomorrow is better because intertemporal utility is then $\kappa\delta \cdot (-11) = -9.7$. Waiting for two days is worse again, $\kappa\delta^2 \cdot (-12) = -10.4$, waiting three days even more so, $\kappa\delta^3 \cdot (-13) = -11.0$. So you decide to do it tomorrow. Yet, the next day, the decision problem is the same: the utility of doing the work now is $-11$. If you wait one more day the utility will be $-10.6$, which is better, so you delay the unpleasant work for one more day. The trouble is that these preferences induce the decision maker to procrastinate forever, which is certainly not optimal by any criterion. So, even though the decision maker maximizes utility, he ends up in a far less than optimal situation. This behavior certainly has descriptive appeal. But it also embodies a form of irrationality or inconsistency. Working with such a model of intertemporal preferences is difficult. It requires you to think of the decision maker as a player in a game where different selves act strategically.

The problem of time inconsistency necessarily occurs if discounting one period twice, $\delta(1)^2$, is not the same as discounting two periods, $\delta(2)$. We conclude that, within the additively separable model that is formulated in relative time, (6.1), the only time-consistent models are the ones that discount exponentially, $\delta(t) := \delta^t$.

Largely because of its simplicity, exponential discounting is the mainstream model of intertemporal preferences, but it has the drawback that it mingles two rather distinct economic concepts, namely impatience and risk aversion, as was already noted by Lucas (1978, see his footnote 8). The curvature of the utility function (typically interpreted as a measure of risk aversion) also influences the intertemporal rate of substitution if future consumption is not equal to present consumption. Epstein & Zin (1989) show how to disentangle these distinct economic concepts; see section 8.2.2 below.

### 6.1.4 *Equilibrium SDF and the fundamental pricing formula*

Our model is dynamic in the sense that it features time (just like the model of chapter 5), but it is static in the sense that we stick with the assumption that all assets can be traded "at the beginning of time" (meaning today), and no trade will be necessary later on. In that sense, the "static dynamic model" is just as far from reality as the contingent-claim economy model of chapter 2. In section 6.2 we will study trading arrangements where not all asset markets are open at the beginning but they open up sequentially.

If we assume exponential discounting of a constant period utility function, and also assume that all asset markets are operative today, then not much changes compared with the portfolio problem of the previous chapter. The problem is only marginally more involved because it features many periods,

$$\max \left\{ v(y^0) + \sum_{t=1}^{T} \delta^t E\{v(y^{\langle t \rangle})\} \,\middle|\, y - w \in \mathcal{M}(q) \right\}. \tag{6.2}$$

We assume that all Arrow securities are traded. The first-order conditions of this problem are then

$$v'(w^0) = \lambda, \quad \delta^{\tau(e)} \pi_e v'(w^e) = \lambda \alpha_e,$$

hence

$$\begin{aligned} \frac{\alpha_e}{\pi_e} &= \delta^{\tau(e)} \frac{v'(w^e)}{v'(w^0)} \\ &= \left(\delta \frac{v'(w^{\psi_1(e)})}{v'(w^0)}\right)\left(\delta \frac{v'(w^{\psi_2(e)})}{v'(w^{\psi_1(e)})}\right) \cdots \left(\delta \frac{v'(w^e)}{v'(w^{\psi_{\tau(e)-1}(e)})}\right). \end{aligned} \tag{6.3}$$

The equilibrium "one period ahead" SDF of event $e$ is the marginal rate of substitution of the representative agent between consumption in event $e$ and the predecessor event $\psi_{\tau(e)-1}(e)$, i.e.

$$M_e = \delta \frac{v'(w^e)}{v'(w^{\psi_{\tau(e)-1}(e)})}. \tag{6.4}$$

We can now write (6.3) more compactly as

$$\frac{\alpha_e}{\pi_e} = M_{\psi_1(e)} M_{\psi_2(e)} \cdots M_{\psi_{\tau(e)}(e)} = \prod_{t'=1}^{\tau(e)} M_{\psi_{t'}(e)} =: \mathbf{M}_e. \tag{6.5}$$

As in the static model, we can express all asset prices with the SDF. Consider a multiple period asset $r^j$. Those components of the cash flow of this asset that are due in period $t$—the period $t$ strip $r^j_{\langle t \rangle}$—can be priced like (5.30) as $E\{\mathbf{M}_{\langle t \rangle} r^j_{\langle t \rangle}\}$. The price of the complete asset $j$ is of course simply the sum of the prices of all its strips.

**Box 6.1** ***Fundamental pricing formula***

The equilibrium price of an asset with payoffs $r^j$ is given by

$$q_j = \sum_{t=1}^{T} E\left\{\mathbf{M}_{\langle t \rangle} r^j_{\langle t \rangle}\right\}.$$

If the representative agent is risk neutral, all $M_e$ are equal to $\delta$ (hence $\mathbf{M}_e = \delta^{\tau(e)}$) and the fundamental pricing formula collapses to a simple expected present value relationship,

$$q_j = \sum_{t=1}^{T} \delta^t \, E\left\{r^j_{\langle t\rangle}\right\}. \tag{6.6}$$

### 6.1.5 Lucas's tree metaphor

Think of an economy in which the only endowment of agent $i$ is, metaphorically speaking, a "tree." The tree produces a stochastic amount of fruit each period, $(r_i^0, r_i^{\langle 1\rangle}, r_i^{\langle 2\rangle}, \dots)$. There is nothing the agent can do to affect the harvest. The fruit that the tree produces is exogenous. This tree is the only endowment of the agent, $w_i = r_i$. Some trees may be located at somewhat more or less advantageous locations, giving their owners more or less food on average, so there can be rich and poor agents in the economy. Some trees may be more exposed to the weather than others, exposing their respective owners to more or less volatility. If different trees give an imperfectly correlated stream of food, agents will want to mutually insure each other. We assume that there is a (quasi-)complete market that allows them to do that perfectly. The only risk that is left is aggregate, i.e. the average fruit stream of all trees, or the fruit stream of the forest if you like, $w := \sum_{i=1}^{I} w_i/I$. We also assume that the heterogeneous agents can be aggregated into a representative utility maximizer with exponential discounting (for instance because the Rubinstein conditions are satisfied, Box 5.3). This is the setup of Robert Lucas's (1978) famous "tree model," and we easily recognize it as the standard model we have been using throughout: the endowment process is exogenous, there is a representative agent, and the allocation is Pareto efficient because idiosyncratic risk is washed out and aggregate risk is allocated efficiently. This tree model is perfectly suited to study the equilibrium price of aggregate risk. We can study what the equilibrium price of the forest (the representative tree) is and how this price fluctuates with aggregate fruit availability.

Without any further assumptions, not much can be said except that the equilibrium price of the aggregate or average tree satisfies Box 6.1; for $r^j = w$,

$$q = \sum_{t=1}^{T} E\left\{\mathbf{M}_{\langle t\rangle} w^{\langle t\rangle}\right\}. \tag{6.7}$$

There is one special case in which this gives rise to a very simple closed-form solution. If the representative agent has a constant relative risk aversion of one (i.e. he has Bernoulli's specification, $v = \ln$), the fundamental pricing formula applied to a Lucas tree simplifies dramatically:

$$\begin{aligned} q &= \sum_{t=1}^{T} E\left\{\delta^t \frac{1/w^{\langle t\rangle}}{1/w^0} w^{\langle t\rangle}\right\} \\ &= \sum_{t=1}^{T} \delta^t w^0 \\ &= \frac{\delta(1-\delta^T)}{1-\delta} w^0. \end{aligned} \tag{6.8}$$

The price of a Lucas tree is *proportional* to today's fruit, and completely independent of tomorrow's expected fruit or of any other stochastic properties of the fruit process. $q/w^0$ is the price–dividend ratio. With log utility, it is a constant that depends only on the time preference of the representative agent. With other utility functions, no concrete statements are possible unless we impose some assumptions on the endowment process. This is the route that Lucas (and all the literature since) has taken. Endowment or endowment growth is typically modelled as a Markov process,[6] and equilibrium asset prices are related to properties of this process, such as the mean growth rate, its variance, and its persistence.[7]

## 6.2 Dynamic trading

The "static dynamic" model of the previous section features just one round of trade of financial assets at the beginning of time, and after that only the commodity spot markets open every period in accordance with the Radner equilibrium model. This is, of course, highly unrealistic. It is particularly artificial to assume that spot markets do reopen but financial markets do

[6]Consider some sequence of random variables, $X_1, X_2, \ldots$. We denote the value that was drawn from $X_t$ by $x_t$. In general, the distribution of $X_{t+1}$ depends on the history of draws up to period $t$, $(x_1, x_2, x_3, \ldots, x_t)$. This construction is called a *stochastic process.* The stochastic process has the *Markov property* if the distribution of $X_{t+1}$, given the history $(x_1, x_2, x_3, \ldots, x_t)$, depends only on the last component $x_t$.

[7]Note that modelling the endowment process in this way implies that it is not true that the information partition of the agents becomes increasingly fine as time passes, as depicted in Figure 2.1. In a Markov process, some information is revealed each period (namely today's state), but the amount of uncertainty remains the same as time goes by and every period is essentially identical to all other periods.

not. Empirically, financial assets are traded continuously. This simple fact has significant consequences.

For one thing, if financial markets reopen, it makes sense to study the *time series properties* of financial asset prices, since we can observe these prices at different points in time. Moreover, re-trading assets also provides a channel through which a seemingly incomplete market can be completed. This is called *dynamic completion.* However, re-trade in a model with an infinite horizon has a drawback: it opens up the possibility of a new form of arbitrage which consists of rolling debt over infinitely and thus effectively avoiding redeeming it (so-called *Ponzi schemes*). In addition, the infinitely re-trading of assets opens up the possibility of *price bubbles*, which disconnect the market price from its *fundamental value*.

### 6.2.1 Dynamic completion

It seems natural to assume that there are many states, maybe even a continuum. Does that imply that we need a continuum of assets? The answer is no. The market can be made dynamically complete by allowing trade in only few assets, provided these assets can be traded continuously in time. That is, we match the large set of states by allowing trade at a large set of points in time. There are two ways of achieving this. One is via dynamic completion using only short-lived assets (Guesnerie & Jaffray, 1974). Another possibility that works with even fewer assets uses only long-lived securities; this was devised by Kreps (1982). It is also possible to use a combination of these ideas: the right amalgamation of short- and long-lived assets can constitute a dynamically complete market.

We first consider Guesnerie & Jaffray's (1974) approach, which is an elaboration of Arrow (1953). Using a two-period model, Arrow showed that state-contingent contracts can be replaced by elementary assets delivering state-contingent purchasing power (Arrow securities). Guesnerie & Jaffray extend this idea to multiple periods. Call an asset *short-lived* if it pays out only in the period immediately after it has been issued. Suppose that, for each event $e$ and each immediate successor event $e'$, there is an asset that pays out one unit of purchasing power if event $e'$ materializes tomorrow, and zero otherwise. This constitutes a complete set of short-lived assets in the sense that all immediate uncertainty can be separately insured with short-lived Arrow securities.

For the market to be complete, *all* events—not just the ones of the next period—must be tradeable. This is easily achieved. Consider an event $e$ in period 2. The immediate predecessor event is $\psi_1(e)$. If this predecessor event is reached in period 1, we will buy one short-lived asset that pays out

**Table 6.1.** *Return matrix.*

| *asset* | 1 | 2 | [1,0] | [2,0] | [1,1] | [2,1] | [1,2] | [2,2] |
|---|---|---|---|---|---|---|---|---|
| *event 0* | $-q_{1,0}$ | $-q_{2,0}$ | $-q_{1,0}$ | $-q_{2,0}$ | 0 | 0 | 0 | 0 |
| *event 1* | 0 | 0 | $q_{1,1}$ | $q_{2,1}$ | $-q_{1,1}$ | $-q_{2,1}$ | 0 | 0 |
| *event 2* | 0 | 0 | $q_{1,2}$ | $q_{2,2}$ | 0 | 0 | $-q_{1,2}$ | $-q_{2,2}$ |
| *state 1* | 1 | 0 | 0 | 0 | 1 | 0 | 0 | 0 |
| *state 2* | 0 | 1 | 0 | 0 | 0 | 1 | 0 | 0 |
| *state 3* | 1 | 0 | 0 | 0 | 0 | 0 | 1 | 0 |
| *state 4* | 0 | 1 | 0 | 0 | 0 | 0 | 0 | 1 |

in $e$. This asset costs $q_e$. In order to finance these expenses in period 1, we buy $q_e$ short-lived securities in period 0 that pay out in event $\psi_1(e)$. Therefore, this sequence of trades—buy $q_e$ units of event-$\psi_1(e)$ Arrow securities in period 0, and then in period 1, if event $\psi_1(e)$ occurs, buy one unit of event-$e$ Arrow security—is equivalent to buying an event-$e$ Arrow security in period 0. We see here that repeated trade of short-lived assets is a substitute for a complete market. This construction reduces the number of assets because only those Arrow securities must be traded that are immediate successors of the path that the economy takes through the event tree. But notice that, for this construction to work, we have to assume that the future equilibrium event-contingent asset prices (in the example $q_e$) are known to all agents in advance, just like future event-contingent spot prices must be known to all decision makers in a Radner equilibrium. If we are ready to swallow this assumption, no long-lived securities are needed to make the market complete.

Kreps (1982) has developed the idea that the same effect can be achieved using only long-lived assets. This actually works with fewer assets than dynamic completion with short-lived assets. Call an asset *long-lived* if it pays out only in the very last period $T$, or more generally (with an infinite horizon) if there is no $t$ such that the period $t'$ strip of the asset is zero for all $t' > t$. (A consol would be an example.) It is most easy to see how dynamic completion with long-lived securities works in the absence of uncertainty. To simplify even further, assume a finite horizon, $T < \infty$. There is only one asset, namely a risk-free $T$-period bond. The price of this bond when traded in period $t < T$ is denoted by $\beta_t$. Without uncertainty, a complete market means that wealth must be transferrable between any two periods. This can easily be achieved with the single asset, simply by buying the asset in one period and selling it in another. So, even though the complete market has $T$ dimensions, it can be spanned by repeatedly trading the single long-lived bond, for $T$ different prices, $\beta_0, \ldots, \beta_{T-1}$.

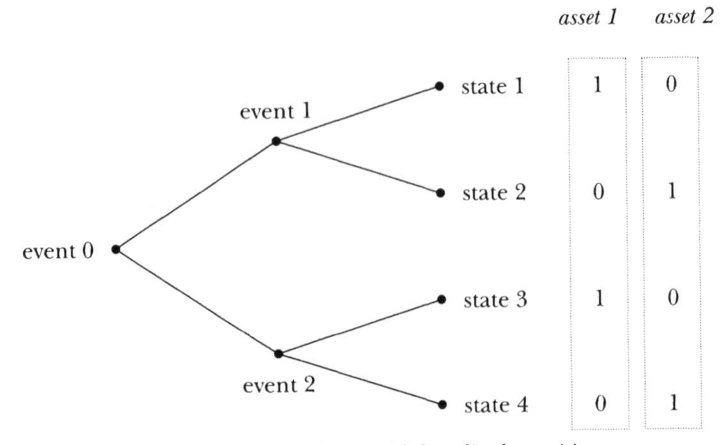


***Figure 6.1.*** *Completion with long-lived securities.*

The argument is more complicated if there is uncertainty. Consider a three-period model with the event tree depicted in Figure 6.1. There are four final states, plus two events in period 1. A complete market requires that payoff in the two events and the four states can be traded separately. This requires six Arrow securities. Yet this economy has only two securities. These two securities can be traded in period 0 and in the two events of period 1, so altogether there are six prices, $q_{j,e}$ for $j = 1, 2$ and $e = 0, 1, 2$. The easiest way to understand why this constitutes a complete market is by generating many short-lived assets from the few long-lived assets. Let "asset $[j, e]$" be the cash flow that results from buying asset $j$ in event $e$, and holding it for one period. This gives rise to six short-lived assets, which is potentially enough to span a complete market. For our example of Figure 6.1, the return matrix of these short-lived assets is shown in Table 6.1. This constitutes a complete market if the bottom-right 6-by-6 sub-matrix has full rank. This is the case if the sub-matrix shown in bold in Table 6.1 has full rank.

The components of this sub-matrix are the prices of the two long-lived assets in the two events of period 1. The market is dynamically incomplete if and only if the rank of this sub-matrix is less than 2, that is if $(q_{1,1}, q_{2,1})$ and $(q_{1,2}, q_{2,2})$ are collinear. In some special cases this will indeed be the case in equilibrium. Suppose that real endowment of each agent is the same in events 1 and 2, in states 1 and 3, and in states 2 and 4, respectively, and that the probability of reaching state 1 after event 1 is the same as that of reaching state 3 after event 2. Then clearly the sub-matrix is singular. This case, however, amounts to saying that events 1 and 2 do not really distinguish themselves in any relevant aspects. By the mutuality principle, in any efficient allocation consumption of everyone is the same in these two events.

To achieve efficiency, agents must be able to transfer purchasing power from event 0 to the two successor events proportionately; i.e., a dynamically quasi-complete market requires only unit rank for the sub-matrix.[8]

Of course, the sub-matrix may be singular even with arbitrary endowments, preferences, and probabilities, simply *by accident*. But this would be very exceptional. By slightly perturbing the cash flows of some assets, the endowments, or the utility functions, we can remove the accidental singularity of the sub-matrix (Kreps, 1982, proposition 3). Thus, we conclude that generically the market is indeed dynamically complete.

Interestingly, in our example just two long-lived assets are (generically) sufficient to span a complete market in an economy with four final states and two additional events. With more complicated event trees, two long-lived assets may not suffice. The number of long-lived assets that are needed to span a complete market is equal to the maximum number of immediate successor events of any non-final event in the game tree.[9] The intuition for this is quite clear: we need to be able to construct short-lived assets that completely span the immediate successor events of any event. We need $n(e)$ assets to do this for an event that has $n(e)$ immediate successors. Thus, in order to construct sufficiently many short-lived assets for all events, we need $\max_{e \in \mathcal{E}} n(e)$ long-lived assets. Duffie & Huang (1985) have extended Kreps's idea to continuous time. They show that a small number of long lived securities (provided they have the right payoff structure) constitute a dynamically complete market if they are continuously traded. The infinite dimensionality of the commodity space is matched with infinitely frequent trading.

### 6.2.2 Sequence of budget constraints and Ponzi schemes

If trade is sequential, and if at any point in time only a limited number of asset markets operate, there is no single budget constraint that restricts the consumption-portfolio path that an agent can afford. Rather, for every period there is one budget constraint that determines the wealth that the agent carries to the next period, and these sequential constraints are connected to each other through the law of motion for the individual wealth. But an infinite horizon opens up an unpleasant possibility. Without any further constraints it is possible for an agent, given market prices, to ensure

[8]Alternatively, we may simply treat events 1 and 2 as a single event, since they are the same in all relevant aspects.

[9]This is the greatest number of rays that fan out from any node in the game tree. In Figure 6.1 it is 2, so in this example two long-lived securities (with the right payoff structure) suffice.

infinite consumption by borrowing an arbitrarily large amount and rolling over the principal and the interest on this debt forever, without effectively repaying it. Such a scheme is known as a *Ponzi scheme.*[10] Despite the fact that all Arrow prices are positive and thus no arbitrage opportunities exist, it is nevertheless possible for an agent to circumvent the budget constraint altogether, destroying the existence of a utility maximum.

No uncertainty is needed to understand the mechanics of this, so consider an infinite horizon model with no uncertainty. The event tree is just a single ray. For each time to maturity, a discount bond is traded. There may also be other assets, but this is not relevant for us. Consider the maximization problem of a single agent (we drop the $i$ index to lighten notation) when only discount bonds are available,

$$\max \left\{ \sum_{t=0}^{\infty} \delta^t v(y^t) \;\middle|\; \begin{array}{ll} y^0 - w^0 \leqslant -\beta_1 z^1 & \\ y^t - w^t \leqslant z^t - \beta_{t+1} z^{t+1} & \text{for } t > 0 \end{array} \right\}. \tag{6.9}$$

$z^t$ is the number of period $t$ discount bonds in his portfolio, and $w^t$ and $y^t$ denote his endowment and consumption, respectively, in period $t$. Excess consumption $y^t - w^t$ in one period is financed either by maturing bonds ($z^t > 0$) or by selling next period's discount bonds short ($z^{t+1} < 0$). Of course, borrowing today will make the constraint more stringent tomorrow, but the infinite nature of the problem allows us to circumvent the budget constraint altogether.

Consider, for instance, a consumption stream where the agent consumes one unit of purchasing power in excess of his endowment *forever*:

$$(y^0, y^1, y^2, \cdots) := (w^0 + 1, w^1 + 1, w^2 + 1, \cdots).$$

This consumption stream can be financed with ever increasing debt: $z^1 := -\beta_1^{-1}$, $z^2 := (-1 + z^1)\beta_2^{-1}$, $z^3 := (-1 + z^2)\beta_3^{-1}$, etc. The budget constraint is satisfied, and the agent always pays back his debt including interest on time. Yet, he consumes more than what he owns. So why stop at one unit of purchasing power in excess of endowment? Why not two ... or ten, or ... ? The Ponzi scheme allows infinite consumption in every period, which is the same as saying that the decision problem has no solution.

Of course, Ponzi schemes can never be part of a general equilibrium, because every agent would accumulate infinite debt (as long as asset prices are finite) and the market would never clear. But that just means that the non-existence of the utility maximum translates into a non-existence of equilibrium.

[10]Charles Ponzi tried to use such a scheme in the 1920s. Initially he was quite successful, but eventually he was sent to jail for it.

To restore the coherence of the model, we need to rule out this possibility and impose a *no Ponzi scheme constraint* onto the individual's decision problem. A simple solution would be to impose a *no short-sale constraint*, $z^t \geqslant 0$, or a *no debt constraint*, $\beta_t z^t \geqslant 0$. But that would be too harsh, since it would shut down all short selling and therefore also all positive asset holdings by other agents in equilibrium (so as to satisfy the zero net supply equilibrium condition), and as a result would destroy Pareto efficiency (if the constraint is binding). A better way of ruling out Ponzi schemes is to require that all debt must be redeemed *eventually*,

$$\lim_{t\to\infty} \beta_t z^t \geqslant 0. \tag{6.10}$$

This *transversality condition* is the same constraint that would be imposed on the agents in a static model without reopening: the present value of consumption may not exceed the present value of endowment. This clearly rules out Ponzi schemes (Gilles & LeRoy, 1997). Magill & Quinzii (1996*a*) have shown that an equilibrium exists if we impose this constraint, and that efficiency is not in jeopardy.

### 6.2.3 Bubbles

When we compute the price of an asset through time (as in a model with reopening financial markets) in an infinite horizon model, something strange can happen. In addition to the *fundamental price*, which is given by the fundamental pricing formula of the "static dynamic" model Box 6.1, other solutions emerge. These other prices have an additional *bubble component* to them.

We study bubbles in the simplest case and discuss only bubbles on consols. The logic is the same with arbitrary assets, however. As for Ponzi schemes, no uncertainty is needed to understand the phenomenon, so we consider an infinite horizon model without uncertainty. Since there is no uncertainty, there is only a single event in every period, and therefore we write $M_t$ and $\mathbf{M}_t$ in place of $M_{\langle t\rangle}$ and $\mathbf{M}_{\langle t\rangle}$, respectively. Because of this, or equivalently following Box 6.1, the price of the consol in the "static dynamic" model is

$$q = \sum_{t=1}^{T} \mathbf{M}_t. \tag{6.11}$$

Consider now the re-opening of financial markets. Let $q_t$ denote the price of the consol *as traded at time* $t$, so $q_0, q_1, q_2, \ldots$ forms a time series of prices.[11] The price of the consol in period $t$ must be equal to the price of all remaining Arrow prices, so

$$\begin{aligned} q_0 &= \sum\nolimits_{t=1}^{T} \alpha_t \\ &= \sum\nolimits_{t=1}^{T} \delta^t \frac{v'(w^t)}{v'(w^0)}. \end{aligned}$$

At $t = 1$, the price of the consol is defined analogously: it is the sum of all marginal rates of intertemporal substitution,

$$\begin{aligned} q_1 &= \sum\nolimits_{t=2}^{T} \delta^{t-1} \frac{v'(w^t)}{v'(w^1)} \\ &= \delta^{-1} \frac{v'(w^0)}{v'(w^1)} \underbrace{\sum\nolimits_{t=2}^{T} \delta^t \frac{v'(w^t)}{v'(w^0)}}_{=q_0 - \delta \frac{v'(w^1)}{v'(w^0)}}. \end{aligned}$$

More generally,

$$q_{t+1} = \delta^{-1} \frac{v'(w^t)}{v'(w^{t+1})} \underbrace{\sum\nolimits_{\tilde{t}=t+2}^{T} \delta^{\tilde{t}-t} \frac{v'(w^{\tilde{t}})}{v'(w^t)}}_{=q_t - \delta \frac{v'(w^{t+1})}{v'(w^t)}}.$$

Therefore,

$$\begin{aligned} q_t &= \delta \frac{v'(w^{t+1})}{v'(w^t)} + \delta \frac{v'(w^{t+1})}{v'(w^t)} q_{t+1} \\ &= M_{t+1} + M_{t+1} q_{t+1}. \end{aligned}$$

We can solve this forward; i.e., we substitute the $t+1$ version of this equation into itself, which gives us $q_t$ as a function of $q_{t+2}$. Then we substitute the $t+2$ version of the equation, and so on:

$$\begin{aligned} q_0 = M_1 + M_1 q_1 = M_1 + M_1[M_2 + M_2 q_2] = \\ M_1 + M_1[M_2 + M_2[M_3 + M_3 q_3]] = \cdots \end{aligned}$$

With a finite horizon model we reach the solution in finitely many steps, i.e.

[11] Even though we use subscripts to denote the time period, $q_t$, and not the asset as before, $q_j$, no ambiguity should emerge.

$$q_0 = \underbrace{\sum_{t=1}^{T} \mathbf{M}_t}_{\text{fundamental value}} + \underbrace{\mathbf{M}_T \, q_T}_{\text{bubble}} . \tag{6.12}$$

If the horizon is infinite we have to take the limit,

$$q_0 = \underbrace{\sum_{t=1}^{\infty} \mathbf{M}_t}_{\text{fundamental value}} + \underbrace{\lim_{T\to\infty} \mathbf{M}_T \, q_T}_{\text{bubble}} . \tag{6.13}$$

The *fundamental value* is the price of the consol in the "static dynamic" model of (6.11). With repeated trading, there is an additional *bubble* component on top of the fundamental pricing formula of Box 6.1. If the horizon is finite, this bubble component must be zero, however, because the price of any asset is zero in the last period. The reason for this is that there is no further chance of consuming and generating utility. No-one wants to save at the eve of the world; thus, $q_T = 0$.

If the horizon is infinite, there is no obvious argument to rule out a bubble, and indeed it has been argued that the value of fiat money can be understood as a bubble (Bewley, 1980). Indeed, as long as there is no deflation, money is an asset that pays no dividends whatsoever. In real terms it even "pays" negative dividends if the inflation rate is positive, as was the case in every country for most of the twentieth century. So, clearly, the fundamental value of money as an asset is zero or even negative. Yet, money has a positive market value: people happily exchange very valuable real goods in exchange for pieces of paper. They do that because they expect to sell those pieces of paper later in exchange for other real goods. No-one thinks of holding on to the money forever. Thus, in the "static dynamic" model of section 6.1 there would be no place for money, because once you have bought it in period 0 there is no way of getting rid of it again, as financial (including cash) markets are closed forever. In the dynamic infinite horizon model, however, money can have value if there is a bubble on it.[12] More generally, it has been shown that bubble equilibria do indeed exist if we impose (6.10) to rule out Ponzi schemes (Kocherlakota, 1992). The bubble equilibria implement the same real allocation as the corresponding fundamental equilibria, so bubbles have no real effects, *as long as markets are complete.* If markets are incomplete, some equilibrium allocations may be supported only with a bubble (Magill & Quinzii, 1996*a*).

[12]Another interpretation of the value of money (and cash in particular) is that it provides access to a transaction technology that other assets do not. It facilitates the bilateral exchange of goods, and thus may be seen as a productive technology or a service rather than as a purely financial asset.

### 6.2.4 Martingales

A stochastic process $x_1, x_2, x_3, \ldots$ is said to be a *martingale* if

$$E\{x_{t+1}|x_t, \ldots, x_1\} = x_t,$$

and, by the law of iterated expectations,

$$E\{x_{t+t'}|x_t, \ldots, x_1\} = x_t \quad \text{for all } t' \geqslant 1.$$

In words, today's observation of $x$ is an unbiased estimate of all future realizations of $x$. Changes of $x$ are not forecastable. Note that this does not imply that higher moments (the variance, for instance) are unforecastable, so forecastable heteroscedasticity is not ruled out by the martingale.

Samuelson (1965) has argued that the discounted prices of financial assets are martingales if agents are risk neutral. The prices have to be discounted to accommodate the intertemporal rate of substitution. To be exact, it is not the prices *per se* that follow a martingale, but rather, as LeRoy (1989, page 1589) explains, the discounted value of a fund that holds an asset and keeps reinvesting the dividends back into the same asset. For this to work we have to assume bubbles away, so that we can use the fundamental pricing formula of Box 6.1.

To derive the martingale property under risk neutrality, we elaborate on (6.6):

$$\begin{aligned} q_{j,0} &= \sum_{t=1}^{T} \delta^t E\{r^j_{\langle t \rangle}\} = E\left\{\sum_{t=1}^{T} \delta^t r^j_{\langle t \rangle}\right\} \\ &= \delta E\left\{r^j_{\langle 1 \rangle} + \sum_{t=2}^{T} \delta^{t-1} r^j_{\langle t \rangle}\right\} \\ &= \delta E\{r^j_{\langle 1 \rangle} + q_{j,\langle 1 \rangle}\}. \end{aligned} \tag{6.14}$$

Consider a fund whose portfolio consists of $z_0$ units of asset $j$ and nothing else. The value of this fund today is $f_0 := q_{j,0} z_0$. Next period it will receive a (state-contingent) dividend $r^j_{\langle 1 \rangle} z_0$ and will use these dividends to purchase more of asset $j$, at (state-contingent) price $q_{j,\langle 1 \rangle}$, so it will then own the (state-contingent) amount $z_{\langle 1 \rangle} := z_0 + z_0 r^j_{\langle 1 \rangle}/q_{j,\langle 1 \rangle}$, which we rewrite as

$$q_{j,\langle 1 \rangle} z_{\langle 1 \rangle} = (q_{j,\langle 1 \rangle} + r^j_{\langle 1 \rangle}) z_0. \tag{6.15}$$

What is the expected discounted value of this fund tomorrow, $\delta E\{f_{\langle 1\rangle}\}$?

$$\begin{aligned}
\delta E\{f_{\langle 1\rangle}\} &= \delta E\{q_{j,\langle 1\rangle} z_{\langle 1\rangle}\} \\
&= \delta z_0 E\{q_{j,\langle 1\rangle} + r^j_{\langle 1\rangle}\} && \text{by (6.15)} \\
&= z_0 q_{j,0} && \text{by (6.14)} \\
&= f_0.
\end{aligned}$$

The discounted value $f$ of the fund is a martingale. This analysis can easily be extended to $E\{f_{\langle t\rangle}\}$ for arbitrary $t$. Notice that it is *not* the prices themselves, $q_j$, that are martingales: rather, it is the return rate of capital gains (change of $q_j$) plus dividends ($r^j$) that has the martingale property.

Equation (6.14) is not valid if the representative agent is risk averse. In that case, the funds' present value lacks the martingale property. Yet, LeRoy (1973) and Lucas (1978) have shown that using a different measure to compute the expectation, one that takes account of risk aversion, restores the martingale property.

By Box 6.1, the price of a risk-free bond is $\beta_t = E\{\mathbf{M}_{\langle t\rangle}\}$. As was done in Boxes 3.3 and 3.4, apply the definition of risk-neutral probabilities to the multiple-period setting,

$$\tilde{\alpha}_{\langle t\rangle} = \alpha_{\langle t\rangle}/\beta_t = \pi_{\langle t\rangle}\mathbf{M}_{\langle t\rangle}/\beta_t. \tag{6.16}$$

The second equality follows from (6.5). Clearly, $\sum_{e\in\mathcal{E}_t} \tilde{\alpha}_e = E\{\mathbf{M}_{\langle t\rangle}\}/\beta_t = 1$, so $\tilde{\alpha}_{\langle t\rangle}$ is a probability distribution. We denote expectations taken with respect to this probability by $\tilde{E}\{\cdots\}$. By definition, $\beta_t\tilde{E}\{x_{\langle t\rangle}\} = E\{\mathbf{M}_{\langle t\rangle}x_{\langle t\rangle}\}$.

With these preliminaries, we can now reformulate the fundamental pricing formula (Box 6.1):

$$\begin{aligned}
q_{j,0} &= \sum_{t=1}^{T} E\left\{\mathbf{M}_{\langle t\rangle} r^j_{\langle t\rangle}\right\} \\
&= E\left\{M_{\langle 1\rangle} r^j_{\langle 1\rangle} + \sum_{t=2}^{T} \mathbf{M}_{\langle t\rangle} r^j_{\langle t\rangle}\right\} \\
&= E\left\{M_{\langle 1\rangle} r^j_{\langle 1\rangle} + M_{\langle 1\rangle} \sum_{t=2}^{T} \left(\prod_{t'=2}^{t} M_{\langle t'\rangle}\right) r^j_{\langle t\rangle}\right\} \\
&= E\left\{M_{\langle 1\rangle}\left(r^j_{\langle 1\rangle} + q_{j,\langle 1\rangle}\right)\right\} \\
&= \beta_1 \tilde{E}\left\{r^j_{\langle 1\rangle} + q_{j,\langle 1\rangle}\right\}.
\end{aligned} \tag{6.17}$$

As before, we consider a fund that holds only asset $j$ and keeps reinvesting all dividends into this same asset. The value of this fund today is $f_0 = z_0 q_{j,0}$

if $z_0$ is the number of shares the fund owns today. We want to compute the expected discounted future value of this fund, but with two alterations: we will discount not with the representative's time preference, but with the risk-free interest rate instead, and we will use the "distorted" measure defined in (6.16) to compute expectations. Thus, we want to compute $\beta_1 \tilde{E}\{f_{\langle 1\rangle}\}$:

$$\begin{aligned} \beta_1 \tilde{E}\{f_{\langle 1\rangle}\} &= \beta_1 \tilde{E}\{q_{j,\langle 1\rangle} z_{\langle 1\rangle}\} \\ &= \beta_1 z_0 \tilde{E}\left\{q_{j,\langle 1\rangle} + r^j_{\langle 1\rangle}\right\} && \text{by (6.15)} \\ &= z_0 q_{j,0} && \text{by (6.17)} \\ &= f_0. \end{aligned}$$

The properly discounted (with $\beta_t$ instead of $\delta^t$) and properly expected (using the measure $\tilde{\alpha}_{\langle t\rangle}$ instead of $\pi_{\langle t\rangle}$) value of the fund is indeed a martingale. For this reason, the risk-neutral probability distribution $\tilde{\alpha}_{\langle t\rangle}$ is also called the *equivalent martingale measure*. As explained in Box 5.8, this measure is the same as the objective probability distribution if the representative if risk neutral, because then $\mathbf{M}_{\langle t\rangle} = \delta^t$, and thus $\tilde{\alpha}_{\langle t\rangle} = \pi_{\langle t\rangle}\delta^t/\beta_t = \pi_{\langle t\rangle}$. If the representative agent is risk averse, however, then $\tilde{\alpha}_{\langle t\rangle}$ is pessimistic, in the sense that it puts more weight on low-income states (and accordingly less weight on the high-income states) than $\pi$ does.

### 6.2.5 Rates of return

In the two-period model, we defined the gross return rate of an asset $j$ as

$$R^j_s := \frac{r^j_s}{q_j}.$$

This was perfectly appropriate because the asset was worthless after the second period. (In fact, there was no "after.") Similarly, we can define the return rate of an asset in a multiple-period model, *provided the asset pays out only at one point in time.* Let $j$ be an asset that pays out only in period $t$, so $e \notin \mathcal{E}_t$ implies $r^j_e = 0$. The per period gross real return rate of this asset in event $e \in \mathcal{E}_t$ is defined as

$$R^j_e := \left(\frac{r^j_e}{q_j}\right)^{1/t}.$$

This is perfectly appropriate because the asset is worthless after period $t$.

But now consider an asset that delivers at different points in time—a share, for instance, that you buy today for \$48 (= $q$). Tomorrow you will receive a dividend of \$3 ($= r$). It would not be correct to say that the gross rate of return of this share is \$3/\$48 = 0.0625, implying a net return rate of −93.75%. This is not sensible because the share does not expire after period 2. It will (presumably) deliver more dividends in the more distant future.

Without any further information, the return rate of an asset that delivers purchasing power at different points in time is not a well defined concept. But suppose that this asset is traded (and thus has a market price) in every period. For instance, the share we considered before that costs \$48 today may also be traded tomorrow for a price of, say, \$50. In that case we can compute the return rate of buying the share today and holding it for one period only. The cash flow of this plan is −\$48 today and \$50+\$3 tomorrow. Accordingly, the gross one-period return rate of this share is (\$50+\$3)/\$48 = 1.104, and the net return rate is 10.4%.

More generally, let $q_{j,e}$ denote the price of asset $j$ in event $e$. Let $R_e^j$ denote the average per period gross return rate of asset $j$ between today and event $e$ (in period $\tau(e)$). The gross per period return rate is defined as

$$R_e^j := \left(\frac{q_{j,e} + r_e^j}{q_{j,0}}\right)^{1/t}. \tag{6.18}$$

To understand what $q_{j,e}$ is we can use the logic of Box 6.1. Assuming bubbles away, $q_{j,e}$ is the marginal rate of substitution between consumption in all events after $e$, weighted with the cash flow that asset $j$ generates in these future events, and consumption in event $e$; that is to say,

$$q_{j,e} = \frac{\sum_{t=\tau(e)+1}^{T} E\{\mathbf{M}_{\langle t\rangle} r_{\langle t\rangle}^j \mid e\}}{\mathbf{M}_e}. \tag{6.19}$$

Using this, we can rewrite (6.18) as

$$M_e R_e^j = \frac{M_e r_e^j + \sum_{t=2}^{T} E\{\mathbf{M}_{\langle t\rangle} r_{\langle t\rangle}^j \mid e\}}{E\{M_{\langle 1\rangle} r_{\langle 1\rangle}^j\} + \sum_{t=2}^{T} E\{\mathbf{M}_{\langle t\rangle} r_{\langle t\rangle}^j\}}, \quad \text{for} \quad e \in \mathcal{E}_1. \tag{6.20}$$

Taking expectations over all events of period 1 yields a version of (5.31) for the first future period of the dynamic model,

$$E\{M_{\langle 1\rangle} R_{\langle 1\rangle}^j\} = 1. \tag{6.21}$$

Define the *discount bond yield to maturity*, or simply the *yield* $\rho_t$ as the per period gross interest rate of a risk-free discount bond that matures at $t$:

$$\beta_t =: (\rho_t)^{-t}, \quad \text{hence } \rho_t = \beta_t^{-1/t}. \tag{6.22}$$

This is analogous to (3.1) for the two-period model. We can now express (6.21) with the martingale measure, giving us (using (6.22))

$$\tilde{E}\{R^j_{\langle 1\rangle}\} = \rho_1, \tag{6.23}$$

which is the same as in Box 3.5.

This form does *not* carry over to $t > 1$, because cash flows in the periods 1 to $t-1$ affect today's price of the asset, $q_{j,0}$, but not the price in period $t$, $q_{j,\langle t\rangle}$. Formally,

$$\mathbf{M}_e\left(R^j_e\right)^t = \frac{\mathbf{M}_e r^j_e + \sum_{t'=\tau(e)+1}^{T} E\{\mathbf{M}_{\langle t'\rangle} r^j_{\langle t'\rangle} \mid e\}}{\sum_{t'=1}^{\tau(e)} E\{\mathbf{M}_{\langle t'\rangle} r^j_{\langle t'\rangle}\} + \sum_{t'=\tau(e)+1}^{T} E\{\mathbf{M}_{\langle t'\rangle} r^j_{\langle t'\rangle}\}}, \tag{6.24}$$

$$\Rightarrow E\left\{\mathbf{M}_{\langle t\rangle}\left(R^j_{\langle t\rangle}\right)^t\right\} \neq 1, \tag{6.25}$$

unless $r^j_{\langle t'\rangle} = 0$ for all $t' < t$. The reason for this failure is of course that this definition of the return rate fails to take into account the effect of reinvesting dividends into the asset. The contingent return rate of a fund that keeps reinvesting all cash flows into the asset $j$ is $f_{\langle t\rangle}/f_0$, using the notation of the previous section. The expectation of this, using the martingale measure, is constant and equal to the risk-free interest rate for all horizons, $\tilde{E}\{f_{\langle t\rangle}/f_0\} = \beta_t^{-1} = (\rho_t)^t$.

## 6.3 Models of the real interest rate

### 6.3.1 Cross section properties: The term structure of real interest rates

Risk-free bonds are an especially interesting application of the model because they measure only the equilibrium intertemporal price of consumption and are affected by risk considerations only indirectly. For that reason, bond prices for different times to maturity can carry much useful information about the expected future development of consumption per capita. We have seen this nexus in Box 5.9: higher expected growth tends to make present consumption relatively more valuable, thus increasing the real interest rate. In a multiple-period model, this insight translates into the statement that greater expected future growth makes interest rates with long maturities higher than interest rates with short maturities. Thus, we can try to estimate market business cycle expectations from such interest rates, and in fact these data are routinely used for forecasting and policy making.

To begin the analysis of the term structure of interest rates, consider a period $t$ discount bond. By Box 6.1, the price of such a bond is

$$\beta_t = E\{\mathbf{M}_{\langle t\rangle}\}, \tag{6.26}$$

which is equivalent to the expression for the two-period economy (5.29). The price of a consol is $\sum_t \beta_t$. The price of a coupon bond (with coupon $c$) is $\beta_t + c\sum_{t'\leqslant t}\beta_{t'}$. This demonstrates most clearly that consols and coupon bonds are nothing more than particular portfolios of discount bonds. It seems therefore appropriate to focus on discount bonds when analyzing interest rates, since they are simple and contain all the information on prices of all kinds of risk-free bonds.

Using the first-order conditions (6.3) we can express the yields associated with these bond prices in terms of aggregate data,

$$\rho_t = \delta^{-1}\left[\frac{E\{v'(w^{\langle t\rangle})\}}{v'(w^0)}\right]^{-1/t}. \tag{6.27}$$

The collection of all such interest rates, $(\rho_1, \rho_2, \ldots, \rho_T)$, is called the *term structure of interest rates* or the *yield curve.* It is the cross-section of all yields to maturity at a given point in time.

Let $g_e$ be the average per period growth rate of per capita consumption between today and event $e$, so $w^e/w^0 =: (1+g_e)^{\tau(e)}$. With this we can rewrite (6.27) as

$$\rho_t = \delta^{-1}\left[\frac{E\{v'((1+g_{\langle t\rangle})^t w^0)\}}{v'(w^0)}\right]^{-1/t}.$$

In the two-period model we derived an explicit approximate formula for the risk-free interest rate assuming CRRA utility, equation (5.38). This equation relates the interest rate to the time preference, the growth rate, and the coefficient of relative risk aversion. Uncertainty does not affect the equilibrium interest rate according to this equation, but this is only because the effect of uncertainty is second order and has disappeared in the approximation. We can perform the same approximation steps for the multi-period version of this equation. (That is, we assume CRRA utility, use the equilibrium SDF, take logs, and apply first-order approximations.) This yields

$$\ln \rho_t \approx \gamma E\{g_{\langle t\rangle}\} - \ln \delta, \tag{6.28}$$

which is only marginally more complicated than (5.38). We conclude from this that the yield curve is upward sloping if long-term expected growth exceeds short-term expected growth: the yield curve forecasts business cycles or, more precisely, measures expectations of business cycles.

Although (6.28) was derived from CRRA utility, we can draw conclusions from this equation about the shape of the yield curve even if we drop the CRRA assumption. Suppose the expected growth rate is positive and constant through time. Then expected consumption per capita is larger the further we go into the future. Suppose moreover that relative risk aversion is decreasing with consumption;[13] that is, for large $t$, the relevant value of $\gamma$ in (6.28) is smaller than from small $t$. As a result, the interest rates for long times to maturity will be smaller than those for short times to maturity. In other words, the yield curve is downward sloping.

**Box 6.2** ***Qualitative features of the term structure of interest rates***

If the representative agent is risk neutral, the term structure of interest rates is flat: $\rho_t = \delta^{-1}$ for all $t$. Suppose now that the representative agent is risk averse but there is no uncertainty.

- If aggregate endowment is constant through time (zero growth rate), the term structure is flat.
- If the growth rate of aggregate endowment is constant through time and the representative has CRRA utility, the term structure is flat.
- If the representative has CRRA utility and the growth rate increases (decreases) over time, the term structure is upward (downward) sloping.
- If utility is DRRA (IRRA) and there is a constant positive growth rate, then the term structure is downward (upward) sloping.

By using first-order approximations, we have shut off the effect of uncertainty, but Box 5.10 provides a hint. Suppose the representative agent is prudent ($v''' > 0$), expected growth is zero, but there is uncertainty. Then the interest rate will be lowest for those times to maturity for which the average per year growth rates $g_{\langle t \rangle}$ are subject to the greatest uncertainty. For instance, if uncertainty increases with the horizon, the yield curve is downward sloping; if uncertainty decreases with the horizon (say, because the period growth rate is mean reverting), then the yield curve is upward sloping.

[13]Remember that there is some empirical evidence for DRRA, see footnote 25 on page 92.

### 6.3.2 Time series properties: Expected term premia and the expectations hypothesis

In some sense, the term structure of the yields to maturity described in Box 6.2 compares incomparable things. It does not really answer the question of a borrower as to whether he should take a loan with a short or with a long maturity, or what the best investment horizon is for a person who wants to save. For instance, suppose you have some money that you will not need during the next four years, but will need afterwards. You could buy bonds with a four-year time to maturity. Suppose the yield of such bonds is 5% per year. Of course, if bonds can be traded not only today, but also four years from now, then you could also buy 10-year bonds instead, since their yield to maturity is, say, 7% per year. Because your plan is to use the money for other purposes four years from now, you will of course have to sell the 10-year bonds before they reach their maturity. Yet another alternative is to buy one-year bonds and roll over the investment four times when the bonds come due. There are thus three distinct strategies that would free up the invested capital after four years, and that we can therefore compare: (*i*) invest into four-year bonds; (*ii*) buy longer maturity bonds and sell them after four years; (*iii*) buy shorter maturity bonds and roll them over. The differences of the expected yields of these strategies are the *expected term premia.*

Note that, unlike the yield curve we have studied before (which is a cross-section of interest rates), a theory about expected term premia makes statements about how interest rates are expected to move in the future, so these are *time series models* of interest rates. The *expectations hypothesis of the term premium* is one such theory. It states that all three of the above strategies are equivalent on average; i.e., the expected term premia are nil. Yet, note that only strategy (*i*) is risk-free. The other strategies are risky because, in the case of (*ii*), the price of the long maturity bond after four years is not known, and, in the case of (*iii*), the price of the short maturity bond used for rolling over the investment is not known. Accordingly, these risky strategies should carry some risk premium, at least if their risk is correlated with aggregate risk. Thus, we can identify two cases in which the expectations hypothesis holds. The first arises if the risks of strategies (*ii*) and (*iii*) are uncorrelated with aggregate risk (for instance, because there is no aggregate risk, then the covariance is necessarily zero). The second case arises if the price of risk is zero, because the representative agent is risk neutral.

More formally, let $\beta_{e,t}$ be the price of a risk-free discount bond that is traded in event $e$ and that matures in period $t$, with $\tau(e) < t$. $\beta_{0,t}$ is the price of such a bond that is traded today. $\beta_{\langle t \rangle,t'}$, with $t < t'$, is a random variable consisting of all $\beta_{e,t'}$ for all $e \in \mathcal{E}_t$ that belong to period $t$. Thus, $E\{\beta_{\langle t\rangle,t'}\}$ is the unconditional expected value (i.e. given today's information) of the price that a discount bond maturing in period $t'$ will have in period $t$. Then, in analogy to (6.26), we can express the price of bonds conditional on future events as

$$\begin{aligned} E\{\beta_{\langle t\rangle,t'}\} &= \delta^{(t'-t)}\, E\left\{\frac{v'(w^{\langle t'\rangle})}{v'(w^{\langle t\rangle})}\right\} \\ &= E\left\{\left(\delta\frac{v'(w^{\langle t+1\rangle})}{v'(w^{\langle t\rangle})}\right)\left(\delta\frac{v'(w^{\langle t+2\rangle})}{v'(w^{\langle t+1\rangle})}\right)\cdots\left(\delta\frac{v'(w^{\langle t'\rangle})}{v'(w^{\langle t'-1\rangle})}\right)\right\} \\ &= E\{M_{\langle t+1\rangle}M_{\langle t+2\rangle}\cdots M_{\langle t'-1\rangle}M_{\langle t'\rangle}\}. \end{aligned} \tag{6.29}$$

To simplify, consider today's price of a bond that matures in two periods,

$$\begin{aligned} \beta_{0,2} &= E\{M_{\langle 1\rangle}M_{\langle 2\rangle}\} \\ &= E\{M_{\langle 1\rangle}\}E\{M_{\langle 2\rangle}\} + \operatorname{cov}(M_{\langle 1\rangle}, M_{\langle 2\rangle}) \\ &= \beta_{0,1}E\{\beta_{\langle 1\rangle,2}\} + \operatorname{cov}(M_{\langle 1\rangle}, M_{\langle 2\rangle}). \end{aligned} \tag{6.30}$$

$\beta_{0,1}E\{\beta_{\langle 1\rangle,2}\}$ is the expected price of the targeted cash flow (one unit of purchasing power in period 2) if it is financed with rolling over short-term bonds. We see that this strategy need not have the same (expected) cost as buying the two-period bond, $\beta_{0,2}$. The difference, $\operatorname{cov}(M_{\langle 1\rangle}, M_{\langle 2\rangle})$, is a risk premium. The expectations hypothesis is the assertion that this premium is zero.

More generally, the price of a $t$-period bond is

$$\beta_{0,t} = E\{\mathbf{M}_{\langle t\rangle}\} = E\{M_{\langle 1\rangle}\cdots M_{\langle t\rangle}\}.$$

If all $M_{\langle s\rangle}$ are pairwise uncorrelated, for $s = 0, \ldots, t$, this expression reduces to $\beta_{0,t} = E\{M_{\langle 1\rangle}\}\cdots E\{M_{\langle t\rangle}\}$.

**Box 6.3** ***The expectations hypothesis of the term structure***

The expectations hypothesis of the term structure states that expected term premia are zero. This hypothesis is true if and only if the per period SDF is serially uncorrelated [$\operatorname{cov}(M_{\langle s\rangle}, M_{\langle t\rangle}) = 0$ for all $(s,t)$, $s \neq t$]. In particular, the hypothesis is true if the SDF is not stochastic, either because the representative agent is risk neutral or because there is no aggregate risk.

We have seen in the previous section that risk neutrality also implies that the term structure is flat, $\rho_{0,t} = \delta^{-1}$. Moreover, this is true for all points in time, $\rho_{t',t} = \delta^{-1}$, so the term structure is also constant through time. As a result, the expectations hypothesis is trivially fulfilled: all interest rates are the same, they are not stochastic (either through time or across events), and they are equal to the rate of time preference.

Equation (6.6) is helpful in developing intuition for this finding. If the representative agent is risk neutral, we have

$$q_{j,e} = \sum_{t=t'+1}^{T} \delta^{t-t'} E\left\{ r^j_{\langle t\rangle} \;\middle|\; e \right\} \quad \text{for } e \in \mathcal{E}_{t'}$$

for an arbitrary asset, so the only source of price variation stems from event-contingent variations of $r^j$ and from the horizon. A risk-free discount bond does not have any cash flow variations. For a risk-free discount bond that matures in period $t^*$, the formula simplifies to

$$\beta_{j,e} = \delta^{t^*-t'} \quad \text{for all } e \in \mathcal{E}_{t'},$$

so the price is independent of the event $e$ and is an exponential function of the time to maturity $t^* - t'$.

Consider risk aversion now. Specifically, consider a CRRA representative agent. In this case, the one-period SDF is a function of the per capita growth rate only. The expectations hypothesis will be valid if today's growth rate contains no information about tomorrow's growth rate, for instance if log real per capita consumption is difference-stationary with white noise residuals. If, however, real per capita consumption is trend-stationary (with white noise errors), then the growth rates will be negatively serially correlated, because a high growth rate today (a boom) will boost consumption above trend and thus lead to weaker expected growth in the future. In that case the covariance term in (6.30) will be negative, and accordingly the term premium will be positive; that is, long maturity bonds will be cheaper (have a higher yield) than today's and tomorrow's expected short maturity bonds.[14] Another way to explain this is to say that a boom is bad news for future growth in that case (because of the negative serial correlation), so that interest rates will be low in a boom, and accordingly bonds will be expensive. Thus, long-term bonds that are sold before maturity are like "good weather assets": they are most valuable when you do not need it (during a boom). They provide no hedge against aggregate risk and are therefore cheap, which is tantamount to saying that the expected term premium is positive (LeRoy, 1982).

[14]Difference stationarity means that $\Delta \ln w^t$ is a stationary stochastic process. Here we require it actually to be white noise, so that today's growth carries no information about tomorrow's growth. Trend stationarity means that $\ln w^t - f(t)$ is stationary for some deterministic trend function $f$. See Harvey (1981) for details.

## 6.4 Portfolio selection

Financial planners often recommend that customers decrease the share of wealth invested into risky assets, such as equities, with age. The usual, but questionable argument to support such an advice is that equities carry less risk over a longer horizon. Yet, there may be a more sophisticated argument for such a strategy.

Consider a risky bet that is beneficial on average, like owning a share as opposed to a bond. Holding the equity for two periods is the same as taking this bet twice (if the returns to equity are serially uncorrelated, which we assume here). Since young people have presumably (at least in expectations) longer remaining life spans, it is optimal for a young investor to hold the equity, but for an old investor not to hold it, if and only if one such bet produces a negative expected utility (because it contains too little reward on average, given its risks) but two such bets produce a positive expected utility. Paul Samuelson has argued that, under some condition, this is impossible:

> Recalling a conversation a few years ago I offered some lunch colleagues to bet each $200 to $100 that the side of a coin they specified would not appear at the first toss. One distinguished scholar—who lays no claim of advanced mathematical skills—gave the following answer: "I won't bet because I would feel the $100 loss more than the $200 gain. But I'll take you on if you promise me to make 100 such bets." What was behind this interesting answer? He, and many others, have given something like the following explanation. "One toss is not enough to make it reasonably sure that the law of averages will turn out in my favor. But in a hundred tosses of a coin, the law of large numbers will make it a darn good bet. I am, so to speak, virtually sure to come out ahead in such a sequence, and that is why I accept the sequence while rejecting the single toss." (Samuelson, 1963, page 50f.)

Samuelson argues that this is a fallacious application of the law of large numbers. Indeed, it is true that the probability of coming out on the positive side increases with the number of tosses. In fact, as the number of tosses goes to infinity, you will gain *almost surely*. This is the law of large numbers. Yet, the potential loss—that is, the lower bound of the support of the payoff of a sequence of tosses—diverges to minus infinity as the number of tosses increases indefinitely. Samuelson then proves the following result:

> If at each income or wealth level within a range, the expected utility of a certain investment or bet is worse than abstention,

> then no sequence of such independent ventures (that leaves one within the specified range of income) can have a favorable expected utility. (Samuelson, 1963, page 53)

Of course, the range that Samuelson talks about must be unbounded if no limit is put on the maximum number of repetitions of the coin toss, since in his example each toss enlarges the range of possible payoffs by \$200 on the upside and \$100 on the downside. Thus, Samuelson's result says that, if the investor rejects a single instance of the bet at all wealth levels, then the investor also rejects any sequence of such bets.

Ross (1999) has recently pointed out that the assumption that the single bet be rejected at all wealth levels puts a strong restriction on the admissible utility functions. Whether you accept the lottery $[w - 100, 0.5; w + 200, 0.5]$ or not depends on your absolute risk aversion, since it is an additive risk. If you reject this bet at all wealth levels $w$, your absolute risk aversion must be constant. The consequence of this analysis is that a person with non-CARA utility may very well accept a long enough sequence of (on average) beneficial bets, while rejecting a single such bet. And since DARA is a very convincing assumption about human (and, remember, animal) behavior, there seems to be some logic in the advice to vary with age the amount of wealth invested in equity.

But the folklore financial advice concerns the *share* of wealth invested into equity. If an investor holds constant over several periods the share of wealth invested into risky assets, he faces a sequence of multiplicative risks, $[w(1 - d), 0.5; w(1 + u), 0.5]$ (assuming a binomial process for simplicity), where $d$ and $u$ are the percentage decrease or increase of the value of the equity over one period. Essentially, our conclusion with respect to additive risk and CARA utility functions translates into an equivalent statement about multiplicative risk and CRRA utility functions: an investor with CRRA utility function who rejects some multiplicative risk at all wealth levels also rejects an arbitrary sequence of such (serially independent) risks.[15] Mossin (1968) has concluded from this that myopic behavior is optimal for a CRRA agent: such an agent decides on the basis of current wealth and maximizes expected utility over one period, so that there is no intrinsic difference between young and old investors. When faced with the same prices, they will choose the same risk exposure independent of their remaining horizon. Mossin shows

[15] Ross's proof of the additive case (his theorem 1) is easily amended to the multiplicative case. Let $x$ be a random variable with strictly positive support. Let $P(n) := x_1 x_2 \cdots x_n$ be the product of $n$ draws of this random variable. We assume that the investor rejects a single instance of this multiplicative risk, $E\{v(wx)\} < v(w)$, for all $w$. Then $E\{v(wP(n))|P(n-1)\} = E\{v(wP(n-1)x)|P(n-1)\} < v(wP(n-1))$. Hence, $E\{v(wP(n))\} < v(w)$; that is to say, the investor rejects $n$ repetitions of this multiplicative lottery.

that CRRA is not only sufficient, but also necessary for myopia. An agent with DRRA, such as the power utility function with subsistence consumption that we have already encountered, $(x-\underline{x})^{1-\gamma}/(1-\gamma)$ with $\underline{x} > 0$, gives rise to a decreasing exposure to risk with age, as long as the real risk-free interest rate is positive. If the real risk-free interest rate is negative, the opposite is true. Gollier & Zeckhauser (1997) have recently analyzed this problem outside the class of HARA utility functions.

Empirically, the results on the age-contingent behavior of investors is mixed. Ameriks & Zeldes (2001) stress the identification problem that time, cohort, and age effects cannot be separated without imposing arbitrary assumptions, because age is by definition the difference between the observation period and the date of birth. A cohort effect, for instance, would be that investors born in the late 1900s or early 1910s may be more reluctant to hold equity because they made very negative experiences with these types of asset early in their career as potential investors. A time effect would be a general trend to put a larger or smaller share of wealth into equities. For instance, it is easily conceivable that during the bullish market of the 1990s investors became increasingly willing to participate in the stock market, thus increasing the share of wealth invested into equities over time. Different assumptions about the presence of time and cohort effects will obviously affect the assessment of age effects. Ameriks & Zeldes find that individuals tend to readjust their portfolios very rarely, so there is very strong inertia in individuals' portfolios. However, their data does not allow them to know whether the share of equity held by an investor is decreasing or constant or increasing as a function of age.

## Notes on the literature

LeRoy (1989) is an exceptionally lucid discussion of the martingale model and its relation to the efficient market hypothesis. Campbell (1995) provides a very accessible introduction to yield curves. A more in-depth textbook treatment is provided by Campbell et al. (1997, chapters 10 and 11), and Duffie (2001, chapter 7), who also features an extensive guide to the literature of this large field.

## Problems

**Problem 6.1** Consider an economy with a representative CRRA agent. Per capita endowment growth follows a random walk,

$$G_t = G_{t-1} + \varepsilon_t,$$

where $\varepsilon_t \sim N(0, \sigma^2)$ and $\mathrm{cov}(\varepsilon_t, \varepsilon_{t'}) = 0$ for all $(t, t')$. $G_t := \ln(w^t/w^{t-1})$ is the (stochastic) growth rate of per capita endowment between period $t-1$ and period $t$.

($a$) Compute the yield curve using (6.28). How does this depend on the current growth rate $G_0$?

($b$) Does the yield curve predict the business cycle?

**Problem 6.2** Redo problem 6.1, but assume instead that per capita endowment growth is difference-stationary with AR(1) disturbances,

$$G_t = \mu + \phi(G_{t-1} - \mu) + \varepsilon_t.$$

$\mu$ is the trend growth rate and $\varepsilon$ is white noise. Compute the yield curve. How does it depend on the current growth rate ($G_0$) and on the parameters of the model $(\gamma, \delta, \mu, \phi, \sigma^2)$? Are interest rates procyclical or countercyclical Does the yield curve predict the business cycle?

**Problem 6.3** Redo problem 6.1 once more, but this time assume that per capita endowment is trend-stationary; i.e.,

$$\ln w^t = \mu t + \eta_t, \qquad \eta_t := \phi\eta_{t-1} + \varepsilon_t,$$

where $\mu t$ is the log-linear trend. Accordingly, today's log endowment is equal to today's deviation from the trend, $\ln w^0 = \eta_0$. Compute the yield curve. How does this depend on the current deviation from trend ($w^0$) and on the parameters of the model ($\gamma$, $\delta$, $\mu$, $\phi$, $\sigma^2$)? Are interest rates procyclical or countercyclical? Does the yield curve predict the business cycle?

# 7
# Empirics and the puzzles

The time has come to confront the empirical evidence. In this chapter you will be told that the theory you have learned so far fails miserably when confronted with the data! The empirical failure of the model, whose most famous incarnation is the *equity premium puzzle*, was a great disappointment for the profession. But of course, scientists are not inclined to give up when an intellectual puzzle emerges. In hindsight, the puzzles have generated a rich research effort that has produced many new and interesting ideas.

## 7.1 Collecting the right data

### *7.1.1 The risk-free rate—$\rho$*

An asset is free of risk if the cash flow it delivers in the future is independent of the state of the world, $r_s^j = r_{s'}^j$ for all $s, s'$. This obviously rules out shares and all sorts of options. Furthermore, it rules out assets that imply a payment obligation by an agent who may default in some states of the world. For instance, a corporate bond is not risk free because the corporation that issued the bond could go bankrupt. Government bonds also are not truly default risk free—there have been defaults of sovereign debtors. Although government bonds of stable and well developed economies are close to being default risk free they are not truly risk free, because for an asset to be risk free it must deliver not just constant money cash flows, but constant purchasing power among states. Since inflation can be state dependent, the return of a government bond is not risk free in terms of the purchasing power of its cash flow. From the creditor's point of view, inflation is really much like partial default. Instead of receiving the cash necessary to buy one week's vacation, you can buy only four days' worth if inflation turns out to be high.

So, ideally, we would like to consider inflation indexed government bonds. But such bonds have become available only recently. Alternatively, we can consider bonds (or bills, or notes) with a short time to maturity, and subtract from their return rate the realized inflation rate. The advantage of this is that there is very little uncertainty about the inflation rate over the next few months. Thus, the nominal return rate minus the realized inflation rate (the ex post real return rate) is almost free of inflation risk and is close to the true real return rate.

### 7.1.2 *Stock indices: capital versus wealth*—$R$

The CCAPM is supposed to work with arbitrary assets, so in principle we could choose an arbitrary risky asset and use it to test the model. One specific asset that is at the center of much empirical research is a diversified portfolio of stocks, such as the stocks contained in the indices that are supposed to represent a significant part of the market (S&P 500, FTSE 100, Nikkei, DAX, CAC 40, SMI, etc). Most of these are capital indices: weighted averages of the prices at which the stocks contained in the respective index are traded.

But in order to compute rates of return, we have to add dividends. A capital index with added dividends is called a wealth index. It measures the wealth that an investor accumulates over time by holding the stocks contained in the index and reinvesting all dividends.[1]

### 7.1.3 *Endowment or output or consumption?*—$w$ *and* $g$

Our model is an exchange economy; it contains no production. The economy's output is therefore by definition equal to the consumption of the population, which in turn is equal to aggregate endowment. But if we want to do empirical work, we have to decide what to measure, because consumption is not the same as output or endowment.

Our asset pricing theory explains saving and risk taking in terms of marginal rates of substitution through time and across states. Consumption enters utility, and thus our model is "consumption based." But a more precise description would really be "utility based." Two questions emerge here: what do we mean by "consumption," and do things other than consumption enter utility as well?

[1] See Clarke & Statman (2000) for an attempt to make a wealth index out of the Dow Jones Industrial Average.

Regarding the first question, it should be clear that expenses for non-durable consumption goods, such as food and clothing, certainly are part of it. But durable consumption goods also enter utility. A refrigerator enhances the well-being of its owner for many years, a house for even longer. Similarly, government consumption may enter the utility of the agents. Better hospitals or better public television might increase your well-being, whether it is paid for by taxes or by private means.[2]

As for the second question, according to mainstream views, consumption is not the only element that enters people's preferences. Leisure is another prominent candidate. Thus, instead of measuring the covariance of return rates by consumption growth, we should measure it by a composite of consumption growth and leisure. Empirical investigations have detected that employment is largely procyclical (Kydland & Prescott, 1990), hence leisure is countercyclical. But that implies, we might think, that a composite good consisting of consumption and leisure is even less volatile than consumption alone. As a result, aggregate risk should be even smaller when measured by this composite good.

But wait: what really matters is marginal utility. Since leisure and consumption are negatively correlated, a composite good consisting of both components is less volatile than consumption alone *only if* consumption and leisure are substitutes. Only in that case does more leisure reduce the marginal utility of consumption. If, however, consumption and leisure are complements, then the composite good is more volatile than consumption alone, because in a slump consumption is small and leisure is large, and both contribute to a high marginal utility of consumption. Finally, if leisure and consumption are additively separable, then the amount of leisure has no effect on the marginal utility of consumption, and variations in consumption then have no effect on the SDF and thus none on asset prices.

The empirical evidence on this issue is inconclusive (Mankiw et al., 1985; Eichenbaum et al., 1988). The same thoughts apply to durables and their relation to non-durable consumption. It is quite clear that purchasing some durable today decreases the marginal utility of durables later, so durables are intertemporal substitutes. But it is not so clear that durables and non-durables are substitutes as well. The empirical evidence on this issue is weak as well (Mankiw, 1982). Maybe for that reason it has become accepted

[2]The gross benefit of such goods is independent of the way they are financed. The net benefit, of course, does depend on who pays for it.

practice, for the purpose of empirical asset pricing, to identify consumption with the expenses for non-durable consumption goods.[3]

### 7.1.4 Stylized facts

Several researchers have collected time series for testing the CCAPM. A prominent data set is the one compiled by Mehra & Prescott (1985). For the risk-free nominal interest rate, for dates from 1931 onwards they use the yield of 3-month government Treasury bills, for 1920–1930 they use the yield on Treasury certificates, and for dates prior to 1920 they use the yield on 60- to 90-day Prime Commercial Paper. From this they subtract the inflation rate of the consumer price index, thereby generating ex post real interest rates.

Although our asset pricing theory is supposed to be valid for arbitrary assets, it has become customary to focus on a broad portfolio of risky assets when trying to measure the market price of risk. Mehra & Prescott use the annual averages of the Standard & Poor 500, which is a nominal capital index of the stock market. They add a series of dividends of the S&P 500 stocks, and divide by the consumer price index (defined as the quotient of nominal aggregate consumption of non-durables and services divided by real aggregate consumption). This is the cumulative return on a risky asset. The real return rates on the risky asset are computed as the growth rate of this cumulative return.

Finally, endowment (consumption) growth is measured as the growth rate of real consumption of non-durables and services divided by total population.

The period studied by Mehra and Prescott is 1889–1978. They find the following statistics based on their data. Real per capita consumption grows 1.83% per year on average, with a standard deviation of 3.57%. The real risk-free return rate is 0.80% on average, with a standard deviation of 5.67%. The real return rate on the risky asset is 6.98%, with a standard deviation of 16.54%. Thus, the equity premium equals a hefty $6.98\% - 0.80\% = 6.18\%$ on average. The standard deviation of the equity premium is 16.67%.

Other popular data sets include Siegel's (1992; 1998; 1999) extended sample covering almost 200 years of American data. A comprehensive collection

[3]See Pakos (2003) for an exception. He assumes that the service flow from durables and consumption of non-durables are tight complements. Because the stock of durables can be adapted only slowly, a small variation of non-durable consumption (due to business cycle variation) implies a substantial change of marginal utility, thereby effectively making the agents highly risk averse to non-durable consumption fluctuations.

of international financial market data (unfortunately lacking consumption data) has been put together by Dimson, Staunton & Marsh (2002).

## 7.2 The equity premium puzzle

### 7.2.1 *One parameter for two equations*

The benchmark model of utility is the CRRA specification. We have seen in chapter 5 that this model implies a specific equation for the risk-free rate and for the risk premium,

$$\ln \rho \approx \gamma E\{g\} - \ln \delta, \tag{5.38}$$

$$E\{R^j\} - \rho \approx \gamma^* \mathrm{cov}(g, R^j), \tag{5.39}$$

with

$$\gamma^* := \frac{\gamma}{1 - \gamma E\{g\}}.$$

Remember that these are all real per capita measures, so we need to correct nominal interest and growth rates for inflation and population growth.

Equation (5.38) is not at all absurd. Table 7.1 contains a few back-of-the-envelope calculations. Column ($a$) reports the maximum $\gamma$ that is compatible with (5.38), assuming that $\delta \leqslant 1$. If $\delta < 1$, a smaller $\gamma$ is required. The Boskin commission (Boskin et al., 1996) suggested that true inflation was about 1.1% smaller than measured, which implies that the real interest rate and the real consumption growth rate both exceed official data. Column ($b$) reports the maximum $\gamma$ assuming $\delta \leqslant 1$ and correcting for the inflation bias. The results establish that (5.38) requires coefficients of relative risk aversion of between 0.4 and 2.5, which is compatible with our discussion in section 4.5.

The problem lies with equation (5.39),

$$\underbrace{E\{R^j\} - \rho}_{\text{large}} \approx \gamma^* \underbrace{\mathrm{cov}(g, R^j)}_{\text{small}}.$$

The historical return premium between an equity index and government bonds is rather large. The covariance between the return rate of equity and aggregate consumption is small simply because consumption is so smooth. This implies a huge $\gamma^*$.

Of course, one straightforward solution is to argue that our presumption that $\gamma$ should be small is not vindicated by the data. The empirical estimation

**Table 7.1.** *Relative risk aversion implied by equation (5.38).*

| country | sample | $\rho$ | $E\{g\}$ | $\gamma$ | |
|---|---|---|---|---|---|
| | | | | $(a)$ | $(b)$ |
| *Australia* | 1970.1 to 1998.4 | 1.02054 | 2.071% | 0.98 | 0.98 |
| *Canada* | 1970.1 to 1999.1 | 1.02713 | 2.170% | 1.23 | 1.14 |
| *France* | 1973.2 to 1998.3 | 1.02715 | 1.212% | 2.21 | 1.62 |
| *Germany* | 1978.4 to 1997.3 | 1.03219 | 1.673% | 1.89 | 1.52 |
| *Italy* | 1971.2 to 1998.1 | 1.02371 | 2.273% | 1.03 | 1.01 |
| *Japan* | 1970.2 to 1998.4 | 1.01388 | 3.233% | 0.43 | 0.57 |
| *Netherlands* | 1977.2 to 1998.3 | 1.03377 | 1.671% | 1.99 | 1.58 |
| *Sweden* | 1970.1 to 1999.2 | 1.01995 | 1.001% | 1.97 | 1.45 |
| *Switzerland* | 1982.2 to 1998.4 | 1.01393 | 0.559% | 2.47 | 1.48 |
| *U.K.* | 1970.1 to 1999.1 | 1.01301 | 2.235% | 0.58 | 0.71 |
| *U.S.A.* | 1970.1 to 1998.3 | 1.01494 | 1.802% | 0.82 | 0.88 |
| *U.S.A.* | 1947.2 to 1998.3 | 1.00896 | 1.951% | 0.46 | 0.65 |

*Note*: Column $(a)$ reports the maximum coefficient of relative risk aversion that is compatible with (5.38), assuming that $\delta \leqslant 1$. Column $(b)$ reports the same assuming that true inflation is 1.1% smaller than measured, as suggested by the Boskin report. The data for $\rho$ and $E\{g\}$ are taken from table 5 of Campbell (2003).

of (5.39) simply suggests that society is extremely risk averse. Rather than relying on our intuition for "reasonable" values of $\gamma$ we should take this evidence seriously (Kandel & Stambaugh, 1991). The problem with this argument is that it leads directly to the empirical failure of (5.38), as can be seen from Table 7.1. If $\gamma$ is very large, then not only do people dislike risk, but they also dislike intertemporal variations of consumption. As a result, there is a very strong incentive to smooth intertemporally. Yet, smoothing intertemporally is not possible in the aggregate. Therefore, if the economy grows ($E\{g\} > 0$) and if $\gamma$ is large, we should observe a very large risk-free rate. The bottom line is this: either we assume that $\gamma$ is moderately small, in which case (5.39) fails, or we assume that $\gamma$ is very large, in which case (5.38) fails. The true puzzle is that there is no $\gamma$ that satisfies these two equations simultaneously.

Note, however, that we do in fact have two parameters to match the risk-free rate and the risk premium: namely, the coefficient of relative risk aversion $\gamma$ and the time preference $\delta$. According to (5.39), we could set

$$\gamma^* := \frac{E\{R^j\} - \rho}{\operatorname{cov}(g, R^j)},$$

and compute $\gamma$ from this

$$\gamma := \frac{\gamma^*}{1 + \gamma^* E\{g\}}.$$

This yields a very large $\gamma$. Provided we are ready to accept such a large coefficient of risk aversion, we can make it compatible with the risk-free rate (5.38) by an appropriate choice of $\delta$:

$$\ln \delta := \gamma E\{g\} - \rho = \frac{\gamma^* E\{g\}}{1 + \gamma^* E\{g\}} - \rho.$$

The problem is that this requires $\ln \delta > 0$, hence $\delta > 1$. What does this mean? We could say that an agent with $\delta = 0$ is infinitely impatient, and does not care about the future at all, an agent with $0 < \delta < 1$ is moderately patient or impatient, and an agent with $\delta = 1$ is infinitely patient because he does not care about the timing of consumption. An agent with $\delta > 1$ is more than infinitely patient: he actually likes waiting! Surely this is not a feeling that is familiar to many of us (but see Benninga & Protopapadakis, 1990; Kocherlakota, 1990).

### 7.2.2 *Mehra and Prescott's binomial formulation*

Mehra & Prescott (1985)[4] use the standard general equilibrium model of chapter 5 and assume constant relative risk aversion. Since with this specification all asset prices are invariant to the *level* of endowments, we can just normalize today's endowment to unity. Only state-contingent growth rates are relevant.

Rather than work with many states, Mehra and Prescott simplify the model by assuming that there are only two states of the world, each with equal probability ($\pi_1 = \pi_2 = 1/2$). They calibrate the growth rates of these two states so that the mean and the variance of their binomial model fits the empirical mean and variance of U.S. per capita consumption growth. Specifically, set $g_1 := +5.4\%$ and $g_2 := -1.8\%$. Thus, mean per capita growth is $+1.8\%$,

[4]Mehra & Prescott were not the first to discover that implausibly high relative risk aversion was needed to make the theory compatible with the data. It was reported earlier by Grossman & Shiller (1981), Mankiw (1981), and Shiller (1982).

and the standard deviation is 3.6%, which almost matches the empirical moments of real per capita consumption.[5]

The approximate solutions of the risk-free rate and the equity premium we have developed, (5.38) and (5.39), are helpful if we work with many states. With just two states, there is really no point in using these approximations; we can easily compute the exact solutions. Note that $M_s = \delta(1+g_s)^{-\gamma}$ and $\beta = E\{M\} = \rho^{-1}$, thus

$$\rho = \frac{1}{\delta[(1+g_1)^{-\gamma} + (1+g_2)^{-\gamma}]/2} = \frac{1}{\delta[1.054^{-\gamma} + 0.982^{-\gamma}]/2}. \tag{7.1}$$

Besides the risk-free bond, Mehra and Prescott consider only one additional asset: a very broadly defined "equity"—a Lucas tree—whose cash flow equals state-contingent per capita consumption, $r_s := w^s$. The price of a risky asset is $q = E\{Mr\}$, so for this broad equity, using the equilibrium SDF of the CRRA specification, we have

$$q = \delta E\left\{\frac{w^{-\gamma}}{(w^0)^{-\gamma}} w\right\} = \delta E\{(1+g)^{1-\gamma}\}w^0.$$

The return rate is given by $R_s := w^s/q$; thus,

$$R_s = \frac{(1+g_s)w^0}{\delta E\{(1+g)^{1-\gamma}\}w^0},$$

and the expected return rate is

$$E\{R\} = \frac{E\{1+g\}}{\delta E\{(1+g)^{1-\gamma}\}} = \frac{1+(g_1+g_2)/2}{\delta[(1+g_1)^{1-\gamma} + (1+g_2)^{1-\gamma}]/2} = \frac{1.018}{\delta[1.054^{1-\gamma} + 0.982^{1-\gamma}]/2}. \tag{7.2}$$

[5] Mehra and Prescott use a Markov chain with a symmetric transition matrix. In this sense both states are equally likely. They assume, however, some serial correlation of endowments, meaning that the probability that the state tomorrow is the same as the state today need not be 0.5. Specifically, they set $g_1 := +5.4\%$ and $g_2 := -1.8\%$, and assume that the probability of switching states is 0.57, while the probability of remaining in the same state is 0.43, so endowments are negatively serially correlated. For simplicity, we disregard serial correlation here.

Subtracting (7.2) from (7.1) yields the equity premium,

$$E\{R\}-\rho=\frac{1.018}{\delta[1.054^{1-\gamma}+0.982^{1-\gamma}]/2}-\frac{1}{\delta[1.054^{-\gamma}+0.982^{-\gamma}]/2}. \qquad (7.3)$$

Using (7.1) and (7.3), Mehra & Prescott plot the risk-free rate against the equity premium, varying $\delta$ and $\gamma$. They conclude that they can justify a risk premium of at most 0.35% with the theoretical model if they constrain $\delta \leqslant 1$, $\gamma \leqslant 10$, and $\rho \leqslant 1.04$.[6] Figure 7.1 is an extended version of figure 4 of the Mehra–Prescott paper that contains these data. All points below the lines are combinations of interest rates and equity premia which can be predicted by the model by an appropriate choice of $\delta$ and $\gamma$. Comparing these admissible regions with the historical data, it becomes apparent that there is no way to make this model fit the data.[7]

### 7.2.3 Hansen–Jagannathan bounds

An alternative view of the equity premium puzzle was given by Hansen & Jaganathan (1991). They use the CCAPM to put a bound on the volatility of the SDF. Observe that by definition

$$\operatorname{cov}(-M, R^j)=\sigma_M\cdot\sigma_{R^j}\cdot\operatorname{corr}(-M, R^j),$$

where $\sigma$ denotes the standard deviation and "corr" is the correlation coefficient. From this and the first line of the equation in Box 5.11, we have

$$\underbrace{\frac{E\{R^j\}-\rho}{\sigma_{R^j}}}_{\text{Sharpe ratio}}=\underbrace{\operatorname{corr}(-M, R^j)}_{\leqslant 1}\cdot\frac{\sigma_M}{E\{M\}}\leqslant\frac{\sigma_M}{E\{M\}}=\rho\sigma_M. \qquad (7.4)$$

The Sharpe ratio (Sharpe, 1966) measures the price of risk. Since the correlation coefficient cannot exceed one, the coefficient of dispersion of the SDF, $\sigma_M/E\{M\}$, puts a restriction on the maximum price of risk. Put the other way around, the large Sharpe ratio we observe in the market implies a large volatility of the SDF.

[6] $\gamma = 10$ is certainly an outrageously large number, but the bound on $\gamma$ is actually not binding. The maximum premium subject to $\rho \leqslant 1.04$ and $\delta \leqslant 1$ materializes if $\delta = 1$ and $\gamma = 2.5$. If we allow the interest rate to go up to 6%, then the maximum premium is achieved with $\delta = 1$ and $\gamma = 4.0$. The equity premium is then 0.5%. With $\delta \leqslant 1.05$ and $\rho \leqslant 1.06$, the premium becomes 1.2% if $\gamma = 9.3$.

[7] An Excel file containing a program for computing bounds as shown in Figure 7.1 can be downloaded from the book's website.

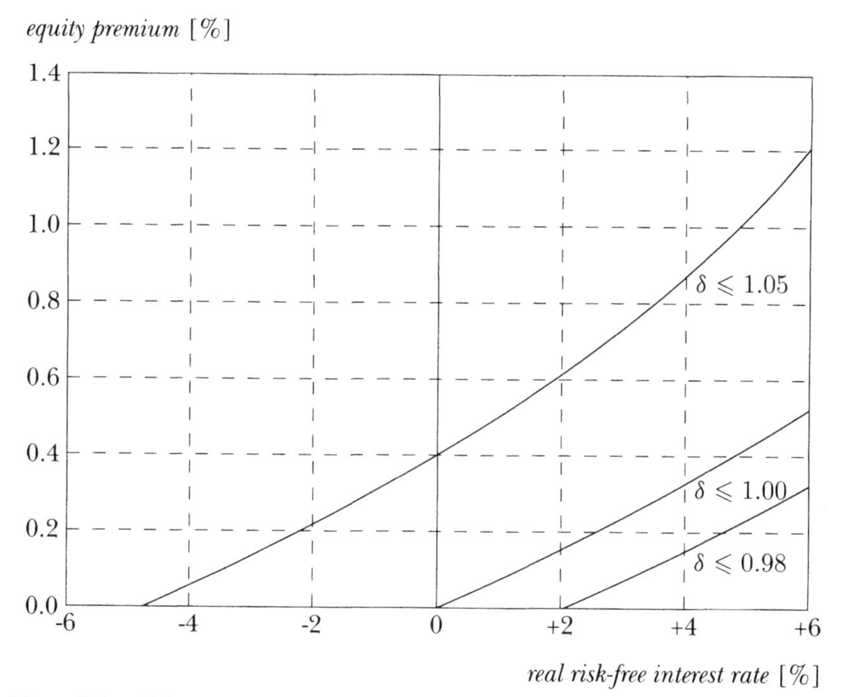


***Figure 7.1.*** *Mehra and Prescott's (1985) plot (based on model without serial correlation).*

To a first-order approximation, $\sigma_M$ equals $\gamma\sigma_g$.[8] Thus,

$$\text{Sharpe ratio} \leqslant \rho\gamma\sigma_g. \tag{7.5}$$

We know that the right-hand side is small in the data. According to the Mehra–Prescott data, $\rho = 1.008$ and $\sigma_g = 3.57\%$, but the Sharpe ratio of the risky asset they study (S&P 500 including dividends) is $6.18\%/16.54\% = 0.37$. Thus, $\gamma \approx 10$ is required to make (7.5) compatible with the data. And even though this is much greater than what seems reasonable, it is only a lower bound. Since consumption growth and return rates of the S&P 500 are hardly correlated, the $\gamma$ that makes the theory hold has to be multiplied accordingly, thereby reaching ridiculous proportions.

The smoothness of consumption growth together with the assumption of moderate risk aversion imply a small volatility of the SDF. Yet, the high

[8]Let $x$ be a random variable with values in the neighborhood of 1; then a first-order Taylor approximation reveals that $\text{var}(x) \approx \text{var}(\ln x)$. Applied to our problem, this implies $\text{var}((1+g)^{-\gamma}) \approx \text{var}(-\gamma\ln(1+g)) \approx \gamma^2\text{var}(g)$; hence $\sigma_M \approx \gamma\sigma_g$.

Sharpe ratios observed in the data suggest a very volatile SDF. The incompatibility of these statements is an alternative way of stating the equity premium puzzle.

### 7.2.4 Mean reversion

We know from (6.14) and (6.17) that there is no reason to expect asset prices (even if corrected for dividends) to follow a martingale. They are a martingale only with respect to the martingale measure, not with respect to the objective process governing the evolution of the states. Empirically, equity returns are positively autocorrelated over a short horizon, but negatively autocorrelated over a long horizon (Fama & French, 1988; Poterba & Summers, 1988). Bad times are likely to be followed, on average, by better times. That implies that stocks are actually less risky for long-term investors than what the one-period standard deviation of the return rate suggests.

To understand this, suppose that return rates were not serially correlated. Consider then the version of (7.4) for an investor with a $T$-period horizon. The expected equity premium is just $T$ times the one-period expected premium, $T(E\{R^j\} - \rho)$.[9] The variance also grows linearly with the horizon, implying that the standard deviation grows with the square root, $\sqrt{T}\sigma_{R^j}$. The $T$-period version of (7.4) is therefore

$$\frac{T(E\{R^j\} - \rho)}{\sqrt{T}\sigma_{R^j}} \leqslant \rho\sqrt{T}\sigma_M, \tag{7.6}$$

which is independent of $T$ and thus identical to (7.4).

Negative serial autocorrelation has no effect on the expected return rate, but it does affect its standard deviation. It implies that the standard deviation of the return rate is actually smaller than $\sqrt{T}\sigma_{R^j}$ if $T$ is large enough. Accordingly, the Sharpe ratio increases faster with $T$ than (7.6) suggests. As a result, the Hansen–Jagannathan bound becomes more difficult to fulfill as the horizon lengthens. The puzzle becomes worse, because even more risk aversion is required to satisfy the bound.

How important is this effect quantitatively? Poterba & Summers (1988, p. 36) report that "eight-year returns are about four rather than eight times as variable as one-year returns." But this result applies only to U.S. data from 1926 to 1985 (see their table 2). The result becomes much weaker when extending the sample backwards. For data covering 1871 to 1985

[9] This is exact only if we use continuously compounded return rates. For discrete return rates, the exact formula is $E\{(R^j - \rho)^T\}$. To a first order approximation, the two formulas are the same.

they find variance ratios of about 0.8, implying that the standard deviation of eight-year returns is about 90% of what it should be, based on the one-year standard deviation (see their table 3). The authors also extend their analysis to other countries, with mixed results. For some countries they find evidence of strong negative autocorrelation (Colombia, Switzerland), for some they find no serial correlation (Finland, South Africa), and for one country (Spain) they find evidence of positive serial correlation even at the eight-year horizon (see their table 4).

A fair conclusion therefore would be that negative serial correlation does indeed make the puzzle worse in theory, but the empirical evidence is sufficiently weak that we may be allowed to disregard it.

### *7.2.5 Production*

It should also be noted that production was not part of our model. We have worked with exchange economies only. In our model people are simply forced to consume their endowment in the aggregate. Introducing production (with capital as an input) into the model frees up the equality between aggregate endowment and aggregate consumption. There can be aggregate saving, which is invested into productive capital—something that is impossible in an exchange economy. Consumption becomes an endogenous variable, just like prices.

Rouwenhorst (1995) has noted that the endogeneity of consumption can make the equity premium puzzle *harder* to solve, because any increase in the effective coefficient of risk aversion, whether by introducing habits[10] or any other device, will also make consumption smoother. More fundamentally, production allows us to get rid of some of the aggregate risk by shuffling capital between states. Thus, if aggregate consumption is subject to less risk, the equity premium will be smaller. A model with production will therefore need to assume that capital adjustments are costly in order to explain the large equity premium. Jermann (1998, page 258f.) put it best:

> with no habit formation, marginal rates of substitution are not very volatile since people do not care very much about consumption volatility; with no adjustment costs, they choose consumption streams to get rid of volatility of marginal rates of substitutions. They have to both care and be prevented from doing anything about it.

[10]See section 8.2.3.

Consequently, Jermann finds that a real business cycle model that features either habit formation or capital market frictions cannot explain the equity premium, whereas a model that features both can.

The extent to which production is able to reduce aggregate risk and thereby affect asset pricing depends essentially on how easily the production technology allows transformation of output through time and across states. A production technology that allows easy transformation through time has an effect on the interest rate because it smoothes the intertemporal rate of substitution. But a major effect on the risk premium would be obtained only if the production technology also allowed for transformation across states of nature. A possible solution to the equity premium puzzle and the risk-free rate puzzle may therefore lie in the introduction of a production technology that allows for easy intertemporal substitution, but not for easy transformation across states (see Cochrane, 2001, p. 483).

## 7.3 Alternative interpretations of the data

One strategy of resolving the puzzle is to say that it does not exist. The data, so the story goes, do not truly reveal the existence of a puzzle. Rather, it is our interpretation of the data that is at fault.

Several attempts in this direction are discussed here. We will see that it is indeed possible to reduce the measured equity premium by alternative interpretations of the data, but the equity premium remains significantly greater than what can be reconciled with the theory, at least for the data up to 1980. Since then, the expected equity premium seems to have declined considerably.

### *7.3.1 Siegel's extended sample*

Siegel (1992) has argued that Mehra & Prescott's sample from 1889 to 1979 covered an exceptional period.[11] He argues that the risk-free interest rate was substantially lower between 1926 and 1980 than the long-term historical average owing to unanticipated inflation after World War II and in the 1970s. Ex post real interest rates, so the argument goes, are therefore biased estimates of the real returns that investors expected during that time. This argument is certainly valid for long-term bonds—inflation is easily able to wipe out the value of non-indexed long-term bonds. But this argument is not fully convincing with respect to short maturities. The nominal yields of

[11] See also his book on the topic: Siegel (1998), and an update in Siegel (1999).

short maturities continually adjust to expected inflation, and it seems unlikely that there is much surprise about the inflation rate over short horizons. This is precisely why we use assets with a short time to maturity to measure real interest rates. Thus, while it is true that inflation soared after World War II and in the 1970s, it is not clear why *real* return rates of short-term assets should have declined.

Based on previous work by Schwert (1990), who had pieced together various time series, Siegel extended the sample to almost two hundred years, spanning the period from 1802 to 1998. He also corrected Mehra & Prescott's measurement of the risk-free rate for the period 1889–1920. They used the Prime Commercial Paper rate, which Siegel corrected for a risk premium. For Siegel's whole sample the average real return rate of stocks was 7.0%, which is equal to Mehra & Prescott's estimate for their shorter sample. The real return on risk-free bills, however, was 2.9%, significantly larger than Mehra & Prescott's estimate of 0.8%. Because of this, the equity premium measured by Siegel (1999) is 4.1%, as opposed to almost 6.2% reported by Mehra & Prescott (1985).

### *7.3.2 Unobserved disaster state and survival bias*

The equity premium puzzle basically says that the price of risk is much higher than what can be justified by our beliefs about the behavior of people facing uncertainty. Rietz (1988) was the first to advance the idea that it is not that the price of risk that is high, but that the effective risk is much larger than what we measure. He entertains the idea that there is a disaster state in which endowment falls dramatically. This state, however, has a very small probability, which is why it was not observed. Krebs (2001) demonstrates that, by adding personal disaster states to the model (one for each agent), the CCAPM retains no testable hypothesis whatsoever, meaning that all data are compatible with the model, and the model cannot be falsified. The theory is "saved," but it is also without content.

Adding such a third disaster state to Mehra & Prescott's binominal formulation clearly increases the risk and therefore the equity premium, without increasing the price of risk. Rietz calibrates a three-state model which generates interest rates and equity premia that are comparable to the ones reported by Mehra & Prescott. But his third "disaster" state is always very extreme. For instance, the following parameters would do the trick (cf. Rietz's table 3): the representative agent has a coefficient of relative risk aversion somewhat in excess of 5 (still high!); he is rather impatient ($\delta < 0.9$); and every year, with 0.3% probability, 50% of output is destroyed. The problem with this construction is that it is very difficult to test empirically, and Rietz's idea clearly does not convince everyone (Mehra & Prescott, 1988).

Significant catastrophes, however, have been observed outside the United States. Many financial markets worldwide experienced more or less complete breakdowns, so the question is whether the U.S. market really is representative. Most of the research on the puzzle focuses on U.S. data. This is certainly due to the fact that the United States is the most successful economy today. As a result, most research economists work in the United States, and U.S. data offer the longest observed sample. But a hundred years ago it was not so clear that the American market would enjoy such a rosy future. As Cochrane (1997, page 7) noticed,

> perhaps it was not in fact obvious in 1945 that rather than slipping back into depression, the U.S. would experience half a century of growth never seen before in human history. If so, much of the equity premium was unexpected; good luck.

In hindsight, investing in American stocks was very profitable. But if the success of the American market was not fully expected, the expected rate of return on stocks was smaller than it turned out to be. In other words, the historic experience overstates the expected performance of American stocks, and underestimates the expected performance of less lucky markets, such as those of Germany or Japan. This is the survival bias. If we study only the market that turned out to be successful, we miss an important source of loss (Brown et al., 1995).

Siegel (1998) has constructed return series for British, German, and Japanese stocks for the period of 1926–1997. Comparing this with the performance of American stocks, he concludes that the performance of German stocks fell 60 basis points short of American ones, that of British stocks was 100 basis points, and that of Japanese stocks 380 basis points worse than American stocks. This clearly justifies the hypothesis of a survival bias.

But Siegel also claims that the survival bias cannot explain why the true equity *premium* should be overestimated by the historic data. It is true that realized returns of American stocks exceeded expected returns because of the survival bias. But all economies whose financial markets experienced serious disruptions experienced very high rates of inflation, some even hyperinflation. This hurt bond-holders much more than stock-holders. As Siegel (1999, page 13) put it,

> Although stock returns may be lower in foreign countries than in the U.S., the real returns on foreign bonds are substantially lower. Almost all disrupted markets experienced severe inflation, in some instances wiping out the value of fixed-income

> assets. ... It is my belief that if one uses a world portfolio of stocks and bonds, the equity *premium* will turn out higher, not lower than in the U.S."

And in Siegel (1998, page 26), he writes,

> The fact that stocks, in contrast to bonds or bills, have never offered investors a negative real holding period return yield over periods of 17 years or more is extremely significant. Although it might appear to be riskier to hold stocks than bonds, precisely the opposite is true: the safest long-term investment for the preservation of purchasing power has clearly been stocks, not bonds.

This argument basically says that historically, stocks have provided much better insurance against inflation than bonds, so "risk-free" bonds are actually riskier than risky stocks in this respect.[12] This is especially true for bonds with long times to maturity. Correcting for the risk embodied in bonds would make the true equity premium even larger.

This argument is clearly not valid if we measure the risk-free rate with short-term maturities. Except for hyperinflationary states, there is not much uncertainty about inflation over the next month. Thus, ex ante real rates are almost identical to ex post real rates. The argument has much more power if we work with long-term bonds. Non-indexed long-term nominal bonds are indeed very risky assets owing to unexpected inflation.

Recently, however, inflation-indexed bonds issued by the U.S. Treasury have become available. Such *Treasury Inflation Protected Securities*, so-called TIPS, are bonds whose cash flow is indexed to the price level. These are usually coupon bonds, many with long times to maturity. Siegel (1999) reports that they yield about 4%, which is significantly more than historic real ex post yields of non-indexed bonds. Indexed bonds are not subject to inflation risk, so we can take this 4% as an accurate measurement of the real risk-free interest rate.[13] Subtracting the 4% from Siegel's estimate of the long-run real return of American stocks of 7% decreases the equity premium of the U.S. market to 3%. Taking into account that the expected real return of stocks is probably smaller than 7% because of the survival bias decreases the true equity premium further.

[12]See Danthine & Donaldson (1986) for a theoretical model in which stocks are a perfect hedge against inflation that is due purely to monetary expansion.

[13]See http://www.publicdebt.treas.gov/gsr/gsrlist.htm. TIPS actually also contain an option feature. At maturity the bonds are redeemed at either the inflation-adjusted original principal or the original principal, whichever is greater. TIPS therefore provide insurance in nominal terms (over-insurance in real terms) for the unlikely event of an overall deflation over their life span.

### 7.3.3 *Forward-looking return rates*

Our asset pricing relationships concern expected values: the risk-free interest rate is a function of *expected* consumption growth, and the *expected* equity premium is a function of the covariance of consumption growth and the stochastic discount factor. Yet, we test these relationships work with historical averages. One reason for the puzzle may therefore be that the historical average equity premium is an imprecise or even distorted proxy for the expected premium. The survival bias argument mentioned before is based on such a reasoning. Using TIPS instead of the ex post real interest rate is another example in the same spirit.

One obvious way of measuring expectations is by asking professionals. Welch (2000) reports that popular views about the equity premium are extremely optimistic (or, rather, were optimistic in the second half of the 1990s). Surveys performed between October 1997 and November 1999 by the *New York Times*, *Fortune*, and *Gallup/Paine-Webber* report expected premia of between 16% and 22%! Welch conducted two surveys himself, but he restricted participation to academic financial economists. His first survey took place end of 1997 (226 respondents), the second about one and a half years later (112 respondents). His results indicate that academic financial economists are far more conservative than the broad public. The large chunk of forecasts for the 30-year horizon equity premium was between 4% and 11% (the minimum was −2%, the maximum 15%), and the median was 7.1%. The results of the two surveys differed only marginally.

Welch (2001) has recently updated his survey and conducted a third one in August 2001, after the stock market had started to decline. This time 597 subjects responded, 510 of which identified themselves as finance or economics professors (only these were kept for the analysis). This time the forecasts were more pessimistic. The 30-year equity premium forecast of all respondent was 5% on average, the median was 5.5%. Of those responding, 112 reported having participated in the earlier survey. The mean and median of the 30-year equity premium forecast of this sub-group was exactly the same as that of all respondents together.

It is not too courageous a hypothesis to suggest that the recent events that had affected the stock market in the meantime directed the change of respondents' long-term forecasts. Expectations seem to be driven much more by history than by theory.

### 7.3.4 *The equity size puzzle*

Welch (1999) has forcefully argued that the law of motion of market capitalization provides a good reason for not expecting such a large equity premium to pertain forever. His argument is that a large premium will soon cause aggregate returns on stocks to exceed GDP. He aptly calls this the *equity size puzzle.* The argument is simple: market capitalization is driven by the following law of motion,

$$K_{t+1} = R_t K_t - L_t. \tag{7.7}$$

$K$ is the total value of stocks, $R$ is the return rate (either in the form of capital gains or paid out as dividends), and $L$ is net outflows (or *leakage*) out of the stock market. Leakage is zero if all dividends are reinvested into stocks. It is positive if some dividends are consumed rather than invested or if firms buy back stock, it is negative if firms issue new shares. Suppose that leakage is a constant share of market capitalization, $L_t := \lambda K_t$; then market capitalization grows at a rate $R_t - \lambda$. Suppose further that potential GDP grows at some constant rate $g$, $Y_{t+1} = gY_t$. Let $k_t := K_t/Y_t$ denote the capitalization–GDP ratio. Then, from (7.7),

$$gk_{t+1} = (R_t - \lambda)k_t. \tag{7.8}$$

This difference equation is unstable if $R_t - \lambda > g$. In this case, the capitalization–GDP ratio increases without bounds and total return on stocks eventually exceeds GDP. While this may be possible sporadically, surely aggregate returns cannot exceed GDP forever. To avoid this, the return rate on equity is bounded above by the growth rate of the economy plus leakage. More generally, Welch's argument implies that the population average return rate of *any* asset is bounded above by the growth rate of the economy plus leakage out of this asset.

For example, if the potential GDP growth rate is, say, 2%, the leakage out of the stock market is 2.5% annually (as estimated by Welch), and the real risk-free interest rate is 3%, then the maximum long-run equity premium is $2\% + 2.5\% - 3\% = 1.5\%$. A persistently higher premium is possible only if potential growth of the economy accelerates, if leakage out of the stock market increases, or if the real interest rate decreases. However, long-run GDP growth and the interest rate are related by (5.38). Unless $\gamma$ is substantially different from one (which does not seem reasonable, section 4.5), the net effect of potential growth on the long-run equity premium is small. Therefore, a persistently large equity premium requires an increased leakage out of the stock market. Are respondents who report a 7% long-run expected premium (or even a 22% premium) aware of this?

### 7.3.5 The recent decline of the equity premium

No strong consensus has emerged yet about the true size of the equity premium. This is still an intensely discussed matter among professional economists and practitioners. Siegel (1992) has argued that Mehra & Prescott's (1985) estimate of the equity premium may be exaggerated because the 90-year period on which they based their calculations was, though quite long, still somewhat unusual. By going further back into the past, he was able to reduce the average equity premium significantly.

The idea that the data underlying the Mehra–Prescott study are exceptional is also verified by the fact that the expected equity premium has recently declined (or shall we say, *normalized*?). Fama & French (2002) have recently made this point. The rate of return on an asset is given by the dividend it pays plus the capital gains (change of market price), divided by the purchasing price. From (6.18), we can write

$$R_t := \frac{r_t}{q_{t-1}} + \frac{q_t}{q_{t-1}}, \tag{7.9}$$

where $R_t$, $r_t$, $q_t$ denote realized values. Taking averages over many periods, we can write

$$\frac{1}{T}\sum_{t=1}^{T} R_t \approx \frac{1}{T}\sum_{t=1}^{T} \frac{r_t}{q_{t-1}} + \frac{1}{T}\sum_{t=1}^{T} \frac{q_t}{q_{t-1}}. \tag{7.10}$$

Now suppose that log dividends and log market prices are cointegrated, so that the price–dividend ratio is stationary. Then the return through capital gains, $q_t/q_{t-1}$, must in the long run be equal on average to the growth rate of dividends, $r_t/r_{t-1}$. Hence we can write

$$\frac{1}{T}\sum_{t=1}^{T} R_t \approx \frac{1}{T}\sum_{t=1}^{T} \frac{r_t}{q_{t-1}} + \frac{1}{T}\sum_{t=1}^{T} \frac{r_t}{r_{t-1}}, \tag{7.11}$$

an equation that Fama & French call the *dividend growth model*. They compute these averages with U.S. data from 1872 to 1950 and from 1951 to 2000. From these computations they subtract the yield of six-month Commercial Paper, which gives an estimate of the equity premium. For the early sample, the results are similar when using (7.10) or (7.11); they find an equity premium of 4.40% and 4.17%, respectively. For the later sample, the results diverge significantly. Using (7.10) the equity premium is 7.43%, whereas for the dividend growth model (7.11) it is only 2.55%. The reason for this difference is that the price–dividend ratio has greatly increased in the fifty years covered by this sample. In other words, equity prices increased much faster than dividends.

The price–dividend ratio may have increased because firms replaced dividends with share repurchases as a means of paying out earnings to shareholders. Such change of behavior implies that dividends and prices are not cointegrated. The price–*earnings* ratio should be integrated, though, and should be immune to the way firms transfer payoffs to shareholders. Replacing dividend growth with earning growth in (7.11) yields an equation that Fama & French call the *earnings growth model.* Earnings data are not available for the 1872–1950 period. For 1951–2000, the earnings growth model yields an estimate of the equity premium of 4.32%, somewhere between the average stock return and the dividend growth model, but closer to the latter, and close to the estimate of the earlier sample using the dividend growth model.

There are three possible explanations for the discrepancy between the return due to earnings and the realized stock return. The first possibility is that there is a bubble on equity prices. That would destroy the stationarity of the price–earnings ratio. The second possibility is that earnings expectations are much greater today than they were earlier. This is the "new economy" explanation: if the information technology revolution increases productivity growth, then future earnings growth will be higher. This would justify a large price–earnings ratio today. The third possibility is that the expected equity premium has decreased. A smaller equity premium is compatible with unchanged earnings on average if equity is more expensive. In this interpretation, the bullish market since the 1980s is simply a result of the transition to a higher price level for equities. Fama & French do not consider the bubble explanation. They dismiss the new economy interpretation because they find no evidence that earnings can be forecast, and hence earnings growth cannot be expected to accelerate. As a result, they conclude that the expected equity premium has decreased.

Other researchers have reached the same conclusion. Blanchard (1993) computes the expected return rate of equity using a refined version of Gordon's (1959) formula and assuming that "profits will grow at the same rate as the economy" (Blanchard, 1993, p. 83f). He reports that the expected equity premium has more or less steadily declined since the 1950s, and "today [1993] appears to be around 2 to 3%" (Blanchard, 1993, page 113), yet his figure 11 suggests that the premium was not significantly different from zero since the early 1980s. Jagannathan, McGrattan & Scherbina (2000) report that the premium was 7% on average between 1926 and 1970, but has since declined to about 0.7%; again, the premium for two of their equity measures do not seem to be significantly positive since the 1980s (see their chart 5).

The diagnosis that the equity premium has dramatically declined has recently surfaced also in the investment community (Arnott & Ryan, 2001; Best & Byrne, 2001). But it would be wrong to say that this has become the new consensus view. Some authors are still quite upbeat about the prospects of investing into equity (Ibbotson & Chen, 2003).

### 7.3.6 Conclusion

Careful examination suggests that the huge premium postulated by Mehra & Prescott (1985) is exaggerated. One reason for this is the survival bias: the large return that American stocks have achieved in the last century may have been to a significant extent the result of unforeseeable good luck. In addition, as we now know from the prices of inflation-protected government bonds, the real risk-free interest rate seems to be much greater than the ex post real interest rate on short-term government debt. The expected equity premium is probably more in the neighborhood of 2% than in excess of 6%, as originally measured by Mehra & Prescott.

This is still significantly more than what can be explained by the mainstream model. But the equity premium puzzle seems to be dissolving, as the premium has declined dramatically since the 1980s. The question now is: is this decline here to stay, and if so why was the premium so enormous for such a long time? Or, are stock prices highly overvalued now, so that a return to smaller price–earnings ratios (and hence larger premiums) is imminent?

It seems reasonable to believe that the high stock price/low premium is here to stay, since this is what theory predicts. And yet, eminent financial economists disagree. In fact, the views about the future performance of the stock market are as diverse today as they can possibly be. At the peak of the stock price level the most extreme optimists, Glassman & Hassett (2000), argued that stock prices would continue to rise substantially, because the forward looking equity premium was—according to them—still too high. At the same time, Shiller (2000) argued that a very large correction was due. Between these extremes there is McGrattan & Prescott (2000) who argued that the stock market was, on the whole, correctly valued.

## 7.4 Excessive volatility

### 7.4.1 Early variance bounds tests

LeRoy & Porter (1981) and Shiller (1979, 1981) were the first to notice that the theory makes strong predictions about the volatility of asset prices, and that empirically asset prices are more volatile than what is compatible with the theory. Following this early literature, we start by assuming risk neutrality. In the absence of bubbles, the current price of an asset is simply the discounted value of its dividends, given today's information:

$$q = \sum_{t=1}^{\infty} \delta^t E\left\{r_{\langle t \rangle}\right\}. \tag{6.6}$$

Notice that, according to this equation, the price changes only if there is new information so that expectations change. Suppose for a moment that investors had perfect foresight. Following Shiller (1981), we call the resulting asset price the "ex post rational price,"

$$q^* := \sum_{t=1}^{\infty} \delta^t r_t, \tag{7.12}$$

where $r_1, r_2, \ldots$ denotes the realized dividend sequence. If agents had perfect information, then $q = q^*$. In general however, there is uncertainty, and thus $q$ will be a noisy estimate of $q^*$,

$$q^* = q + \varepsilon. \tag{7.13}$$

Rational expectations dictates that the expected dividends are an unbiased but possibly noisy estimate of the true dividends, and expectations errors are orthogonal. Formally, $E\{\varepsilon\} = 0$ and $\mathrm{cov}(q, \varepsilon) = 0$. This implies that

$$\mathrm{var}(q^*) = \mathrm{var}(q) + \mathrm{var}(\varepsilon) \geqslant \mathrm{var}(q). \tag{7.14}$$

The more accurate the information that investors have about future dividends (implying a small variance of the expectation error $\varepsilon$), the more volatile the stock price ($q$) should be. If information is perfect, the observed stock price $q$ is as volatile as the ex post rational price $q^*$. If information is less than perfect, $q$ is less volatile than $q^*$. Thus, the present value relation (6.6) implies that the volatility of the ex post rational price is an upper bound for the volatility of the stock price.

The trouble with testing this prediction is that $q^*$ is not observable since it is an infinite sum, (7.12). Shiller (1981) constructs an estimate of $q^*$ by applying $q_t^* = \delta(q_{t+1}^* + r_{t+1})$ recursively for $t = 1, \ldots, T-1$, and imposing the terminal condition $\sum_{t=1}^{T} q_t^* = \sum_{t=1}^{T} q_t$, which says that the observed price is equal on average to the ex post rational price. Visual inspection of $q$ and $q^*$ suggests that $q^*$ is conspicuously smoother than $q$—see Shiller's figures 1 and 2—so that (7.14) seems flagrantly violated.

LeRoy & Porter's (1981) approach is somewhat different and has the advantage of producing confidence intervals. They prove that, subject to some conditions on the dividend process, the coefficient of dispersion of dividends exceeds that of the stock price. In other words, stock prices must be smoother than dividends. They test this implication of the present value relation and find that it is violated empirically. Yet, although most stock prices appear much more volatile than their respective dividends, the tests are rejected with only borderline significance.

### 7.4.2 *Critics and improved tests*

These early results have given rise to an extensive literature further exploring the apparent violation of the present value relation, and several econometric objections have been raised.

The first objection was formulated by Flavin (1983). She points out that the sample variances of $q$ and $q^*$ are both biased downwards, but the bias is larger for $q^*$ than for $q$, thus leading to a test that is biased toward rejection of the null hypothesis of no excess volatility. The reason for this bias is that $q$ and $q^*$ are both serially correlated, but $q^*$, being a moving average, is more serially correlated, and thus its sample variance is a more biased estimate of the population variance.

The second objection is based on the time series properties of dividends. Note that, according to the present value equation (assuming a constant discount factor), it is only the information about future dividends that drives today's price. Past dividends are of course observable, so they are included in the information set. From this it follows that the stochastic process one assumes for the discount process is of utmost importance for relating current dividend to expected future dividends, and thus for the relationship between the relative variances of dividends and stock prices. For instance, if dividends have no serial correlation, they cannot have any effect on price. On the other hand, if dividends follow a random walk, then any small change of dividend (which is perceived as permanent) has a large effect on the corresponding stock price.

More generally, to make the argument as simple as possible, assume that expected dividends grow at a constant rate, $E\{r_{t+1}/r_t\} = x$. Assume also an infinite horizon and the absence of bubbles. Then, the present value relationship (6.6) simplifies to

$$q = \sum_{t=1}^{\infty} \delta^t r_0 x^t = \frac{\delta r_0 x}{1 - \delta x} = \frac{r_0 x}{\rho - x} = \frac{E\{r_1\}}{\rho - x}, \qquad (7.15)$$

since $\delta = \beta = \rho^{-1}$. This equation is known as the Gordon (1959) model. Given today's information, the price of the equity equals expected dividends, $E\{r_1\}$, divided by the constant factor $\rho - x$. But now suppose that uncertainty prevails not only with respect to future dividend levels ($r$), but also with respect to future dividend growth ($x$). Notice that dividend *growth* has much more leverage on the present value of a stock than dividend *levels*. For instance, suppose $\rho - x$ is 2%; then the appropriate price–dividend ratio is 50. But if agents reduce their expectation of $x$ by one percentage point (so $\rho - x$ is now 3%), then the appropriate price–dividend ratio is only 33, implying a 34% drop in the value of stocks.

Empirically, asset prices are typically not stationary, so intertemporal population means and variances are not defined. Moreover, the management of a firm may choose to smooth dividends, so it is very likely that dividends are highly serially correlated. LeRoy & Porter (1981) and Shiller (1981) were of course aware of this fact. LeRoy & Porter (1981) first correct for inflation by dividing by the GNP deflator, and they also correct for retained earnings. They assume that the resulting return series are stationary.[14] Shiller (1981) simply corrects for an estimated exponential trend.

Kleidon (1986), relating only to Shiller's work, demonstrates that this correction is inappropriate. He points out that (7.14) is an inequality that must hold across states, yet the variance bounds tests compare intertemporal variances. He reports Monte Carlo simulations of dividends following a geometric random walk, and corresponding prices that satisfy the present value relation by definition and to which Shiller's computations are applied. The resulting graphs look just like the ones Shiller produces: the generated ex post rational price looks much smoother than the generated share price, and we may be led to conclude that the variance bound seems to be violated "simply by looking at the graph," but in fact the present value relation holds.[15]

LeRoy & Parke (1992) address the non-stationarity problem more directly. Since asset prices are typically not stationary, intertemporal population means and variances are not defined. Instead, they study price–dividend ratios, which are more likely to be stationary. They assume that dividends follow a geometric random walk, thus avoiding Kleidon's critique. Even so, they are able to reject the variance bound on the price–dividend ratio implied by the present value model.

[14]The authors are quite frank about possible problems: "There appears to be some evidence of downward trends, although they are not clearly significant. We have decided to neglect such evidence and simply assume that the series are stationary ... We do not argue that this treatment is entirely adequate, nor do we in any way minimize the problem of nonstationarity; the dependence of our results on the assumption of stationarity is probably the single most severe limitation" (LeRoy & Porter, 1981, page 569).

[15]Compare his figures 1 (real data) and 2 (artificial data satisfying the present value model and the variance bound by definition).

Another critique that has been raised is that agents may be risk averse, which would invalidate the constant discount factor assumption. In terms of the theory as we have developed it, we should test not (6.6), but the fundamental pricing equation of Box 6.1. This critique has been addressed quite early in this literature (LeRoy & LaCivita, 1981; Grossman & Shiller, 1981; Michener, 1982). If the discount factor is stochastic, prices may become more volatile. LeRoy & LaCivita (1981) generalize LeRoy & Porter's (1981) result on the relative coefficients of dispersion of dividends and stock prices. They show that the coefficient of dispersion of the stock price is smaller than the coefficient of dispersion of dividends if and only if the coefficient of relative risk aversion is smaller than one. Thus, risk aversion alone already justifies more volatile stock prices. The intuitive reason for this result is that risk-averse agents try to smooth consumption, but aggregate risk cannot be smoothed in equilibrium. Thus, asset prices have to behave in such a way that the representative agent willingly abstains from consumption smoothing and instead consumes his endowment. For this to happen, stocks must be expensive in a boom, to prevent agents from buying stocks in order to save, and they must be cheap in a recession, to prevent agents from selling stocks in order to dissave. Thus, the more risk averse the representative is, the more volatile and procyclical stock prices must be. The problem is, just as with the equity premium puzzle, that, in order to induce enough volatility of the SDF to make relative stock price and dividend volatility compatible with each other, we need to assume a very large risk aversion parameter, simply because consumption growth is so smooth. The problem is precisely the same as with the equity premium puzzle.

### *7.4.3 Conclusion*

Initially, stock prices looked just too volatile to be compatible with the view that they reflect only news about future dividends. But the research that has been conducted since the discovery of excess volatility has made this diagnosis much less clear cut than it used to be. The introduction of risk aversion allows for somewhat more volatile stock prices. Allowing for more persistence in the dividend process helps a great deal more. Even so, it seems that we are still missing some variability of the theoretical SDF to make the model work.

Some have argued that this missing volatility of the theoretical SDF should be interpreted as a challenge to our imagination and should push us to come up with more sophisticated utility functions, or perhaps with some sort of market frictions that would make the SDF violate the simple frictionless first-order condition. Others seem to believe that the rationality assumption itself is proven wrong by the excess volatility diagnosis. Rather than maximizing utility, the argument goes, people's investment behavior is driven by fads, not by ratio. Of course, without any further specification, "fads" is just another name for "unexplained residual," and as such not that helpful. Only if we can explain fads as social psychological phenomena might we get a better model of asset pricing out of it.

An alternative route, less psychological and closer to mainstream economics, has been taken by information economics. Gennotte & Leland (1990) demonstrate how the mixture of better and less informed agents in the market can cause sudden price drops. These crashes are due to the informational content of prices. Less informed agents try to infer the hedging activity of insiders from publicly observable prices. In their model, a small piece of information can unravel a high price equilibrium and lead to a sudden drop to a much lower price. The system features some hysteresis, too. It is possible to get back to the high-price equilibrium, but it requires a much bigger opposing shock than the one that triggered the crash.

## 7.5 Anomalies

An enormous equity premium and excessively volatile stock prices may make one wonder about the way financial markets function. But researchers have uncovered an impressive collection of even stranger patterns in financial market data. To name just the most famous anomalies, there are the weekend, the size, and the January effects.

The weekend effect was discovered by French (1980). He reports that S&P 500 returns are significantly negative between Fridays and Mondays. The size effect, due to Banz (1981) and Reinganum (1981), states that shares of firms with small capitalization earn abnormal returns. The January effect, discovered by Keim (1983) and Reinganum (1983), refers to the fact that many of these abnormal returns occur in January. Such patterns seem difficult or even impossible to reconcile with the mainstream model of rational behavior, because they seem to offer arbitrage opportunities. For instance, a rational investor who knows about French's weekend effect should sell his portfolio on Friday and buy it back on Monday. Such crazy patterns are therefore often called anomalies, because standard theory predicts that we should not observe such things. Is it true that the anomalies offer risk-free arbitrage opportunities, and if so, why are these patterns not arbitraged away? The literature offers two quite opposing answers.

One possibility is that arbitrage is limited because rational investors face noise trader risk when trying to make an arbitrage profit. The argument is simple. If prices offer risk-free arbitrage opportunities, then we are off equilibrium—a situation that should never be observed. But if we do observe off equilibrium prices, how can we be sure that prices return to their arbitrage-free equilibrium position? Thus, harvesting apparent risk-free arbitrage opportunities may not be risk free after all. Consequently, the fact that no arbitrage is undertaken does not imply that prices are "right" in the sense of allocating scarce resources to the most valuable projects (Barberis & Thaler, 2003). If this is so, then we should not rely on the first welfare theorem. But then, the validity of the mutuality principle or Wilson's theorem—even as an approximation—is in jeopardy.

On the other hand, Schwert (2003) has observed that, after the anomalies have been discovered, some professional investors tried to exploit them, but the anomalous returns did not materialize in these portfolios. Schwert argues as follows. If many researchers shuffle the same data around with great intensity, the probability of finding "anomalous" statistics is quite high. The real test is off sample: do the anomalies exist in samples of data that have not been used when searching for anomalies? He argues that none of the anomalies has proved to be reliably present out of sample. This means that the anomalies have never in fact really been there, or have been arbitraged away since their discovery.[16] If this is so, then we may witness only the search and discovery process of financial market participants that makes this institution more and more efficient. In that case, the mainstream efficient market model may be a good model for the steady state of the market.

## Notes on the literature

Abel (1991) is an easy introduction into the equity premium puzzle. Cornell (1999) offers a non-technical discussion of many aspects of measurement, of the puzzle itself, and of solutions that have been proposed in the literature, and AIMR (2002) is quite a deep *tour d'horizon* written in a conversational style. Dimson et al. (2002) offer an international view by covering sixteen countries. The survey by Gilles & LeRoy (1991) and the review by Cochrane (1991) contain the essence of the literature on excessive volatility. The asset pricing puzzles that we have discussed in this chapter are also investigated in depth by Campbell (2003) and Cochrane (2001, chapters 20 and 21).

[16]The only exception, according to Schwert, is the small-firm January effect, which has been much weaker recently, but does not seem to have disappeared completely.

# 8
# Adapting the theory

Even though the asset pricing puzzles are, by their very nature, negative results, they have been seminal in the sense of launching an intensive search for their resolution. We discussed one branch of this research in the last chapter. This entails regarding the puzzle as misinterpretation the data. One can claim that the arguments put forth by these researchers justify a significantly reduced estimate of the equity premium, from more than 6% to about 2%. But 2% is still too much, so a puzzle remains, at least for the data up to about 1980. Since then the forward looking premium seems to have diminished significantly, although there is anything but a consensus on what return to expect from equities.

In this chapter we consider several promising avenues researchers have taken in the quest to resolve the puzzles. Some of these routes are well understood now; other possibilities, also to be discussed below, still seem to be in their infancy.

## 8.1 Assumptions of the mainstream model

The standard model is built on the following assumptions.

1. Markets work without frictions. There are no transaction costs, no bid–ask spreads, and the law of one price holds.
2. All agents are price takers. Prices are such that all markets clear.
3. Expectations are rational in the following sense:
   (a) everyone agrees on the state space;
   (b) everyone agrees on the state-contingent cash flows of all assets;

(c) if there are multiple equilibria, everyone agrees on which one is being played.

- ► *The data we observe are generated by a Radner equilibrium.*
- ► *There is a representative commodity (wealth).*

4. Financial markets are complete or quasi-complete.

- ► *There is a representative agent with ordinal utility.*

5. People maximize a time-separable NM expected utility.
6. People share common beliefs about the probability distribution of the states.

- ► *There is a representative NM agent, $v(w^0) + E\{u(w)\}$, (5.3), but his utility function today and tomorrow are generally different, $v \neq u$.*

7. People share a common discount factor.

- ► *There is a representative NM agent with the same common discount factor, $v(w^0) + \delta E\{v(w)\}$, and the same NM utility function in both periods (Box 5.3).*

8. All agents have HARA utility with a common slope parameter.

- ► *The representative agent, and thus the equilibrium prices, are independent of the inter-personal distribution (Rubinstein aggregation).*

9. The coefficient of relative risk aversion of the representative agent is moderate.[1]
10. The representative's utility function is CRRA.

The assumptions that have drawn most attention for being potentially responsible for the empirical failure of the model are 1, 4, and 5, but other assumptions such as 7 or 8 could probably also be held responsible.

Fundamentally, what we need to justify a larger equity premium is more volatility of the SDF. This can be achieved by amending the utility function (somehow people are more risk averse than we think) or by arguing that individual consumption is more volatile than suggested by aggregate data (people bear some undiversified idiosyncratic risk). Or one can break the close link between the SDF and asset prices by arguing that the simple first-order condition captured by the SDF does not hold because of frictions of

[1] This may be interpreted as $\gamma < 4$, since experiments rarely detect a larger coefficient, or, following evolutionary finance, it may mean that $\gamma \approx 1$.

some sort. All these strategies have been pursued in the literature, and we discuss some of the contributions in this chapter.

## 8.2 Non-standard preferences

In this section we examine several departures from the standard time- and state-separable power utility function that have been pursued in the literature, in an attempt to bring the theory more in to line with empirical observations. Typically this research works with a single agent, or with a large number of identical agents. Aggregation is rarely, if ever, dealt with in a careful manner. For instance, it is not clear how a population of decision makers, all behaving according to prospect theory, behaves in the aggregate. I mention this as a general caveat, but will make no attempt to shed light on aggregation issues involved when using these more exotic preferences.

### *8.2.1 Non-HARA utility*

There is no reason to believe *a priori* that the inter-personal income distribution does not affect asset prices. In principle, the income distribution can affect the properties of the representative agent's utility function or time preference and thus can have an influence on equilibrium prices. Yet, if the conditions for Rubinstein's aggregation are valid (Box 5.3), the distribution has no effect because the risk tolerance of the representative agent is unaffected by a change of the inter-personal income distribution.

Gollier (2001*b*) has recently elaborated on the effect of income distribution on the equity premium and on the risk-free rate. He assumes that all agents have identical preferences (not just a representative agent), but have non-HARA utility. Instead, he assumes that absolute risk tolerance is a concave function of wealth. He finds that in this case more inter-personal wealth heterogeneity (a less egalitarian distribution) increases the equity premium. This result comes straight out of Wilson's theorem and Jensen's inequality. If risk tolerance is a concave function of wealth, then average risk tolerance is smaller than the risk tolerance of a person with average wealth, by Jensen's inequality. This effect is the stronger the larger the dispersion of individual wealth. Consequently, greater inequality decreases the representative agent's risk tolerance, and thus increases the market price of risk. For realistic parameters, Gollier estimates that this effect alone may double the theoretical equity premium.

The effect of the wealth distribution on the risk-free interest rate is more difficult to evaluate. Gollier assumes that absolute imprudence (the reciprocal of absolute prudence) is a concave function of wealth as well.[2] Under this condition he shows that a mean preserving spread of the inter-personal income distribution reduces the risk-free rate. Thus, wealth heterogeneity may help to lower the theoretical prediction about the risk-free rate and to increase the prediction about the market price of risk.

### 8.2.2 Separating cross-state from intertemporal substitution

The *elasticity of substitution* is typically used in production theory to measure the substitutability of two production factors. It is defined as the percentage change of the proportion in which two factors are optimally employed as the result of a change of their marginal rates of substitution (say, a change in the relative price of the two factors). Formally, if $f(L, K)$ is a production function with two factors (e.g., labor and capital), then the elasticity of substitution is defined as[3]

$$\frac{1}{\varepsilon} := -\frac{d\ln(K/L)}{d\ln(\partial_2 f(L, K)/\partial_1 f(L, K))}. \tag{8.1}$$

If the relative price of labor and capital changes by 1%, the profit-maximizing capital–labor ratio changes by a factor $1/\varepsilon$.

The same idea can be applied to utility maximization problems. In particular, consider a two-period problem without uncertainty and with additively separable preferences and CRRA period felicity function,

$$V(y_0, y_1) := \frac{y_0^{1-\gamma}}{1-\gamma} + \delta\frac{y_1^{1-\gamma}}{1-\gamma}.$$

The elasticity of substitution is

$$\frac{1}{\varepsilon} = -\frac{d\ln(y_1/y_0)}{d\ln(\partial_2 V(y_0, y_1)/\partial_1 V(y_0, y_1))}.$$

We have

$$\frac{\partial_2 V(y_0, y_1)}{\partial_1 V(y_0, y_1)} = \delta\left(\frac{y_1}{y_0}\right)^{-\gamma},$$

hence

$$\ln\left(\frac{\partial_2 V(y_0, y_1)}{\partial_1 V(y_0, y_1)}\right) = \ln\delta - \gamma\ln\left(\frac{y_1}{y_0}\right).$$

[2]Note that this entails a condition on the fifth derivative of the utility function.

[3]$\varepsilon$ denotes the reciprocal of the elasticity of substitution.

Rearranging yields

$$-\ln\left(\frac{y_1}{y_0}\right) = \frac{1}{\gamma}\left(\ln\left(\frac{\partial_2 V(y_0, y_1)}{\partial_1 V(y_0, y_1)}\right) - \ln\delta\right).$$

Interpreting the right-hand side as a function of $\ln(\partial_2 V/\partial_1 V)$ and differentiating with respect to this argument, we find that

$$\varepsilon = \gamma. \tag{8.2}$$

The elasticity of intertemporal substitution is intimately related to the coefficient of relative risk aversion. This seems overly restrictive, since the two concepts capture quite distinct and unrelated aspects of preferences. One can easily be only moderately averse to cross-state risk (small $\gamma$), but at the same time be very averse to intertemporal fluctuations of consumption (large $\varepsilon$). In fact, a small $\gamma$ and a large $\varepsilon$ is exactly what experimental and empirical evidence suggests.[4] Yet, the mainstream specification cannot accommodate such tastes. Thus, the standard specification seems to have too few degrees of freedom, which potentially explains its empirical failure.

Several authors have developed a generalization of the standard model that allows us to separate these two distinct aspects of preferences (Epstein, 1988; Epstein & Zin, 1989, 1991; Weil, 1989, 1990). The approach is based on a generalization of von Neumann–Morgenstern utility theory which was developed by Kreps & Porteus (1978) and Selden (1978). The punchline of this research is that separating risk aversion from intertemporal substitution does not resolve the equity premium puzzle. Instead, it produces a second puzzle, the *risk-free rate puzzle* (Weil, 1989). If agents are only moderately risk averse but are highly averse to intertemporal fluctuations, then the equity premium should be much smaller than measured in the data, and the risk-free rate should be much larger than observed. As we will see, the reason for this is that the risk-free rate is a function only of the intertemporal elasticity of substitution (and of the mean growth rate and the discount factor), but is unrelated to the coefficient of relative risk aversion. If people are highly averse to substitute intertemporally and the economy grows on average, then the risk-free interest rate should be large. On the other hand, the risk premium is unrelated to the intertemporal elasticity of substitution and is a function only of relative risk aversion. Extending the standard specifications

[4]We have discussed the evidence for moderate risk aversion in section 4.5. Empirical evidence about the intertemporal elasticity of substitution in consumption suggests that it is close to zero (Hall, 1988); recently, however, Beaudry & van Wincoop (1996) have produced an estimate in the neighborhood of one. Abdulkadri & Langemeier (2000) use data on farm household consumption and estimate the intertemporal elasticity of substitution to be between 0.16 and 0.35.

with a separate parameter for intertemporal substitution is therefore unable to increase the theoretical risk premium. This can be achieved only by increasing the risk aversion coefficient.

In the following, we study this approach in a simple two-period setting. Let $y = (y_0, \ldots, y_S)$ denote present and state contingent future consumption as usual, and let $V$ be a utility function mapping consumption bundles into the real line. $V$ is additively separable through time in the sense that there are functions $u$ and $v$ such that

$$V(y) := u(y_0) + \delta u(v^{-1}(E\{v(y)\})). \tag{8.3}$$

As before, $E$ is the expectations over the states $1, \ldots, S$; $v$ is tomorrow's period NM felicity function; and $\delta v^{-1}(E\{v(y)\})$ is the certainty equivalent, discounted back to the present, of future consumption. Thus, $V(y)$ is the sum of present and discounted future utility $u(\cdots)$, as in the standard two-period problem without uncertainty. But unlike the standard case, the argument that is used to evaluate future utility is the certainty equivalent of future state-contingent consumption, computed using a *different* utility function $v$. This function $v$ captures the preferences of the agent for cross-state variability (his risk aversion). The different function $u$ captures his preferences for intertemporal variability (his elasticity of intertemporal substitution).

A straightforward specification for $u$ and $v$ which keeps the useful property of scale invariability is to make them CRRA:

$$u(z) := \frac{z^{1-\varepsilon}}{1-\varepsilon}; \quad v(z) := \frac{z^{1-\gamma}}{1-\gamma}. \tag{8.4}$$

Then $\gamma$ is the coefficient of relative risk aversion and $1/\varepsilon$ is the elasticity of intertemporal substitution. The special case $\varepsilon = \gamma$ gives rise to the standard model, section 5.8.4, because then $u(v^{-1}(E\{v(y)\})) = E\{v(y)\}$ in (8.3).

These preferences give rise to an SDF of the following form:

$$\begin{aligned}
M_s &= \delta \overbrace{\frac{u'(v^{-1}(E\{v(y)\}))v'(y_s)}{v'(v^{-1}(E\{v(y)\}))}}^{[\partial V(y)/\partial y_s]/\pi_s} \frac{1}{u'(y_0)} \\
&= \delta[v^{-1}(E\{v(y)\})]^{-\varepsilon+\gamma} y_s^{-\gamma} y_0^{\varepsilon} \\
&= \delta E\{y^{1-\gamma}\}^{\frac{\gamma-\varepsilon}{1-\gamma}} y_s^{-\gamma} y_0^{\varepsilon} \\
&= \delta E\{(1+g)^{1-\gamma}\}^{\frac{\gamma-\varepsilon}{1-\gamma}} y_0^{\gamma-\varepsilon} y_s^{-\gamma} y_0^{\varepsilon} \\
&= \delta E\{(1+g)^{1-\gamma}\}^{\frac{\gamma-\varepsilon}{1-\gamma}} (1+g_s)^{-\gamma}.
\end{aligned} \tag{8.5}$$

Approximately, then,

$$-\ln M_s \approx \varepsilon E\{g\} + \gamma(g_s - E\{g\}) - \ln \delta. \tag{8.6}$$

Thus, the risk-free interest rate is, approximately,

$$\ln \rho \approx -E\{\ln M\} \approx \varepsilon E\{g\} - \ln \delta. \tag{8.7}$$

As claimed above, the risk-free interest rate is independent of risk aversion $\gamma$. Comparing this with (5.38), we see that it is really the elasticity of intertemporal substitution rather than the degree of risk aversion that determines the interest rate.

Substituting (8.5) into the CCAPM formula (Box 5.11) yields the equilibrium risk premium of an asset $j$ with state-contingent return rates $R_s^j$,

$$\begin{aligned} E\{R^j\} - \rho &= \rho \mathrm{cov}(-M, R^j) \\ &= \rho\delta \underbrace{E\{(1+g)^{1-\gamma}\}^{\frac{\gamma-\varepsilon}{1-\gamma}}}_{\approx e^{(\gamma-\varepsilon)E\{g\}}} \underbrace{\mathrm{cov}(-(1+g)^{-\gamma}, R^j)}_{\approx \gamma \mathrm{cov}(g, R^j)}. \end{aligned}$$

From (8.7) we have $\rho \approx e^{\varepsilon E\{g\}}\delta^{-1}$; thus,

$$E\{R^j\} - \rho \approx \gamma^{**}\mathrm{cov}(g, R^j), \tag{8.8}$$

with

$$\gamma^{**} := \gamma e^{\gamma E\{g\}}.$$

The claim made above is verified: the equilibrium risk premium is independent of $\varepsilon$. Given the small covariance between $g$ and $R^j$, the premium can be large only if $\gamma$ is large.[5]

### 8.2.3 *Habits and the Joneses*

Most of us would probably agree that it is very hard to reduce consumption a lot from one year to the next. Doing this is painful. We develop standards and habits that we are not easily willing to give up. Suppose you moved to a bigger house a few years ago, but suddenly you are forced to move back into the small house you were living before: this smaller house would feel tiny, maybe unbearably so, despite the fact that you lived there for many

[5] Comparing (5.39) with (8.8), we notice some difference between $\gamma^*$ and $\gamma^{**}$ due to taking different first-order approximations. For reasonable parameters, the difference is small, though. For instance, if $\gamma = 4$ and $E\{g\} = 4\%$ (two rather large numbers), then $\gamma^* = 4.76$ and $\gamma^{**} = 4.69$.

years and never found it extremely small before. This is referred to as *habit formation.*

Mathematically, this is modelled by making utility a function of consumption $y$ and of some habit stock $x$, $v(y, x)$, with $\partial_1 v > 0$ and $\partial_2 v < 0$. Habit usually enters utility in either an additive or a multiplicative fashion. The power specification of the CRRA utility function can conveniently be maintained. Thus, the standard habit specification is

$$v(y, x) := \frac{z(y, x)^{1-\gamma}}{1-\gamma}, \tag{8.9}$$

where $z$ is a function, $y$ is consumption, and $x$ is some reference (or habit) level. The equilibrium SDF is the marginal rate of substitution between consumption in state $s$ tomorrow and consumption today. The power specification (8.9) implies that the SDF is given by

$$M_s = \delta \left( \frac{z(y_s, x_s)}{z(y_0, x_0)} \right)^{-\gamma} \times \frac{\partial_1 z(y_s, x_s) + \partial_2 z(y_s, x_s) \frac{\partial x_s}{\partial y_s}}{\partial_1 z(y_0, x_0) + \partial_2 z(y_0, x_0) \frac{\partial x_0}{\partial y_0} + \delta z(y_1, x_1)^{-\gamma} \partial_2 z(y_1, x_1) \frac{\partial x_s}{\partial y_0}}. \tag{8.10}$$

The $\partial x / \partial y$ terms capture the idea that the consumption choice of the agent ($y$) might affect his reference level ($x$). This connection makes the maximization problem more complicated, because today's consumption decision has an effect on today's or tomorrow's habit. A forward-looking rational agent takes this into account, much like Becker & Murphy's (1988) rational addict. For instance, an agent may delay the purchase of some luxury good because this would increase his habit and thus hurt his felicity later on. The presence of lagged consumption in today's felicity function implies a positive effect of today's consumption on tomorrow's marginal utility. This should increase the volatility of the SDF.

Two functional forms for the relation between $z$ and $y$ have been pursued in the literature. Some authors relate the two variables in an additive, others in a multiplicative, way,

$$z := y - hx, \qquad \textit{additive habits}, \tag{8.11}$$

or

$$z := yx^{-h}, \qquad \textit{multiplicative habits}. \tag{8.12}$$

$0 \leqslant h \leqslant 1$ is a parameter that governs the strength of the habit motive, and $x$ is the habit level. For $x$, also, different specifications have been pursued in the literature. One possibility is to set the habit level equal to the consumption of the previous period, $x_t := y_{t-1}$. For example, Sundaresan (1989) and Constantinides (1990) work with an exponential lag structure in continuous time, $x_t := \int_{-\infty}^{t} e^{\ln(h)(t-s)} y_s ds$. If $h \to 0$, then $x_t \to 0$ for all $t$; if $h = 1$, then $x_t$ equals cumulative consumption up to time $t$.

A variation of this idea is to specify the reference consumption level not as past own consumption, but as the average consumption of other people. This specification has the advantage of being easier to work with, because the reference level is exogenous from the individual's point of view (at least in a "large" economy). The interpretation too is somewhat different, but it can be motivated by an appealing example as well. Imagine a situation in which you are earning \$100,000 a year, and you feel pretty comfortable. Then suppose you learn that all your colleagues at work earn 50% more than you. Suddenly you feel very dissatisfied. Depending on character and temper, you may become bitter or aggressive or depressed. What matters to you is not only absolute wealth, but also wealth relative to your neighbors. This observation is captured by the idea that people have a motivation for *keeping up with Joneses*. People define themselves not (only) in absolute terms, but in relation to others. If your neighbors become richer, you want to be wealthier too, just to maintain the previous standards.

This idea can be modelled in the same way as habits ((8.9)–(8.12)), except that the habit level is defined as the consumption of the decision maker's peers, or, more easily, as average per capita consumption of the whole population. In equilibrium, per capita consumption is equal to per capita endowment. Joneses' preferences (or *external* habits, as they are sometimes called) are simpler than the internal habit model discussed earlier because the individual's consumption decision has no effect on the habit level. Thus, all $(\partial x/\partial y)$ terms in (8.10) vanish, making the Euler equation much simpler:

$$M_s = \delta \left( \frac{z(y_s, x_s)}{z(y_0, x_0)} \right)^{-\gamma} \frac{\partial_1 z(y_s, x_s)}{\partial_1 z(y_0, x_0)}. \tag{8.13}$$

As before, the habit level can enter additively or multiplicatively. Moreover, some authors have used lagged per capita endowment while others have used contemporaneous endowment. Abel (1990) aptly names these choices "catching up with the Joneses" and "keeping up with the Joneses," respectively. Gali (1994), for instance, uses a multiplicative keeping up with the Joneses model, i.e. (8.9), (8.12), and $x_t := w_t$. Abel (1990) uses a combined multiplicative catching up with the Joneses and internal habit model. The Joneses part of his utility function is given by (8.9) and (8.12), together with $x_t := w_{t-1}$. Finally, Campbell & Cochrane (1999) use an additive catching up model, (8.9), (8.11), and $x_t := w_{t-1}$. The asset pricing implications of these models are quite different. We start with the multiplicative model and go on to study the additive model.

Consider a multiplicative Joneses model that contains keeping up and catching up at the same time:

$$z_t(i) := \frac{y_t(i)}{(w_t)^{(1-\lambda)h}(w_{t-1})^{\lambda h}}. \tag{8.14}$$

$0 \leqslant h \leqslant 1$ is again the strength of the Joneses motive, and $0 \leqslant \lambda \leqslant 1$ is the lag of the reference level.

Looking at the representative agent ($y = w$), we get, from (8.13) and (8.14),

$$M_s = \delta(1+g_s)^{-\gamma-(1-\lambda)h(1-\gamma)}(1+g_0)^{-\lambda h(1-\gamma)},$$

or, in logs, approximately

$$\ln M_s \approx \ln\delta - [\gamma + (1-\lambda)h(1-\gamma)]g_s - \lambda h(1-\gamma)g_0. \tag{8.15}$$

We see that, for a short lag ($\lambda \to 0$), the stronger the habit motive ($h \to 1$), the more the representative agent behaves like a person with log utility, *independently of the curvature parameter* $\gamma$. Thus, if $\gamma > 1$, multiplicative Joneses preferences with a contemporaneous reference level (or with a short enough lag) *reduce* the equilibrium price of risk, and thus deepen the equity premium puzzle.

A long lag, in contrast, does not affect the curvature, so, to a first-order approximation, the equilibrium risk premium is not changed by multiplicative lagged Joneses preferences. The time preference, however, is affected. For $\lambda = 1$, we have

$$\ln M_s \approx \underbrace{\ln\delta - h(1-\gamma)g_0}_{=:\ln\tilde{\delta}} - \gamma g_s.$$

The representative agent behaves like a person with relative risk aversion $\gamma$, just as if there were no Joneses motive. The effective time preference, however, is increased: $\tilde{\delta} > \delta$ if $h > 0$ and $\gamma > 1$ and $g_0 > 0$. That is, the Joneses motive increases patience. In fact, the effective discount factor $\tilde{\delta}$ can easily exceed unity in this case. This helps solving the risk-free rate puzzle by keeping the interest rate low, even if risk aversion is high.[6]

[6]This is in accordance to what Siegel & Thaler (1997, page 196) conclude: "Catching up with the Joneses reduces an individual's desire to borrow against higher future consumption and hence lowers the real rate, but leaves an investor just as risk averse to contemporaneous shocks."

What is the intuition for this? If it is not only absolute consumption that matters to you, but also consumption relative to other people, then you will *want to consume more tomorrow than today* (effectively raising the time preference above one) if aggregate consumption grows through time, because if you do not you will fall back relative to the mean, and this will hurt if you are trying to catch up with the Joneses. In other words, such preferences increase the incentive to save, and thus keep the equilibrium interest rate low.

Next we consider the implications of the additive lagged Joneses model used by Campbell & Cochrane (1999). The additive model (8.11) seems easier at first sight because $\partial_1 z(y, x) = 1$, so that the SDF formula (8.13) is simplified further. But additive habits, together with the power specification (8.9) induces the problem that utility is not defined if consumption drops below the reference level, $y_s(i) \leqslant hx_s$. If this is the case for some event, intertemporal utility is not defined. So we assume that $y_s(i) > hx_s$ for all $s$. We follow Campbell & Cochrane and define the *consumption surplus ratio,*

$$\psi_s(i) := \frac{y_s(i) - hx_s}{y_s(i)} > 0. \tag{8.16}$$

By definition, $z = \psi y$. Moreover, if we look at the representative agent ($y_s(i) = w_s$), the SDF (8.10) can then be written as

$$M_s = \delta \left( \frac{\psi_s w_s}{\psi_0 w_0} \right)^{-\gamma}. \tag{8.17}$$

The SDF is driven, as usual, by the growth rate of consumption ($w_s/w_0$), but also by the growth rate of the consumption surplus ratio ($\psi_s/\psi_0$). Campbell & Cochrane specify the habit level as a non-linear function of lagged consumption with slowly decreasing weights as the lag lengthens. We simplify here by specifying that the habit level is simply last period's per capita consumption, $x_t := w_{t-1}$. In that case,

$$\psi_s = \frac{w_s - hw_0}{w_s} = \frac{w_s - hw_0}{w_0}(1 + g_s)^{-1} = \frac{1 - h + g_s}{1 + g_s}.$$

If habits are strong, for simplicity assume $h = 1$, then $\psi_s \approx g_s$, and $\psi_s/\psi_0$ is essentially the *growth rate of the growth rate* of consumption. This variable is much more volatile than $g$ itself, thereby increasing the volatility of the SDF immensely. Unlike the multiplicative specification, additive Joneses preferences are therefore able to increase the equilibrium price of risk considerably.

The intuition for this result is that the additive Joneses model effectively makes $h$ times lagged per capita endowment ($hw_{t-1}$) act as a subsistence level.[7] Thus, agents have a DRRA utility function like the one discussed on page 92. If habits are strong ($h$ close to unity) and growth is moderate ($g$ close to zero), the representative agent will be quite close to his subsistence level, making him very risk averse.

### 8.2.4 *First-order risk aversion*

Kandel & Stambaugh (1991) have argued that the power specification of the utility function is defective because there does not seem to exist a coefficient of relative risk aversion that fits different sizes of gambles.

> Inferences about $\gamma$ are perhaps most elusive when pursued in the introspective context of thought experiments. It seems possible in such experiments to choose the size of a gamble so that *any value of* $\gamma$ *seems unreasonable.* (Kandel & Stambaugh, 1991, page 68, emphasis added).

They give the following example. Consider a person with wealth of $75,000 who faces a 50–50 chance of winning or losing $25,000, which is a third of his initial wealth and therefore a substantial risk. If $\gamma = 30$, which the authors say is sufficient to explain the large equity premium found by Mehra & Prescott (1985), then the agent is willing to pay $24,000 to avoid the risk. This is clearly absurd, since it transforms a downside risk and upside chance into a sure loss almost as large as the worst case of taking the risk. $\gamma = 2$ gives rise to a more sensible decision, because the willingness to pay for an insurance against this risk then drops to $8,333. But now consider a small risk, a lottery in which the agent stands to win or lose $375, or 0.5% of his wealth. $\gamma = 2$ now induces a willingness to pay for insurance of only $1.88, which seems too small. $\gamma = 30$ induces a reservation insurance premium of $28, which seems a more reasonable number. This example suggests that most people are much more averse (in the sense of relative risk aversion) to small gambles than to large gambles.

Segal & Spivak (1990, 1997) discuss this idea more formally. Consider a fair gamble $x_1, \ldots, x_S$ (fair in the sense that $E\{x\} = 0$), and a scaled version of it, $tx$, for an arbitrary scalar $t$. Then, if the NM utility is differentiable, the risk premium an agent is prepared to pay to avoid this gamble is approximately proportional to $t^2$, for small $t$. This is the result of Box 4.9: the

[7] The same is true for the additive internal habit model. Consider (8.9) and (8.11) with the habit level equal to last period's consumption, $x_t := y_{t-1}$. Then $hy_{t-1}$ is like a subsistence level.

risk premium for small gambles is proportional to the *variance* of the lottery. Segal & Spivak therefore call such preferences *second-order risk averse*. In contrast, they call preferences for which the risk premium is proportional to $t$ (for small $t$) *first-order risk averse*. Such preferences give rise to indifference curves in state space (cf. Figure 4.3) that have a kink along the certainty line. For such preferences, the risk premium is approximately proportional (for small gambles) to the *standard deviation* of the lottery.

Epstein & Zin (1990) apply this idea to asset pricing. An alternative, non-von Neumann–Morgenstern, risk utility theory that does feature first-order risk aversion is Yaari's (1987) rank-dependent probabilities. Essentially, bad states are given a larger weight than their true probabilities, and good states are given a smaller weight. In Yaari's model this distortion is computed in a very specific way, but the details are not important. What matters is only that the distribution that is applied when computing expected utility is made more pessimistic. This is tantamount to increasing the effective relative risk aversion, and thus the equilibrium risk premium, at least as long as only small risks are involved.[8]

### 8.2.5 Prospect theory and the house money effect

In order to address several experimental shortcomings of received theory, Kahneman & Tversky (1979) have proposed a far more general theory of risky decision making than the mainstream von Neumann–Morgenstern model. *Prospect theory* departs from NM in the following ways:

- Agents draw utility not from wealth, but from gains and losses defined with respect to some reference level (typically assumed to be the status quo). This is called the *endowment effect*.
- A loss hurts more than an equally large gain produces joy. This is called *loss aversion*.[9]
- Agents are risk averse over gains, but risk loving over losses.[10]
- Agents weight low probability states too much, and high probability states too little.

[8]It is noteworthy that Epstein & Zin's (1990) model retains the constant relative risk aversion property in the sense that relative risk aversion is the same for all wealth levels, *given a certain size of the gamble*. But, unlike the standard specification, the coefficient of relative risk aversion is not the same for differently sized gambles.

[9]Loss aversion is modelled as a utility function (defined over gains and losses, not over final wealth) which is kinked at zero, $\lim_{z\uparrow 0} v'(z) > \lim_{z\downarrow 0} v'(z)$.

[10]This feature means that $v''(z) < 0$ for $z > 0$, but $v''(z) > 0$ for $z < 0$.

Two of these departures are reminiscent of ideas discussed earlier. The endowment effect is essentially the same as the idea of habits. In both cases, the outcome is evaluated with respect to a reference level of some sort. Loss aversion is a particular form of first-order risk aversion. It is different in the sense that the utility function has a kink at only one point (at the reference level), and not along all points on the certainty line. But it is similar in the sense that it induces a very severe aversion to small fair gambles around the reference level. Since both ideas—habits and first-order risk aversion—are potentially helpful in justifying a larger premium, prospect theory should be expected to deliver this as well.

Barberis et al. (2001) apply these ideas to equilibrium asset pricing. They simplify prospect theory in that they do not use the assumption of a partly risk loving, partly risk averse, utility function. Instead, they assume that the utility function is piecewise linear. They also do not use the assumption of prospect theory that probabilities are distorted. Barberis et al. model an economy with a risk-free asset and one risky asset. The reference point, which is key in prospect theory because it determines the location of the kink in the utility function, is assumed to be the wealth that the agent could have achieved by investing 100% of his wealth into the risk-free bond. The agent experiences a loss if the risky asset's return falls short of the risk-free interest rate; in the opposite case he experiences a gain. To sum up, the utility function they use is

$$v(s, r) := \begin{cases} s(R - \rho) & \text{if } R > \rho, \\ \lambda s(R - \rho) & \text{if } R < \rho, \end{cases} \tag{8.18}$$

where $s$ is the amount of wealth invested in the risky asset, $R$ is the return rate of the risky asset, $\rho$ is the return rate of the risk-free bond, and $\lambda := 2.25$ is a parameter that determines by how much losses cause more disutility than gains cause utility.

Surprisingly, Barberis et al. find that they can explain only a marginally larger equity premium with this first-order risk aversion. They identify the reason for this in the fact that equity returns are not volatile enough in their model, so that the prospect of possibly experiencing a (small) loss does not scare the investor enough. He will happily hold the equity in exchange for a small premium. The solution, they conclude, is to make equity returns more volatile. This they achieve by adding another idea of behavioral finance.

In a series of experiments, Thaler & Johnson (1990) found that the risk-taking behavior of subjects depends on previous gains and losses. A person who has made a gain in the recent past is more likely to take risks than a person who has not. They call this the *house money effect.* Similarly, a person who has made a loss in the recent past becomes generally more risk averse, although deals that offer the opportunity to break even (i.e. to recover the previous loss) are particularly attractive. These findings are closely related to the reference point idea of prospect theory, and may be understood as a more concrete model of how this reference point is determined. Essentially, Thaler & Johnson's theory states that the reference point is *not* the status quo: rather, it takes some time for gains and losses to be absorbed into the reference point. Interpreted in this way, the house money effect amounts to justifying a lagged habit as opposed to the contemporaneous habit (reference level = status quo) of ordinary prospect theory.

The interaction between lagged habit (in the form of the house money effect) and first-order risk aversion (in the form of loss aversion) yields a varying degree of willingness of the investor to take risks. Because current performance is not immediately absorbed into the reference point, a recent gain moves actual wealth into the gain zone ($R > \rho$). This decreases the risk aversion of the decision maker because it moves the actual point away from the reference point.[11]

The situation is less clear after a loss. After all, a prior loss also moves the actual wealth level away from the reference point and thus into a locally linear region of the utility function. Yet, Barberis et al. argue that it seems more realistic to assume that investors who have recently experienced losses will be more risk averse. They model this in a somewhat ad hoc fashion by amending the utility function,

$$v(s, r, z) := \begin{cases} s(R - \rho) & \text{if } R > \rho, \\ \lambda(z)s(R - \rho) & \text{if } R < \rho, \end{cases} \tag{8.19}$$

where $z$ measures prior gains or losses: $z$ is between 0 and 1 if the has previously experienced a gain and is greater than 1 if he agent has previously experienced a loss. $\lambda$ is now a function of $z$. They assume that $\lambda(z) = 2.25$ for $z < 1$, but $\lambda(z) > 2.25$ and $\lambda'(z) > 0$ for $z > 1$. Thus, prior losses increase loss aversion.

Finally, some sluggish process is defined which governs how the reference point is driven by past gains and losses. This process has to be sluggish to have the effect of lagged habits. Otherwise, the model would degenerate to contemporaneous habits and the agent would always sit on the kink of his utility function, thereby preventing the model from generating varying degrees of risk aversion.

The intuition for the model is now quite clear: increase in stock prices (for instance because of a positive dividend surprise) leads to a gain, making

[11] Given the assumed piecewise linearity of the utility function, it even makes the investor locally risk neutral.

investors less risk averse. They want to increase their exposure to the risky asset, which happens automatically through the inflated price of the equity, but if the reduction of risk aversion is strong enough, the investor might want to buy more of the stock, thereby increasing the price further. On the other hand, a loss increases risk aversion and makes investors want to decrease their exposure to the risky asset. Again, if the effect is strong enough, a loss will incite the investor to sell some of the risky asset, thereby depressing the price still further. The result is a very volatile stock price. This large volatility then makes a large equity premium necessary in order for stocks to be held in equilibrium. Thus, the model explains a large premium and a large volatility.

## 8.3 Heterogeneity

### 8.3.1 Cautiousness

Rubinstein's (1974) aggregation theorem (Box 5.3) allows aggregation independent of wealth distribution, but does so at the cost of not allowing much heterogeneity in other dimensions. Agents are all supposed to have the same cautiousness and patience. If we relax these assumptions, a representative agent will still exist, but he will not be independent of the interpersonal wealth distribution. In that case, we will have to keep track of which agent owns how much when developing an asset pricing theory. Since the distribution changes as we move through the event tree, the properties of the representative agent also change in that case. This can give rise to changing degrees of risk aversion of the representative agent, which can contribute to increased volatility and possibly also to a larger theoretical risk premium.

The competitive NM SWF of chapter 5 helps us understand what is going on:

$$V(z) := v(z^0) + E\{u(z)\}, \tag{5.3}$$

with

$$\begin{aligned} v(z) &:= \max\left\{ \frac{1}{I} \sum_i \lambda_i^{-1} v_i(y(i)) \;\middle|\; \sum_i (y(i) - z) \leqslant 0 \right\}, \\ u(z) &:= \max\left\{ \frac{1}{I} \sum_i \lambda_i^{-1} \delta_i v_i(y(i)) \;\middle|\; \sum_i (y(i) - z) \leqslant 0 \right\}. \end{aligned} \tag{5.9}$$

$\lambda_i$ is $i$'s shadow price of wealth. This formulation is valid in a two-period model, but it is suggestive for the mechanics of a multi-period economy.

Consider a population of CRRA people, all with the same patience, but who do not share the same degrees of relative risk aversion. In an efficient equilibrium, the more risk averse agents will be less exposed to aggregate risk, and the less risk-averse agents will bear more of it. That implies that the less risk-averse ones become relatively poorer in a slump, and relatively richer in a boom, than the rest of society. The opposite is true for the more risk-averse agents.

It is unclear *a priori* what this implies for the relative weight of the different types of agents in the SWF. Certainly, $\lambda_i$ co-varies negatively with individual wealth for a risk-averse person, and, according to (5.9), the weight of agent $i$ is inversely related to $\lambda_i$. Therefore, since the wealth of less than average risk-averse agents varies more with aggregate shocks, we may be tempted to conclude that their weight in the SWF is countercyclical. But there is a countervailing effect: the smaller curvature of the utility function of the less risk-averse agents implies that $\lambda_i$ becomes less volatile for a given variation of wealth. In fact, for a risk-neutral agent, $\lambda_i$ is completely independent of his wealth. Therefore, the relative weight of a risk-neutral person living in a society of risk-averse fellows is small in a slump and large in a boom, hence procyclical. We will see that this second effect dominates.

More formally, consider the decision problem of a CRRA person,

$$\max \begin{cases} \frac{(y^0)^{1-\gamma}}{1-\gamma} + \delta E\left\{\frac{y^{1-\gamma}}{1-\gamma}\right\}, & \text{if } \gamma \neq 1, \\ \ln(y^0) + \delta E\{\ln y\}, & \text{if } \gamma = 1, \end{cases}$$

$$\text{s.t.} \quad \begin{bmatrix} 1 & \alpha \end{bmatrix} \cdot y \leqslant \bar{w},$$

where $\bar{w} := \begin{bmatrix} 1 & \alpha \end{bmatrix} \cdot w$ is the present value of the endowment. An unusual way of writing the first-order conditions of this problem is,

$$y^0 = \lambda^{-b}, \quad \alpha_s y^s = \alpha_s^{1-b} \delta^b \pi_s^b \lambda^{-b},$$

where $b := 1/\gamma$ is cautiousness. Using the budget constraint, we can express the reciprocal of the shadow price of wealth for this agent as

$$\lambda^{-1} = \left( \frac{\bar{w}}{1 + \delta^b \sum_{s=1}^{S} \alpha_s^{1-b} \pi_s^b} \right)^{1/b}. \tag{8.20}$$

From (5.14), (5.16), and (5.18), we know the optimal exposure to aggregate risk for this agent (the optimal portfolio of Arrow securities after hedging all his idiosyncratic risk):

$$y^s = \frac{\delta^b \alpha_s^{-b} \pi_s^b}{1 + \delta^b \sum_{\tilde{s}=1}^{S} \alpha_{\tilde{s}}^{1-b} \pi_{\tilde{s}}^b} \bar{w}. \tag{8.21}$$

Using (8.20), (8.21), and the power specification of the $v_i$ function, we can write the objective function in the $u$-function of (5.9) as

$$\frac{1}{I}\sum_i \lambda_i^{-1}\delta_i v_i(y^s(i)) =: \frac{1}{I}\sum_i \psi_i^s, \tag{8.22}$$

where

$$\psi_i^s := \begin{cases} \bar{w}_i \delta_i^{b_i} \frac{b_i}{b_i-1}\left(\frac{\pi_s}{\alpha_s}\right)^{b_i-1}\left[1+\delta_i^{b_i}\sum_{\bar{s}=1}^S \alpha_{\bar{s}}^{1-b_i}\pi_{\bar{s}}^{b_i}\right]^{-1}, & \text{if } b_i \neq 1, \\ \bar{w}_i \frac{\delta_i}{1+\delta_i}\ln\left(\frac{\delta_i}{1+\delta_i}\right)\ln\left(\frac{\pi_s}{\alpha_s}\right), & \text{if } b_i = 1. \end{cases} \tag{8.23}$$

Remember that the risk-neutral probabilities are pessimistic. Thus, $\pi_s/\alpha_s$ tends to be greater than unity in a boom, and smaller than unity in a recession.[12] Consider then the *relative* weight of an agent,

$$\frac{\psi_i^s}{\sum_j \psi_j^s} = \frac{\bar{w}_i \delta_i^{b_i} \frac{b_i}{b_i-1}\left(\frac{\pi_s}{\alpha_s}\right)^{b_i-1}\left[1+\delta_i^{b_i}\sum_{\bar{s}=1}^S \alpha_{\bar{s}}^{1-b_i}\pi_{\bar{s}}^{b_i}\right]^{-1}}{\sum_j \bar{w}_j \delta_j^{b_j} \frac{b_j}{b_j-1}\left(\frac{\pi_s}{\alpha_s}\right)^{b_j-1}\left[1+\delta_j^{b_j}\sum_{\bar{s}=1}^S \alpha_{\bar{s}}^{1-b_j}\pi_{\bar{s}}^{b_j}\right]^{-1}}, \tag{8.24}$$

assuming that no $b_j$ equals 1. This ratio is procyclical for agents who are especially cautious (large $b_i$, thus small $\gamma_i$), and countercyclical for agents who are less cautious (hence more risk averse). The cyclicality (positive or negative) is stronger for exceptionally patient (large $\delta_i$) and for exceptionally wealthy (large $\bar{w}_i$) agents. Thus, in a boom the social welfare function (and thus the properties of the representative agent) is dominated by less than average risk-averse, more than average patient, and more than average rich people. As a result, the representative agent tends to become less risk averse and more patient during a boom, and more risk averse and less patient during a recession. More generally, the way the representative agent depends on the aggregate state of the economy is a function of the joint distribution of risk aversion, patience, and wealth across the whole population.

Dumas (1989) studies an economy populated by two CRRA persons with different coefficients of relative risk aversion. Among other results, he finds that such an economy gives rise to a varying market price of risk, as a function of aggregate shocks. Using the argument above, we can see why. Ignoring wealth and time preference heterogeneity, we can conclude that the representative agent becomes less risk averse in a boom and more risk

[12] This is not completely correct, because $\alpha$ are the Arrow prices, not the risk-neutral probabilities. Thus, on average, $\pi_s/\alpha_s > 1$ if the real risk-free interest rate is strictly positive. But it is still true that $\pi_s/\alpha_s$ is positively correlated with the business cycle.

averse in a recession, essentially because less risk-averse agents are voluntarily more exposed to aggregate risk, and therefore own a larger share of total wealth in a boom than in a recession. This is compatible with the results of Benninga & Mayshar (2000) and of Hara & Kuzmics (2002) that heterogeneous cautiousness implies DRRA. This pattern is precisely the kind of countercyclical risk aversion that generates more volatile asset prices, for the reasons discussed in the sections on habits, first-order risk aversion, and prospect theory. More volatile stock prices then require a larger expected equity premium for agents voluntarily to hold all the aggregate risk.[13]

### 8.3.2 Patience

Equation (8.24) shows that heterogeneous patience (or heterogeneous wealth) does affect equilibrium asset prices, but it is heterogeneous cautiousness that is responsible for making the representative agent's properties a function of the aggregate state of the economy. If $b_1 = \cdots = b_I$, then (8.24) simplifies to

$$\frac{\psi_i^s}{\sum_j \psi_j^s} = \frac{\bar{w}_i \delta_i^b \left(1 + \delta_i^b \sum_{\tilde{s}=1}^S \alpha_{\tilde{s}}^{1-b} \pi_{\tilde{s}}^b\right)^{-1}}{\sum_j \bar{w}_j \delta_j^b \left(1 + \delta_j^b \sum_{\tilde{s}=1}^S \alpha_{\tilde{s}}^{1-b} \pi_{\tilde{s}}^b\right)^{-1}} \tag{8.25}$$

The relative weights of the agents still depend on $\delta$ and on $\bar{w}$ and $b$, but no longer on the business cycle.[14] Thus, if we look for countercyclical risk aversion and procyclical patience, we primarily need heterogeneous risk aversion. Heterogeneous patience can enhance these cyclical properties, but only in conjunction with heterogeneous risk aversion.

Heterogeneous patience, however, has another long-term effect on asset prices, which is not business cycle related and not visible in (8.24). It is simply due to the fact that more patient people tend to save more. Thus, if patience is heterogeneous, asymptotically, all the wealth of the economy is concentrated in the hands of the most patient agent (Becker, 1980). In the long run, therefore, the prime factor determining interest rates should be the smallest individual discount rate in the population. This certainly justifies a very low interest rate for long maturities. For shorter maturities,

[13] Other research investigating the implications of heterogeneous cautiousness is Chan & Kogan (2001), who study a model with heterogeneous cautiousness *and* multiplicative habits; Wang (1996) studies the implications of heterogeneous cautiousness on the term structure of interest rates.

[14] $\pi_s/\alpha_s$ is taken as a proxy for the business cycle in (8.24).

this may not be the case, as less patient agents are prepared to pay substantial interest on loans with a short or medium time to maturity. We would therefore expect an inverse term structure of real interest rates.

More generally, society as a whole may discount the near future with a higher rate than the more distant future. Intuitively, impatient people put almost no weight on returns that accrue in the far future. Consequently, the longer the horizon, the larger is the impact of the relatively patient subjects, and the average discount rate becomes a decreasing function of the horizon. Weitzman (1998, 2001) explores this idea. He defines social discounting as the average weight that people give to returns in different points in time. Following Weitzman we will work in continuous time and with a measure space of agents $[0, 1]$. Each agent discounts the future exponentially, but with different rates, $\exp(-xt)$, where each agent may use a different discount rate $x$. Let $f$ be the density function of $x$, with support in $[0, \infty)$. The average discount rate $x^*$ is the discount rate that corresponds to the average weight given by all members of the group,

$$e^{-x^*t} := \int_0^\infty e^{-xt} f(x)dx. \tag{8.26}$$

Weitzman (2001) performed a survey among academic economists to get some information about a reasonable range and distribution of discount rates. Luckily, the distribution he found looks reasonably similar to the Gamma distribution. This simplifies the mathematics a lot. So assume

$$f(x) := \frac{m^k}{\Gamma(k)} x^{k-1} e^{-mx},$$

where $\Gamma(k) := b^k \int_0^\infty z^{k-1} e^{-bz} dz$ is the Gamma function. This is the same function *for arbitrary* $b > 0$,[15] so we are free to choose this parameter in a suitable manner. Then (8.26) becomes

$$\begin{aligned} e^{-x^*t} &= \int_0^\infty \frac{e^{-xt} m^k x^{k-1} e^{-mx}}{b^k \int_0^\infty z^{k-1} e^{-bz} dz} dx \\ &= \left(\frac{m}{b}\right)^k \frac{\int_0^\infty x^{k-1} e^{-x(m+t)} dx}{\int_0^\infty z^{k-1} e^{-bz} dz} \\ &= \left(\frac{m}{m+t}\right)^k, \end{aligned} \tag{8.27}$$

[15]To see why, define $G(b, k) := b^k \int_0^\infty z^{k-1} e^{-bz} dz$ and $\Gamma(k) := G(1, k)$. Integration by parts reveals that $G(b, k) = (k-1)G(b, k-1)$. Differentiating $G$ with respect to $b$ yields $(k/b)G(b, k) - (1/b)G(b, k+1)$. Combining the two results implies that $\partial G(b, k)/\partial b = 0$, and therefore $G(b, k) = G(1, k) = \Gamma(k)$.

where the last line follows from setting $b := m + t$. Solving for $x^*$,

$$x^* = \frac{k}{t} \ln \left( \frac{m+t}{m} \right), \tag{8.28}$$

and differentiating with respect to $t$ yields

$$\frac{dx^*}{dt} = \left[ \ln \left( \frac{m}{m+t} \right) + \frac{t}{m+t} \right] \frac{k}{t^2} < 0, \tag{8.29}$$

because $\ln(m/(m+t)) < m/(m+t) - 1 = -t/(m+t)$. This is the essence of hyperbolic discounting: the average discount rate $x^*$ is a decreasing function of the horizon.

The question remains of what Weitzman's insight implies for asset prices.[16] After all, the *average* time preference of all agents is not the same as the *representative* time preference. Simply computing the average discounting is not an appropriate way for computing the equilibrium yield curve.

In order to explore the asset pricing implications of heterogeneous patience more carefully, and to bring to the surface these implications most forcefully, we will work with the most simple model possible. We start with a two-period model without uncertainty and a single asset (a risk-free bond). There are arbitrarily many households $i$, all with the same time-contingent wealth $(w_0, w_1)$ and log felicity function, $v(z) := \ln(z)$. However, households have different time preferences, $\delta(i)$. The decision problem of agent $i$ is

$$\max \{ \ln(x_0(i)) + \delta(i) \ln(x_1(i)) \mid x_0(i) + \beta x_1(i) \le w_0 + \beta w_1 \}, \tag{8.30}$$

where $\beta$ denotes the price of the bond, as usual. The first-order conditions boil down to $\beta x_1(i) = \delta(i) x_0(i)$. Taking expectations over all agents $i$ yields

$$\beta E\{x_1\} = E\{\delta\} E\{x_0\} + \text{cov}(\delta, x_0). \tag{8.31}$$

Market clearing requires that, on average, a household consumes per capita endowment. Thus,

$$E\{x_0\} = w_0; \quad E\{x_1\} = w_1. \tag{8.32}$$

Therefore, in equilibrium

$$\beta(1+g) = E\{\delta\} + \text{cov}\left( \delta, \frac{x_0}{w_0} \right), \tag{8.33}$$

where $1 + g := w_1/w_0$ is the gross growth rate of endowment. As in a model with homogenous patience, the bond price is a function of the growth rate

[16]The remaining of this section is based on Lengwiler (2003).

and average discount factor. But here, the bond price is also a function of the covariance of the consumption share of agents today ($y_0/w_0$) and their individual discount factor ($\delta$).

Given the log felicity function, the optimal consumption plan of agent $i$ is easily computed,

$$(x_0(i), x_1(i)) = \left( \frac{w_0 + \beta w_1}{1 + \delta(i)}, \frac{\delta(i)(w_0 + \beta w_1)}{\beta(1 + \delta(i))} \right). \tag{8.34}$$

Substituting this into (8.33) and solving for $\beta$ yields

$$\beta = \frac{E\{\delta\} + \text{cov}(\delta, (1 + \delta)^{-1}))}{(1 + g)(1 - \text{cov}(\delta, (1 + \delta)^{-1}))}, \tag{8.35}$$

or in logs

$$\begin{aligned} \ln \rho := -\ln \beta &= -\ln(E\{\delta\} + \text{cov}(\delta, (1 + \delta)^{-1})) \\ &\quad + \ln(1 + g) + \ln(1 - \text{cov}(\delta, (1 + \delta)^{-1})) \\ &\approx -\ln(E\{\delta\} + \text{cov}(\delta, (1 + \delta)^{-1})) \\ &\quad + g - \text{cov}(\delta, (1 + \delta)^{-1}). \end{aligned} \tag{8.36}$$

As in the standard model with unit intertemporal elasticity of substitution, the interest rate (approximately) equals the sum of the average discount rate of the population ($-\ln(E\{\delta\})$) and the growth rate of per capita consumption ($g$). But in addition, there is a covariance term (entering twice) which is a function only of the extent to which agents have heterogeneous patience. This covariance is always negative, and therefore necessarily increases the interest rate.

This is an *endogenous timing effect.* Impatient people consume early, patient people defer more consumption into the future. This choice of timing of consumption increases the intertemporal rate of substitution of patient people, and decreases the intertemporal rate of substitution of impatient people. In equilibrium, the Euler equations of everyone—the patient and the impatient—must be met, and the intertemporal rate of substitution is the same for everyone, and equal to the equilibrium interest rate for cash flows at different points in time. We see from (8.33) that this means that the yield is increased ($\beta$ is decreased) because the covariance between patience and early consumption is negative. Thus, a mean preserving spread of the discount factor increases the equilibrium interest rate.

It may seem surprising that heterogeneous time preference should increase the equilibrium interest rate. After all, we argued that the more patient people should dominate, at least in the long run. Due to the limitation of a two-period model, this is not visible here, so let us extend the model to multiple periods. We keep log utility, equal endowment, and absence of uncertainty, and we assume that per capita endowment grows at a constant rate, $w_{t+1} = (1+g)w_t$ for all $t \in \{1, \dots, T\}$. There are $T$ risk-free bonds, one for each possible time to maturity, with prices $\beta_1, \dots, \beta_T$. With this extension, the analogue to (8.33) is

$$\beta_t(1+g)^t = E\{\delta^t\} + \operatorname{cov}\left(\delta^t, \frac{x_0}{w_0}\right), \qquad \text{for} \quad t = 1, \dots, T. \tag{8.37}$$

The optimal consumption path of an agent with time preference $\delta(i)$, given market prices $\beta_1, \dots, \beta_T$ (and with $\beta_0 := 1$ by definition), is

$$x_0(i) = \frac{w_0 \sum_{s=0}^{T} \beta_s (1+g)^s}{\sum_{s=0}^{T} \delta(i)^s}, \quad \text{and} \quad x_t(i) = \frac{\delta(i)^t}{\beta_t} x_0(i), \text{ for } t = 1, \dots, T. \tag{8.38}$$

Therefore,

$$\beta_t(1+g)^t = E\{\delta^t\} + \operatorname{cov}\left(\delta^t, \left(\sum_{s=0}^{T} \delta^s\right)^{-1}\right) \sum_{s=0}^{T} \beta_s (1+g)^s. \tag{8.39}$$

Next we sum over all $t$, solve for $\sum_t \beta_t(1+g)^t$, and substitute this into (8.39). This gives us closed forms for all bond prices,

$$\beta_t(1+g)^t = E\{\delta^t\} + \underbrace{\frac{\operatorname{cov}\left(\delta^t, \left(\sum_{s=0}^{T} \delta^s\right)^{-1}\right) \sum_{s=0}^{T} E\{\delta^s\}}{1 - \sum_{s=0}^{T} \operatorname{cov}\left(\delta^s, \left(\sum_{s'=0}^{T} \delta^{s'}\right)^{-1}\right)}}_{=: \mathcal{C}(t)}. \tag{8.40}$$

This is the $T$-period model generalization of (8.35). What can be said about this? First, the timing effect $\mathcal{C}(t)$ is negative for all $t$. It depresses all bond prices and accordingly increases all interest rates. Second, if $\delta(i) < 1$ for all $i$, the timing effect disappears asymptotically for long maturities, that is, $\mathcal{C}(t) \to 0$ as $t \to \infty$.[17]

The yields of the different bonds are

$$\rho_t := (\beta_t)^{-1/t} = (1+g)[E\{\delta^t\} + \mathcal{C}(t)]^{-1/t}. \tag{8.41}$$

[17]The reason for this is that $\mathcal{C}(t)$ is a constant times $\operatorname{cov}(\delta^t, (\sum_s \delta^s)^{-1})$. If all $\delta(i) < 1$, this covariance vanishes for large $t$, because the range of $\delta^t$ collapses to $[0, \varepsilon]$ with $\varepsilon \to 0$ as $t \to \infty$.

This is the analog of (6.28). It is more special because here we assume no aggregate risk and $\gamma = 1$. It is more general because we allow for heterogeneous time preference. As $T \to \infty$, the return rate of the longest maturity bond $\rho_T$ converges to the discount rate of the most patient person in the economy (plus the growth rate of the economy),[18]

$$\begin{aligned} \rho_\infty &:= \lim_{T\to\infty} \rho_T \\ &= (1+g) \lim_{T\to\infty} [E\{\delta^T\} + \mathcal{C}(T)]^{-1/T} \\ &= (1+g) \max\{\delta\}^{-1}. \end{aligned} \tag{8.42}$$

The yield on a bond with infinite maturity equals the per capita growth rate of the economy plus the discount rate of the most patient person. Why? We have already argued that $\mathcal{C}(T) \to 0$ as $T$ grows indefinitely, so for large enough $T$ we can ignore this term. We need to show that $E\{\delta^T\}^{1/T} \to \max\{\delta\}$. This is so because the largest discount factor dominates ever more as $T$ grows ever larger.[19] This is the Becker–Weitzman effect. The price of a bond with infinite maturity is determined only by the most patient person (and by the growth rate of the economy, of course).

We calibrate the model as follows: let there be ten types of agents (all equally weighted), with discount rates of 0.7%, 1.3%, 1.8%, 2.3%, 2.8%, 3.4%, 4.0%, 4.9%, 6.7%, and 13.0%, respectively. The average discount rate of this population is 4.1%. This calibration matches the distribution found by Weitzman (2001) in his survey quite closely. We also set $g = 1\%$. The resulting equilibrium term structure is quite inverse.[20] Interestingly, the Becker–Weitzman effect and the consumption timing effect contribute more or less equally in making the term structure inverse. It is particularly remarkable how long reaching the inversion effect is. With this calibration, $\rho_\infty = 1.7\%$.[21] Yet, a bond with one year to maturity yields 7.75%, a 25-year bond yields about 6.0%, and a 50-year bond still yields 5.1%.[22]

[18]In this formula $\max\{\delta\}$ denotes the largest discount factor in the population.

[19]Proof: Let $\varepsilon(i) := \delta(i)/\max\{\delta\} \in [0,1]$. Then $E\{\delta^T\}^{1/T} = \max\{\delta\}(\Sigma_i\, \varepsilon(i)^T/n)^{1/T} \to \max\{\delta\}$ as $T \to \infty$ because $\Sigma_i\, \varepsilon(i)^T/n \in [1/n, 1]$ for arbitrary $T$.

[20]The resulting yield curve is computed in an Excel file that is available for download from the book's website.

[21]There is one caveat with this calibration. In Weitzman's survey, six out of 2160 respondents reported negative discount rates, with a minimum of −3%. Forty-six more reported zero discounting. If the support of $\delta$ includes unity or even numbers greater than that, then the yield impact of the consumption timing effect does not vanish even for arbitrarily long maturities. In that case, $\rho_t$ stays bounded away from the sum of the growth rate and the smallest discount rate, so in that case $\rho_\infty > (1+g)\max\{\delta\}^{-1}$.

[22]5.1% is also the interest rate that a naive observer might expect, summing the growth rate (1%) and the average discount rate (4.1%) of the population.

We can compute a representative agent that produces this term structure. However, this representative agent does not discount exponentially. Consider an agent with average endowment, $w_t = w_0(1+g)^t$, and who uses uses the discount factor $\tilde{\delta}_t := (1+g)/\rho_t$ for consumption in period $t$. The maximization problem of this agent is

$$\max \left\{ \sum_{t=0}^{T} (\tilde{\delta}_t)^t \ln(x_t) \,\middle|\, \sum_{t=0}^{T} \beta_t x_t \leqslant \sum_{t=0}^{T} \beta_t w_t \right\}. \tag{8.43}$$

$x = w$ is a solution to this problem, which establishes that this agent is a local representative. The discount rate that corresponds to the representative's discount factor is given by $-\ln(\tilde{\delta}_t) \approx \ln(\rho_t) - g$. This rate is decreasing in $t$ because the equilibrium term structure is inverse. We can therefore conclude that the representative discounts hyperbolically (Laibson, 1997). In other words, a population of exponentially discounting agents aggregates into a representative agent that discounts in a hyperbolic fashion. *Hyperbolic discounting is an aggregation phenomenon.*

In an individual, hyperbolic discounting gives rise to time inconsistency. Nothing of this sort happens here: the representative is not a real person in this economy. It is only a technical tool that relates asset prices to aggregate endowment. Therefore, hyperbolic discounting in the aggregate does not give rise to time inconsistency for any individual member of the economy.

### *8.3.3 Age (demography)*

Another dimension in which agents may differ, and which departs even more deeply from the mainstream model, is age. The age of a decision maker is irrelevant in the standard model because everyone is supposed to be existing at some common point in time ("period 0," or "today") and no new agents show up in the course of events. Yet, a typical life—from a purely financial point of view—consists of first accumulating assets when young and working, and then living off these assets when old and retired.

Maybe a more realistic model, one that captures this *life cycle*, is one that features partially overlapping generations of agents (Samuelson, 1958; Diamond, 1965). At any point in time there are young agents, old agents, possibly also middle-aged agents. Some of them work, some do not, depending on age. Some live off the proceeds of the wealth they have accumulated, others are still in the process of accumulating wealth. To be more concrete, consider an overlapping generations (OG) model featuring agents who live for two periods. They are called "young" in the first period of their lives and "old" in the second. At each point in time, an old and a young generation is present. The economy functions without capital. The young produce a consumption good (food), which is not storable. The old are retired and produce nothing. But the old own a number of green pieces of paper that are of no intrinsic value. They trade these pieces of paper with the young in exchange for a share of the food they produce. The young agree to this trade because they are after the green pieces of paper, which will allow them to live off the next generation's production one period later. These pieces of paper—money, or more generally financial assets—allow intertemporal smoothing of consumption. This is essentially the same role that a pension system fulfills. Without this institution, consumption would be possible only for those who grow food, that is, the young. "If Crusoe were alone, he would obviously die at the beginning of his retirement" (Samuelson, 1958, page 468).

It is easily conceivable that a change in the age composition of the population, perhaps resulting from a demographic shock, can have a strong impact on the exchange rate between food and money, i.e. on asset prices. Consider an extreme situation when everyone is old and no one works. Assets are worth nothing and consumption is zero. If everyone is young, on the other hand, assets are worth infinitely much, except that there are no assets to be found. From these extreme cases, we may tentatively conclude that an economy that grows younger should experience rising asset prices, and an economy that grows older should experience falling asset prices.

Under this interpretation, the bullish housing market of the 1970s, when the earliest baby boomers were in their thirties, was an aftermath of the baby boom (Mankiw & Weil, 1989). Similarly, the bullish stock market of the 1980s and 1990s was driven by the baby boomers' search for investment opportunities in anticipation of retirement (Bakshi & Chen, 1994). But birth control ended the baby boom. When the baby boomers start liquidating (roughly from 2010 onwards), they will have trouble selling their assets to the next generation, because the next generation is so much smaller.

Several factors can attenuate these dire impacts. First, we assumed that goods are not storable, so that all of the old generation's consumption has to come from the young. If some goods are storable this is not true, because consumption can then be moved through time. In that case, Crusoe would not have to die when he retired, even if he were alone. Capital that is not in fixed supply, but can be accumulated and decumulated, is just such a good. Abel (2003) studies an OG model with endogenous capital and social security. He uses a log-linear specification of the capital production function (the function that maps existing capital and investment into the amount of capital available in the next period),

$$K_{t+1} = I_t^{\phi} K_t^{1-\phi}.$$

If $\phi = 0$, capital supply cannot be altered by investments and is simply fixed. If $\phi = 1$, all the existing capital depreciates within a period and today's capital stock equals yesterday's investment. The most realistic cases are those in between, $0 < \phi < 1$. Abel finds that the price of capital is an increasing function of the birth rate if $\phi < 1$. The effect is the strongest if $\phi = 0$, so the ability to accumulate capital smoothes movements of the price of capital as a result of demographic shocks. But the effect does not go away completely unless $\phi = 1$. He also finds that the price of capital is mean reverting if $0 < \phi < 1$. Therefore, a baby boom inflates asset prices only temporarily.

Second, the baby boom and baby bust is a demographic shock that occurred primarily in the industrial countries of the Western hemisphere. But the world is a larger place. Maybe the Chinese will buy the assets of American and European baby boomers. In that case, the meltdown of asset prices could be avoided and the baby boomers would be bailed out. Perhaps the lurking crisis is a chance for emerging economies to aquire the capital they need to grow. This scenario implies radical movements. Capital will flow from the West to the emerging economies. Accordingly, the West will run large trade deficits. Siegel (1998, page 42) says it well: "First they [the emerging economies] will pay off their debts, then acquire ownership of their own capital and eventually buy the assets of the developed world." In the end, the world will be a more equitable place. But, of course, that requires that global markets for goods and capital remain open.

## 8.4 Efficiency failure

Aggregate risk is small, as measured by the national consumption statistics, but the premium on risky assets is large. This implies a very large price of risk. The implied price of risk would be smaller if somehow we could justify that people bear more than just aggregate risk. If idiosyncratic risk were not fully diversified away, people would bear more than just the small aggregate risk. As a consequence, the large equity premium would be compatible with a smaller price of risk.

The failure of complete diversification of idiosyncratic risk amounts to a failure of the mutuality principle (section 5.2). This principle requires two conditions in order to hold: agents must share common beliefs, and the equilibrium allocation must be Pareto efficient. If beliefs are not common, efficiency does not imply complete diversification of idiosyncratic shocks, because agents want to bet on the states they consider more likely. If the equilibrium allocation is not Pareto efficient, idiosyncratic risk will not be fully diversified away, even with common beliefs.

There are several reasons why the equilibrium allocation may not be Pareto efficient. The two most important ones are transaction costs and incompleteness of markets.[23] Transaction costs make the simple unconstrained first-order condition fail by placing a wedge between the rates of substitution (the SDF) and the asset prices. Incomplete markets preclude full mutual insurance in a very direct way. We explore these possibilities in the rest of this section.

### *8.4.1 Incomplete markets*

Mankiw (1986) presents a very stylized (and therefore very instructive) model of asset pricing with incomplete markets. There are two equally likely aggregate states, a good and a bad one. Aggregate wealth in the good state is $\mu$, and in the bad is $(1-\phi)\mu$, with $0 < \phi < 1$. Everyone has the same utility function. The aggregate endowment is of course simply the mean endowment of the population. But Mankiw assumes that the individual endowment shocks, which sum up to the aggregate endowment shock, are concentrated on a portion $\lambda$ of the population. That is to say, besides the aggregate state there are idiosyncratic states. If the good aggregate state materializes, everyone receives endowment $\mu$. If the bad state materializes, there is a chance $1-\lambda$ for each agent to get $\mu$ anyway. But with probability $\lambda$ the agent receives $(1-\phi/\lambda)\mu$. If $\lambda = 1$ shocks are not concentrated. If $\lambda < 1$ only a (random) part of the population is hit by the endowment shock. If $\lambda = \phi$, the endowment of the unlucky ones drops to zero if the bad aggregate state occurs.

A good way to think about the aggregate and idiosyncratic states is to view the aggregate state as business cycles (aggregate consumption may be low or high tomorrow) and idiosyncratic states as unemployment risk. People will be laid off only in a recession, but this will affect only a small part of the population.

Mankiw assumes that there are assets to trade only aggregate risk; there are no markets for idiosyncratic risks. In other words, there is no unemployment insurance. He finds that the equilibrium equity premium increases with the concentration of endowment shocks (the smaller $\lambda$, the larger the risk premium) if the utility function is prudent ($v''' > 0$, which is weaker than DARA). The numerical examples he provides suggest that with CRRA utility quite a strong concentration (a small $\lambda$) is needed to produce a large risk premium. Nevertheless, the effect works well.

[23]Danthine, Donaldson & Mehra (1992) argued quite early that Keynesian features such as frictions and incomplete mutual insurance are able to enhance the success of RBC models in terms of describing business cycles as well as asset prices.

Now, put this model in an environment with many periods. Suppose that idiosyncratic endowment shocks are not very persistent, meaning that if you were unlucky last time (if you were one of those who suffered the endowment loss in the last recession), it does not mean that you will be unlucky forever. Then the incompleteness of the insurance that is possible using financial assets can partially be circumvented by *self-insurance*. How does that work? Agents can largely wash away the effects of idiosyncratic risk by mutually borrowing and lending some asset among each other (a government bond, for instance). In the idiosyncratically bad state, the risk-free asset is sold short (or if the agent has a stock of it, it is simply sold); in the idiosyncratically good state, the risk-free asset is bought. Such a strategy allows individuals to eliminate much of the idiosyncratic risk. It will not eliminate all of it, however, if there is an upper bound on short selling, and if there is a positive probability of running into this bound. In that case, agents would optimally increase savings to some extent in order to decrease the probability of hitting the constraint. Yet, in the aggregate, saving is zero in equilibrium (in an exchange economy), so the increased demand for saving arising from a desire to self-insure provides an explanation for the low risk-free rate.

What about the equity premium? If endowment shocks are not very persistent, self-insurance works in that it allows agents to largely eliminate idiosyncratic risk. In this case agents do not bear much more than just aggregate risk in equilibrium. Consequently, equilibrium asset prices will be very similar to those applying in the complete market case (Telmer, 1993; Lucas, 1994). Thus, it seems that the lack of a complete financial market per se cannot explain the large equity premium, unless idiosyncratic risk is highly persistent. Microeconometric evidence does not support the hypothesis of highly persistent idiosyncratic shocks, though, thereby more or less shutting down Mankiw's channel (Heaton & Lucas, 1996).

Constantinides & Duffie (1996) show how far incomplete consumption insurance is able to explain the risk premium puzzle if individual endowment shocks are very persistent (in fact, permanent in their case). They work with an economy consisting of agents with identical standard preferences. They show that it is possible to construct individual income processes that are compatible with a given aggregate income process and with given asset price processes, for any (non-zero) degree of risk aversion. The key is that the cross-sectional income variance must be negatively correlated with aggregate endowment. A recession is not bad primarily because it reduces income on average, but because it amplifies risk. This makes shares unattractive for saving for bad times, thereby raising the equity risk premium. Brav et al. (2002) test this model and find it to be compatible with the data if one accepts a coefficient of relative risk aversion between 3 and 4. Cogley (2002), on the other hand, finds that an equity premium of at most 2% can be justified by the data if risk aversion is constrained to be below 5.

### *8.4.2 Credit constraints*

Can the Mankiw channel be reactivated if self-insurance is difficult for some reason? An agent who is credit constrained, for instance, will find it difficult to self-insure. Such constraints are not natural in a Walrasian model, but they are very natural outcomes if we consider asymmetric information (Stiglitz & Weiss, 1981). A credit-constrained agent, living in a world with highly incomplete financial markets, will not be able to smooth consumption much or to hedge idiosyncratic risk. Such an agent will be subject to much more than just aggregate risk and may therefore be highly averse to bearing marginally more risk. However, Lettau (2002) computes an upper bound of the effect of incomplete markets by assuming that agents cannot smooth consumption at all. Instead, they are forced to consume their current income. Yet, even with this extreme assumption he finds that income volatility is too small to explain the large Sharpe ratios that we measure in the data.

Constantinides, Donaldson & Mehra (2002) have proposed a model in which not all agents are credit constrained, but only those who would value equities particularly strongly. They consider a model with three overlapping generations. The young and the middle-aged generations work, the old generation is retired; they have no labor income anymore but just live off their accumulated wealth. The young have no current wealth and a low wage. They also face idiosyncratic labor income risk for the middle age period. This is supposed to capture the idea that an agent, when entering the labor market, does not know how his career will develop. The middle-aged—the established workers—do not face labor income uncertainty anymore.The trouble is that the young cannot hedge their labor income risk because financial markets are not complete. The individual endowment processes (consisting of just two numbers $(w_t, w_{t+1})$ for generation $t$) are not traded. If the market were complete, the optimal portfolio of the young would be to hedge labor income risk. Since the middle-aged generation is the only one that has a high wage, the young would like to borrow against their future labor income, and the middle-aged would like to save for their old age. But only the middle-aged are allowed to do this, because by assumption future labor income cannot be used as collateral owing to credit market imperfections, and therefore the young are credit constrained.

The authors consider a calibration of this model in which the young, if they were not constrained, would borrow by shorting the risk-free bond and would invest some of this loan into risky equities.[24] Once we impose the credit constraint on the young, they cannot borrow anymore and consequently they cannot buy equities. In this constrained equilibrium the young do not hold any assets in equilibrium. Saving begins only when middle-aged. The middle-aged buy the bonds and the equities from the old generation in order to smooth consumption. Inter-generational exchange takes place only between the middle-aged and the old. The young are excluded, so at any point in time one third of the population is not participating in the financial markets. Constantinides et al. find that, with their calibration, this friction reduces the risk-free interest rate and increases the equity premium, although the effect is not overly strong.

Bequests are assumed away in this model. If the young inherit from the old that will help them overcome the constraint. They may then be able to buy shares which would reduce the equity premium. Yet, note that bequests do not change anything if the children inherit from their parents, because in this case wealth is transferred from the dying old generation to the newly old generation. If the grandchildren inherit from their grandparents, the assets are transferred to the newly middle-aged generation. Either way, the young will not benefit. Bequests would diminish the credit constraint only if the old generation bequested to the *newly young* generation, that is to say, to the generation that starts life when the testator generation dies. In the calibration of the model, where one generation spans twenty years, this means that the heirs are sixty years younger than the testators, which is probably quite untypical.

### 8.4.3 Transaction costs

Transaction costs put a wedge between the rates of substitution and the asset prices. If transaction costs have a fixed component, independent of the traded quantity, then the simple first-order conditions do not hold. This is reminiscent of the menu cost literature in macroeconomics (Sheshinski & Weiss, 1977, and the literature that followed). A small quantity-independent transaction cost is sufficient to make it optimal for an investor not to adjust his portfolio when prices change. This is because the objective function of the investor (his expected utility) is almost flat near the maximum. Deviations from the optimal portfolio therefore have only a second-order effect on the objective, and it is not worth adjusting to shocks (in the language

[24]Whether this is a particularly compelling choice seems debatable.

of our theory, to the realization of specific events in the uncertainty tree) in the presence of transaction costs, unless the shock is sufficiently large or else several small shocks, all requiring a change in the same direction, have accumulated. Thus, a second-order transaction cost can induce first-order deviations from the optimal portfolio.

Yet, it seems that the utility cost of these deviations should be small, since they cannot exceed the transaction cost. (Otherwise it would be optimal to adjust despite the transaction cost.) However, the New Keynesian macroeconomic theory has shown that there is an externality inherent in this problem. In the new Keynesian imperfect competition macro models, the firms' price decisions are strategically complementary. As a result, if one firm fails to adjust, the others won't either. What appears to be small losses arising from menu costs on an individual basis then sum up to considerable losses for society as a whole. Something similar might happen in asset markets. If investors' portfolio decisions are strategic complements, then individually small transaction costs may cause significant departures from Pareto efficiency, thereby invalidating the mutuality principle and effectively increasing the amount of risk borne by all agents.

Such a New Keynesian asset pricing theory has not yet been fully formulated. Instead, the pricing implications of transaction costs are analyzed in a much simpler fashion, without reference to the effect on equilibrium allocations and departures from efficiency. The classic contribution here is Demsetz (1968). After studying the market for transaction services on the New York Stock Exchange (NYSE), he estimates the cost function of traders in this market from bid–ask spreads, and finds evidence for scale economies. A later important contribution is Amihud & Mendelson (1986). In their model each asset has an an exogenously given transaction cost associated with it. In equilibrium, investors are compensated for these costs. As a result, high transaction cost assets earn a larger return (before correcting for transaction costs) than low transaction cost assets. Amihud & Mendelson assume that there are different types of investor, distinguished by investment horizon (or trading affinity). With this assumption they identify a *clientele effect.*[25] Investors with a short horizon trade more often and therefore are hurt more by transaction costs. In equilibrium, therefore, low transaction cost assets are allocated to short-horizon investors. The long-horizon investors are happy to buy the high transaction cost assets in exchange for a higher return, because they can spread the transaction costs over a longer period of time. Because short-horizon investors are affected more by transaction costs, the pricing effect is marginally the greatest in those asset classes

[25]This is a general equilibrium endogenous sorting effect, similar to the consumption timing effect of section 8.3.2.

held by the short-term investors, i.e. the low transaction cost assets. For this reason, the expected return rate is not linear, but concave in transaction costs. That is to say, the increase in the expected return that is due to transaction costs is the largest for small transaction cost assets. This is a testable implication, which is verified empirically by Amihud & Mendelson.

There is some consensus that transaction costs explain the small firm anomaly (section 7.5), because the market for small firm equity is typically less liquid and therefore exhibits greater bid–ask spreads. But it is not so clear that transaction costs can explain the general equity premium. It is true that government bonds markets are more liquid than equity markets, but is the difference sufficient to explain a very large premium? This seems to be an unsettled issue. Fisher (1994) reports that observed bid–ask spreads justify an equity premium of 3%–4% in an otherwise mainstream model featuring a representative agent with a constant relative risk aversion coefficient of 2. Luttmer (1999), on the other hand, estimates that an investor with logarithmic utility function who consumes per capita endowment and can trade Treasury bills and an index of the NYSE must face a fixed transaction cost (independent of quantity) of 3% of monthly consumption. But this result is highly sensitive to the risk aversion parameter, the possibility of habit persistence or short-sale constraints, and the kind of information that investors observe before trading. Perhaps it is a question of the historical period under study. Spending 3% of your monthly budget for just one transaction (buying or selling the NYSE index in Luttmer's model) seems excessive for today's technology. But maybe this figure makes more sense for the early part of the period studied by Mehra & Prescott (1985). If the transaction cost explanation is correct, we should expect the equity premium to be much smaller today and in the future than it used to be.

There is, however, a serious problem with the Amihud & Mendelson model. Asset-specific transaction costs basically amount to an asset-specific tax—the risk premia before tax are anomalous, the risk premia after correcting for taxes are not. It is unclear, though, why investors should not try to avoid these taxes. In the language of the model, all investors should become less eager to trade and should use a longer horizon in their portfolio decisions. Of course, this is not part of the model, because trading activity of the investors is exogenous, so "extending one's horizon" is not in the realm of possible choices. Yet, a more complete model would allow for this. There is little doubt that the high transaction costs postulated here would provide a strong an incentive to trade much less than what we observe in the data. Essentially, the asset pricing puzzle is transformed into a *trade volume puzzle.*

Moreover, even if most assets are subject to considerable transaction costs, the price implications of this friction will be limited as long as one asset is traded at negligible cost.[26] The reason for this is the same as in the case of incomplete markets. The liquid asset can be traded dynamically to self-insure. So, generally speaking, transaction costs might not be such a good explanation of the large risk premium.

### *8.4.4 Taxes and inflation*

Transaction costs can be circumvented simply by trading less. Taxes, in contrast, also put a wedge between asset returns and marginal utility, but these costs cannot easily be circumvented. If different assets are taxed differently by the government, this could easily explain pre-tax anomalies. Thus, it appears that taxes could play a more prominent role for asset pricing than mere transaction costs.

McGrattan & Prescott have recently explored this possibility and report their results in two papers. McGrattan & Prescott (2000) compare the value of U.S. corporate capital with the value of U.S. corporate equity. If debt is small, the two should be roughly identical. After estimating non-tangible capital (such as organizational structure or brand names), the authors find that total value of corporate capital is indeed roughly equal to the value of corporate equity. The ratio of corporate capital or corporate equity to GDP, however, has changed a lot. Between 1946 and the mid-1990s this ratio fluctuated between 0.4 and 1.0. Since then it has suddenly increased to 1.8, a figure that is compatible with the calibration of their model. This development has basically reduced the equity premium to nil.

McGrattan & Prescott (2001) argue that this reduction is due to unexpected changes in tax rates. They observe that U.S. tax rates on dividends have been massively reduced over that last forty years. The marginal income tax rates on the highest tax bracket have fallen from 91% in 1960 to 33% in 1986. (Since then, they have been increased somewhat again, along with a rise of state income tax rates.) They argue, however, that a second channel of tax reduction is more important. Retirement accounts are tax free and have been available for a long time. Yet before 1960 almost no equity was held in such accounts because of legal restrictions. With the liberalization of such regulations, this is no longer the case. Moreover, for savings outside of retirement accounts, mutual funds have become available that transform dividends into capital gains, which are much less heavily taxed. As a consequence, return on equity is nowadays much less subject to taxation than it used to be.

[26]The liquid asset should be such that it pays out in all events. A risk-free consol would be ideal, but a family of government bonds, maturing at various points in time, would do as well. Even cash would be fine, provided inflation is moderate.

The authors argue that the after-tax return rate on equity is the sum of two factors: the return generated by dividends, and the return generated by anticipated growth of the capital stock (capital gains). They compute that in the postwar period the dividend yield has decreased from 3% to 1% essentially because of the increase in equity prices. Expected growth of productive assets (tangible and intangible) has been about 3.5% and has not changed much. In addition to these two factors, the pre-tax return rates on equity are also affected by unanticipated growth in the value of stocks arising from reductions in the tax rate. They argue that the relevant tax rates have decreased from 44% to 18% during this time span, giving rise to an additional return rate of almost 2% per year on average. Yet, if no further tax reductions are forthcoming, this additional factor should vanish. Thus, all three factors together justify a return rate on equity that declined from $3\% + 3.5\% + 2\% = 8.5\%$ after the war to $1\% + 3.5\% + 0\% = 4.5\%$ today. This is roughly what we see in the data, so the authors conclude that "there is no equity premium puzzle in the postwar period" (McGrattan & Prescott, 2001, abstract).

This is a surprising and very thought provoking result. Maybe all the confusion about why the equity premium was so high is simply due to an oversight? Yet, one might be tempted to quarrel with McGrattan & Prescott's (2001) computation of the relevant tax rates. Is it really true that taxation has been reduced as much as the authors claim? After all, retirement accounts are not really tax free:

> Contributions to most retirement accounts are not taxed and grow tax-free until they are withdrawn for consumption. Although these funds are taxed upon withdrawal, this tax is in effect a consumption tax, not a dividend tax. Consequently, the marginal tax rates on these distributions have no consequence for the steady-state value of corporate equity relative to GDP. (McGrattan & Prescott, 2001, page 2)

This is an odd argument. After all, a utility maximizing agent who draws utility only from consumption and leisure does not care whether it is his dividends or his consumption that are being taxed. Consider an extreme case. Suppose the tax on retirement accounts upon withdrawal is 100% on capital gains, dividends, and principal. Then putting an asset into such an account is like burning it. It is clearly not right to say that such a tax would have no consequence for the equilibrium value of corporate equity. In general, the fact that the investor who saves for his retirement will not be able to transform the returns on equity *completely* into consumption reduces his willingness to pay for equity, and therefore should increase the equilibrium equity premium.

Another aspect of taxation is the fact that it is random, at least over longer horizons. Sialm (2002) explores the asset pricing implications of this additional risk factor using an infinite-horizon model with a private and a public good and with transfers. Many implications of taxation on asset pricing can be understood within a much simpler two-period model, however.[27] There is a proportional state-contingent tax on consumption. Suppose that all agents have the same CRRA utility function but possibly different state-contingent endowments, and that idiosyncratic risk can be hedged using a complete set of financial markets. Suppose also that taxation is not progressive but linear. Then, Rubinstein aggregation applies (Box 5.3), and we can ignore inter-personal distribution and work with a single CRRA agent.

Note that progressive income taxation destroys distribution-independent aggregation because it implies that different agents face different after-tax returns from the same financial assets. So, for aggregation to work we assume that all agents face the same tax rate in a given state. But that doesn't mean that the tax rate cannot vary with the state. There can be high-tax and low-tax states of the world.

Let $\mathbf{t}_s$ denote the tax rate in state $s$. The portfolio problem of the representative agent is then

$$\max\left\{v(y^0)+\delta E\{v(y)\}\;\middle|\;(1-\mathbf{t}_0)(y^0-w^0)+\sum_{s=1}^{S}\alpha_s(1-\mathbf{t}_s)(y^s-w^s)\leqslant 0\right\}, \tag{8.44}$$

and the first-order conditions are

$$\delta\frac{v'(w^s)}{v'(w^0)}\frac{1-\mathbf{t}_s}{1-\mathbf{t}_0}=\frac{\alpha_s}{\pi_s}=:M_s. \tag{8.45}$$

The SDF can be decomposed into two components,

$$\mathbb{M}_s:=\delta\frac{v'(w^s)}{v'(w^0)}\quad\text{and}\quad\mathbb{F}_s:=\frac{1-\mathbf{t}_s}{1-\mathbf{t}_0}, \tag{8.46}$$

so that $M_s=\mathbb{M}_s\mathbb{F}_s$, where $\mathbb{F}_s$ denotes the gross rate of change of the share of income that is available after taxation. $\mathbb{F}_s=1$ if tax rates in state $s$ are

[27] Sialm (2002) adds a public good that enters total utility in an additively separable fashion. He also adds a parameter that determines the shares of the tax receipts that are used to produce the public good and that are returned to the agents as transfers, respectively. All of this is irrelevant for asset pricing, though. Taxes that are transferred back to the representative agent are equivalent to a reduction of the tax rate, and the public good has no effect on asset prices due to the assumed separability. For that reason, we leave these items out and simply think of tax revenues as being burned.

the same as today (in state 0); $\mathbb{F}_s > 1$ means that the tax rate is smaller, and $\mathbb{F}_s < 1$ implies that the tax rate is larger than today.

A truly risk-free asset in this model would be an asset that never defaults and whose payoff is indexed to the price level and the tax rate. But such assets do not exist. Instead, consider a bond that is inflation-indexed and free of default risk, but is not indexed to the tax rate. The equilibrium price of such an asset is

$$\beta = E\{\mathbb{M}\mathbb{F}\} = E\{\mathbb{M}\}E\{\mathbb{F}\} + \operatorname{cov}(\mathbb{M}, \mathbb{F}). \tag{8.47}$$

Compare this with (5.29). Tax rates that are expected to decrease through time ($E\{\mathbb{F}\} > 1$) reduce the default-risk free interest rate, as do procyclical tax rates ($\operatorname{cov}(\mathbb{M}, \mathbb{F}) > 0$). The intuitive reason for this last effect is that a procyclical tax rate reduces aggregate risk because high-income states are taxed more heavily than low-income states. Thus, a default-risk free bond acts as a hedge against aggregate risk.

Assuming a CRRA representative with a coefficient of relative risk aversion $\gamma$ and acyclical tax rates yields

$$\ln \rho + \ln \mathbb{F} \approx \gamma E\{g\} - \ln \delta. \tag{8.48}$$

The real default-risk free interest rate is as in the standard model (5.38) after correcting for the expected change of tax rates. So taxation affects the real interest rate via two channels. A tax rate that changes through time puts a wedge between pre- and after-tax interest rates. A stochastic tax rate adds a positive or negative risk premium to the default-risk free asset, which is risk free only in pre-tax terms.

The equilibrium pricing formula (5.31) for an asset with state-contingent return rates $R$ becomes

$$\begin{aligned} 1 &= E\{\mathbb{M}\mathbb{F}R\} \\ &= E\{\mathbb{M}\mathbb{F}\}E\{R\} + \operatorname{cov}(\mathbb{M}\mathbb{F}, R) \\ &= \beta E\{R\} + \operatorname{cov}(\mathbb{M}\mathbb{F}, R). \end{aligned} \tag{8.49}$$

This implies

$$E\{R\} - \rho = \rho \operatorname{cov}(-\mathbb{M}\mathbb{F}, R), \tag{8.50}$$

similar to (5.36). Assuming that the representative agent is CRRA with coefficient of relative risk aversion $\gamma$ and taking first-order approximations, this becomes

$$E\{R\} - \rho \approx \rho\delta\gamma \operatorname{cov}(g\mathbb{F}, R). \tag{8.51}$$

The risk premium depends on the covariance of the return rate with after-tax endowment growth. As in (5.39), we can substitute $\rho$ on the right-hand side of (8.51) with its equilibrium value implied by (8.47).[28] We then get

$$E\{R^j\} - \rho \approx \tilde{\gamma}\,\mathrm{cov}(g\mathbb{F}, R), \tag{8.52}$$

with

$$\tilde{\gamma} := \frac{\gamma}{E\{\mathbb{F}\}(1 - \gamma E\{g\}) - \gamma\,\mathrm{cov}(g, \mathbb{F})}.$$

If taxation is not stochastic, (8.52) collapses to (5.39). Non-stochastic tax rates have no effect on the risk premium; as a consequence of the CRRA assumption.[29] This is so even if the future tax rate differs from the present tax rate ($\mathbb{F}_1 = \cdots = \mathbb{F}_S \neq 1$), because then the expected return rates of all assets are affected in precisely the same way, leaving the risk premium unchanged.

The same is approximately true for stochastic tax rates that are uncorrelated with endowment. Define $\mathfrak{F}_s := \mathbb{F}_s / E\{\mathbb{F}\}$; then $\mathrm{cov}(g\mathbb{F}, R) = \mathrm{cov}(g\mathfrak{F}, R)E\{\mathbb{F}\}$ and $E\{\mathfrak{F}\} = 1$. Then,

$$\begin{aligned}
\mathrm{cov}(g\mathfrak{F}, R) &= \mathrm{cov}((1+g)\mathfrak{F} - \mathfrak{F}, R)\\
&= \mathrm{cov}((1+g)\mathfrak{F}, R) - \mathrm{cov}(\mathfrak{F}, R)\\
&\approx \mathrm{cov}(\ln(1+g), R) + \mathrm{cov}(\ln \mathfrak{F}, R) - \mathrm{cov}(\mathfrak{F}, R)\\
&\approx \mathrm{cov}(g, R).
\end{aligned}$$

The first-order Taylor approximations used in this derivation are approximately correct if the cross-state variance of $g$ and of $\mathfrak{F}$ are small. In that case we conclude that

$$\mathrm{cov}(g, \mathbb{F}) = 0 \Longrightarrow \tilde{\gamma}\,\mathrm{cov}(g\mathbb{F}, R) \approx \gamma^* \mathrm{cov}(g, R). \tag{8.53}$$

Acyclical tax rates have only second-order effects on the risk premium.

Tax rates that are correlated with endowment, however, have a first-order effect on the risk premium. Procyclical tax rates ($\mathrm{cov}(g, \mathbb{F}) < 0$) make $\tilde{\gamma}$ smaller and thus decrease the equity premium. Countercyclical tax rates have the opposite effect. The intuition is the same as for bond pricing.

[28]With the CRRA-assumption, (8.47) becomes $\rho^{-1} = \beta = \delta E\{(1+g)^{-\gamma}\}E\{\mathbb{F}\} + \delta\mathrm{cov}((1+g)^{-\gamma}, \mathbb{F}) \approx \delta[(1 - \gamma E\{g\})E\{\mathbb{F}\} - \gamma\mathrm{cov}(g, \mathbb{F})]$.

[29]In that case, $\tilde{\gamma} = \gamma^*/E\{\mathbb{F}\}$ and $\mathrm{cov}(g\mathbb{F}, R) = E\{\mathbb{F}\}\mathrm{cov}(g, R)$.

Procyclical tax rates reduce the effective (after-tax) amount of aggregate risk, and therefore reduce the market premium paid for carrying this risk.

It is convenient that the effects of inflation on asset pricing can be explained using exactly the same model, simply by interpreting $(1 - \mathbf{t}_s)$ as the index of the purchasing power of money instead of the purchasing power of real income net of taxes. Let payoffs and return rates be measured in nominal (money) terms, but let endowments and consumption denote real (utility-generating) quantities, and assume regular taxation away. Then, $(1 - \mathbf{t}_s)$ can be interpreted as the link connecting nominal to real terms. In this interpretation, $\mathbb{F}^{-1}$ is the inflation rate between today and tomorrow. Expected inflation ($E\{\mathbb{F}\} < 1$) depresses the price of a nominal risk-free bond and thus increases the nominal risk-free interest rate. Countercyclical inflation has the same effect.[30] If we assume that inflation is not correlated with the growth rate of the economy, then (8.47) implies Irving Fisher's equation, i.e.

$$\ln \rho \approx \ln E\{\mathbb{M}\} - \ln E\{\mathbb{F}\}. \tag{8.54}$$

Here, $\ln \rho$ is the nominal interest rate (because all asset payoffs and prices are in nominal terms), $\ln E\{\mathbb{M}\}$ is the intertemporal rate of substitution for consumption and thus is equal to the real interest rate, and $(-\ln E\{\mathbb{F}\})$ is the expected rate of inflation, so the nominal interest rate is approximately equal to the sum of the real interest rate and the expected inflation rate. Compared with this benchmark, countercyclical inflation reduces the nominal interest rate to something smaller than the sum of real interest rate and expected inflation rate.

Inflation also has the same effect as taxation on the price of risky assets. Non-stochastic inflation has no effect on the equity premium, and uncorrelated stochastic inflation has only a second-order effect. Procyclical inflation, on the other hand, decreases the equilibrium equity premium and countercyclical inflation increases this premium.

Contrary to widespread preconceptions, Cooley & Ohanian (1991) find that U.S. inflation seems to be acyclical or countercyclical most of the time, except for the Great Depression, when it was procyclical. This might help to explain a greater equity premium than we would expect when ignoring the effect of stochastic inflation. In any case, our results relate to the *conditional cross-state covariance,* not to the ex post realized intertemporal covariance.

[30]Inflation is countercyclical if $\mathrm{cov}(\mathbb{M}, \mathbb{F}) < 0$, because $\mathbb{M}$ is negatively related to the business cycle and $\mathbb{F}$ is negatively related to the inflation rate.

## Notes on the literature

This is a very active research area. We have discussed several important contributions in this chapter. There is little doubt that more will be published in the future in the pertinent professional journals.

# 9
# Epilog

The gross empirical failure of the CCAPM that was most visibly identified by Mehra & Prescott (1985) was a shock to the profession. This failure has potentially serious consequences, not only for finance, but for macroeconomics as a whole, because much of modern macroeconomics is built on basically the same model that underlies the CCAPM: the stochastic competitive general equilibrium of an economy populated by a representative von Neumann–Morgenstern expected utility maximizer. So, if the CCAPM is to be discarded, much of macroeconomic theory will go with it. This is clearly true for real business cycle theory, which was built on this paradigm from its very beginning. The conclusion is somewhat less true for modern Keynesian theory, because this is general equilibrium theory with imperfections, such as transaction costs, menu costs, or asymmetric information—just the ingredients that may be needed for explaining the quantitative aspects of empirical asset pricing that more simple models cannot elucidate.

An example of a conclusion whose validity depends on how the puzzles are explained is Lucas's (1987) estimation of the social costs of business cycles. Lucas concludes that these costs are essentially zero, because the amount of aggregate risk caused by business cycles is small and the price of risk should be moderate, given that high degrees of risk aversion are unlikely. Yet, if new asset pricing theories are able to justify a larger equilibrium price of risk, or if the effective amount of risk borne by the agents is greater than just the risk measured by aggregate consumption statistics, then our estimate of the true cost of business cycles will be affected. More generally, the gross inability of the theory to explain fundamental prices such as the price of time and the price of risk casts doubt on the general validity of the model for all other purposes as well.

This serious threat to the theory explains the extraordinary research effort that has gone into resolving this particular puzzle as well as the other asset pricing puzzles. I believe that three approaches can be identified. A first view sees the equity premium puzzle as a mystery, a very deep problem for which we have not yet developed any good ideas. The second view is that the puzzle is indeed a challenge, but one that will eventually be resolved. The third view is that the puzzle has disappeared (or, according to McGrattan & Prescott (2001), has never been there): stock prices have adjusted so that there is no longer a puzzle, or, as Irving Fisher once said, stock prices have settled on a "permanently high plateau."

## 9.1 A mystery

The asset pricing puzzles have proved tough. Despite the extraordinary research effort that has been concentrated on this problem, they still have not been resolved. This has led some researchers to paint a grim picture of the state of macroeconomic and financial theory. Kocherlakota (1996), for instance, identifies the equity premium puzzle as a special case of the old challenge of monetary economics—that is to say, to explain why people hold fiat money despite the fact that it is return-dominated by bonds:

> Like fiat money, the equity premium appears to be a widespread and persistent phenomenon of market economies. The *universality* of the equity premium tells us that, like money, the equity premium must emerge from some primitive and elementary features of asset exchange ... we cannot hope to find a resolution to the equity premium puzzle by continuing in our current mode of patching up the standard models of asset exchange with transaction costs here and risk aversion there. (Kocherlakota, 1996, page 67)

The fact that fiat money has value and that people willingly hold it despite the availablility of return-dominating alternatives (such as bonds) can be viewed as one instance of the asset pricing puzzles. Money is a consol with zero coupon. Its return rate is therefore minus the rate of inflation, and therefore was almost always negative in all countries throughout much of the twentieth century. But at the same time, almost risk-free government bonds were available which yielded a higher return. To the professionally less deformed mind, the reason for this is obvious: money facilitates transactions that bonds do not. You cannot settle your purchases at the grocery store with bonds.[1] So money seems to provide a particularly efficient transaction technology which other assets miss, and that makes money valuable.[2] If similar effects are at work when comparing bonds with equity, then only an integrated theory of relative prices and the price level, a theory that has overcome the classical dichotomy, will be able to solve the equity premium puzzle. Financial economics will fulfill its objective only when monetary economics has. Clearly, we are still far away from formulating such an integrated model. As a consequence, a resolution of the puzzle is not likely in the near future.

## 9.2 A challenge

Despite the fact that asset prices are not well understood, some significant progress can be reported. The huge premium originally identified by Mehra & Prescott (1985) has been reduced by extending the sample, by looking at expected premia rather than realized premia and by considering inflation indexed bonds; and new theoretical ideas have been developed that help us understand why the market price of risk may exceed what the most simple standard theory predicts.

The question is not whether we will be able to explain the premium. The question is *how* we will explain it. Which combination of ideas will turn out to be the right one? This choice among explanations will affect our modelling decisions for many other problems as well, most notably in macroeconomics, but also in economics at large. Moreover, it will affect our assessment of the social cost of aggregate risk, and thus of the value of policies designed to reduce this risk.

Maybe the puzzles can be solved by amending the simplest mainstream model with the right combination of non-standard preferences, heterogeneity, and frictions. If this is the case, the asset pricing puzzles will have been the source of a much more precise, but still standard, model of the economy. The kind and extent of amendments will of course affect our view about the social costs and benefits of public policy measures. But the fundamental view about the mechanics of a market economy will be essentially untouched.

[1] ... Or can you? What about check deposits or debit cards? In fact, what is happening here is that wealth that is placed in an interest-bearing account, and which the bank reinvests in the financial markets (for instance in bonds), is being withdrawn *on demand and just in time* for the transaction, and is credited to the account of the grocer. When you write out a personal check or pay for a transaction with your debit card at point of sale, it is as if you handed over a fraction of a government bond to your grocer.

[2] This effect is being explored by the search models of money that emerged after the Kiyotaki & Wright; Kiyotaki & Wright's (1989; 1993) contributions.

On the other hand, if the best way to explain the puzzles is by dropping the rationality assumption, as the behavioral finance literature seems to advocate, then quite radical changes of all economic theory is in order. In fact, rationality is no longer the holy grail of the profession that it used to be. But there are so many ways in which to depart from the maximizing *homo economicus*. Should we pursue models that combine insights of psychology or sociology into economics? Or is a collaboration with biology (by introducing evolutionary mechanisms) the better way? Surely, these decisions will have a profound impact on the future shape of economic theory, on the way economists interpret the data we observe, and on our views about appropriate public policy.

## 9.3 The party's over

One possible reason for the large equity premium that existed for a good part of the last two hundred years or so is that it was difficult for investors to hold a diversified portfolio. Transaction costs were high, so that it was not feasible to purchase many different stocks. Index-linked funds offered a low transaction cost way of holding a diversified portfolio, but they became available only fairly late. Moreover, simply holding a diversified portfolio may not be enough. The mutuality principle says that in any efficient allocation all agents bear only aggregate risk. But to implement this, agents must be able to hedge their own idiosyncratic risk. For instance, a cashier/worker/banker has to be able to hedge the risk of his shop/factory/bank going out of business and his losing his labor income as a result. This requires a specific portfolio quite distinct from a globally diversified portfolio. If such hedging is not possible, agents are not able to diversify their idiosyncratic risk, and thus will have to bear more than just aggregate risk.

Technological progress has transformed the way financial markets operate, and this progress has made such hedging at least partially feasible. As a result, our asset pricing theory should now be more correct than it used to be. Consequently, the equity premium should have fallen. This is precisely what has happened. The huge stock market rally we have witnessed (sometimes with disbelief) in the 1990s has reduced the forward looking premium to levels close to zero (Blanchard, 1993; Siegel, 1999; Jagannathan, McGrattan & Scherbina, 2000; McGrattan & Prescott, 2000). The extraordinary return on equities was therefore, in this interpretation, a *one-time windfall* from the technological improvements that took place in the financial markets. The flip-side of this interpretation is of course that, if equities are now more or less correctly valued, then in the future we should see the small equity premium predicted by theory. In other words, the 7% or 8% long-term real returns on equity are gone forever.

The same conclusion applies if McGrattan & Prescott's (2001) tax explanation is correct. The bull market was just a reflection of the reduction in tax rates. Unless taxes are reduced further, we should not expect anymore large risk-adjusted returns on any asset. And in fact, if this is true, then the large premium was only a figment: it existed only before tax, not after tax.

The demographic explanation of the runup of asset prices is only slightly more cheery. This explanation implies that asset prices will be depressed when the baby boomer generation starts to retire (unless the emerging economies bail us out). Prices will recover only when the baby boom generation has vanished and has transferred its assets to the next generation. The party is not over for good, but it is over for quite a while. Either way, the financial implications of these scenarios for public or private pension systems and investors in general are simply overwhelming.

# Appendix A

## Symbols and notation

| | |
|---|---|
| $\mathbb{R}$ | set of real numbers |
| $\partial_i f$ | partial derivative of function $f$ with respect to the $i$th argument |
| $\nabla$ | gradient |
| $\leqq$ | $\forall i (x_i \leqslant y_i)$ |
| $\leq$ | $x \leqq y$ and $x \neq y$ |
| $\ll$ | $\forall i (x_i < y_i)$ |
| $\arg_{\langle t \rangle}$ | components of arg that belong to events in period $t$ |
| | |
| $\mathcal{E}_t$ | set of events that belong to period $t$ |
| $\mathcal{L}$ | set of lotteries |
| $\mathcal{M}(q)$ | market span |
| $\mathcal{S}$ | set of states, $\{1, \ldots, S\}$ |
| $\mathcal{V}$ | ordinal utility over a set of lotteries |
| | |
| $\alpha$ | price vector of Arrow securities, state prices |
| $\alpha_+$ | $:= [1 \quad \alpha]$ |
| $\tilde{\alpha}$ | risk-neutral probabilities, equivalent martingale measure |
| $\beta$ | price of a risk-free bond |
| $\varepsilon$ | reciprocal of the elasticity of intertemporal substitution |
| $\gamma$ | parameter of utility function (e.g., coefficient of risk aversion) |
| $\delta$ | discount factor |
| $\mu$ | mean |
| $\pi$ | probabilities |
| $\psi_t(e)$ | event of period $t$ on the path leading to event $e$ |
| $\rho$ | gross risk-free return rate |
| $\sigma$ | standard deviation |
| $\tau(e)$ | period to which event $e$ belongs |

| | |
|---|---|
| $\omega$ | initial endowment |
| $\Omega$ | total initial endowment |
| | |
| $a$ | absolute risk tolerance at wealth level zero |
| $A$ | absolute risk aversion |
| $b$ | slope of absolute risk tolerance, cautiousness |
| $c$ | commodities, $1, \ldots, \ell$ |
| $e$ | event, $e \in \mathcal{E}$ |
| $\mathbf{e}$ | identity matrix |
| $g$ | real per capita growth rate |
| $i$ | agents, $1, \ldots, I$ |
| $j$ | assets, $1, \ldots, J$ |
| $m$ | state-contingent commodities (chapters 2 and 4) |
| $M$, $\mathbf{M}$ | stochastic discount factors |
| $p$ | vector of commodity prices |
| $P$ | prudence |
| $q$ | vector of asset prices |
| $r_s^j$ | cash flow of asset $j$ in state $s$ |
| $R_s^j$ | gross return rate of asset $j$ in state $s$ |
| $R$ | relative risk aversion |
| $s$ | state, $s \in \mathcal{S}$ |
| $T$ | risk tolerance |
| $u$ | utility function (over commodity bundles) |
| $U$ | utility function of representative agent |
| $v$ | indirect utility function (Chapter 3);<br>NM utility function (Chapters 4 and 5) |
| $V$ | representative indirect utility function |
| $w$ | initial wealth (market value of $\omega$) |
| $W$ | total initial wealth |

# Appendix B

## Solutions to the problem sets

### Chapter 2

**Solution 2.1** (*a*) Let $w := p \cdot \omega$ be the agent's wealth. The budget constraint says

$$p \cdot x = p \cdot x' = w,$$

hence

$$\begin{aligned} p \cdot z &= p \cdot (\lambda x + (1 - \lambda)x') \\ &= p \cdot (\lambda x) + p \cdot ((1 - \lambda)x') \\ &= \lambda(p \cdot x) + (1 - \lambda)(p \cdot x') \\ &= \lambda w + (1 - \lambda)w \\ &= w, \end{aligned}$$

so $z$ satisfies the budget constraint with equality.

(*b*) The argument is the same as above, except that the equality on the fourth row of the formula is replaced with a $\leqslant$.

**Solution 2.2** There is no point in giving you the result here. Just follow the instructions. The aim of this exercise is to convince yourself that a price vector is orthogonal to the budget line, and that the utility gradient is orthogonal to the indifference curve.

**Solution 2.3** (*a*) We apply (2.5) and (2.6). The marginal rate of substitution is

$$\frac{\partial_1 u}{\partial_2 u} = \frac{1/x_1}{\beta/x_2} = \frac{x_2}{\delta x_1} = \frac{\rho s}{\delta(w - s)} = \frac{p_1}{p_2}.$$

In optimum this must equal $\rho$; thus, $s = \delta(w - s)$, or

$$s = \frac{\delta}{1+\delta}w, \quad x_1 = \frac{1}{1+\delta}w, \quad x_2 = \frac{\delta}{1+\delta}\rho w.$$

Interestingly, in this special case, savings are unaffected by the interest rate. $\rho$ does not affect today's consumption either. Only tomorrow's consumption depends on the interest rate. The reason for this is that with log utility the income effect and the substitution effect of changes in the interest rate cancel out, leaving optimal saving unchanged.

(*b*) Consider the monotonic transformation of the utility function,

$$v(x_1, x_2) := f(\tilde{u}(x_1, x_2)), \quad \text{with } f(z) := {}^{\ln z}/_{\gamma}.$$

$f$ is a monotonic function, hence $\tilde{u}$ and $v$ represent the same preferences. But

$$v(x_1, x_2) = \ln x_1 + \delta \ln x_2 = u(x_1, x_2), \quad \text{with } \delta := {}^{\varepsilon}/_{\gamma},$$

hence $v$ is the same as $u$, and $u$ represents the same preferences as $\tilde{u}$. Accordingly, the preference maximizing saving must be the same.

*Keep in mind*: With ordinal utility, Cobb–Douglas is the same as additively separable log utility. (This will not be true with von Neumann–Morgenstern utility.)

## Chapter 3

**Solution 3.1** (*a*) The real interest rate this year is \$100/\$97.73 − 1 = 2.32%.

(*b*) The real interest rate next year is \$97.73/\$95.02 − 1 = 2.85%, and so is higher than this year.

**Solution 3.2** Buy 200 shares and sell 30 risky bonds short. The cash flow of these positions are

| asset | amount | cash flow in ... state 1 | state 2 |
|---|---|---|---|
| shares | 200 | 4000 | 7000 |
| risky bonds | −30 | 0 | −3000 |
| portfolio | | 4000 | 4000 |

Note that, by investing into risky shares and selling bonds short, you end up with a risk-free portfolio!

**Solution 3.3** (*a*) A risk-free bond costs $\beta = \sum_s \alpha_s = 0.9803 = \rho^{-1}$; thus, the risk-free interest rate $\rho$ equals 2.0%.

(*b*) $\tilde{\alpha} = (1.02)\alpha = (12.50\%, 25.00\%, 37.50\%, 6.25\%, 18.75\%)$.

(*c*) Using the decomposition idea, we get a price of

$$5 \times \alpha_1 + 5 \times \alpha_2 + 2 \times \alpha_3 + 7 \times \alpha_4 + 4 \times \alpha_5 = 3.7375.$$

**Solution 3.4** (*a*) Yes. There are five assets, just sufficient to span the five states at least potentially. There is no obvious collinearity between different rows or columns, so the payoff matrix appears to be regular. To test this hunch we use Excel's MDETERM function (or the corresponding function of any other spreadsheet software) and find that the determinant of the payoff matrix is $-24$, so different from zero, indicating that $r$ is indeed regular; and thus the market is complete.

(*b*) By reverse decomposition (Box 3.11), we have $\alpha = q \cdot r^{-1}$. Inverting a $5 \times 5$ matrix is not trivial without the help of a computer. With a computer, however, it's a snap. For instance, with Excel's functions MINVERSE and MMULT you can easily compute the vector of Arrow prices. In this specific example it is

$$\alpha = (0.1197, 0.2370, 0.3573, 0.0600, 0.1790).$$

(*c*) All Arrow prices are positive; therefore there are no arbitrage opportunities.

(*d*) The price of a risk-free bond equals $\beta = \sum_s \alpha_s = 0.9530$. The gross risk-free rate of return $\rho$ is $\beta^{-1} = 1.0493$. Thus, in this example, the risk-free rate of return is 4.93%.

(*e*) The risk-neutral probabilities are simply $\rho$ times the Arrow prices, so

$$\tilde{\alpha} = 1.0493\alpha = (12.56\%, 24.87\%, 37.50\%, 6.30\%, 18.78\%).$$

(*f*) The payoff of a call option is $\max\{q - e, 0\}$, where $e$ is the exercise price and $q$ is the state-dependent price of the underlying asset. Applied to this example, a call option on a share of company Y with exercise price 5 gives rise to a state-dependent cash flow of $(7, 3, 0, 0, 0)$.

The most straightforward way to compute the price of this option is by the decomposition idea (see Box 3.2). The price is simply the price of seven state 1 Arrow securities plus three state 2 Arrow securities,

$$price = 7 \times 0.1197 + 3 \times 0.2370 = 1.549.$$

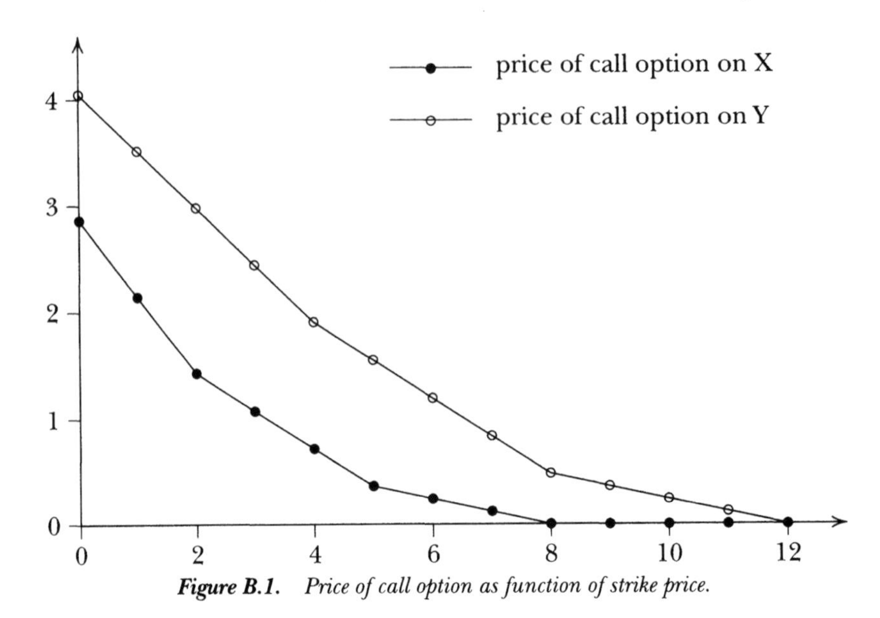


*Figure B.1. Price of call option as function of strike price.*

Alternatively, we can use the risk-neutral pricing formula, Box 3.4,

$$\textit{price} = \frac{1}{1.0493} \times (7 \times 12.56\% + 3 \times 24.87\%) = 1.549.$$

(*g*) The solution is given in Figure B.1.

**Solution 3.5** (*a*) The option is "out of the money" if $q(s) < x$, in which cases the payoff is zero. The option is "at the money" if $q(s) = x$. The payoff then is also zero. The option is "in the money" if $q(s) > x$. In those states the payoff is $q(s) - x$. Let $\alpha(s)$ be the state $s$ Arrow price. Thus, by decomposition, the price of the option is

$$c(x) = \int_{q^{-1}(x)}^{\infty} \alpha(s)(q(s) - x)ds.$$

$q^{-1}(x)$ is the state in which the option is at the money. For all states greater than this the payoff is $q(s) - x$, so we integrate this over the interval $[q^{-1}(x), \infty)$.

With the simplification of naming the state after the price of the asset, $s = q(s)$, we have $q^{-1}(x) = x$.[1] This simplifies the pricing equation,[2]

$$c(x) = \int_x^\infty \alpha(s)(s - x)ds.$$

($b$) Differentiating $c$ yields[3]

$$c'(x) = -\int_x^\infty \alpha(s)ds - \underbrace{\alpha(x)(x - x)}_{=0} < 0.$$

This proves that the option price is a decreasing function of the strike price.

The second derivative (again using Leibnitz's Rule) is

$$c''(x) = \alpha(x) > 0.$$

This is always positive, so $c$ is a convex function. Interestingly, we can measure the Arrow prices directly from the curvature of the option price (Breeden & Litzenberger, 1978; Merton, 1973).[4]

($c$) The curvature of this schedule is the Arrow prices. In this example curvature is negative in some region; thus, some Arrow prices are negative. This implies arbitrage opportunities. We can exploit them and become rich.

How would we do that in this specific example? We want to buy the Arrow securities that have negative prices. This gives us money now (as we purchase something with a negative price), and possibly also later (if the Arrow securities pay out). The Arrow securities with negative prices are the ones where the schedule is locally concave. Those are numbers 4 and 5.

Arrow securities as such are not traded in the market, but we can synthesize them with a portfolio of call options. If you like catchy phases, what we do is

[1]Redefining a state in this way is an appropriate procedure if there is a bijection between the original states and the price, which is what we assumed when we said that $q(s)$ is strictly monotonic.

[2]Note that this redefinition of the state affects the Arrow prices: the state $s$ Arrow price after the redefinition is the same as the state $q^{-1}(s)$ Arrow price before the redefinition. Thus, $\alpha(s)$ does not denote the same thing in the two formulas above.

[3]We use Leibnitz's Rule here,

$$\frac{d}{dx}\int_{f(x)}^{g(x)} h(x, z)dz = \int_{f(x)}^{g(x)} \partial_1 h(x, z)dz + h(x, g(x))g'(x) - h(x, f(x))f'(x).$$

[4]As mentioned before, we are working here not with states of the world, but rather with a partition of the set of states of the world defined by the price of some asset. Let $S$ be the complete set of states of the world, and let $T \subset S$ be those states in which the asset has price $x$. Then $c''(x)$ is the *sum* of all Arrow prices in $T$, $\sum_{s\in T} \alpha_s$.

to construct two "butterfly spreads," one for state 4 and one for state 5. We buy $x$ call options with strikes 3 and 6 and sell $x$ call options with strike 4 and 5. This portfolio costs $-1.33x$. The payoff of this portfolio is $x$ if the price of the underlying asset turns out to be between 4 and 5, and zero otherwise. So not only is this portfolio free, but it pays cash now, and with luck may even pay cash tomorrow as well. [*Note*: There are many more arbitrage portfolios.]

## Chapter 4

**Solution 4.1** ($a$) This utility function is risk averse. I will therefore buy full coverage if the premium is actuarially fair.

($b$) My answer does not depend on $\gamma$ ...

($c$) ... or on my initial wealth. I will always buy full insurance if the premium is fair.

($d$) Now the premium is larger than the actuarially fair premium. This implies that I will buy less than full coverage, $c < 1$.

$\gamma$ is the coefficient of relative risk aversion. The smaller is $\gamma$, the less coverage I will buy, $dc/d\gamma > 0$.

The coverage I buy as a function of initial wealth depends on whether the risk is additive (risk of losing \$1000) or multiplicative (risk of losing 10% of my wealth). If the risk is additive, I will buy less coverage the larger my initial wealth is because this function exhibits *decreasing* absolute risk aversion, DARA. If the risk is multiplicative, the coverage does not depend on my initial wealth because this function exhibits *constant* relative risk aversion, CRRA.

**Solution 4.2** ($a$) This is the result of Box 4.3. The maximization problem is a special case of (4.1). Let $t$ be the amount of tickets for this lottery that you choose to hold. $t$ can be any real number, not just integers. $w$ is your initial wealth. Expected payoff is then

$$\max_{c} \,(1-\pi)v(w-tL)+\pi v(w+tH).$$

The first-order condition of this problem is

$$-L(1-\pi)v'(w-tL)+H\pi v'(w+tH)=0.$$

Rearranging yields

$$\left(\frac{v'(w-tL)}{v'(w+tH)}-1\right)L(1-\pi)=\pi H-(1-\pi)L.$$

The right-hand side of this equation is the expected payoff of this lottery. If it is zero the left-hand side must also vanish, which implies that $v'(w-tL) = v'(w+tH)$, or, by monotonicity, $t = 0$. If expected payoff is positive, we must have $v'(w-tL) > v'(w+tH)$ to make the left-hand side positive as well. But by risk aversion ($v$ is concave, hence $v'$ is a decreasing function) this implies $w - tL < w + tH$, or $t > 0$.

(*b*) This behavior is not compatible with von Neumann–Morgenstern utility. Since we observe this behavior, we know that NM theory cannot be the complete story. One explanation may be to say that people who participate in the national lottery "buy hope." Another is that people overestimate small probabilities. Yet another is that people do not buy lottery tickets for the possibility of an outcome per se, but rather they "consume" the thrill of gambling. This is a direct violation of "consequentialism": not only the consequences (outcomes) matter, but also the act of gambling.

**Solution 4.3** Combining the first-order condition (4.2) with the definition of the markup (4.5) yields

$$\frac{v'(w - c(1+m)\pi d)}{v'(w - c(1+m)\pi d - (1-c)d)} = \frac{1-(1+m)\pi}{(1+m)(1-\pi)}.$$

We will show the steps involved in solving for $c$ only for the CRRA-utility, so we follow the hint given in the problem and substitute $rw$ for $d$. The first-order condition then becomes

$$\frac{v'(w(1 - c(1+m)\pi r))}{v'(w(1 - c(1+m)\pi r - (1-c)r))} = \frac{1-(1+m)\pi}{(1+m)(1-\pi)}.$$

For the CRRA utility, this becomes

$$\left[\frac{1 - cr\pi(1+m)}{1 - c(1+m)\pi r - (1-c)r}\right]^{-\gamma} = \frac{1-(1+m)\pi}{(1+m)(1-\pi)}.$$

We reorder,

$$\frac{1 - c(1+m)\pi r - (1-c)r}{1 - cr\pi(1+m)} = \left[\frac{1-(1+m)\pi}{(1+m)(1-\pi)}\right]^{\frac{1}{\gamma}} =: \xi$$

and solve for $c$,

$$c = \frac{\xi - (1-r)}{r[1 - (1-\xi)\pi(1+m)]}. \qquad \text{(CRRA)}$$

Analogous transformations give us the demand function for insurance for the other specifications. We get

$$c = \frac{r(1-\pi)(1+m)-m}{r(1+m)(1-\pi(1+m))}, \qquad \text{(Bernoulli)}$$

$$c = 1 - \frac{\ln(1+m)+\ln(1-\pi)-\ln(1-\pi(1+m))}{d\gamma}, \qquad \text{(CARA)}$$

$$c = \frac{2b[mw+d(1-\pi(1+m))]-am}{2bd(1-\pi(1-m^2))}, \qquad \text{(quadratic)}$$

$$c = \begin{cases} +\infty & \text{if } m < 0, \\ \text{any real number} & \text{if } m = 0, \\ -\infty & \text{if } m > 0. \end{cases} \qquad \text{(affine)}$$

**Solution 4.4** (*a*) Variance is $(5.21\%)^2 = 0.27\%$. Using (4.15) we compute the cost of business cycles in terms of growth rates as

$$1-\kappa = 2 \cdot \frac{0.27\%}{2} = 0.27\%.$$

In other words, an average growth rate of 2.24% that is subject to business cycles is equivalent in terms of social welfare (as measured by the competitive SWF) to a growth rate of 1.97% (= 2.24% − 0.27%) that is free of business cycles.

(*b*) The difference would become smaller because consumption is much smoother than GDP.[5]

(*c*) According to this estimate, business cycles are not an overwhelming problem.

(*d*) An empirical argument against this analysis may be the significant news coverage of business cycles. Is such coverage evidence against the low estimate of the social cost of business cycles? After all, extensive news coverage suggests significant public interest; would the business cycle be interesting for people if its social cost were so low? Well, maybe: a low cost of business cycles in equilibrium does not imply that business cycles do not require changes in behavior. It is conceivable that familiarity with business cycles may be important for making appropriate decisions, even if the effect on utility, subject to choosing the optimal behavior, is small.

[5]The computations with consumption instead of GDP for the same period of time are as follows: average growth rate is 2.07%, standard deviation is 3.15%, and $1-\kappa = 0.10\%$ if $\gamma = 2$. Thus, the variable consumption growth rate of the data is welfare equivalent to a steady growth rate of 2.07% − 0.10% = 1.97%.

Two theoretical arguments against this analysis come to (my) mind. One is that we assume that there is a representative agent whose preferences can be described by a von Neumann–Morgenstern utility function, and this representative NM utility should have properties that we deem reasonable for individuals. But the representative agent we have constructed so far has only an ordinal utility representation. What do we know about the expected utility representation of the agent, and about properties of his cardinal utility function? We have not dealt with this topic yet, but we will in the next chapter.

The second, possibly more significant, argument is the following. It is true that the local representative agent used in this analysis can be used to price assets. The representative has a positive content. But that does not imply that the representative also has a normative content; that is to say, it is not clear whether the evaluation of the representative's utility tells us anything about social welfare. Just consider this: the competitive SWF is a local representative only insofar as it represents the marginal rates of substitution of everyone in the economy. Suppose there is a NM representation of this utility. Does that imply that the curvature of the NM utility of the representative is the same as the curvature of each individual agent in equilibrium? If not, then small business cycles might be very costly for the very risk averse among us. Aggregating these individual costs of business cycles would entail taking account of the distribution of individuals' relative risk aversion.

**Solution 4.5** There are many such utility functions. The sum of two (or more) risk-averse NM utility functions is itself a risk-averse NM utility function. But the sum of HARA utility functions is typically not HARA. Here are some examples,

$$\begin{aligned}
&-e^{-y}+y, \\
&\ln(y)+y, \\
&\ln(y)-e^{-y}, \\
&-e^{-\gamma_1 y}-e^{-\gamma_2 y}, && \gamma_1 \neq \gamma_2, \\
&\frac{y^{1-\gamma_1}}{1-\gamma_1}+\frac{y^{1-\gamma_2}}{1-\gamma_2}, && \gamma_1 \neq \gamma_2, \\
&\ln(y)+\ln(y+\alpha), && \alpha \neq 0.
\end{aligned}$$

These functions, and many other similar sums, are all monotonic and risk averse, but they are not HARA, as is easy to verify.

Another non-HARA class of utility functions is Saha's (1993) *expo-power class.* As the name suggests, this utility function nests an exponential and a power function,

$$v(y) := -e^{-\alpha y^{\gamma}}.$$

Absolute risk tolerance for this function is

$$T(y) = y(1 - \gamma + \alpha\gamma y^{\gamma})^{-1}.$$

This utility function is risk averse for sufficiently large $y$, but risk tolerance is not an affine function.

Yet another class is that of *nested log or nested power functions.* The simplest such function is the double-log utility function $v(y) := \ln(\ln(1 + y))$. Absolute risk tolerance of this function is

$$T(y) = \frac{(1 + y)\ln(1 + y)}{1 + \ln(1 + y)},$$

which is not affine. More generally, the nested generalized power function has the following structure:

$$v(y) := \frac{(u(1 + y) - \alpha)^{1-\gamma_1} - 1}{1 - \gamma_1},$$

$$\text{with} \quad u(y) := \frac{y^{1-\gamma_2} - 1}{1 - \gamma_2}.$$

Absolute risk tolerance of $v$ is

$$T(y) = \frac{(1 + y)[(1 + y)^{1-\gamma_2} - (1 + \alpha(1 - \gamma_2))]}{(1 + y)^{1-\gamma_2}(\gamma_1 + \gamma_2 - \gamma_1\gamma_2) - \gamma_2(1 + \alpha(1 - \gamma_2))},$$

which is not affine if $\gamma_1$ and $\gamma_2$ are both strictly positive. If $\gamma_1 = 0$ or $\gamma_2 = 0$, however, then $v$ reduces to the simple generalized power utility function, and then $T$ is an affine function of $y$.

Combining these ideas, one can specify a sum of nested power functions, or of exponentials of nested power functions.

## Chapter 5

**Solution 5.1** (*a*) The indifference curves of the risk-neutral agent are just the iso-expected income lines, since this person cares about expected income only. These indifference curves have constant slope $-\pi_1/\pi_2$. Pareto

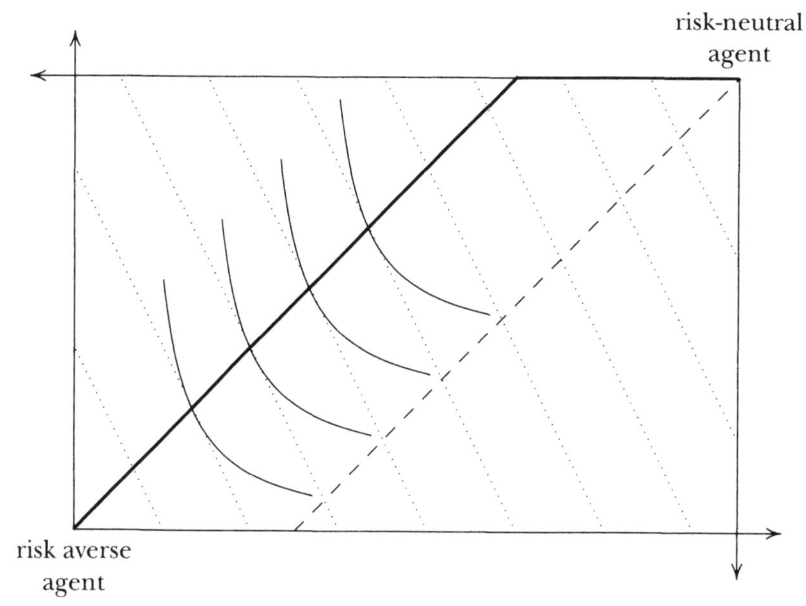


***Figure B.2.*** *Contract curve if one agent is risk neutral.*

efficiency thus requires the indifference curve of the risk-averse agent to be tangent to the iso-expected income line. This implies that the risk-averse agent is on his certainty line (on the 45° line of his coordinate system). The solution is depicted in Figure B.2. All the risk is borne by the risk-neutral agent, since he does not care about the risk. The risk-averse agent bears no risk. We could say that the risk-neutral agent provides full insurance to the risk-averse agent.

(*b*) The representative is risk neutral because the risk-averse agent does not bear any risk, and all the risk is borne by someone who does not mind. One can see this also from (5.7) and (5.8). Mean risk tolerance is infinite, hence the representative is infinitely risk tolerant. The example also demonstrates that the representative's risk aversion is *not* the average risk aversion of the population. Diversity of the degree of risk aversion within the population normally tends to make the representative less averse to risk, because those people who are hurt most by the risk (i.e. the especially risk averse among us) bear only small amounts of risk in any Pareto efficient allocation.

(*c*) Since by definition absolute risk aversion is constant with a CARA utility function, and absolute risk tolerance is the reciprocal of absolute risk aversion, risk tolerance of a CARA utility function is also constant. Wilson's

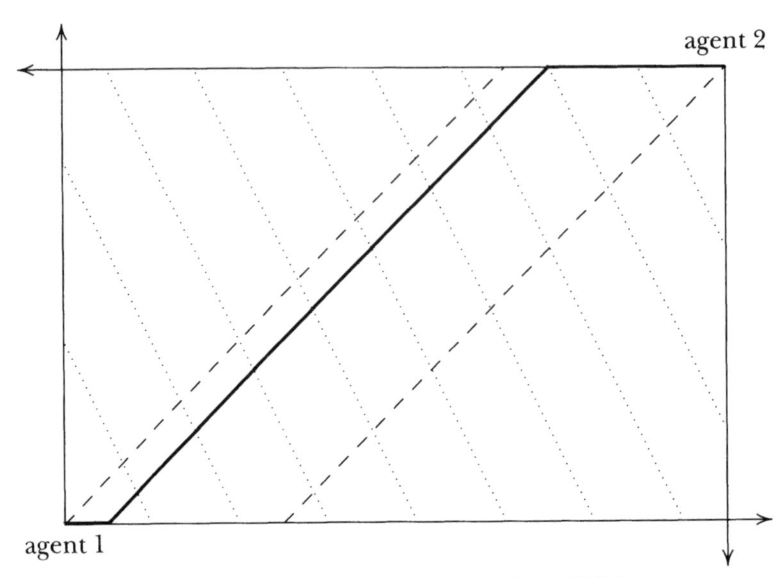


*Figure B.3.* *Contract curve of an economy with two CARA agents.*

theorem says that the marginal share of aggregate risk borne by an agent is proportional to his absolute risk tolerance. With CARA utility, this marginal share is constant, which means that the total aggregate risk share borne by an agent is equal to his marginal aggregate risk share.

Start with an economy that has no aggregate risk. The contract curve is just the security line, Figure 5.1. Now add some aggregate risk. For instance, add one unit to aggregate income in state 1, but not in state 2. This risk will be borne by both agents in proportion to their risk tolerance. As a result, the contract curve is a straight line with 45° slope, which is between the certainty lines of the two agents. The distance from these two certainty lines is determined by the absolute risk tolerance of the two agents. The contract curve will be closer to the certainty line of the less risk-tolerant agent, indicating that he will bear a smaller share of the risk. The solution depicted in Figure B.3 assumes that agent 2 is four times as risk tolerant as agent 1.

**Solution 5.2** The cash flow of this Arrow security is negatively correlated with aggregate risk. For this reason, it will carry a negative risk premium (this asset is a hedge against aggregate risk); thus, $E\{R\} < \rho$.

**Solution 5.3** We know that there is full mutual insurance in cases $(a)$ and $(b)$ by the mutuality principle, so we know that the equilibrium allocation (since it is efficient) will assign the same amount to an agent in both states, although possibly different amounts to each agent. We also know the equilibrium prices, $\tilde{\alpha} = \pi$. Since the budget constraints bind in equilibrium we can directly compute the equilibrium allocations. In (*a*) this is

$$y(1) = \begin{bmatrix} 2 \\ 2 \end{bmatrix}, \quad y(2) = \begin{bmatrix} 2 \\ 2 \end{bmatrix}.$$

In (*b*) the equilibrium allocation is

$$y(1) = \begin{bmatrix} 5/3 \\ 5/3 \end{bmatrix}, \quad y(2) = \begin{bmatrix} 7/3 \\ 7/3 \end{bmatrix}.$$

Initial utilities are smaller than equilibrium utilities. In case (*a*) we have

$$E\{v_1(w(1))\} = \frac{1}{2}\ln 1 + \frac{1}{2}\ln 3 = 0.549 < 0.693 = \ln 2 = E\{v_1(y(1))\},$$
$$E\{v_2(w(2))\} = \frac{1}{2}\ln 3 + \frac{1}{2}\ln 1 = 0.549 < 0.693 = \ln 2 = E\{v_1(y(2))\},$$

and in case (*b*),

$$E\{v_1(w(1))\} = \frac{2}{3}\ln 1 + \frac{1}{3}\ln 3 = 0.366 < 0.511 = \ln 5/3 = E\{v_1(y(1))\},$$
$$E\{v_2(w(2))\} = \frac{2}{3}\ln 3 + \frac{1}{3}\ln 1 = 0.732 < 0.847 = \ln 7/3 = E\{v_1(y(2))\}.$$

(*c*) $i$'s maximization problem is

$$\max\left\{\pi \ln y^1(i) + (1-\pi)\ln y^2(i) \;\middle|\; \alpha_1(y^1(i) - w^1(i)) + \alpha_2(y^2(i) - w^2(i)) \leqslant 0\right\}.$$

The first-order conditions of this problem are

$$\frac{\pi}{y^1(i)} = \lambda\alpha_1, \quad \frac{1-\pi}{y^2(i)} = \lambda\alpha_2.$$

At first sight this case seems to entail more work, because we do not know the equilibrium allocation and prices off-hand, so it looks as if we will have to compute aggregate demand and solve for market-clearing prices. But because of the log utility we can take a shortcut. Notice that the first-order conditions imply

$$y^1(i) = sy^2(i), \quad \text{with} \quad s := \frac{\pi\alpha_2}{(1-\pi)\alpha_1}. \tag{B.1}$$

Summing over both agents and imposing market clearing,

$$W^1 = sW^2.$$

Thus, $s = {}^{W^1}/_{W^2} = {}^3/_5$, and accordingly,

$$^{\alpha_2}/_{\alpha_1} = {}^3/_5. \tag{B.2}$$

To compute the equilibrium allocation, we substitute (B.1) and (B.2) into $i$'s budget constraint:

$$[sy^2(i) - w^1(i)] + \frac{\alpha_2}{\alpha_1}[y^2(i) - w^2(i)] = 0.$$

We can solve this for $y^2(i)$, and using (B.1) also for $y^1(i)$. Substituting the numbers of the example yields

$$y(1) = \begin{bmatrix} 7/5 \\ 7/3 \end{bmatrix}, \quad y(2) = \begin{bmatrix} 8/5 \\ 8/3 \end{bmatrix}.$$

Here, too, there are gains from trade in terms of ex ante expected utility:

$$E\{v_1(w(1))\} = 0.549 < 0.592 = E\{v_1(y(1))\},$$
$$E\{v_2(w(2))\} = 0.693 < 0.725 = E\{v_1(y(2))\}.$$

**Solution 5.4** (*a*) There is no aggregate risk, but the mutuality principle does not apply because of the heterogeneity of the beliefs. As a result, the equilibrium allocation will not be on the security line. Agents will bear some (countervailing) risk, even though there is no risk in the aggregate.

From the solution of the previous problem, we know that the first-order conditions imply

$$y^1(i) = s_i y^2(i), \quad \text{with} \quad s_i := \frac{\pi(i)\alpha_2}{(1 - \pi(i))\alpha_1}. \tag{B.3}$$

But now, because $s_1 \neq s_2$, there is no shortcut. We have to solve for the demand functions first.

We substitute (B.3) into $i$'s budget constraint

$$[s_i y^2(i) - w^1(i)] + \alpha[y^2(i) - w^2(i)] = 0,$$

where $\alpha := {}^{\alpha_2}/_{\alpha_1}$ is the relative price. We solve for $i$'s demand for commodity 2:

$$y^2(i) = \frac{w^1(i) + \alpha w^2(i)}{s_i + \alpha}.$$

Market clearing requires $y^2(1) + y^2(2) = w^2(1) + w^2(2) =: W^2$,

$$\frac{w^1(1) + \alpha w^2(1)}{s_1 + \alpha} + \frac{w^1(2) + \alpha w^2(2)}{s_2 + \alpha} = W^2.$$

The $\alpha$ that solves this is the equilibrium relative price. With the numbers of this example ($s_1 = 2\alpha$, $s_2 = \alpha/2$, and the endowments as defined in the problem) we get $\alpha = 1$, i.e. $\alpha_1 = \alpha_2$.

The equilibrium allocations can be computed by substituting the equilibrium prices and the endowments into the demand functions:

$$y(1) = \begin{bmatrix} 8/3 \\ 4/3 \end{bmatrix}, \quad y(2) = \begin{bmatrix} 4/3 \\ 8/3 \end{bmatrix}.$$

Agents bear risk, even though there is no aggregate risk. Each agent bets (to some extent) on the state he considers to be more likely.

Here, too, there are gains from trade, i.e.

$$E^i\{v_i(w(i))\} = 0.366 < 0.750 = E^i\{v_i(y(i))\},$$

for both agents $i$.

($b$) Suppose you do not know the endowments, preferences, and beliefs of the other people in the economy, but you know the aggregate endowment.[6] For simplicity, assume that there is no aggregate risk, as is the case in this example. By the mutuality principle and the properties of the indifference curves, you know that in this case equilibrium prices are collinear to probabilities, so if you observe $\alpha_1 = \alpha_2$ you should conclude $\pi_1 = \pi_2$, which is different from your own beliefs.[7] As a consequence, you know that beliefs are not common, and thus you cannot expect the mutuality principle to hold. But the prices nevertheless tell you something about the "average" beliefs of the other people in the economy. You know that they put more probability on state 2 than you do.

There are two ways to react to this information. Either you continue to uphold your beliefs, thinking that you have evaluated all the information that was available to you and made the best estimate, and that the new information coming from the equilibrium prices does not alter your estimate; or you revise your beliefs. But revising your beliefs will make you choose a different portfolio. And if an agent revises his beliefs from observing the market prices, demand will no longer equal supply for all assets, the equilibrium will break down, and new market prices will emerge.

[6] In the two-person economy of this example, this implies that you know your fellow's endowment; but if there are many agents you would know close to nothing about the distribution.

[7] Such information may come to you in the form of a report of some quantitative section of your bank, stating that "financial market data suggest that state 1 is equally likely as state 2."

What would constitute an equilibrium in such a situation? It would be an "equilibrium of plans, prices, price expectations, *and beliefs*," that is, a situation in which all markets clear, everyone has correct state-contingent price expectations, and no agent has an incentive to revise his beliefs about the probabilities, given the public information (the market prices) he observes. Such an equilibrium is called a *rational expectations equilibrium*, or *REE*. (See Brunnermeier (2001) for an extensive survey of this field.)

**Solution 5.5** (*a*) Compare the risk-neutral probabilities,

$$\tilde{\alpha} = (12.56\%, 24.87\%, 37.50\%, 6.30\%, 18.78\%)$$

with the objective ones

$$\pi = (20.42\%, 28.96\%, 36.08\%, 2.97\%, 11.57\%).$$

The risk-neutral probabilities are pessimistic in the sense that they put more weight on the poor states (states 4 and 5) than the objective probabilities, and less weight on the rich states (states 1 and 2). Hence the representative agent is risk averse.

(*b*) Compute the stochastic discount factors by dividing the Arrow prices (from the solution to Problem 3.5) by the objective probabilities, $M_s := \alpha_s/\pi_s$. It will be useful to have the log of the SDF as well. We get

| $w$ | 7 | 8 | 10 | 11 | 13 |
|---|---|---|---|---|---|
| $M$ | 2.0202 | 1.5471 | 0.9904 | 0.8184 | 0.5860 |
| $\ln M$ | 0.7032 | 0.4364 | −0.0097 | −0.2004 | −0.5344 |

This is precious information about the shape of the utility function.

A CARA utility function takes the form $v(w) := -(\alpha/\gamma)e^{-\gamma w}$ (see Table 4.2). Thus $M_s := \delta e^{-\gamma(w_s - w_0)}$. This implies that there is an affine relationship between log SDF and the level of income,

$$\ln M_s = (\ln \delta + \gamma w_0) - \gamma w_s.$$

Thus, by regressing $w$ on $\ln M$ we can determine $\gamma$ as the negative of the slope coefficient. Doing this yields

$$\ln M_s = 2.1022 - 0.2065 w_s + \text{error}.$$

The slope and the constant are highly significant, and the adjusted $R^2$ equals 0.9894. By any means this is a very good fit, but it is not perfect. In fact, graphing $\ln M_s$ versus $w_s$ we should get a downward sloping straight line if utility is CARA, with the slope being equal to minus the coefficient of absolute risk aversion $\gamma$. When we do this here, however, we get a downward

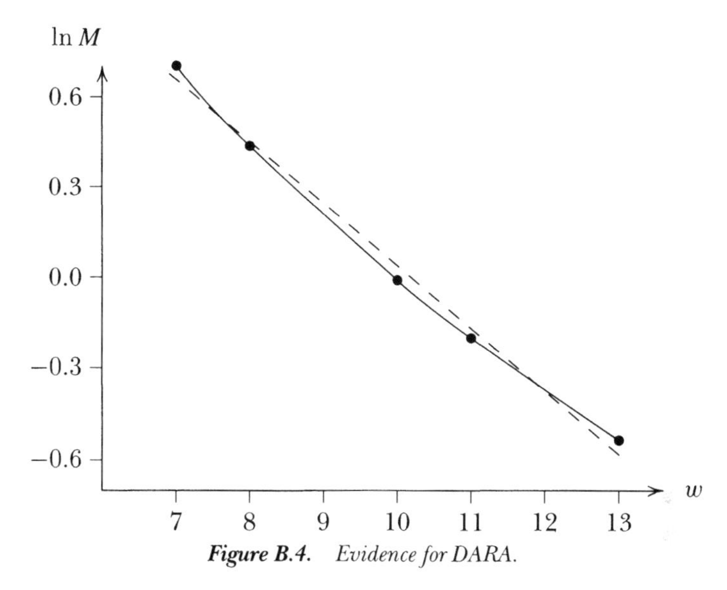


***Figure B.4.*** *Evidence for DARA.*

sloping but convex relationship (Figure B.4). This means that the measured $\gamma$ decreases with income, suggesting that the utility we look for exhibits DARA, not CARA.

(*c*) A CRRA utility function is of the form $v(w) := (\alpha/(1-\gamma))w^{1-\gamma}$ (see Table 4.2). Thus $M_s := \delta(w_s/w_0)^{-\gamma}$. This implies that there is an affine relationship between log SDF and the log of income,

$$\ln M_s = (\ln \delta + \gamma \ln w_0) - \gamma \ln w_s.$$

Regressing $\ln w$ on $\ln M$ yields

$$\ln M_s = 4.5937 - 1.9993 \ln w_s.$$

This fit is almost perfect. EViews reports an adjusted $R^2$ of almost 1.[8] Thus, the example is almost perfectly compatible with a CRRA utility function with a coefficient of relative risk aversion of almost 2.[9]

(*d*) We know the shape of the utility function now, and we also know that the constant in the CRRA-regression equals $\ln \delta + \gamma \ln w_0$, i.e.

$$\ln \delta + 1.9993 \ln w_0 = 4.5937.$$

But these are two unknowns ($\delta$ and $w_0$) and only one equation. Thus, we cannot determine $\delta$.

[8] 0.99999994, to be precise.

[9] In fact, the example was constructed with a CRRA function with $\gamma = 2.0$. The slight deviation is due to the computational inaccuracy of my computer equipment.

If we know that $w_0 = 10.1$, then we can solve the equation above and get $\delta = 0.9707$.

**Solution 5.6** (*a*) The cash flow of IT consulting's bond is not correlated with aggregate endowment, $\text{cov}(r^j, w) = 0$; thus, the expected rate of return must equal the risk-free interest rate,

$$\rho = \frac{100}{96.15} = 1.04 = E\{R^j\} = (1 - \pi) \cdot \frac{100}{76.92},$$

if $\pi$ is the probability of failure. Solving for $\pi$ yields

$$\pi = 20\%.$$

(*b*) Assets that are positively correlated with aggregate endowment are less expensive because they pay off in times of low marginal utility (in the boom) and fail in times of high marginal utility (in the trough). Thus, with 20% failure probability, IT consulting's bond should be cheaper than 76.92 if its success is positively correlated with the business cycle. If its price is still 76.92, this means that the failure probability must be less than 20%.

**Solution 5.7** Owing to the absence of uncertainty, the yield of a bond that expires the next period can simply be written as $\ln \rho = -\ln M$. With this utility function, and a per period growth rate of $g$, we have

$$M := \delta \left( \frac{(1+g)w^0 - \underline{w}}{w^0 - \underline{w}} \right)^{-\gamma}.$$

Therefore,

$$\ln \rho = \gamma \ln \left( \frac{(1+g)w^0 - \underline{w}}{w^0 - \underline{w}} \right) - \ln \delta.$$

Consider the $\ln(\cdots)$ term in the middle of this formula. Initially it is larger than $g$, but through time (as current endowment $w^0$ grows) it converges to $g$ (approximately). Accordingly, the interest rate initially exceeds $\rho^* := \gamma g - \ln \delta$, but eventually converges to this number.

This economy features a monotonically decreasing interest rate which is nevertheless bounded from below and away from zero. The intuition for this finding is as follows. This utility function exhibits decreasing relative risk aversion (DRRA). Initially, when the economy is relatively poor, it is also more relatively risk averse. As a result, the interest rate is high. As this economy becomes richer, it also becomes less relatively risk averse, and the interest rate decreases. Eventually, the subsistence level $\underline{w}$ becomes effectively irrelevant, and the representative is very similar to a CRRA person, when the interest rate (basically) stops decreasing.

# Chapter 6

**Solution 6.1** (*a*) In order to apply (6.28) we need to compute the expected average growth rate over all possible horizons,

$$E\{g_t\} = \frac{1}{t}\sum_{k=1}^{t} E\{G_k\}.$$

Since $G$ is assumed to be a random walk, $E\{G_t\} = G_0$ for all $t > 0$; thus, $E\{g_t\} = G_0$. Consequently, the yield curve is flat,

$$\ln \rho_t \approx \gamma G_0 - \ln \delta.$$

The level of the interest rates correlates perfectly with the current growth rate.

(*b*) Does the yield curve predict the business cycle? Well, yes and no. The current level is the best estimate of tomorrow's endowment. But there are no "booms" or "recessions" because exceptionally high or low income levels do not tend to return to more "normal" rates. In this sense, there is nothing to predict.

**Solution 6.2** [*Note:* An Excel worksheet with the solution to this problem can be downloaded from the book's website.]

Given this process, the expected growth rate (given today's information) between period $t-1$ and period $t$ is given by

$$E\{G_t\} = \mu + \phi^t(G_0 - \mu).$$

Accordingly, the expected average growth rate over an arbitrary horizon is

$$E\{g_t\} = \mu + \frac{G_0 - \mu}{t}\sum_{k=1}^{t}\phi^k = \mu + \frac{G_0 - \mu}{t} \cdot \frac{\phi(1-\phi^t)}{1-\phi}.$$

Using (6.28), we compute the yield curve as

$$\ln \rho_t \approx \gamma\left[\mu + \frac{G_0 - \mu}{t} \cdot \frac{\phi(1-\phi^t)}{1-\phi}\right] - \ln \delta.$$

$\mu$ and $\delta$ affect the level of the yield curve. The variance $\sigma^2$ has no influence because we use only first-order Taylor approximations of the interest rates. The variance does have a second-order effect and will lead in general to a non-flat yield curve on average. $\gamma$ affects the intensity by which interest rates are moved by deviations of the current growth rate from the trend growth rate. The sign and intensity of this effect depends crucially on $\phi$.

$\phi = 0$: The yield curve is always flat and is not stochastic. Interest rates do not vary and therefore are unable to forecast the business cycle.

$\phi > 0$: If the current growth rate ($G_0$) exceeds the trend rate ($\mu$), then the yield curve is monotonically downward sloping, $\rho_t > \rho_{t'}$ for $t < t'$. A boom ($G_0 > \mu$) is associated with an inverted yield curve (i.e. one with a negative slope). For ever longer horizons, the interest rate approaches $\ln \rho_\infty = \gamma\mu - \ln \delta$. If the current growth rate falls short of the trend rate ($G_0 < \mu$), then the yield curve is monotonically increasing but converges to the same infinite-horizon interest rate. Thus, short rates are more volatile than long rates, but all interest rates correlate perfectly with today's growth rate. (All interest rates are procyclical.)

$\phi < 0$: If $\phi$ is negative, then the short real interest rate is smaller than the long real interest rate whenever the current growth rate exceeds the trend growth rate ($\rho_1 < \rho_\infty \iff G_0 > \mu$), so in this case a boom is associated with a normally shaped (i.e. increasing) yield curve. As before, all interest rates are perfectly correlated with current growth, but unlike before, interest rates are countercyclical. Moreover, the yield curve need not be monotonic anymore. If $\phi$ is sufficiently negative, then the yield curve may "wiggle" and change slope between any consecutive times to maturity.

For all cases, however, the expected endowment growth over a given horizon can be computed directly from the interest rate over this horizon,

$$E\{g_t\} = \mu + \frac{\ln \rho_t - \ln \rho_\infty}{\gamma},$$

so the yield curve indeed forecasts the business cycle. The difference is the following: if $\phi > 0$, then high current growth implies high interest rates and is also a good signal for future growth. Thus, high interest rates signal high future growth. If $\phi < 0$, then high current growth implies low interest rates, but is also a bad signal for future growth. So again, high current interest rates (this time due to low current growth) are a good signal for future growth.

**Solution 6.3** [*Note:* An Excel worksheet with the solution to this problem can be downloaded from the book's website.]

Note that $\ln w^0 = \eta_0$. This is the current deviation of log per capita endowment from trend, so $\eta_0 > 0$ is a boom, $\eta_0 < 0$ is a recession. Given this process, the expected level of per capita endowment is

$$E\{\ln w^t\} = \mu t + \phi^t \eta_0.$$

Accordingly, the expected average growth rate over some horizon $t$ is

$$E\{g_t\} = \mu - \frac{1 - \phi^t}{t} \eta_0.$$

Thus, the yield curve is given by

$$\ln \rho_t = \gamma \left[ \mu - \frac{1 - \phi^t}{t} \eta_0 \right] - \ln \delta.$$

As in problem 6.2, $\mu$ and $\delta$ affect the level of the yield curve. But now, the interest rates are all countercyclical, independently of $\phi$. If $\eta_0 > 0$ (boom), then the short-horizon interest rate is smaller than the long-term interest rate, $\rho_t < \rho_\infty$ for all $t < \infty$. This is true whether the AR(1) process governing the deviations from trend is positively or negatively correlated. The intuition for this is as follows. According to (6.28), the interest rate is a function of the expected growth rate. If endowment is trend-stationary, then there is a tendency for deviations to self-correct. For this reason, a positive gap ($\eta_0 > 0$) is a bad signal for future growth. In the long run the growth rate is $\mu$, but in the short run the growth rate is smaller than $\mu$ if the endowment were currently above trend.

If we define the business cycle as the gap between per capita endowment and its trend, then the business cycle can be forecast simply from the current gap, $E\{\ln w^t\} - \mu t = \phi^t \eta_0$. As before, the yield curve predicts the expected endowment growth over a given horizon using the very same formula as in the solution to problem 6.2, $E\{g_t\} = \mu + (\ln \rho_t - \ln \rho_\infty)/\gamma$.

# Bibliography

Abdulkadri, A. O. & Langemeier, M. R. (2000), 'Using Farm Consumption Data to Estimate the Intertemporal Elasticity of Substitution and Relative Risk Aversion Coefficients', *Agricultural Finance Review* **60**, 61–70.

Abel, A. B. (1990), 'Asset Pricing under Habit Formation and Catching Up with the Joneses', *American Economic Review (Papers and Proceedings)* **80**(2), 38–42.

———. (1991), 'The Equity Premium Puzzle', *Business Review, Federal Reserve Bank of Philadelphia* pp. 3–14.

———. (2003), 'The Effects of a Baby Boom on Stock Prices and Capital Accumulation in the Presence of Social Security', *Econometrica* **71**(2), 551–578.

AIMR (2002), *Equity Risk Premium Forum,*, AIMR On Line Publication. www.aimrpubs.org/ap/issues/v2002n1/toc.html.

Aliprantis, C. D. & Tourky, R. (2002), 'Markets That Do Not Replicate Any Options', *Economics Letters* **76**(3), 443–447.

Ameriks, J. & Zeldes, S. P. (2001), How Do Household Portfolio Shares Vary With Age? Working paper, Columbia Business School.

Amihud, Y. & Mendelson, H. (1986), 'Asset Pricing and the Bid-Ask Spread', *Journal of Financial Economics* **17**(2), 223–249.

Arnott, R. D. & Ryan, R. J. (2001), 'The Death of the Risk Premium', *Journal of Portfolio Management* **27**(3), 61–74.

Arrow, K. J. (1953), 'Le Rôle des Valeurs Boursières pour la Répartition la Meilleure des Risques', *Econométrie,* Colloques Internationaux du Centre National de la Recherche Scientifique, Paris **11**, 41–47. Published in English as "The Role of Securities in the Optimal Allocation of Risk-Bearing" in the *Review of Economic Studies,* April 1964, *31* (2), 91–96.

———. (1965), *Aspects of the Theory of Risk-Bearing,* Yrjö Jahnsson Foundation, Helsinki.

______ . (1971), The Theory of Risk Aversion, *in* 'Essays in the Theory of Risk-Bearing', North-Holland, Amsterdam, pp. 90–120.

Arrow, K. J. & Debreu, G. (1954), 'Existence of an Equilibrium for a Competitive Economy', *Econometrica* **22**, 265–290.

Bachelier, L. (1900), *Théorie de la Spéculation*, Annales de l'École normale supérieure, Paris.

Bakshi, G. S. & Chen, Z. (1994), 'Baby Boom, Population Aging and Capital Markets', *Journal of Business* **67**(2), 165–202.

Banz, R. W. (1981), 'The Relationship between Return and Market Value of Common Stocks', *Journal of Financial Economics* **9**(1), 3–18.

Barberis, N. & Thaler, R. H. (2003), A Survey of Behavioral Finance, *in* G. Constantinedes, M. Harris & R. Stulz, eds, 'Handbook of the Economics of Finance', North-Holland, Amsterdam.

Barberis, N., Huang, M. & Santos, T. (2001), 'Prospect Theory and Asset Prices', *Quarterly Journal of Economics* **116**(1), 1–53.

Bartle, R. G. (1976), *The Elements of Real Analysis*, 2nd edition, John Wiley & Sons, New York.

Basu, K. (1992), 'A Geometry for Non-Walrasian General Equilibrium Theory', *Journal of Macroeconomics* **14**(1), 87–103.

Beaudry, P. & van Wincoop, E. (1996), 'The Intertemporal Elasticity of Substitution: An Exploration using a US Panel of State Data', *Economica* **63**(251), 495–512.

Becker, G. S. & Murphy, K. M. (1988), 'A Theory of Rational Addiction', *Journal of Political Economy* **96**(4), 675–700.

Becker, R. A. (1980), 'On the Long-Run Steady State in a Simple Dynamic Model of Equilibrium with Heterogeneous Households', *Quarterly Journal of Economics* **95**(2), 375–382.

Benninga, S. & Mayshar, J. (2000), 'Heterogeneity and Option Pricing', *Review of Derivatives Research* **4**(1), 7–27.

Benninga, S. & Protopapadakis, A. (1990), 'Leverage, Time Preference and the 'Equity Premium Puzzle'', *Journal of Monetary Economics* **25**(1), 49–58.

Bernoulli, D. (1954), 'Exposition of a New Theory on the Measurement of Risk', *Econometrica* **22**(1), 23–36. Translation from Latin by Dr. Louise Sommer of work first published 1738.

Best, P. & Byrne, A. (2001), 'Measuring the Equity Risk Premium', *Journal of Asset Management* **1**(3), 245–256.

Bewley, T. (1980), The Optimum Quantity of Money, *in* J. Kareken & N. Wallace, eds, 'Models of Monetary Economics', Federal Reserve Bank, Minneapolis.

Blanchard, O. J. (1993), 'Movements in the Equity Premium', *Brookings Papers on Economic Activity* **2**, 75–118.

Blume, L. & Easley, D. (1992), 'Evolution and Market Behavior', *Journal of Economic Theory* **58**(1), 9–40.

Boskin, M. J., Dulberger, E. R., Gordon, R. J., Griliches, Z. & Jorgenson, D. (1996), The Boskin Commission Report — Toward a More Accurate Measure of the Cost of Living, Final report to the senate finance committee. www.ssa.gov/history/reports/boskinrpt.html.

Brav, A., Constantinides, G. M. & Geczy, C. C. (2002), 'Asset Pricing with Heterogenous Consumers and Limited Participation: Empirical Evidence', *Journal of Political Economy* **110**(4), 793–824.

Breeden, D. T. (1979), 'An Intertemporal Asset Pricing Model with Stochastic Consumption and Investment Opportunities', *Journal of Financial Economics* **7**(3), 265–296.

Breeden, D. T. & Litzenberger, R. H. (1978), 'Prices of State-Contingent Claims Implicit in Option Prices', *Journal of Business* **51**(4), 621–651.

Brennan, M. J. & Kraus, A. (1976), 'The Geometry of Separation and Myopia', *Journal of Financial and Quantitative Analysis* **11**(2), 171–193.

Brennan, M. J. & Solanki, R. (1981), 'Optimal Portfolio Insurance', *Journal of Financial and Quantitative Analysis* **16**(3), 279–300.

Bronzin, V. (1908), *Theorie der Prämiengeschäfte*, Verlag Franz Deuticke, Leipzig und Wien.

Brown, S. J., Goetzmann, W. N. & Ross, S. A. (1995), 'Survival', *Journal of Finance* **50**(3), 853–873.

Brunnermeier, M. K. (2001), *Asset Pricing under Asymmetric Information — Bubbles, Crashes, Technical Analysis, and Herding*, Oxford University Press, Oxford.

Burk, A. (1936), 'Real Income, Expenditure Proportionality, and Frisch's 'New Methods of Measuring Marginal Utility", *Review of Economic Studies* **4**(1), 33–52.

Campbell, J. Y. (1995), 'Some Lessons from the Yield Curve', *Journal of Economic Perspectives* **9**(3), 129–152.

——— . (2000), 'Asset Pricing at the Millennium', *Journal of Finance* **55**(4), 1515–1567.

——— . (2003), Consumption-Based Asset Pricing, *in* G. Constantinides, M. Harris & R. Stulz, eds, 'Handbook of the Economics of Finance', North-Holland, Amsterdam.

Campbell, J. Y. & Cochrane, J. H. (1999), 'By Force of Habit: A

Consumption-Based Explanation of Aggregate Stock Market Behavior', *Journal of Political Economy* **107**(2), 205–251.

Campbell, J. Y., Lo, A. W. & MacKinlay, A. C. (1997), *The Econometrics of Financial Markets*, Princeton University Press, Princeton.

Cass, D. & Stiglitz, J. E. (1972), 'Risk Aversion and Wealth Effects on Portfolios with Many Agents', *Review of Economic Studies* **39**(3), 331–354.

Chambers, R. G. & Quiggin, J. (2000), *Uncertainty, Production, Choice, and Agency — The State-Contingent Approach*, Cambridge University Press, Cambridge.

Chan, Y. L. & Kogan, L. (2001), Catching Up with the Joneses: Heterogenous Preferences and the Dynamics of Asset Prices, Working Paper 8607, NBER.

Clarke, R. G. & Statman, M. (2000), 'The DJIA Crossed 652,230', *Journal of Portfolio Management* **26**(2), 89–93.

Cochrane, J. H. (1991), 'Volatility Tests and Efficient Markets : A Review Essay', *Journal of Monetary Economics* **27**(3), 463–485.

______ . (1997), 'Where is the Market Going? Uncertain Facts and Novel Theories', *Federal Reserve Bank of Chicago Economic Perspectives* **21**(6), 3–37.

______ . (2001), *Asset Pricing*, Princeton University Press, Princeton and Oxford.

Cogley, T. (2002), 'Idiosyncratic Risk and the Equity Premium: Evidence from the Consumer Expenditure Survey', *Journal of Monetary Economics* **49**(2), 309–334.

Cohn, R. A., Lewellen, W. G., Lease, R. C. & Schlarbaum, G. G. (1975), 'Individual Investor Risk Aversion and Investment Portfolio Composition', *Journal of Finance* **30**(2), 605–620.

Constantinides, G. M. (1990), 'Habit Formation: A Resolution of the Equity Premium Puzzle', *Journal of Political Economy* **98**(3), 519–543.

Constantinides, G. M. & Duffie, D. (1996), 'Asset Pricing with Heterogenous Consumers', *Journal of Political Economy* **104**(2), 219–240.

Constantinides, G. M., Donaldson, J. B. & Mehra, R. (2002), 'Junior Can't Borrow: A New Perspective on the Equity Premium Puzzle', *Quarterly Journal of Economics* **117**(1), 269–296.

Cooley, T. F. & Ohanian, L. E. (1991), 'The Cyclical Behavior of Prices', *Journal of Monetary Economics* **28**(1), 25–60.

Cornell, B. (1999), *The Equity Risk Premium — The Long-Run Future of the Stock Market*, John Wiley & Sons, Inc., New York.

Danthine, J.-P. & Donaldson, J. B. (1986), 'Inflation and Asset Prices in an Exchange Economy', *Econometrica* **54**(3), 585–605.

——— . (2002), *Intermediate Financial Theory*, Prentice Hall, Upper Saddle River, NJ.

Danthine, J.-P., Donaldson, J. B. & Mehra, R. (1992), 'The Equity Premium and the Allocation of Income Risk', *Journal of Economic Dynamics and Control* **16**(3–4), 509–532.

Debreu, G. (1959), *Theory of Value — An Axiomatic Analysis of Economic Equilibrium*, Cowles Foundation Monograph # 17, Yale University Press.

Demsetz, H. (1968), 'The Cost of Transacting', *Quarterly Journal of Economics* **82**(1), 33–53.

Diamond, P. A. (1965), 'National Debt in a Neoclassical Growth Model', *American Economic Review* **55**(5), 1126–1150.

Dimson, E., Staunton, M. & Marsh, P. (2002), *Triumph of the Optimists: 101 Years of Global Investment Returns*, Princeton University Press, Princeton and Oxford.

Duffie, D. (1988), *Security Markets — Stochastic Models*, Economic Theory, Econometrics, and Mathematical Economics, Academic Press, San Diego.

——— . (2001), *Dynamic Asset Pricing Theory*, 3rd edition, Princeton University Press, Princeton.

Duffie, D. & Huang, C.-F. (1985), 'Implementing Arrow-Debreu Equilibria by Continuous Trading of Few Long-Lived Securities', *Econometrica* **53**(6), 1337–1356.

Duffie, D. & Shafer, W. (1985), 'Equilibrium in Incomplete Markets I: A Basic Model of Generic Existence', *Journal of Mathematical Economics* **14**(3), 285–300.

——— . (1986), 'Equilibrium in Incomplete Markets II: Generic Existence in Stochastic Economies', *Journal of Mathematical Economics* **15**(3), 199–216.

Dumas, B. (1989), 'Two-Person Dynamic Equilibrium in the Capital Market', *Review of Financial Studies* **2**(2), 157–188.

Eichberger, J. & Harper, I. R. (1997), *Financial Economics*, Oxford University Press, New York.

Eichenbaum, M. S., Hansen, L. P. & Singleton, K. J. (1988), 'A Time Series Analysis of Representative Agent Models of Consumption and Leisure Choice under Uncertainty', *Quarterly Journal of Economics* **103**(1), 51–78.

Ekern, S. & Wilson, R. (1974), 'On the Theory of the Firm in an Economy with Incomplete Markets', *Bell Journal of Economics and Management Science* **5**(1), 171–180.

Epstein, L. G. (1988), 'Risk Aversion and Asset Prices', *Journal of Monetary Economics* **22**(2), 179–192.

Epstein, L. G. & Zin, S. E. (1989), 'Substitution, Risk Aversion, and the Temporal Behavior of Consumption Growth and Asset Returns I: A Theoretical Framework', *Econometrica* **57**(4), 937–969.

______ . (1990), "First-Order' Risk Aversion and the Equity Premium Puzzle', *Journal of Monetary Economics* **26**(3), 387–407.

______ . (1991), 'Substitution, Risk Aversion, and the Temporal Behavior of Consumption Growth and Asset Returns II: An Empirical Analysis', *Journal of Political Economy* **9**(2), 263–286.

Fama, E. F. & French, K. R. (1988), 'Permanent and Temporary Components of Stock Prices', *Journal of Political Economy* **96**(2), 246–273.

______ . (2002), 'The Equity Premium', *Journal of Finance* **57**(2), 637–659.

Fisher, I. (1907), *The Rate of Interest: Its Nature, Determination and Relation to Economic Phenomena,* Macmillan, New York.

Fisher, S. J. (1994), 'Asset Trading, Transaction Costs and the Equity Premium', *Journal of Applied Econometrics (Supplement: Special Issue on Calibration Techniques and Econometrics)* **9**, 71–94.

Flavin, M. A. (1983), 'Excess Volatility in the Financial Markets: A Reassessment of the Empirical Evidence', *Journal of Political Economy* **91**(6), 929–956.

French, K. R. (1980), 'Stock Returns and the Weekend Effect', *Journal of Financial Economics* **8**(1), 55–69.

Friend, I. & Blume, M. E. (1975), 'The Demand for Risky Assets', *American Economic Review* **65**(5), 900–922.

Fullenkamp, C., Tenorio, R. & Battalio, R. (2003), 'Assessing Individual Risk-Attitudes Using Field Data from Lottery Games', *Review of Economics and Statistics.*

Gali, J. (1994), 'Keeping Up with the Joneses: Consumption Externalities, Portfolio Choice, and Asset Prices', *Journal of Money, Credit, and Banking* **26**(1), 1–8.

Gennotte, G. & Leland, H. (1990), 'Market Liquidity, Hedges, and Crashes', *American Economic Review* **80**(5), 999–1021.

Gilles, C. & LeRoy, S. F. (1991), 'Econometric Aspects of the Variance-Bounds Tests: A Survey', *Review of Financial Studies* **4**(4), 753–791.

______ . (1997), 'Bubbles as Payoff at Infinity', *Economic Theory* **9**(2), 261–281.

Glassman, J. K. & Hassett, K. A. (2000), *Dow 36,000 — The New Strategy for Profiting from the Coming Rise in the Stock Market,* Crown Publishing Group, New York.

Gollier, C. (2001*a*), *The Economics of Risk and Time,* MIT Press, Cambridge and London.

——— . (2001*b*), 'Wealth Inequality and Asset Pricing', *Review of Economic Studies* **68**, 181–203.

Gollier, C. & Zeckhauser, R. J. (1997), Horizon Length and Portfolio Risk, Technical Working Paper 216, NBER.

Gordon, M. J. (1959), 'Dividends, Earnings, and Stock Prices', *Review of Economics and Statistics* **41**(2), 99–105.

Grossman, S. J. (1976), 'On the Efficiency of Competitive Stock Markets Where Trades Have Diverse Information', *Journal of Finance* **31**(2), 573–585.

Grossman, S. J. & Shiller, R. J. (1981), 'The Determinants of the Variability of Stock Market Prices', *American Economic Review (Papers and Proceedings)* **71**(2), 222–227.

Guesnerie, R. & Jaffray, J.-Y. (1974), Optimality of Equilibrium of Plans, Prices, and Price Expectations, *in* J. Drèze, ed., 'Allocation under Uncertainty: Equilibrium and Optimality', MacMillan, London, pp. 71–86.

Hakansson, N. H. (1971), 'Multi-Period Mean-Variance Analysis: Toward a General Theory of Portfolio Choice', *Journal of Finance* **26**(4), 857–884.

Hall, B. J. & Murphy, K. J. (2002), 'Stock Options for Undiversified Executives', *Journal of Accounting and Economics* **33**(1), 3–42.

Hall, R. E. (1988), 'Intertemporal Substitution in Consumption', *Journal of Political Economy* **96**(2), 339–357.

Halmos, P. R. (1993), *Finite-Dimensional Vector Spaces*, Springer, New York.

Hansen, L. P. & Jaganathan, R. (1991), 'Implications of Security Market Data for Models of Dynamic Economies', *Journal of Political Economy* **99**(2), 225–262.

Hara, C. & Kuzmics, C. (2002), Representative Consumer's Risk Aversion and Efficient Risk-Sharing Rules, mimeo., Cambridge University.

Hart, O. D. (1975), 'On the Optimality of Equilibrium when the Market Structure is Incomplete', *Journal of Economic Theory* **11**(3), 418–443.

Harvey, A. C. (1981), *Time Series Models*, Philip Allan, New York, London.

Heaton, J. & Lucas, D. J. (1996), 'Evaluating the Effects of Incomplete Markets on Risk Sharing and Asset Pricing', *Journal of Political Economy* **104**(3), 443–487.

Hicks, J. R. (1937), 'Mr. Keynes and the 'Classics' — A Suggested Interpretation', *Econometrica* **5**(2), 147–159.

Hildenbrand, W. & Kirman, A. P. (1988), *Equilibrium Analysis — Variations on Themes by Edgeworth and Walras*, Advanced Textbooks in Economics, North-Holland, Amsterdam.

Hirshleifer, J. (1965), 'Investment Decision under Uncertainty: Choice-Theoretic Approaches', *Quarterly Journal of Economics* **79**(4), 509–536.

_____. (1966), 'Investment Decision under Uncertainty: Applications of the State-Preference Approach', *Quarterly Journal of Economics* **80**(2), 252–277.

Huang, J. (2002), Who Buys Options from Whom? The Role of Options in an Economy with Heterogeneous Preferences and Beliefs, Working paper, Lancaster University.

Ibbotson, R. G. & Chen, P. (2003), 'Long-Run Stock Returns: Participating in the Real Economy', *Financial Analysts Journal* **59**(1), 88–98.

Ingersoll, J. E. J. (2000), 'Digital Contracts: Simple Tools for Pricing Complex Derivatives', *Journal of Business* **73**(1), 67–88.

Jagannathan, R., McGrattan, E. R. & Scherbina, A. (2000), 'The Declining U.S. Equity Premium', *Federal Reserve Bank of Minneapolis Quarterly Review* pp. 3–19.

Jermann, U. J. (1998), 'Asset Pricing in Production Economies', *Journal of Monetary Economics* **41**(2), 257–275.

Kagel, J. H., Battalio, R. C. & Green, L. (1995), *Economic Choice Theory: An Experimental Analysis of Animal Behavior*, Cambridge University Press, New York and Melbourne.

Kahneman, D. & Tversky, A. (1979), 'Prospect Theory: An Analysis of Decision under Risk', *Econometrica* **47**(2), 263–292.

Kandel, S. & Stambaugh, R. F. (1991), 'Asset Returns and Intertemporal Preferences', *Journal of Monetary Economics* **27**(1), 39–71.

Karni, E. (1979), 'On Multivariate Risk Aversion', *Econometrica* **47**(6), 1391–1402.

Keim, D. B. (1983), 'Size-Related Anomalies and Stock Return Seasonality: Further Empirical Evidence', *Journal of Financial Economics* **12**(1), 13–32.

Keynes, J. M. (1936), *General Theory of Employment, Interest and Money*, Cambridge University Press, Cambridge.

Kihlstrom, R. E. & Mirman, L. J. (1974), 'Risk Aversion with Many Commodities', *Journal of Economic Theory* **8**(3), 361–388.

Kimball, M. S. (1990), 'Precautionary Saving in the Small and in the Large', *Econometrica* **58**(1), 53–73.

Kiyotaki, N. & Wright, R. (1989), 'On Money as a Medium of Exchange', *Journal of Political Economy* **97**(4), 927–954.

_____. (1993), 'A Search-Theoretic Approach to Monetary Economics', *American Economic Review* **83**(1), 63–77.

Kleidon, A. (1986), 'Variance Bounds Tests and Stock Price Valuation Models', *Journal of Political Economy* **94**(5), 953–1001.

Kocherlakota, N. R. (1990), 'On the 'Discount' Factor in Growth Economies', *Journal of Monetary Economics* **25**(1), 43–47.

———. (1992), 'Bubbles and Constraints on Debt Accumulation', *Journal of Economic Theory* **57**(1), 245–256.

———. (1996), 'The Equity Premium: It's Still a Puzzle', *Journal of Economic Literature* **34**(1), 42–71.

Krasa, S. & Werner, J. (1991), 'Equilibria with Options: Existence and Indeterminacy', *Journal of Economic Theory* **54**(2), 305–320.

Krebs, T. (2001), Testable Implications of Consumption-Based Asset Pricing Models with Incomplete Markets, mimeo., Brown University.

Kreps, D. M. (1982), Multiperiod Securities and the Efficient Allocation of Risk: A Comment on the Black-Scholes Option Pricing Model, *in* J. McCall, ed., 'The Economics of Uncertainty and Information', University of Chicago Press, Chicago.

———. (1988), *Notes on the Theory of Choice*, Underground Classics in Economics, Westview Press.

———. (1990), *A Course in Microeconomic Theory*, Princeton University Press, Princeton and Oxford.

Kreps, D. M. & Porteus, E. L. (1978), 'Temporal Resolution of Uncertainty and Dynamic Choice Theory', *Econometrica* **46**(1), 185–200.

Kydland, F. E. & Prescott, E. C. (1990), 'Business Cycles: Real Facts and a Monetary Myth', *Federal Reserve Bank of Minneapolis, Quarterly Review* **14**(2), 3–18.

Laibson, D. I. (1997), 'Golden Eggs and Hyperbolic Discounting', *Quarterly Journal of Economics* **112**(2), 443–477.

Leland, H. E. (1980), 'Who Should Buy Portfolio Insurance?', *Journal of Finance* **35**(2), 581–594.

Lengwiler, Y. (2003), Heterogenous Patience and the Term Structure of Real Interest Rates, Working paper, University of Basel.

LeRoy, S. F. (1973), 'Risk-Aversion and the Martingale Property of Stock Prices', *International Economic Review* **14**(2), 436–446.

———. (1982), 'Risk-Aversion and the Term Structure of Real Interest Rates', *Economics Letters* **10**(3–4), 355–361. See also the "Correction" in *Economics Letters*, 1983, *12* (3–4), 339–340.

———. (1989), 'Efficient Capital Markets and Martingales', *Journal of Economic Literature* **27**(4), 1583–1621.

LeRoy, S. F. & LaCivita, C. J. (1981), 'Risk Aversion and the Dispersion of Asset Prices', *Journal of Business* **54**(4), 535–547.

LeRoy, S. F. & Parke, W. R. (1992), 'Stock Price Volatility: Tests Based on the Geometric Random Walk', *American Economic Review* **82**(4), 981–992.

LeRoy, S. F. & Porter, R. D. (1981), 'The Present-Value Relation: Tests Based on Implied Variance Bounds', *Econometrica* **49**(3), 555–574.

LeRoy, S. F. & Werner, J. (2001), *Principles of Financial Economics,* Cambridge University Press, Cambridge and New York.

Lettau, M. (2002), 'Idiosyncratic Risk and Volatility Bounds, or, Can Models with Idiosyncratic Risk Solve the Equity Premium Puzzle?', *Review of Economics and Statistics* **84**(2), 376–380.

Ljungqvist, L. & Sargent, T. J. (2000), *Recursive Macroeconomic Theory,* MIT Press, Cambridge and London.

Lucas, D. J. (1994), 'Asset Pricing with Undiversifyable Risk and Short Sale Constraints: Deepening the Equity Premium Puzzle', *Journal of Monetary Economics* **34**(3), 325–342.

Lucas, R. E. J. (1978), 'Asset Prices in an Exchange Economy', *Econometrica* **46**(6), 1429–1445.

______ . (1987), *Models of Business Cycles,* Yrjö Jahnsson Lectures Series, Blackwell, London and New York.

Luenberger, D. G. (1998), *Investment Science,* Oxford University Press, New York.

Luttmer, E. G. J. (1999), 'What Level of Fixed Costs can Reconcile Consumption and Stock Returns?', *Journal of Political Economy* **107**(5), 969–997.

Magill, M. & Quinzii, M. (1996*a*), 'Incomplete Markets over Infinite Horizon: Long-Lived Securities and Speculative Bubbles', *Journal of Mathematical Economics* **26**(1), 133–170.

______ . (1996*b*), *Theory of Incomplete Markets, Volume 1,* MIT Press, Cambridge and London.

Magill, M. & Shafer, W. (1991), Incomplete Markets, *in* W. Hildenbrand & H. Sonnenschein, eds, 'Handbook of Mathematical Economics', Vol. IV, North-Holland, Amsterdam, chapter 30, pp. 1523–1614.

Malinvaud, E. (1969), 'First Order Certainty Equivalence', *Econometrica* **37**(4), 706–718.

Mankiw, N. G. (1981), 'The Permanent Income Hypothesis and the Real Interest Rate', *Economics Letters* **7**(4), 307–311.

______ . (1982), 'Hall's Consumption Hypothesis and Durable Goods', *Journal of Monetary Economics* **10**(3), 417–425.

——— . (1986), 'The Equity Premium and the Concentration of Aggregate Shocks', *Journal of Financial Economics* **17**(1), 211–219.

Mankiw, N. G. & Weil, D. N. (1989), 'The Baby Boom, the Baby Bust, and the Housing Market', *Regional Science and Urban Economics* **19**(2), 235–258.

Mankiw, N. G., Rothemberg, J. J. & Summers, L. H. (1985), 'Intertemporal Substitution in Macroeconomics', *Quarterly Journal of Economics* **100**(1), 225–251.

Markowitz, H. (1952), 'Portfolio Selection', *Journal of Finance* **7**(1), 77–91.

Mas-Colell, A., Whinston, M. D. & Green, J. R. (1995), *Microeconomic Theory*, Oxford University Press.

McGrattan, E. R. & Prescott, E. C. (2000), 'Is the Stock Market Overvalued?', *Federal Reserve Bank of Minneapolis Quarterly Review* pp. 20–40.

——— . (2001), Taxes, Regulations, and Asset Prices, Working Paper 8623, NBER.

Mehra, R. & Prescott, E. C. (1985), 'The Equity Premium: A Puzzle', *Journal of Monetary Economics* **15**(2), 145–161.

——— . (1988), 'The Equity Risk Premium: A Solution?', *Journal of Monetary Economics* **22**(1), 133–136.

Menger, K. (1967), The Role of Uncertainty in Economics, *in* M. Shubik, ed., 'Essays in Mathematical Economics in Honor of Oskar Morgenstern', Princeton University Press, Princeton and Oxford.

Merton, R. C. (1971), 'Optimum Consumption and Portfolio Rules in a Continuous-Time Model', *Journal of Economic Theory* **3**(4), 373–413.

——— . (1973), 'Theory of Rational Option Pricing', *Bell Journal of Economics and Management Science* **4**(1), 141–183.

——— . (1974), 'On the Pricing of Corporate Debt: The Risk Structure of Interest Rates', *Journal of Finance* **29**(2), 449–470.

Meyer, J. (1987), 'Two-Moment Decision Models and Expected Utility Maximization', *American Economic Review* **77**(3), 421–430.

——— . (1989), 'Two-Moment Decision Models and Expected Utility Maximization: Reply', *American Economic Review* **79**(3), 603.

Michener, R. (1982), 'Variance Bounds in a Simple Model of Asset Pricing', *Journal of Political Economy* **90**(1), 166–175.

Mossin, J. (1968), 'Optimal Multiperiod Portfolio Policies', *Journal of Business* **41**(2), 215–229.

Negishi, T. (1960), 'Welfare Economics and Existence of an Equilibrium for a Competitive Economy', *Metroeconomica* **12**, 92–97.

Neumeyer, P. A. (1999), 'Inflation-Stabilization Risk in Economies with

Incomplete Asset Markets', *Journal of Economic Dynamics and Control* **23**(3), 371–391.

Ogaki, M. & Zhang, Q. (2001), 'Deceasing Relative Risk Aversion and Tests of Risk Sharing', *Econometrica* **69**(2), 515–526.

Pakos, M. (2003), Asset Pricing with Durable Goods and Non-Homothetic Preferences, mimeo., Graduate School of Business, University of Chicago.

Patinkin, D. (1965), *Money, Interest, and Prices,* 2nd edition, Harper and Row.

Polemarchakis, H. & Ku, B.-I. (1990), 'Options and Equilibrium', *Journal of Mathematical Economics* **19**(1–2), 107–112.

Poterba, J. M. & Summers, L. H. (1988), 'Mean Reversion in Stock Prices: Evidence and Implications', *Journal of Financial Economics* **22**(1), 27–59.

Pratt, J. W. (1964), 'Risk Aversion in the Small and in the Large', *Econometrica* **32**, 122–136.

Pye, G. (1967), 'Portfolio Selection and Security Prices', *Review of Economics and Statistics* **49**(1), 111–115.

Radner, R. (1972), 'Existence of Equilibrium of Plans, Prices, and Price Expectations in a Sequence of Markets', *Econometrica* **40**(2), 289–303.

______ . (1974), 'A Note on Unanimity of Stockholders' Preferences Among Alternative Production Plans: A Reformulation of the Ekern-Wilson Model', *Bell Journal of Economics and Management Science* **5**(1), 281–184.

Ramsey, F. P. (1928), 'A Mathematical Theory of Saving', *Economic Journal* **38**(152), 543–559.

Reinganum, M. R. (1981), 'Misspecification of Capital Asset Pricing: Empirical Anomalies Based on Earnings' Yields and Market Values', *Journal of Financial Economics* **9**(1), 19–46.

______ . (1983), 'The Anomalous Stock Market Behavior of Small Firms in January: Empirical Tests for Tax-Loss Selling Effects', *Journal of Financial Economics* **12**(1), 89–104.

Rietz, T. A. (1988), 'The Equity Premium: A Solution', *Journal of Monetary Economics* **22**(1), 117–131.

Ross, S. A. (1976), 'Options and Efficiency', *Quarterly Journal of Economics* **90**(1), 75–98.

______ . (1999), 'Adding Risks: Samuelson's Fallacy of Large Numbers Revisited', *Journal of Financial and Quantitative Analysis* **34**(3), 323–339.

Rouwenhorst, K. G. (1995), Asset Pricing Implications of Equilibrium Business Cycle Models, *in* T. F. Cooley, ed., 'Frontiers of Business Cycle Research', Princeton University Press, Princeton, pp. 294–330.

Rubinstein, M. (1974), 'An Aggregation Theorem for Securities Markets', *Journal of Financial Economics* **1**(3), 225–244.

———. (1976), 'The Strong Case for the Generalized Logarithmic Utility Model as the Premier Model of Financial Markets', *Journal of Finance* **31**(2), 551–571.

Saha, A. (1993), 'Expo-Power Utility: A 'Flexible' Form for Absolute and Relative Risk Aversion', *American Journal of Agricultural Economics* **75**(4), 205–213.

Samuelson, P. A. (1958), 'An Exact Consumption-Loan Model of Interest with or without the Social Contrivance of Money', *Journal of Political Economy* **66**(6), 467–482.

———. (1963), 'Risk and Uncertainty: A Fallacy of Large Numbers', *Scientia* **98**(6th Series, 57th Year), 108–113.

———. (1965), 'Proof that Properly Anticipated Prices Fluctuate Randomly', *Industrial Management Review* **6**, 41–49.

———. (1970), 'The Fundamental Approximation Theorem of Portfolio Analysis in Terms of Means, Variances and Higher Moments', *Review of Economic Studies* **64**(4), 537–542.

Sargent, T. J. (1987), *Dynamic Macroeconomic Theory*, Harvard University Press, Cambridge and London.

Schwert, G. W. (1990), 'Indexes of U.S. Stock Prices from 1802 to 1987', *Journal of Business* **63**(3), 399–426.

———. (2003), Anomalies and Market Efficiency, *in* G. Constantinides, M. Harris & R. Stulz, eds, 'Handbook of the Economics of Finance', North-Holland, Amsterdam.

Segal, U. & Spivak, A. (1990), 'First Order versus Second Order Risk Aversion', *Journal of Economic Theory* **51**(1), 111–125.

———. (1997), 'First-Order Risk Aversion and Non-Differentiability', *Economic Theory* **9**(1), 179–183.

Selden, L. (1978), 'A New Representation of Preferences over 'Certain × Uncertain' Consumption Pairs: The 'Ordinal Certainty Equivalent' Hypothesis', *Econometrica* **46**(5), 1045–1060.

Sharpe, W. (1964), 'Capital Asset Prices: A Theory of Market Equilibrium under Conditions of Risk', *Journal of Finance* **19**(3), 425–442.

———. (1966), 'Mutual Fund Performance', *Journal of Business* **39**(1), 119–138.

Sheshinski, E. & Weiss, Y. (1977), 'Inflation and Costs of Price Adjustment', *Review of Economic Studies* **44**(2), 287–303.

Shiller, R. J. (1979), 'The Volatility of Long-Term Interest Rates and Expectations Models of the Term Structure', *Journal of Political Economy* **87**(6), 1190–1219.

______. (1981), 'Do Stock Prices Move Too Much to Be Justified by Subsequent Changes in Dividends?', *American Economic Review* **71**(3), 421–436.

______. (1982), 'Consumption, Asset Markets, and Macroeconomic Fluctuations', *Carnegie-Rochester Conference Series on Public Policy* **17**, 203–238.

______. (1993), *Macro Markets — Creating Institutions for Managing Society's Largest Economic Risks,* Clarendon Lectures in Economics, Oxford University Press, Oxford.

______. (2000), *Irrational Exuberance,* Princeton University Press, Princeton.

______. (2003), *The New Financial Order — Risk in the 21st Century,* Princeton University Press, Princeton.

Sialm, C. (2002), Stochastic Taxation and Asset Pricing in Dynamic General Equilibrium, Working Paper 9301, NBER.

Siegel, J. J. (1992), 'The Real Rate of Interest from 1800 to 1990: A Study of the U.S. and U.K.', *Journal of Monetary Economics* **29**(2), 227–252.

______. (1998), *Stocks for the Long Run,* McGraw-Hill, New York.

______. (1999), 'The Shrinking Equity Premium', *Journal of Portfolio Management* **26**(1), 10–17.

Siegel, J. J. & Thaler, R. H. (1997), 'Anomalies: The Equity Premium Puzzle', *Journal of Economic Perspectives* **11**(1), 191–200.

Simon, C. P. & Blume, L. (1994), *Mathematics for Economists,* W. W. Norton & Co., New York.

Sinn, H.-W. (1989), 'Two-Moment Decision Models and Expected Utility Maximization: Comment', *American Economic Review* **79**(3), 601–602.

______. (2002), Weber's Law and the Biological Evolution of Risk Preferences: The Selective Dominance of the Logarithmic Utility Function, Working Paper 770, CESifo.

Sinn, H.-W. & Weichenrieder, A. J. (1993), Biological Selection of Risk Preferences, *in* B. Rückversicherung, ed., 'Risk is a Construct: Perceptions of Risk Perceptions', Knesebeck, Munich, pp. 67–86. www.cesifo.de/pls/ifo_app/LinkSwitch?setPage=publ-special-sinn-biologic.pdf.

Stiglitz, J. E. (1969), 'Behavior Towards Risk with Many Commodities', *Econometrica* **37**(4), 660–667.

______. (1970), 'A Consumption-Oriented Theory of the Demand for Financial Assets and the Term Structure of Interest Rates', *Review of Economic Studies* **37**(3), 321–351.

Stiglitz, J. E. & Weiss, A. (1981), 'Credit Rationing in Markets with Imperfect Information', *American Economic Review* **71**(3), 393–410.

Sundaram, R. K. (1996), *A First Course in Optimization Theory*, Cambridge University Press, Cambridge and New York.

Sundaresan, S. M. (1989), 'Intertemporally Dependent Preferences and the Volatility of Consumption and Wealth', *Review of Financial Studies* **2**(1), 73–89.

Telmer, C. I. (1993), 'Asset-Pricing Puzzles and Incomplete Markets', *Journal of Finance* **48**(5), 1803–1832.

Thaler, R. H. & Johnson, E. J. (1990), 'Gambling with the House Money and Trying to Break Even: The Effects of Prior Outcomes on Risky Choice', *Management Science* **36**(6), 643–660.

Townsend, R. M. (1994), 'Risk and Insurance in Village India', *Econometrica* **62**(3), 539–591.

———. (1995), 'Consumption Insurance: An Evaluation of Risk-Bearing Systems in Low-Income Economies', *Journal of Economic Perspectives* **9**(3), 83–102.

Van Praag, B. M. S. & Booji, A. S. (2003), Risk Aversion and the Subjective Time Discount Rate: A Joint Approach, Discussion Paper TI 2003–018/3, Tinbergen Institute.

Von Neumann, J. & Morgenstern, O. (1944), *Theory of Games and Economic Behavior*, Princeton University Press, Princeton.

Walras, L. (1874), *Éléments d'Économie Politique Pure, ou Théorie de la Richesse Sociale*, Corbaz, Lausanne.

Wang, J. (1996), 'The Term Structure of Interest Rates in a Pure Exchange Economy with Heterogenous Investors', *Journal of Financial Economics* **41**(1), 75–110.

Weil, P. (1989), 'The Equity Premium Puzzle and the Risk Free Rate Puzzle', *Journal of Monetary Economics* **24**(3), 401–421.

———. (1990), 'Non-Expected Utility in Macroeconomics', *Quarterly Journal of Economics* **105**(1), 29–42.

Weintraub, E. R. (1982), *Mathematics for Economists — An Integrated Approach*, Cambridge University Press, Cambridge and New York.

Weirich, P. (1984), 'The St. Petersburg Gamble and Risk', *Theory and Decision* **17**, 193–202.

Weitzman, M. L. (1998), 'Why the Far-Distant Future Should Be Discounted at Its Lowest Possible Rate', *Journal of Environmental Economics and Management* **36**(3), 201–208.

———. (2001), 'Gamma Discounting', *American Economic Review* **91**(1), 260–271.

Welch, I. (1999), A Note on the 'Equity Size Puzzle', mimeo., Anderson Graduate School of Management at UCLA. welch.som.yale.edu/academics/macroperspective.pdf.

———. (2000), 'Views of Financial Economists on the Equity Premium and on Professional Controversies', *Journal of Business* **73**(4), 501–537.

———. (2001), The Equity Premium Consensus Forecast Revisited, Discussion Paper No. 1325, Cowles Foundation.

Werner, J. (1985), 'Equilibrium in Economies with Incomplete Financial Markets', *Journal of Economic Theory* **36**(1), 110–119.

Wilson, R. (1968), 'The Theory of Syndicates', *Econometrica* **36**(1), 119–132.

Woodford, M. (forthcoming), Revolution and Evolution in Twentieth-Century Macroeconomics, *in* P. Gifford, ed., 'Frontiers of the Mind in the Twenty-First Century', Harvard University Press.

Yaari, M. E. (1987), 'The Dual Theory of Choice under Risk', *Econometrica* **55**(1), 95–115.

# Index